George Burrowes

A Commentary on the Song of Solomon

Second Edition

George Burrowes

A Commentary on the Song of Solomon
Second Edition

ISBN/EAN: 9783337020736

Printed in Europe, USA, Canada, Australia, Japan

Cover: Foto ©Thomas Meinert / pixelio.de

More available books at **www.hansebooks.com**

ON THE

SONG OF SOLOMON.

BY

Rev. GEORGE BURROWES, D. D.

PROFESSOR OF BIBLICAL INSTRUCTION IN LAFAYETTE COLLEGE.

SECOND EDITION, REVISED.

PHILADELPHIA:
JAMES S. CLAXTON,
SUCCESSOR TO WM. S. & ALFRED MARTIEN,
1214 Chestnut Street.
1867.

Entered according to Act of Congress, in the year 1853, by

WILLIAM S. MARTIEN,

In the Clerk's Office of the District Court of the Eastern District of Pennsylvania.

CONTENTS.

	PAGE.
PREFACE	5
INTRODUCTION	9
SUMMARY OF THE SONG	75

TRANSLATION.

Chapter I.	78
Chapter II.	79
Chapter III.	81
Chapter IV.	82
Chapter V.	83
Chapter VI.	85
Chapter VII.	86
Chapter VIII.	87

ANALYSIS OF THE SONG.

Chapter I.	89
Chapter II.	93
Chapter III.	99
Chapter IV.	102
Chapter V.	107
Chapter VI.	110
Chapter VII.	114
Chapter VIII.	115

COMMENTARY ON THE SONG.

Chapter I.	121
Chapter II.	218
Chapter III.	274
Chapter IV.	298
Chapter V.	342
Chapter VI.	383
Chapter VII.	401
Chapter VIII.	424

PREFACE.

THE notes which have grown into the following pages were begun amid the pious exercises and duties connected with the pastoral charge of a retired congregation, and without any idea of making a volume for the press. They have gradually taken their present form. The Analysis now stands, with no material alteration, as it was written some years ago; and subsequent research has brought to light no reason for changing the views then adopted concerning the general meaning of this portion of Scripture. To those who consider the misapprehension that has prevailed in reference to the Song, the Introduction may not seem unnecessarily long, inasmuch as an answer to objections, an argument in defence of the allegorical meaning, and a statement of the principles of interpretation, are required before proceeding to the exposition. The Summary and Analysis give the writer's idea of the meaning of the Song. In the exposition, the aim has been to unfold the truth, in the way supposed the most desirable to a soul animated with fervent love for the Lord Jesus, and craving the hidden manna which the Holy Spirit has lodged in this precious portion of the Scriptures. The heart hungering and thirsting for righteousness, does not rest satisfied with the stalk and husks, but is anxious for the luscious kernel, of these fruits of eternal life. As here viewed, the Song is a continuous and coherent whole, illustrating some of the most exalted and delightful exercises of the believing heart. According to our exposition, there will not be found in the book a single passage to which the most fastidious taste can take the least exception. A correct interpretation of the book is its only proper vindication. Those who engage in the work of Scripture exposition, become best aware of the difficulties of the undertaking; and while the writer is sensible of the difficulty attending a Commentary on the Song, and submits this volume with diffidence to those who love the adorable Redeemer, he shall be happy if anything has been done, in however humble a degree, for enabling them to value this book, and draw herefrom truth for nourishing a more vigorous affection for their Beloved and their Friend.

INTRODUCTION.

The effect of sin has been to destroy in the human heart the love of God, and substitute for it the love of unworthy things. The object of redemption is the restoration of man from his condition of enmity against God, and from all the consequences of sin, to the possession and enjoyment of perfect love to God. Hence, as hatred of God is the spirit of sin, love is represented as the essential grace, as the fulfilling of the law. The growth of the soul in holiness must be estimated, not by deep excitement, whether of ecstasy or of overwhelming sorrow, not by burning zeal or untiring activity, not by acquaintance with all mysteries and all knowledge, not by giving our goods to feed the poor and our body to be burned; but by the love which beareth all things, believeth all things, hopeth all things, endureth all things. Long before the time of the apostle Paul, Plato had celebrated the excellence of this affection, though exercised in an inferior sphere. "It is proper to exhort every man to behave in all things piously towards the gods, that we may escape from the ills and obtain the good to which Love is our guide and commander; who confers on us the greatest benefits for the present, and for the future gives us the strongest hopes that if we pay the debt of piety to heaven, he will restore us to our original nature, and make us happy by healing our ills.

Love appears to be himself the most beautiful and best; and to be the cause of such like beautiful things in other beings. He it is who produces

> Peace amongst men, upon the sea a calm;
> Stillness on winds, on beds of sorrow sleep.

It is he who divests us of all feelings of alienation, and fills us with those of friendship; gracious to the good; looked up to by the wise; admired by the inhabitants of heaven; the parent of refinement, of tenderness, of elegance, and of grace; in labour, in fear, in wishes, and in discourse, the pilot, the encourager, the assistant, and best protector; of gods and men, taken altogether, the ornament; a leader the most beautiful and best, in whose train it is the duty of every one to follow, bearing a part in that sweet song which he sings himself when soothing the mind of every one among divinities and men."*

To this love we are restored in sanctification. Perfect sanctification carries with it perfect love. The death of Christ, the agency of the Holy Spirit, all the means of grace, all the dealings of Providence with the saints, converge on this one point, the forming anew in man of this lost love. As the sanctification of the soul is through the truth, we might therefore suppose, that in giving us the Scriptures, God would give full elucidations of this very important principle or affection. This he has been careful to do. He has shown love to be not only important but essential, 1 Cor. xiii. 1—3; has

---

* Banquet, Stallbaum's ed., p. 156.

"Love is the leading passion of the soul; all the rest conform themselves to it, desire and hope and fear, joy and sorrow."—*Leighton.*

"The entire economy of salvation is constructed on the principle of restoring to the world the lost spirit of love."—*Harris.*

given a full and excellent definition of it as the root of our best and holy feelings, 1 Cor. xiii. 4—7; has shown its perpetuity, its superiority to knowledge, faith, and hope, and its inseparable connection with the happiness and existence of the soul of man, 1 Cor. xiii. 8—13; he has embodied it for our benefit in the living example of Jesus Christ; has shown that God, to whose image we must be restored, is love, 1 John iv. 8; has given the blood of his Son for removing the difficulty in the way of establishing in us this principle; and has sent his Spirit for forming it within us by a new creation, and for opening channels in the heart, through which its influence may reach and control all our other powers. All this has been necessary, because divine love is so perfectly opposite to our natural disposition. Its presence makes us new creatures, gives us new workings of the affections, and prompts to new language from the lips.

Now, it is not unreasonable to suppose that He who has given us such means for cherishing this heavenly affection would go farther, and add a description of the actual operations of a heart in which this love is found, and would give us language such as these emotions would naturally adopt in using the words of men; so that in giving utterance to this love, the saints should not be left to the uncertainty and danger of adopting such words as human error might suggest; but have readily furnished language of precision and beauty made ready to our hands by the same Spirit who is working within us this affection. Much of the difficulty and uncertainty of metaphysical disquisitions arises from the imperfection of language, and the want of precision in its use. Words are the signs of ideas, and if the language in which we hear or speak on any subject, be imperfect, our apprehension, as thus got on that subject, must be incorrect. It is important that those who have received a spiritual discernment of the things which are freely given to us of God, should be able to speak of them, not in words which man's wisdom teacheth, but in words which the Holy Ghost teacheth, 1 Cor. ii. 13, that the Spirit who prompts the emotion should furnish the language in which such emotion may find suitable utterance for showing forth the praise of the Redeemer. This has been done for us in a beautiful manner in the Song of Solomon.*

---

* This book is received as canonical for the following reasons.
1. We have seen that there is every ground for the presumption that the Divine Author of the Scriptures would give us a book on the subject with which this is occupied. 2. There can be no presumption against it from the nature of the book, for there are other parts of Scripture containing the same kind of illustrations. 3. "Ezra wrote, and, we may believe," says Warburton, "acted by the inspiration of the Most High, amid the last blaze indeed, yet in the full lustre of expiring prophecy. And such a man would not have placed any book that was not sacred in the same volume with the law and the prophets." 4. The Song of Songs has always been a canonical book in the Jewish church. 5. Our Saviour and his apostles gave their sanction to the canon of the Scriptures received by the Jewish church; in that canon this book had then a place; and therefore, though not quoted by Christ and the apostles, it clearly received their sanction as canonical. 6. In his Antiquities, (viii. 2, 5,) Josephus speaks of Solomon as inspired; and in his work against Apion, gives the number of their canonical books as thirty-nine: the Song is necessary to make up this number. 7. According to Eusebius, (iv. 26,) Melito, Bishop of Sardis, in the second century of the Christian era, went to Palestine for the purpose of ascertaining the sacred books of the Jewish canon, and found the Song of Solomon among the number. 8. Origen in the third century, Jerome, Augustine, and Theodoret in the fifth century, not to mention various others, all testify to the same point. The testimony of the Christian Church on this subject is uniform. This book, illustrating that love which is the very core of the believer's spiritual life, is therefore a part of the Scriptures given by inspiration.

The services of the Jewish ritual point out the way in which this newness of heart, this divine love may be attained by sinners. The Epistle to the Hebrews, as well as the general language of piety, shows how impossible it is to understand the work of Christ and the office of the Holy Spirit, without those typical allusions. The leprosy is the emblem of our spiritual state of nature; the sacrifices show the ground of pardon; the sacred anointing oil, and the water of the laver, illustrate the excellency of the Holy Spirit, and his cleansing power, in developing those fruits, the first of which is love. In the same mode, by allegorical language and emblems, the Song shows what this affection is as already formed and in operation. The heart on which the work of the Spirit has been felt to the greatest extent can best tell how much at a loss we must be in speaking of spiritual exercises and love to Jesus, were we cut off from the language of this Song. Should the soul be influenced to these feelings by the Holy Spirit, and inclined to use such expressions of devoted love, without having at the same time a knowledge of this book as given by inspiration, we would hesitate, would feel ourselves guilty of presumption, and could not answer those who might upbraid us with irreverence or fanaticism. There are persons of undoubted piety, in the early stages of the Christian life, though having long borne the profession, who are as reluctant to believe the reality of the exercises of the most advanced Christians, as is the impenitent to admit the reality of the first emotions attending a change of heart; the error in both instances arises from unwillingness to believe what has not been personally experienced. If, in consequence of having never felt such deep emotions, persons of certain attainments in piety may object to this book as using language too strong, the unrenewed heart may, with the same propriety, doubt the reality of all the exercises of religion. Beyond controversy, there are spiritual exercises which can be better and more naturally expressed in the language of this Song, than in any other portion of the Scriptures. And the Holy Spirit has put into our hands this precious scroll, written full of the characters of love, and whispers to us that we can never do wrong in speaking of Jesus in these terms; and that we may judge of the nature of our love to him by our disposition to speak of him in such language, and by finding in our hearts emotions corresponding with these expressions.

The several books of the word of God have some particular aim and some leading topic. The Gospels furnish the life of God manifest in flesh; the Epistle to the Hebrews opens the doctrine of atonement as vicarious and possessing infinite value from the divine nature of Him who suffered; Proverbs embody the practical duties of daily life; the Psalms are the pious heart's language of devotion; the Song is its language of love. Devotion being the utterance of the different feelings of the soul in combination and resting with reverence on the majesty and goodness of God, and love being the bond which brings us into union with God and gives all our other powers their proper exercise, we find in the Psalms expressions in which to embody our general feelings of repentance, contrition, trust, veneration and praise; in the Song, the expressions are restricted to the various operations of the one exercise of love. These deepest spiritual emotions of the human soul are here exhibited in a way best adapted to the comprehension and wants of man. In the portraits of Shakspeare we have veins of a profound metaphysics, never surpassed, yet so arrayed in flesh and blood, that we overlook the mental abstractions, in the beauty and attractiveness of their guise. And no metaphysical disquisition however laboured, no didactic statement however clear, could give as intelligibly as does this Song, the nature of those exalted exercises of the human soul which constitute love to our redeeming Lord.

Love to Jesus Christ becomes through sanctification, the strongest passion that can take possession of the human heart. Ambition, avarice, and passion may have more of the unnatural vigour attending fever; this carries with it the quiet, enduring energy of health, with sufficient power to consume those unhallowed principles, and bring into captivity every thought to the obedience of Jesus. The power of this love cannot be known without being felt; and none but those who have experienced the greatest intensity of it possible on earth, can be capable judges, whether any language used in expressing it may be exaggerated. The love of the pious heart to God being thus strong, and indeed not utterable even by the strongest terms; the love of God towards us is as incomprehensible as his eternity, omnipresence, or Almighty power. If, therefore, he condescends to illustrate to our comprehension the nature of this reciprocal love, the Holy Spirit must be expected to draw his comparisons from the strongest and tenderest instances of affection known among men, and use, in so doing, all the colouring that can be supplied even from the domains of poetry. Hence, in this Song, the relation of husband and bride is selected. Nor is this comparison peculiar to the Song. It is used throughout the New no less than the Old Testament, and at the close of Revelation the Church is spoken of as the bride, the wife of the Lamb. The relation of father and son, imperfect though it be, is nevertheless the best that language can furnish for setting forth the union between the first and second persons of the Trinity; and the relation between husband and wife is the best known to us, for illustrating the union between Jesus and his redeemed. This union must be far more intimate and far more tender than the marriage relation. The attachment of two persons, strangers perhaps to each other previously during almost their whole life, must, even in its greatest purity, ripeness, and strength, fall very far below the love of Jesus for a soul he has formed for the end of loving him; whose constitution has been framed by sanctification of the Holy Ghost, according to what he can love and desires to love; whom he has allured to himself by overpowering manifestations of love; whom he loved not merely from the first moments of its being, but even before the origin of its being; and who owes its being to his loving it before it was called into existence, even before the world began; over whose course he has watched from its first breath; for whose rescue from misery he did himself submit to death. Besides all this, he has the tender and incomprehensible love of the infinite God. Such love on his part, demands corresponding affection on ours. And how can any earthly comparison reach the measure of this love, when it is such, that if any man hate not his father, and mother, and wife, and children, and brethren, and sisters, yea, and his own life also, he cannot be worthy of the love of his Lord. The comparison of father and son is not more imperfect in expressing the relation of the first and second persons of the Trinity, than is the love of the husband and wife, even when taken in the strongest terms, imperfect in unfolding the love of Christ for his people. This illustration of that love is the best we can now have; but like all human comparisons applied to God, falls very far short of the truth. The expressions in the Song, however hyperbolical they may seem to some minds, give therefore nothing more than a shadow of this love. The language appears strong, not because it is exaggerated, but because we are not capable of appreciating the love of God. Now we see the love of Christ through a glass darkly, even in our brightest hours. Angels, who have a better understanding of the subject, see that this language, instead of being exaggerated, is, as everything heavenly expressed in human language must be, very imperfect. Though the Holy Spirit has selected the most endearing relation on earth, the marriage state, and set forth the reciprocal affections of that relation in the glowing terms, ardent language, and richly coloured imagery of oriental poetry; the whole is not sufficient for enabling us to comprehend, in any other than an indistinct manner, the wondrous love of Christ, which passeth knowledge.

Beset with the inseparable infirmity of human nature, an over estimate of ourselves, and forgetting that the difficulty in understanding it may lie mainly with us, we act as though capable judges of the extent of God's love, and of the way it should be expressed; and we censure the language of the Holy Spirit as improper and extravagant, because we know so little of this love as to be unable to see how incomprehensible its nature.* All the objections brought against the Song, arise from this source. Those who would reject it from the canon of Scripture, or, if retaining it, would pass it over in silence

---

* "Would it not then be a sad thing, if, when there is true and sound reasoning, one should not blame himself and his own want of skill, but should anxiously transfer the blame from himself to the arguments, and thereupon pass the rest of his life in hating and reviling arguments, and so be deprived of the truth and knowledge."—*Plato's Phædo*, 90.

as unfit for use in the present age, do this, not because it has less direct testimony than the other books in favour of its inspiration, but because its general character is not what they would expect to find in writing coming from God. No part of the Scriptures can show more uninterruptedly than this, the concurrent testimony of the Jewish and Christian churches. It bears the clearest internal evidence of having been written by the author of Proverbs and Ecclesiastes. The affection here illustrated is a leading one in the Christian life; the mode of illustrating it is the one generally employed in other parts of the word of God, and is indeed the best that could be used for the purpose. All this, certain opposers of the book will admit, but still object to it strenuously, through prejudices arising from what appears to them exaggerated, if not indelicate expressions. Under these circumstances, and in view of what has been already said concerning the impossibility of doing anything like full justice to the infinite love of God in human language, even adorned with the highest efforts of poetic genius; such persons would do well to reflect that the difficulty lies not in the book, but in themselves; that the Holy Spirit can use no other than the best possible words; and that all these apparent imperfections might vanish under the influence of a keener spiritual discernment, and a deeper love. Different minds in which sin exerts an influence, have an affinity for different kinds of error, and an opposition to different kinds of truths. As sanctification releases us from our native corruptions by degrees, the Christian life is a gradual progress in working the soul loose from the dominion of error. Hence, some men reject the whole word of God; others reject particular books; while some persons who receive as inspired the whole canon of Scripture, can never become reconciled to some of its doctrines. A defect in the intellectual or spiritual man is at the root of all this error. The defect is not in the pages of inspiration, but in the human heart.*

Sir Joshua Reynolds gives this advice to young artists: "With respect to the pictures that you are to choose for your models, I would have you take those of established reputation, rather than follow your own fancy. If you should not admire them at first, you will, by endeavouring to imitate them, find that the world has not been mistaken. The habit of contemplating and brooding over the ideas of great geniuses, till you find yourself warmed by the contact, is the true method of forming an artist-like mind." Thus Dr. Arnold: "The cartoons of Raphael at Hampton Court Palace, the frescoes of the same great painter in the galleries of the Vatican at Rome, the famous statues of the Laocoon and the Apollo Belvidere, and the church of St. Peter at Rome, the most magnificent building perhaps in the world—all alike are generally found to disappoint a person on his first view of them. But let him be sure that they are excellent, and that he only wants the knowledge and the taste to appreciate them properly, and every succeeding sight of them will open his eyes more and more, till he learns to admire them, not indeed as much as they deserve, but

---

* "The very essence of truth is plainness and brightness; the darkness and crookedness is our own. The wisdom of God created understanding fit and proportionable to truth, the object and end of it, as the eye to the thing visible. If our understanding have a film of ignorance over it, or be blear with gazing on other false glistenings, what is that to truth? If we will but purge with sovereign eye-salve that intellectual ray which God hath planted in us, then we would believe the Scriptures protesting their own plainness and perspicuity, calling to them to be instructed, not only the wise and the learned, but the simple."—*Milton, Of Reformation in England*, Book I.

so much as greatly to enrich and enlarge his own mind, by becoming acquainted with such perfect beauty. So it is with great poets; they must be read often and studied reverently, before an unpractised mind can gain any thing like an adequate notion of their excellence. The reader must be convinced that if he does not fully admire them, it is his fault, and not theirs. Here, as in everything else, humility is the surest path to exaltation." These remarks apply with the greatest force to the Scriptures, embodying as they do, in the noblest and most appropriate language, not the conceptions of the human intellect, but truths so unusual, so grand, and so ennobling, that even after having been revealed, they cannot be received by the natural man without a discernment imparted by the Spirit. The truths illustrated in this Song, are pre-eminently among those which are spiritually discerned. They are not so much the principles of the doctrine of Christ, as the things which are brought more particularly into view as we go on unto perfection. The nature of the subject, love, makes it belong to the advanced part of the Christian life more especially; and as sanctification refines our spiritual perceptions, and by raising us from our degradation of darkness towards the condition of saints in light, gives us the ability to appreciate the love of Jesus—we see more and more beauty in this Song; we see in it nothing but beauty; we find our objections against it arose from the corrupt heart rather than from the book; we feel thankful that the Author of our faith has provided for us words so rich, so glowing, and so perfect for giving utterance to our emotions; and we rejoice to find, under the light of the Holy Ghost, our unsanctified misapprehensions giving place to the conviction, that the love of

INTRODUCTION.

Jesus towards us is infinitely greater than is even here expressed.

The Scriptures contain truths, promises, and illustrations, adapted to every variety of circumstances, and to every grade of religious experience. Particular truths can be fully understood, and the power of certain promises can be adequately felt, only by our being brought into situations where the soul is made to feel the need of those truths and those promises. Here are innumerable gradations of truth adapted to the different degrees of the growth of the soul in grace, from the first exercises of conviction to the highest measure of sanctification attainable on earth. A particular development of our spiritual perceptions is requisite for feeling the beauty and power of any one of the portions of truth in this ascending scale; and as the unrenewed man, even with profound learning, fails to apprehend the perfection of holy beauty in passages with which he has a mere scientific acquaintance, the Christian, while understanding all the heart can know of the truths adapted to the steps of religious experience through which he has passed, may yet fail to comprehend and appreciate thoroughly, portions of holy writ lying in regions of pious exercises whereunto he has not attained. Three things are necessary for understanding perfectly the Scriptures: such an acquaintance with them as may be derived from human learning; the illumination of the Holy Spirit; and a position in the circumstances for which those truths were specially given and adapted. The two last are not inferior in importance to the first, and other things being equal, the man who has the advantage not only of the teaching of the Spirit, but of being led by Providence through the circumstances of life in which the want of certain promises is felt, and their comforting power enjoyed, will be better able than other persons to see beauty, and richness, and glory, in many domains of gospel truths, which must have lain unobserved by him, had he not been drawn into these green pastures, and beside these still waters, by the Presence that dwelt amid the pillar of fire in the wilderness.

Hence, this Song is not so much a favourite in the early stage of the religious life, as at subsequent periods when we have grown in grace. It is the manual of the advanced Christian. When love has been more perfected by the Spirit, hither do we come for expressions of that love. When we are anxious to hear from the lips of Jesus the fulness of his love to us, here do we rejoice to sit and listen. The Jews were not wrong when they represented this book as the holy of holies in the fabric of revelation; for assuredly, the voice here speaking, the living oracles here uttered, can be heard only by those who have been initiated into the mysteries of godliness and dwell under the shadow of the Almighty. Accordingly, this book has been a favourite with eminent Christians. While some persons versed in biblical lore, but ignorant of the alphabet of piety, can see nothing further in this Song than an amatory eclogue; and others, whose piety we are far from doubting, can represent these words given by inspiration, as "leading us away from pure and spiritual devotion," by "connecting amatory ideas and feelings with a devotional frame of mind;"* there is, and always has been, in the Church, a class of persons of no questionable character for ability, learning, or holiness, who esteem this book among the choicest portions of the word of God. Were we to speak of the partiality of Lady Guyon for this book, some might reply, she was a mystic. Whether

---

* Stuart on the Old Testament, p. 374.

mystic or not, far better would it be for the world, were the tone of her deep, fervent, energetic piety, more common. But who will bring the charge of mysticism against Leighton, Owen, Romaine, President Edwards, and Chalmers. That most profound of metaphysicians, the immortal author of the treatise on the Freedom of the Will, was peculiarly fond of the book of Canticles, and read and meditated much upon it. "The whole book of Canticles," says he, "used to be pleasant to me, and I used to be much in reading it about that time, and found from time to time an inward sweetness that would carry me away in my contemplations." The great leader of the Free Church of Scotland in her exodus, speaking of Dr. Pye Smith's asserting the non-inspiration of the Song, says: "It would bespeak not only a more pious but a more philosophic docility, to leave that book in undisturbed possession of the place which it now enjoys, where it might minister, as in ages heretofore, to the saintly and seraphic contemplations of the advanced Christian, who discovers that in this poem a greater than Solomon is here, whose name to him is as ointment poured forth, and who, while he luxuriates with spiritual satisfaction over pages that the world has unhallowed, breathes of the ethereal purity of the third heavens, as well as their ethereal fervour." Owen says: "Then may a man judge himself to have somewhat profited in the experience of a mystery of a blessed intercourse and communion with Christ, when the expressions of love in that holy Dialogue, the Song, do give light and life unto his mind, and efficaciously communicate unto him an experience of their power. But because these things are little understood by many, the book itself is much neglected, if not despised." In the words of the saintly McCheyne, "No book furnishes a better test than does the Song, of the depth of a man's Christianity. If his religion be in his head only, a dry form of doctrines; or if it hath place merely in his fancy, like Pliable in Pilgrim's Progress, he will see nothing here to attract him. But if his religion have a hold on his heart, this will be a favourite portion of the word of God." Beza, the friend and associate of Calvin, writes: "Those instructed and advanced in the divine life, the writer of this Song does, as it were, carry away with him beyond the regions of earth to the contemplation of heavenly things—as though being now citizens of heaven, they might knock for admission at its gates." Rutherford's Letters, so rich in pious affection and heavenly unction, take their colouring from the Song; and McCheyne, who found in these "Letters" daily delight, though dying at the age of nine and twenty, had scarcely left himself a single text of the Song on which he had not already discoursed.

When, therefore, this book is admitted to be inspired, and to have been sanctioned and loved by the ablest and most saintly men of even the present age, those who make these concessions, yet hold the book in disesteem, would act with humility and wisdom by feeling that the difficulty in appreciating it lies with themselves. Much of what is censured as exceptionable, disappears from the Song when read in the original, rather than in our translation, and properly understood. There are arguments on this point which we might urge, but on which we do not rely. It might be stated that the Song is in strict accordance with the nature of oriental poetry, and that many things which appear strange to us are but the peculiarities of this oriental costume. The Hebrew modes of thinking and writing, were different from ours; though not more so than the habits of thought and diction yet found in the literature of eastern nations.

Ancient fable mentions a person who possessed the power of turning everything he touched into gold; some minds possess the faculty of turning everything they touch into intellectual gold; others have the characteristic of turning everything into impurity; even the grace of God into lasciviousness, and his truth into a lie. Much of the alleged indelicacy of this book, is the fault not of the author but of the translators, as may be seen by entering into the spirit of the original, or by reading any good translation, like that of Rosenmüller, Dopke, or John Mason Good.

But on the points here mentioned we shall not insist. We take the higher and nobler ground, which we trust the subsequent exposition will show to be truth, that that there is nothing in this Song contrary to delicacy of taste and purity of thought. Even what are called by some persons the indelicate passages of holy writ, are far from being found in this Song. We venture to assert, that the parts looked on with most distrust, are capable of a natural interpretation incapable of offending the most sensitive modesty, and tending directly to our edification in holiness. With the same reasonable spirit which is essential for enjoying the finest works of uninspired genius, let us feel that this Song is everything it has been represented by an innumerable cloud of witnesses; that we are not at liberty to reject or neglect a book so manifestly of Divine origin; that if the Song has been ridiculed by the corrupt heart, or misused to purposes of evil, the same has happened with almost every other portion of the Bible; that all Scripture is given by inspiration of God, and is profitable; and that by patient continuance as learners at the feet of Him who is meek and lowly in heart, we shall become sensible of its beauties, and filled with admiring love.

As the enemy of souls contests every step of our progress from error into the full light of truth, failing to make us reject this book as uninspired, or as improper for the use of the pure in heart, he will be equally satisfied in depriving us of its benefit, by leading to a wrong interpretation. Much of the dislike to this Song, even by Christians, has arisen from the erroneous method pursued in the exposition, by some of the most pious commentators. Even a pious man may go astray, through a false theory of interpretation. There is no book in the Bible further removed than this Song, beyond the capability of an impious man, even of great learning, for giving a proper exposition. There are portions of Scripture containing an unadorned statement of doctrine or facts, which a scholar who takes them up as he would an uninspired classic, may interpret fairly according to the literal meaning. Such a man may be called a commentator on the Scriptures, he can hardly be called an expounder of them. It is a dangerous error, and one into which the unsanctified heart is continually liable to fall, that learning is the one essential thing in biblical interpretation. The importance in this book of a well furnished head, may cause us to undervalue the aid necessary from a pious heart. Bringing to the subject of religion our modes of thinking on common topics, we forget that the Scriptures have difficulties which require spiritual discernment, no less than philological acumen, and that a man may "understand all mysteries and all knowledge," while destitute of the love which is the key to the solution of its deepest and most edifying problems. The mere philologist and antiquary perform an important work in the business of exposition. It is nothing more than the work of hewing the wood and drawing the water. In religious worship, the tendency of the heart, under its corrupt inclinations, is to exalt the ceremonial above the spiritual; and in devotion to the study of the Scriptures, we are in danger of exalting the scientific above the spiritual; of resting in the means, rather than in the end; in learned investigation, rather than in the spiritual apprehension by the heart, of the truths to which those investigations lead. The enemy of holiness and parent of error cares not in what way he succeeds in keeping us from understanding the truth; whether by inducing us to neglect the essential aids of learning and study, under the fanatical impression that the Spirit will give all needed illumination without the use of means, or by leading us to rest in these scientific investigations alone, without the indispensable assistance of the Holy Spirit. Here, especially, must the well furnished head be found in alliance with a heart controlled by grace. There is no portion of the Scriptures which requires more than does this Song, a sanctified state of the affections in him who undertakes the interpretation. Without this, the marrow of the book cannot be relished or detected. Here, especially, are things which must be not so much philologically, as spiritually discerned; and which, to the natural mind, however learned, without the teaching of the Spirit, must appear as absolute foolishness. To such we may say, in the language of Herbert:

> "Slight not these few words;
> If truly said, they may take part
> Among the best in art.
> The fineness which a hymn or psalm affords,
> Is, when the soul unto the lines accords."

In this Song, truth is taught, not by didactic statements, but by figurative illustrations. As the doctrines relating to the person and work of Jesus are not only set forth literally in the New Testament, but are illustrated by the emblems of the Jewish service; so the reciprocal love of Christ and his people, unfolded by plain statement in other portions of the Bible, is here elucidated by poetical imagery and comparisons. The types are correctly interpreted by a knowledge of the doctrines of the New Testament, while those doctrines are in turn made clear only by intelligent acquaintance with the meaning of the types. And the love of the Redeemer and the redeemed, as taught by himself and his inspired disciples, is illustrated in the emblematical language of this Song; while, at the same time, the key to a knowledge of these instructive figures is found in acquaintance with the divine love here so beautifully elucidated. A single emblem or illustration, standing out by itself, is called a type or figure of things to come. When the emblems are multiplied, and the figure continued to some length, the whole becomes an allegory. Such is the nature of this book. It is an allegorical illustration of the operations of love in the bosom of the saint and of the Redeemer.

Lowth defines an allegory to be "a figure, which, under the literal sense of the words, conceals a foreign or a distant meaning." Dividing allegories into three kinds, the continued metaphor, the parabolic allegory, and the mystical or historic allegory, he supposes this Song to belong to the third class, which conveys under the veil of some historical narrative a sacred and more elevated meaning. According to him, the parabolic allegory "consists of a continued narration of fictitious events, applied by way of simile to the illustration of some important truth." The difference between the historic and the parabolic allegory lies in this fact: in the latter, the incidents are partly or wholly fictitious; in the former they are entirely real. We differ from him, in holding this book to belong to the parabolic, rather than the historic allegory. Fairbairn's definition is good:* "An allegory is a narrative, either expressly feigned for the purpose, or, if describing facts which really took place, describing them only for the purpose of representing certain higher truths or principles than the narrative in its immediate representation, whether real or fictitious, could possibly have taught. The immediate representation, therefore, is either invented, or at least used, as a mere cover for the higher sense, which may refer to things ever so remote from those primarily denoted, if only the corresponding relations are preserved." The inquiry then arises—Receiving this book as a part of the canon, what reasons have we for giving it an allegorical interpretation? While proceeding to mention these, we consider the point as incontestably settled, that no portion of the Scriptures has a better right than this Song to a place among the pages of inspiration. Taking this book as canonical, are we to go no further than the literal import, or are we to give it an allegorical meaning? We expound it allegorically for the following reasons.

1. The reception of this book into the canon cannot be accounted for but on the ground that it represents allegorically the reciprocal love of Christ and his people. There must have been some reason for taking it into the canon. It could not have been for singing of carnal love: this the whole aim of the Scriptures opposes. And when such men as Umbreit, Ammon, and Velthusen maintain that it consists of amatory epistles by Solomon, and Michaelis supposes it was placed here to guard against the opinions of those who hold conjugal love inconsistent with the love of God—they forget that a house divided

* Fairbairn's Typology, vol. i. p. 10.

against itself cannot stand; that as the design of the Scriptures is to effect the purity of heart necessary for seeing God, they cannot by any possibility sing of illicit love, or even the praises of conjugal affection. "Impossible! impossible!" says Aben Ezra, the celebrated rabbi, "that the Song of songs should treat of carnal love; everything is expressed in it in the way of allegory. Were not the book of the highest dignity, it could never have been incorporated among the sacred writings. Nor on this point is there any controversy." To all such objections, the answer of Rosenmüller is sufficient: "The universal genius and method of the sacred books exclude the idea of admitting among them songs about the ordinary love of man and woman." The marriage of Solomon was not a thing of such importance, as to warrant the Jews in placing among the sacred Scriptures a song restricted to this topic only, and uninspired. Nothing was admitted into the canon that is not inspired, and that has not a direct bearing on the spiritual improvement of man—that is not profitable for instruction in righteousness. 2 Tim. iii. 16.

2. The allegorical interpretation is in perfect accordance with the spirit of oriental poetry. "The Song of songs is an oriental poem; and this allegoric mode of describing the sacred union subsisting between mankind at large, or an individual and pious soul, and the great Creator, is common to almost all eastern poets, from the earliest down to the present age. It is impossible, without such an esoteric interpretation, to understand many of the passages of the chaste and virtuous Sadi, or the more impassioned Hafiz; and the Turkish commentators, Feridun, Sudi, and Seid Ali, following the example of the ancient Hushangis, have uniformly thus interpreted them, as they have also the writings of all the Sufi poets;

though in many instances they have unquestionably pursued their mystic meaning to an extravagant length. The Leili and Mejnún of the Persians may be contemplated as the royal bridegroom and his beloved spouse of the Hebrews. The former have furnished a subject for a variety of the bards of Iran. But whether, in the instance before us, Solomon intended, or not, to introduce the mystic allegory here assumed, it is incontrovertible that precisely such an allegory exists in the Mesnavi, or poem upon the loves of the same illustrious personages, Leili and Mejnún, by the elegant Nezami, who, as well as Hafiz, in the opinion of Sir William Jones, always appears to apply the name of Leili to the omnipresent Spirit of God. This emblematic mysticism in the bards of Iran, is quite as conspicuous in those of India; and the Vedantis, or Hindu commentators, have been as eager as the Sufis themselves to attribute such a double meaning to their compositions. Of all the poems of the East, by far the nearest in subject, style, and imagery, to the Song of Solomon, are the Gitagovinda,* or Songs of Jayadeva. The subject of the inimitable Jayadeva is the loves of Crishna and Radha, or the reciprocal attraction between the divine goodness and the human soul. His style, like that of the Hebrew bard, is in the highest degree flowery; his poem consists of distinct songs or idyls, some of which are soliloquies, and others dialogues; but all of them, like the Song of songs, confined to the same theme, and in some measure progressive in its history."† Major Scott Waring says: "The Persians insist that we should give them the credit of understanding their own language; that all the odes of their celebrated poets are mystical,

---

* A translation of this may be found in Adam Clark's Commentary on the Song, and in Sir William Jones's Works.

† Song of songs, or Sacred Idyls, by John Mason Good, p. 20.

and breathe a fervent spirit of adoration towards the Supreme Being. They maintain that the poets, being generally Soofees, profess eager desire without carnal affection, and circulate the cup, but no material goblet, since all is spiritual to them, all is mystery within mystery. In fact, they regard the poetry as of the same nature as Solomon's Song; and, indeed, the fact that so large a proportion of the poetry of Western Asia, that is, of Arabia and Persia, is employed in the expression of religious emotions mystically, under the same image that we find there, is a very strong argument for the general opinion that the Canticles form a mystical, or allegorical, or religious poem, the details of which, although they seem to us hard to be understood, are perfectly intelligible, in a sacred sense, to the Persian and Arabian of the present day, as they were to the ancient Hebrew."

In his essay on the mystical poetry of the Persians and Hindus, Sir William Jones says all that need be said on this subject: "A figurative mode of expressing the fervour of devotion, or the ardent love of created spirits towards their beneficent Creator, has prevailed from time immemorial in Asia: particularly among the Persian theists, both ancient Hushangis and modern Sufis. This singular species of poetry consists almost wholly of a mystical religious allegory, though it seems, on a transient view, to contain only the sentiments of a wild and voluptuous libertinism. Passages in Barrow on the love of God, and the mysterious union of the soul with him, border on quietism and enthusiastic devotion; and differ only from the mystical theology of the Sufis and Yogis, as the flowers and fruits of Europe differ in scent and flavour from those of Asia; or as European differs from Asiatic eloquence; the same strain, in poetical measure, would rise up to the odes of Spencer on divine love and beauty; and in a higher key, with richer embellishments, to the songs of Hafiz and Jayadeva, the raptures of the Masnavi, and the mysteries of the Bhagavat. Many zealous admirers of Hafiz insist that by wine he invariably means devotion, by kisses and embraces the raptures of piety. The poet himself gives a colour in many passages to such an interpretation; and without it we can hardly conceive that his poems, or those of his numerous imitators, would be tolerated in a Musselman country, especially at Constantinople, where they are venerated as divine compositions."* The Sufis have a regular lexicon of large size, the express design of which is to give the allegorical meaning of the words most frequently used in this kind of poetry—as in the following specimens: wine means devotion; sleep, meditation; perfume, religious hope; kiss, pious rapture; ebriety, religious ardour; lips, mysteries of God; beauty, perfections of God; tresses, glory of God.

As the Song is an oriental production, the allegorical interpretation is the natural one to a person acquainted with the spirit of oriental literature. To such, the literal interpretation is that which appears far-fetched, vapid, and unnatural.

3. The names employed to designate the two important persons in this Song, prove it to be an allegory. Shelomoh and Shulamith differ from each other only as Cornelius differs from Cornelia. They are in as perfect keeping with the tenor of the allegory as John Bunyan's Christian and Christiana are with the scope of the Pilgrim's Progress. According to prophecy, Jesus was to be called the Prince of Peace; and angels heralded his coming as "peace on earth." The names here adopted

---

* Sir W. Jones's essay on "The Mystical Poetry of the Persians and Hindus."—*Works*, vol. i. p. 445.

are in accordance with such a character—Shelomoh meaning Prince of peace; and Shulamith, the bride of Shelomoh, the Princess of peace.

4. There are many things in the Song which cannot be explained by any knowledge we have of Hebrew customs; nor indeed in any way, without taking the book as an allegory, rather than a personal narrative, without reference to facts as existing, and solely to illustrate truth. Such departure from rigid facts and customs is allowable in an allegory. In reading history, our object is to have reproduced before the mind a picture of events as they really existed: in an allegory we look for nothing further than the illustration of truth; and therefore he who weaves it, is not bound, in bringing together the incidents, to follow any order of nature or of facts; but is at liberty to combine incidents in any way that imagination, guided by reason, sees conducive to the end in view. "By what other means," says Warburton, "except by revelation, can an allegorical writing be known to be allegorical, but by circumstances in it which cannot be reconciled to the story or fable that serves both for a cover and vehicle to the moral? When the allegory is of some length, it can scarce be otherwise but that some circumstances in it must be varied from the fact to adapt it to the moral."* In such compositions as the vision of Mirza or of Theodore, the history of Seged or the Pilgrim's Progress, the adventures of Sir Guyon or of Faustus, we do not expect an adherence to facts, or even to probabilities. "The poet is universally allowed to place his personages, even when strictly historical, in circumstances which we know could not have been those that actually surrrounded them."† And we must notice

---

* Warburton's Divine Legation, book iii. 274.
† Edinburgh Review, No. 181, p. 109.

the difference between an allegory and a type. Types are incidents, personages, or objects, appointed under the Old Dispensation as illustration of truths to be thereafter fully revealed. The meaning conveyed by them is metaphorical, but the incidents in which that meaning is embodied, are not to any degree imaginary, but are throughout real. While an allegory is a continued metaphor, the materials composing it may be drawn indiscriminately from the domains of fact or of fiction. This Song is not a typical, but an allegorical representation of the love of Christ and his Church, a love that existed and needed elucidation under the Old Economy, no less than under the New. Hence many things are found in it that are a deviation from Jewish customs, and from human facts; and are here written down for setting in a clear light this wondrous love. It will be sufficient now to refer to chap. iii. 2, chap. v. 7, and chap. iii. 10, "paved with love." Therefore it is that Rosenmüller says, on chap. iii. 4, *Hinc satis patet ἀλληγορικῶς hæc intelligenda esse.* And it is for obviating the difficulty arising from the disagreement of circumstances here mentioned, with Jewish antiquities, that some commentators have resorted to the supposition that a part of the incidents here recorded, occurred only in a dream. When the book is viewed as an allegory, all these difficulties disappear.

5. The obvious connection of this Song with the forty-fifth and seventy-second psalms, is another claim for giving it an allegorical meaning. The thirty-seventh psalm bears a very strong resemblance to the book of Proverbs, and the thirty-ninth psalm to the book of Job; as the Song does to the psalms just mentioned. There are certainly trilogies to be found in the book of Psalms, though we would run no parallel whatever between them and the trilogy of the Greek drama. Thus, according to

Hengstenberg, psalms cviii. cx. and cxi. form a trilogy. The same is true of the Song of Solomon, and psalm xlv. and lxxii. They are all the parts of a whole, and draw their imagery from the court and reign of Solomon. Psalm lxxii. represents the nature of the reign of the Prince of Peace as righteous, universal, gracious, and enduring; psalm xlv. sets forth, under the marriage of a noble, beauteous, conquering prince with a foreign princess, the relation of the Messiah to his chosen people; the Song of Solomon illustrates under a comparison drawn from the mutual affection of such a king and queen, doubtless the same referred to in psalm xlv.—the reciprocal love of Jesus and his redeemed. The oldest interpreters, both Jewish and Christian, give these two psalms no other than an allegorical interpretation. Considering, therefore, their identity with this book, in imagery, spirit, and aim, all correct principles of exposition require that we give to the Song, equally with them, an allegorical interpretation.

6. The Scriptures apply the spirit of this allegory to Christ and the Church. This is not indeed done within the narrow compass of the book called the Song. It is enough that such application be found in the limits of the Bible. The clew to the meaning of the parable of the sower was not given at the time it was spoken, but afterwards, when the disciples had been made to feel themselves unable to see through the mystery, and had come to Jesus for an explanation. The interpretation of this parable and of others, is as much detached from the parable as the grounds for explaining this Song are detached from the Song. The clew to the whole system of the Jewish ritual is not found till we come to the Epistle to the Hebrews. The solution of many of the prophecies given in allegorical dress, is to be got, not

from any hints appended as to the specific facts pointed out thereby, but only from the general meaning of such symbols in prophetical language, and from the future history of the world, viewed in comparison with such meaning. It is not a thing of the least moment, that the clew to a prophecy, parable, or allegory, be given in the book containing it, or by the man who gave it utterance. The material point is, that it be spoken by the Holy Spirit, and be found within the word of God. The various books of inspiration are merely different chapters in the one great volume of revelation. The whole has one Author, the divine Spirit of Wisdom, and whatever truths are there found, derive their authority, "not of men, neither by man," but from the presence of the Holy Ghost. And according to the laws of poetic composition, we could not expect to find in Canticles itself, an indication that the book is an allegory, and that such is its meaning. The poem is more finished and more pleasant as a study, in its present form, than it could be with the thread of the allegory continually broken by interpolations concerning the meaning. Is it necessary, or in good taste, to write on an allegorical picture or piece of statuary, what it means. The finest allegorical poems, and the finest allegorical passages of poems not wholly allegorical, are framed on the same principle with this Song—of leaving much to be done by the reader towards threading out the literal meaning. Every piece of this kind is a species of enigma: the solution of this is to be sought at the lips of the Holy Spirit; he will lay open the veins of wisdom here contained, to those who search for them as for hid treasures.

The question therefore is, Do we find in the Scriptures any clew to the meaning of an allegory like this? any thing leading us to suppose that such language may be applied to the illustration of the love of Christ and his people? On this point we have full and satisfactory instructions. In many passages, the relation of husband and wife is used for setting forth the love and the relations of the Redeemer and the redeemed. This is, in truth, the leading and standing comparison on this subject, throughout the whole Scriptures. For establishing the inspiration of a book, there is no necessity for it to be quoted by Christ and his Apostles, or for its illustrations to receive such sanction. The Song is not the only book in the Old Testament where this comparison is used. It is the leading and standing comparison on this subject. And how can there be a doubt concerning its meaning, after such language as this: "I have likened the daughter of Zion to a comely and delicate woman." Jer. vi. 2. After such frequent repetition of it through the compass of revelation, one of the last things in the Scriptures is the setting of this allegory beyond all question, by calling the Church "the bride, the wife of the Lamb," Rev. xxi. 9; as though it was said, The bride alluded to in those many passages as the wife of the Lamb, is the redeemed Church. And how could we expect anything more satisfactory than the words of our Saviour, in Matt. xxii. 1—10, and xxv. 1—13? There the meaning is made clear by the restriction, "The kingdom of heaven is like unto a certain king which made a marriage."

Here, therefore, we have a volume which the Holy Spirit has given to man by inspiration, consisting of different chapters, called by us books, published at intervals, through a succession of ages, according to his wise arrangements in unfolding the plan of salvation. One of these chapters is occupied as an elucidation of the love of Christ and his people, by means of a comparison taken from the love of husband and wife. In perfect keeping with the laws of poetry, this allegory is not marred by the introduction of sentences giving a clew to its literal meaning. It lies in the casket of revelation, an exquisite gem, engraved with emblematical characters, with nothing literal thereon to break the consistency of their beauty. But in other parts of this volume, its author, the Holy Spirit, has very distinctly stated that the bride there introduced is the redeemed Church, the sanctified soul; and that "her Maker is her husband, the Lord of Hosts is his name."

7. The Scriptures do more than merely apply the spirit of this allegory to Christ and his Church; they set forth the union of Christ and his Church, as a great fact on which the relation of marriage is founded, for being the illustration of this union to the comprehension of men. In Eph. v. 22—33, the apostle takes the truth of the oneness of Jesus and his people, and makes it the basis of an argument for illustrating and enforcing the duties of the marriage relation. These were very much violated in the heathen world, as they are even at the present day; they lie at the foundation of everything good and stable among men, and therefore required to be set in a very clear light, and on a very strong basis. This has been done. What, therefore, is that basis? It is nothing less than the union existing between Christ and his people, and the likeness of the relation between husband and wife to this union. He does not go from the marriage relation to the union of Christ and the Church, as though the former was the first and better established principle; but he comes down from the union of Jesus and his people, to the marriage relation, inasmuch as that union was the first and best recognized fact, and the ground of the reciprocal duties of the marriage state.

While man was formed in the image of God, and thus bears in his constitution certain endowments which are the likeness of certain attributes of the divine character; in his social relation, the union between husband and wife was intended to be an image of the relation existing between Jesus and the redeemed; just as the relation of father and son is an illustration of the union between two persons of the Trinity. In the purpose of God, this union existed before the creation of man and the institution of the marriage relation. It was an original picture lodged in the mind of God, of a great and glorious fact thereafter to be developed, which it was necessary to unfold to man, and of which the marriage relation was a transcript. God could doubtless have made other arrangements for representing to us this spiritual relation; it is sufficient for us to know that marriage has been shaped with reference to this end. Love in the human soul is the image of love in God, and the love of husband and wife is the image of that love of God in Christ exercised towards his people. This is not an uncertain figment of the fancy, but truth resting on the deliberate purpose of God the Creator.

The apostle brings out distinctly several points on this topic; Christ is the head of the Church;—the Church is his body;—he is the Saviour of this body, by and through him it was created anew from its state of spiritual death;—this salvation or new creation is the result of his love, and is a strong exhibition of that love; —it required him to leave heaven and suffer great sacrifices;—it prompts him to foster and cherish the Church by sanctification;—this is in order that the Church may be without spot or wrinkle, perfectly lovely;—the Church, as a consequence, is subject to Christ. He states these truths as the foundation of the following duties: As Christ is the head of the Church, so the husband is the head of the wife; as the Church is the body of Christ, so the wife is really one with the husband, as truly as the body of an individual is one with the person; —as the Church is formed from Christ, so the wife was formed from the body of the husband;—as this forming of the Church is the result of his love, or for the purpose of gratifying that love, so the existence of the marriage relation calls into exercise the strongest affection of man;—as it required Jesus to leave the glory of the Father and heaven, so must a man leave father and mother and cleave to his wife;—as Christ fosters and cherishes the Church, so should a man foster and cherish his wife, even as his own body;—as this was done in order that the Church might be made more lovely, husbands should so cherish their wives as to bear with infirmities;—as the Church is subject to Christ, so must the wife be subject to the husband. According to the plain purport of this passage, this union is the appointed means for illustrating to us what is the nature of the relation between Christ and his people; and the character of that relation cannot be understood in this world without studying this union. Therefore, in applying to Christ and his Church the language of the Song, we are only using in words prepared for us by the Holy Spirit the illustrations which the Creator established on this subject when the world began.

8. Man was made in the image of God—that is, his nature or soul has been filled up with endowments which represent certain characteristics of the invisible God. These faculties are a living portrait of divine attributes, far from being perfect, yet correct as far as they go, and sufficient for our present wants until we are brought into a more perfect state and a clear vision of the divine

glory. That such a state is before us, is evident from the promises given us of seeing God. Matt. v. 8; 1 Cor. xii. 12. When, therefore, the Scriptures speak of God as hearing, seeing, loving, hating, &c., they do not use illustrations caught up at random, as when we use a common simile; but they are adopting as representations of the divine attributes things which were established for this purpose by the Creator. The furniture of the tabernacle, and the Jewish ritual were not more definitely appointed by God as representations of divine things, than was the fabric of the human soul. And when God said, "Let us make man in our image," he meant, "Let us now form a creature who shall be a portrait, shall combine a likeness, of certain of our intellectual and moral perfections." Of those thus implanted in the soul, a leading one was love. "God is love." This affection was inlaid in the human heart for representing to us the love of God. When we ask of our Creator what is the character of his love to the saints, he replies, that in forming us in his image, he placed in the soul love as the image of his love; and that by studying the workings of this affection in the tenderest and dearest relations, we will see what he intended to be the standing representation of his love to us. Love to God is the gem; and the frame-work of the soul with its curious workmanship and costly finishing, is the setting wherein this brilliant is inlaid for reflecting the splendour of the divine love. This living temple of the human soul, which once stood in perfection, has been laid in ruins by sin; and the sculpture bearing the image of the divine attributes has been lying, like the alabaster slabs and statues of Nineveh, dilapidated, defaced, and hidden from view. Some of the truths originally written on the chambers of the soul, but so sadly lost, have been brought to light again and written in the pages of Scripture—thence to be transferred by the Holy Spirit to the fleshly tablet of the heart. The love of God, engraved so gloriously on the soul at creation, but now so completely lost, has been rescued from ruins, and is set before us in this alabaster tablet of the Song, by the same original image, the love of the human heart—dim and broken indeed, yet the best means possible for illustrating the love of God to us, in our present state. By going down into the ruins of the soul, and exhuming the table on which is wrought in bold relief the affection of husband and wife, we shall find—though in lines broken and decayed—what our Creator has appointed as the image to us of the love of God.

9. Hence, the principle of allegorical instruction is found to be wrought into the very nature of man. The human soul is itself a living allegory: the truths it embodies and represents are truths relating to the character of God.* We are living emblems of the divine perfections. We were formed for being illustrations of the attributes of our invisible, spiritual Creator. Accordingly, when genius would make abstract truths tangible, intelligible, and attractive, resort is at once had to emblems, comparisons, and allegories. These constitute, to a great extent, the embellishments of poetry. Some of the greatest works of genius are pure allegories. This principle pervades the whole Pagan Mythology of all countries and all ages. Even facts have there received an allegorical shape for embalming them in the memory and making them interesting to the curiosity of future ages. "The ancients," says Bryant, "loved to

---

* "The system of the world may be called an allegorical fiction in which there is an outward bodily appearance wherein a meaning lies concealed, as the soul within the body."—*Sallust on the gods.*

wrap up everything in mystery and fable."* Whichever of the two leading theories concerning the origin of Pagan idolatry be adopted, the principle here stated will appear true. The beautiful fable of Cupid and Psyche† has the same aim with the Song of Solomon—the illustration of divine love towards the human soul. The interval between the two allegories is indeed as great as the difference between a state of nature and a state of grace—reason unaided and revelation—the glimmerings of fancy and the effulgence of the Holy Ghost;—they both however point to the one end—the human soul as the object of heavenly love. The pleasure and profit had from poetical personification is allied with this, and has its foundation in the nature of man. Many of the brightest gems of poetry are abstract truths and things personified; and when thus personified, are seen to assume a garb kindred to that of allegory.

Since these principles are thus woven by nature into our being, God acts according to those laws in revealing to us his love through an allegorical guise. The love of God to us and our love to him, lie at the foundation of our eternal happiness. Whatever other knowledge may be possessed, we can never be happy without a practical acquaintance with these. There is, therefore, need that they be unfolded to us in the plainest manner, and according to the laws of our being. Those laws require this to be done by allegory, such as is found in the Song.

10. As Leighton says, "The experimental knowledge of Christ's loveliness and the believer's love, is the best

---

* Analysis of Ancient Mythology, vol. ii. 98; Faber's Horæ Mosaicæ, ii. 231.

† Apuleii Metamorph. lib. iv. See also the remarks in Maurice's Indian Antiquities, vol. v. 655.

commentary on the whole strain of this allegorical Song."* The laying up in the sacred Scriptures, of truths and books that can be comprehended only by developments made in the after-course of the Christian life, was intended to be one of the classes of cumulative proofs of the divine origin of our faith. Different minds require different kinds of proof; and the same mind, passing through various states, as from unbelief to mature holiness, may be more affected at various stages by evidence which, though less satisfactory at a former period, becomes more powerful than any of the preceding, when the heart has been attempered to its nature. The external evidence is more adapted to the unrenewed mind; the internal, requiring a spiritual discernment, is more convincing to the pious heart. There are miracles for the irreligious; prophecies for ages as they pass, and prophecies for the most remote ages; truths revealed by the Holy Spirit, for different stages of growth in grace; and there is this book for the later periods of the Christian life. And when we find its passages opening their meaning in the light of our religious experience, just as prophecies are seen fulfilling in the operation of events in the world, we have another class of proofs for the divinity of our faith and of the Scriptures. Fairbairn lays down the principle, "that in determining the existence and import of particular types, we must be guided, *not so much by any knowledge possessed, or supposed to be possessed, by the ancient worshippers concerning their prospective fulfilment, as from the light furnished by their realization in the great facts and revelations of the gospel.*"† According to this, the design and meaning of such passages of Scripture as this Song, is to be fully

---

* Sermon on Canticles i. 3. † Typology, vol. i., p. 118.

ascertained, not by the impenitent, nor by renewed persons who have not reached the advancement in piety for which they were intended; but by those who have attained that stage of spiritual light and growth in grace for which they were specially designed. The Redeemer has made provision for continually, as it were, feeding our confidence in the divine origin of these words of promise by which our spirits live. Fresh proofs, rich, convincing, and varied, are found along the whole of our way to heaven. Without forgetting those which are behind, or ceasing to feel their force, we find our persuasion on this point unceasingly gathering strength from new evidence coming into view by our advance, and by the brightening dawn. Particular doctrines, which were foolishness to us in our unrenewed condition, and stumbling-blocks on our first coming to Christ, do, as the day breaks over our soul, not only lose their repulsiveness, but, like the headlands rising afar in the ocean, from which the shades of night and mists of morning are rolling away, tower towards heaven with the beauty of Carmel, and the majesty of mountains forming the foundation of the city of the living God. The same principle is true concerning books of Scripture, no less than of the truths contained in those books.

The cure for unbelief is not argument, but the action of the Holy Spirit. To the same source must we look for the removal of unbelieving prejudices, the remnants of native corruption, that linger in the breast of the Christian, against certain truths and portions of the Scriptures. Every objection to this book has been often answered; but after conviction has been carried to the understanding, the old repugnance will remain, till grace has suitably illumined the heart. In the eyes of many who are Israelites indeed, in whom is no guile, this Song is in as bad repute as was Nazareth of old; and when they say, Can any good thing come out of this book? with the feelings of Philip, we reply, Come and see. Here we have found Him of whom Moses in the law and the prophets did write; and as that ancient saint saw in Jesus of Nazareth more than the son of Joseph, even the Messiah—so does the divine illumination cause us to see in this portrait of the Beloved, a greater than Solomon, even him in whom dwells all the fulness of the Godhead bodily.

When, therefore, we are asked what proof we have that this Song is to be interpreted allegorically, our answer is, that among other proofs we have this, viz. There are periods in the Christian life when the soul enlightened by the Holy Spirit, sees a deep, instructive, and glorious meaning in the Song; when the truth thus found here, proves to be the very manna of the heart, the quintessence of spiritual nourishment, with less of the tang of earth and more of the flavour of heaven; and the meaning thus got, and thus delightful, is an allegorical meaning. The persons who see nothing but beauty, instructiveness, and consolation in this book—a class who have pressed into the foreground of holy attainments on earth, and contemplate it from that point of view—are of one mind, in giving it an allegorical interpretation. They testify, that thus understood, the Song has heavenly attractions, but that explained in any other way, it has nothing spiritually beautiful or desirable. In the treatment of persons under disease, there are different medicines, stimulants, and food required for the various steps of their recovery; and it would be preposterous for any invalid to assert that because a particular thing might not be adapted to his infirmity or stage of disease, it could not be useful to any other person, or even to himself at some future time. He must be no less than a madman, who could go over the chest that had been filled with restoratives by an able physician, and break every bottle which might not suit his own fancy. The sick man is not capable of judging for himself, much less for others. The Bible is a depository of medicinal truths for our enfeebled souls and suffering race, in all ages, and during the whole course of our life. There is virtue in every book, and in every verse. They have been filled by the hand of the heavenly Physician, for meeting our spiritual wants in every possible variety of circumstances. Let us beware how we call in question his wisdom—how we throw away books filled with rich infusion of spiritual doctrines for the maladies of man. A healthy person could judge whether the medicine or the chest had evidence of having come from the physician said to have prepared it; the invalid alone could find in the medicine the virtue bespeaking its healing power and fitness for his case. And while any Christian, or even an irreligious man, may judge of the external evidence for this book, the advanced believer only can pronounce properly on the divine virtue herein contained. When the recovering patient finds any medicine benefiting him by its use at any particular stage of his restoration, he has the best proof that it was intended for his cure, and was placed there by wisdom. His sober experience is worth all the conjectural theories of speculative philosophers.

For the foregoing reasons, the Song must have an allegorical interpretation. Hence we must not expect to find here any statement of doctrine in a didactic form. We must here search for truth, not in the form in which it appears in the Epistle to the Romans, but in the guise it assumes in the figures of the Jewish ritual. Beautiful and instructive though the services of the law are to ourselves, how dim was the apprehension Israel had of their significance; and how great is the flood of light poured on them from the knowledge imparted by God manifest in flesh. As mere poetry, this book has transcendent beauty; but when viewed in the light of knowledge of the glorious love of God, shed abroad in our hearts by the Holy Ghost, it assumes a splendour and instructiveness unimagined and unsurpassed.

In the interpretation of this Song, there are therefore two separate lines of investigation, bearing upon each other and converging, though perfectly distinct. There is the study of the language, and the study of the allegorical meaning. After knowing all that can be known of the literal import, and the customs here referred to, there remains the more important task of determining what are the spiritual truths intended to be conveyed to us in this figurative language. The meaning wrapped up in the folds of the allegory is the main object of search.* Speaking of the time and learning thrown away on the inquiry, whether the bride was a daughter of the king of Egypt or a native of Palestine, Kitto says, "We formerly thought this question one of much interest; but latterly this and other external points connected with it, have appeared to us in greatly reduced importance, in our search after the inner meaning, which under this aspect the book presents, the nutritive kernel which this outer husk contains, and to which it is adapted."† Hence the commentators who have gone no further than an elucidation of the literal

---

* The instruction conveyed by the allegory or parable, demands the expositor's chief attention; and the circumstances, just so far as they lead to the right interpretation, and no further."—*Scott on Cant.* i. 2.

† Daily Bible Illustrations, on the Song, p. 382.

meaning, even by all the learning that may here be brought to bear, cannot be considered as having expounded this scripture. The meaning of the allegory yet remains untouched; and to the scholar who has gone thus far, this meaning may be as perfectly unknown as is the narrative of the facts there contained, to him who does not understand the language. Biblical learning furnishes the key to a knowledge of the book as a poem; there is another element necessary for giving us a clew to the spiritual meaning embodied in this mystical poetry. In the words of the eminent scholar just mentioned, "It is only those who are greatly experienced in the mysteries of man's inner life, and whose souls have been tried by passing through many fires, that can truly feel all that this book means, and, feeling, are enabled to understand it."* The mere literal meaning of the prophecy of Isaiah was intelligible to the Ethiopian eunuch; and yet he said, How can I understand, except some man should guide me? Of whom speaketh the prophet thus? of himself, or of some other man? Acts viii. 31. In this Song particularly, a knowledge of the letter gives nothing like the meaning of the book, without a knowledge of the spirit. The words of Jesus are equally applicable here—"It is the Spirit that quickeneth, the flesh profiteth nothing: the words that I speak unto you, they are spirit, and they are life." John vi. 63. This is the key to the whole interpretation of the Song. The meek will he teach his way, and he will show them his covenant. The secret of the Lord is with them that fear him; and as without a parable spake our Lord not unto the multitudes, but when they were alone he expounded all things to his disciples, Mark iv. 34; so must

---

* Kitto's Daily Bible Readings, on the Song, p. 390.

we still, with meekness and godly fear, seek to be alone with him in prayer, that we may ask of him the meaning of the parables contained in the written word, and receive the Holy Ghost for teaching us all things, and guiding us into all truth. A fundamental inquiry in the Song is, Of whom speaketh Solomon this? of himself, or of some other person? And never can we understand what we here read, until after diligent study and humble meditation we have the Holy Spirit to begin at the same scripture and preach unto us Jesus. He must open our eyes before we can behold the wondrous things contained in this portion of God's law. Whatever our knowledge of the word of God, certain it is that our hearts will never burn within us, till Jesus himself open to us the Scriptures. None other can expound to us in all this Song the things concerning himself.

The necessity of the influence of the Holy Spirit in interpreting divine truth, is taught by Peter, who says, we must receive it as a first principle, "that no prophecy of the Scripture is of any private interpretation."* Showing in this passage he had not followed cunningly devised fables, in making known the power and coming of our Lord; he points out two distinct grounds of confirmation for the truth of the gospel. The first is external, and depends on the testimony of the witnesses who were with him in the holy mount of transfiguration, and were there eye-witnesses of the magnificent glory, and heard the voice of the Father from heaven in attestation of the divinity of the Son. The second is internal—the persuasion which every true believer has of the divine origin of the Scriptures, from what he sees and feels of the power of these truths, under the influence of the Holy Spirit. This demonstration, this inward witness of

* 2 Peter i. 20.

the Spirit, is a safer reliance than a voice from heaven; is a more sure word of prophecy, of divine instruction regarding the truth of our faith, an interpretation or expression of the divine will on which we may more certainly rely. Without at all undervaluing the external evidence, the miracles wrought in confirmation of Christianity, the believer finds, as he grows in grace, that his conviction of the inexpressible excellence of his faith, is felt more and more distinctly to rest, not on the testimony adduced from men, so much as on the words which the Holy Ghost speaketh, through the Scriptures, to his sanctified heart. Divine truth kindled to a flame by the Spirit is within his soul as a light shining in a dismal place. To this word, a lamp unto his feet, and a light unto his path, he does well to take heed, until the shadows of error and sin flee away, until the day dawn and the day-star arise in our hearts. But in receiving the advantage and pleasure had from the Scriptures, thus spiritually discerned, we must start with this essential truth, must know this first, that no prophecy of the Scripture, no portion of divine instruction there revealed, is of any private interpretation;* that is, of an interpretation that may be reached by the exercise of any powers peculiar to the unaided human mind by nature; for as prophecy, or the teachings contained in the Scriptures, were not discovered and uttered by the unassisted intellect of man, but were spoken by men borne along by the Holy Ghost,

---

* *Idus, quod animo acquisivimus et possidemus:* That of which one is himself the owner, possessor, and producer. Our exposition of this passage agrees with that of the Romanists, in holding this word to mean, that Scripture cannot be interpreted by man without aid of some kind. According to the fundamental error of their system, in putting the Church in the place of Christ, they hold that this needed assistance must be got from the Church, we say that it can be furnished only by the Holy Spirit.

those truths cannot be understood and interpreted by us, without the enlightening influences of the same Spirit.

The parable of the sower derives its great interest from its instructiveness through the exposition of our Lord. This application of those simple facts to the illustration of spiritual things, invests them with great beauty. Touching as is the parable of the prodigal son, how greatly is the attractiveness of the narrative heightened, when viewed as illustrating the joy there is in heaven over one sinner that repenteth. The types, parables, and allegories of Scripture, rich in literary materials, are like the curiously wrought lanterns of oriental countries, which do not reveal their beauty of transparency and emblems till lighted up within:—these portions of truth, though a light unto our feet and a lantern unto our path, reveal their excellence, splendour, and power to guide, only when, through their divine emblems, streams on us the inner light of the Holy Ghost and the Lamb. An exposition of the sower or of the prodigal son, that might go no farther than an elucidation of the literal meaning, without searching for the golden vein of spiritual instruction there concealed, might be of use as materials ready to the hand of some other person, but would fail to give an idea of the mind of the Spirit. In all our duties, human agency must be blended with divine co-operation. In raising the fruits of the earth, there is a duty for the husbandman, and there is an influence that can be supplied only by the Creator; in spiritual things Paul may plant and Apollos water, but God gives the increase; and in interpreting the Scriptures, in this Song more especially than any other part of them, there is a work to be done by the mind, in gathering all that can be furnished from the stores of biblical learning, and besides this, there must be the aid of the Holy Ghost for rendering our efforts perfect and successful. Here, learning can go no farther than the threshold; the key by which the mysteries within are reached, must be furnished by the Spirit of God. To this subject, apply the words of one of the poems of Gregory Nazianzen, when speaking of the difference between rhetorical display and true spiritual interpretation of the Scriptures:

> "All our discourse is two-fold,
> Words and meaning. Those are like the outward
> Raiment; this, like the body within that is clothed.
> But we take not much account of the external
> How it fares, but very much of the inward.
> For our salvation resides in the meaning,
> So as it be declared, and made manifest."

Like the tabernacle, beautiful in the eyes of the spectator, with its sides overlaid with gold, the Song, unsurpassed in poetic excellence, may fix the admiration of even an unrenewed mind; but when the soul is admitted into the recesses of its interior meaning, and the hand of the Holy Spirit lifts the mysterious veil, we gaze with the trepidation of holy affection on something more entrancing than the ark of the covenant, the cherubim, and the human form seen amid the cloud of glory. Fanaticism and ignorance may undervalue the indispensable and fundamental assistance supplied by learning, but the mind best instructed by the Holy Spirit will be best able to use these aids aright, without unduly exalting them or treating them with neglect.

The error into which many pious commentators have fallen, seems to have sprung mainly from the attempt to make too much out of the allegory. In expounding the types, some of the most learned and pious among the old divines are greatly at fault by the extreme to which they have pushed their principle of interpretation. They appear almost to think, that everything must be a type, in which there can be found even a remote comparison; and in those things which are unmistakenly types, seek for numerous resemblances evidently not intended by the Holy Spirit. As might be expected, this principle has been carried beyond all reasonable bounds in their efforts to expound this Song. A controlling impression with them seems to be, that everything must be drawn from this figurative language, that can be devised by a lively fancy in alliance with a spiritual heart. The duty of an interpreter of Scripture is to search for the mind of the Spirit. The facts and personages, the services and figures of the word of God, may receive applications well nigh innumerable by way of accommodation and illustration; but these uses of sacred truth, however pleasing and instructive, should not be the leading aim of a commentator. Much of what is intended for exposition of the types, viewed as such an exposition, is perfectly worthless; but viewed as an ingenious improvement of Scripture, is edifying and attractive. The use of a fact, or allusion, as a mere literary embellishment or illustration, may be allowable and profitable, when the same fact put forth, in the same way, authoritatively as a type, would be a perversion of Scripture. And when the analogies of the real types are carried too far, we are perverting the Scriptures. In every parable and allegory there is some leading principle running through the illustration, and for this principle we must search, without expecting to find similitudes in the minor incidents introduced as necessary appendages to the narrative. There can be no better models for us to follow in interpreting allegorical scriptures, than the exposition given by our Saviour of the parables of the sower and of the tares of the field.

Perhaps nothing has done more to bring this book into disrepute than the well-meant but ill-judged efforts of pious men to draw some hidden meaning from almost every word. They could hardly have been more minute in dissecting and weighing the didactic portions of the Epistles. Their expositions are often so overloaded with ingenious appropriations of these figures, as to crowd out of sight the one leading truth designed to be taught by the Spirit. Even with the best trained imagination this principle must draw the expositor into offences against good taste. Every word of God is pure—

> "A critic on the sacred book should be
> Candid and learn'd, dispassionate and free:
> Whatever shocks, or gives the least offence
> To virtue, delicacy, truth, or sense—
> Try the criterion—'tis a faithful guide,
> Nor has, nor can have Scripture on its side."*

The words of the Lord are pure words, as silver tried in a furnace of earth, purified seven times. Nothing can therefore be clearer than the truth, that any interpretation of this inspired allegory, which is in the least contrary to delicacy and correctness of taste, cannot be the expression of its meaning. The inspiration of this book is established beyond all cavil; as the word of God it must therefore be very pure. The word of God must be consistent with its author, and consistent with itself. In consequence of the peculiar manner in which truth is taught by allegory, any interpretation of this book must be wrong, which does not harmonize with the rest of the Scriptures. Here we must keep in mind the direction, "Prophecy according to the proportion of

---

* Cowper's Progress of Error.

faith," understanding it, as we do, to mean, Interpret the language of revelation, the will of God, according to the standard of things believed as gathered from the general tenor of revelation. By adhering to this principle, exercising good taste, and not trying to draw too much from the figures, while seeking humbly the guidance of the Holy Spirit, we shall find every anticipated indelicacy to vanish.

The words of chap. i. ver. 13, may be taken as an example. Unto those who believe, Jesus is precious, his presence is delightful. We are asked the question, How precious, how agreeable is the society of our Lord? What are the sensations of pleasure like, that we have in his presence? We reply, What are the sensations of delight you experience from a cluster of camphire blooms, or from the fragrance of a bundle of myrrh, so rich that you love to have it dwelling in your bosom? Now the delights shed abroad in our soul by the presence of Jesus are more pleasant than the exquisite delights thus received through the bodily senses. Such is the language necessary from our present position in the flesh, that we must use such comparisons, or say nothing concerning the loveliness of the presence of Jesus. We imagine that the passages describing the pleasure had by our Lord in contemplating the redeemed soul, chap. iv. 1—5; vi. 4—7; vii. 1—5; and the illustration of the beauty and loveliness of Christ, chap. v. 10—16, were not intended to be dissected so minutely as they have been by some commentators. Like the description of the New Jerusalem, these are representations of spiritual things by clusters of the richest emblems. The elegance and force of such a passage is lost by taking it to pieces, and turning the fragments in every imaginable direction, for finding in them various shades and veins of allegory. It is as unreasonable as tearing a rose to pieces, and examining it leaf by leaf for getting at its beauty; or as breaking portions from a piece of statuary, instead of surveying it as constituting a finished whole. The use to which the emblems in such a description may be applied for illustrating truth by way of accommodation, is one thing; the leading intention had by the Holy Spirit in inditing the passage, is another. The latter is what we must seek for in the interpretation of the book. The appearance of our Lord to John at Patmos, was for representing emblematically the offices now sustained by him, as ascended, in behalf of his persecuted people. Hence, the garment down to the foot, and the girdle about the breast, show him to be still a merciful and gracious High Priest; his head and hair, white like wool, bespeak the eternity of the Son of God, manifest in the human form of Jesus of Nazareth; his eyes as a flame of fire, denote his omniscience. The exhibition of him given in the Song, chap. v. 10—16, is confined to the single idea of illustrating his loveliness. When a beautiful object is contemplated, the sight raises within the mind a train of pleasing sensations. The more these sensations are multiplied, the more intense must be our pleasure. The sight of the Lord Jesus as contemplated by faith, calls up within the soul clusters of ideas of the greatest beauty, and sensations of the greatest pleasure. No one thing will illustrate his loveliness; and therefore many objects of beauty are brought together for showing, by their diversity, the variety of shades of beauty there is in Christ. The white and ruddy colour; the most fine gold and raven locks; the eyes of doves by rivers of water; the bed of spices and sweet flowers; the gold rings set with beryl; the white ivory overlaid with sapphires; the pillars of marble set on sockets of fine gold; the majesty of Lebanon with the excellency of its cedars;—each one of these objects separately pours into the mind a rich stream of beautiful ideas; each reference or emblem forms by itself a pleasing study; all these objects combined and viewed at once, if this were possible, would flood and overpower the heart with beauty. Now, when the inquiry is made, What is the beauty of Christ, of which so much is heard? the Holy Spirit says, View these different objects, each of which is so beautiful; gather into your mind all the ideas of splendour they shadow forth; contemplate them collectively; and then, with your mind thus dazzled and drunk with beauty, think that the single view of Christ alone raises in the soul an overflowing flood of beautiful ideas, visions, and conceptions, so deep, so rich, so captivating, that all these things, with all their resplendent beauty, can only serve unitedly, as one great and glorious, but comparatively dim, emblem for representing the beauty of Jesus. The essential thing the mind must search for in this allegorical description, is the loveliness of our Lord.

The blessed Saviour thinks of us far more constantly, and far more fervently, than we, even in hours of deepest emotion, think of him; he contemplates us with far more steadiness and intense interest than we can contemplate him. How could he illustrate to us the beauty he sees in the saints, the work of his hands, as well as the purchase of his blood? How tell the pleasure he has in dwelling in our souls in process of sanctification? Only by illustrations from the beauties seen around us in the world. The eyes of doves; the flock of goats on Mount Gilead; the flock of sheep coming up from the washing; the thread of scarlet; the piece of pomegranate; the majestic tower of David, whereon hung a thousand shields; the twin roes feeding among the lilies; the city

Tirzah, situated beautifully on Judah's hills; Jerusalem on Mount Zion, magnificent for situation; the jewels wrought by the hands of a cunning workman; the heap of wheat set about with lilies; the tower of ivory; the limpid fish-pools in Heshbon; the tower of Lebanon, which looketh towards Damascus; Carmel crowned with verdure and flowers; the stately palm-trees, with clusters of grapes; the fairness of the moon; the clearness of the sun; the grandeur of an army with streaming banners—all these things are beautiful in themselves, and on any one of them we can dwell long, with great pleasure; what is the measure of the beauty pouring into our mind from them all combined? Yet the Lord Jesus says, by his Spirit, that all the pleasure we can have from contemplating all these objects, is nothing more than a shadow of the pleasure he has in dwelling on the character and ripening graces of his saints. It is no part of our duty, to let the imagination so carry us away from the direct line of interpretation as to inquire, what there is in the renewed soul answering to the teeth in the body, and why believers "have not such teeth as lions and tigers, but such as sheep have; nor tusks like dogs and ravenous beasts, but even shorn:"*—as to inquire what is meant by the head of Jesus, and in what respects that head resembles the most fine gold. In these, and in all the other particulars of the descriptions here given, the material point of the comparison lies in the beauty of the impression made, and the pleasure thereby excited. The spiritual beauty of Christ could not be set forth intelligibly to our dull and carnal comprehension, otherwise than by reference to the beauty of the human form; the same is true concerning the beauty of the renovated soul of man. And it may assuredly encour-

---

* Durham, on chap. iv. 2.

age and gratify us to know, that the soul of the believer excites in the bosom of Jesus, and the loveliness of Christ excites in the heart of the saint, deeper emotions of beauty and delight than can spring from the contemplation of all the objects of splendour mentioned in these descriptions, combined in one dazzling group.*

* The theory we have adopted in explaining these passages, does away with the necessity of resorting to the supposition adopted by Harmer, Kitto, and others, that in these descriptions of the bride and the beloved, the parts of the description which seem not in accordance with our ideas of delicacy, are to be taken as portraying the dress on such parts of the body. We are however obliged to think that the divine poet had in his mind, in these sketches, the bride and bridegroom in their bridal dress. 1. There can be no reason why some parts of the body should be spoken of as ornamented and others not, especially as those thus mentioned are not the parts which delicacy requires to be kept from view. See chapter i. 10, and chapter vii. 1, the feet with sandals. 2. The mention of some, especially under such circumstances, warrants us in concluding that the intention of the poet was, the others should be understood as thus ornamented. 3. The situation in which the parties are placed leads us to look for this, inasmuch as there was no time when they were more carefully adorned, and wore more costly ornaments than at the celebration of nuptials. 4. There is no reason for believing that any parts of the body, beyond those uncovered according to ordinary usage, are intended here to be represented as unprotected by clothing; nor is anything gained by portraying them as destitute of the usual drapery. 5. Other portions of the Scriptures that speak of the redeemed and the Redeemer glorified, portray them in costume correspondingly appropriate and beautiful. Rev. i. 13; vii. 9; xix. 8. 6. This idea is still further confirmed by the fact that these descriptions of the bride and the beloved are in public, and in circumstances where the remarks must refer to impressions of beauty, heightened by the beauty of a bridal dress. In chap. v. 9—16, the words of the spouse are addressed to the daughters of Jerusalem in the street; and in chap. vi. and vii. the language is evidently uttered in the garden among the virgins. See chap. vi. 2, in connection with chap. v. 8, 9. 7. The idea that some parts of the body are here represented as naked, has arisen entirely from misapprehension of the meaning of some passages, such as chap. v. 14, and vii. 2. 8. The end in view here, is to set forth the beauty of the two parties;

Truth lies amid the beauties of allegory as the clusters of grapes hang among the branches and leaves of the vine; and as the good husbandman, instead of cutting down the vine and manufacturing it into various shapes according to his peculiar fancy, will gather the fruit and leave the branches untouched—we are using allegories aright, only when gathering carefully the clusters of truth hid in their rich and luxuriant folds. This Song is a fruitful bough, even a fruitful bough by a well—a choice vine brought out of heaven and planted by the spiritual brook of Eshcol, the waters of life along which are found those trees of life, the diversified books of the Scriptures. He who gave us this spiritual vine, growing so luxuriantly over the fountain of the waters of the Holy Spirit, for our refreshment in this valley of Baca on our weary pilgrimage to the heavenly Zion, intended that we should gather the fruit, not that we should break and destroy the branches; and that with leaf that never withers, these fruits, however frequently gathered by passing pilgrims, should still bud forth in fresh and ripening clusters, beautiful and reviving to each successive generation even to the end of the world. Much is said about the indelicacy of this poem; but these objections have arisen less from an examination of the book on its own merits, than from looking at the fancies of commentators.

Much of the learning gathered around this subject con-

---

elegance of dress, so far from interfering with this splendour of appearance, was the direct means for increasing its effect; everything offensive to our ideas of what is beautiful must be excluded; and when it is said such and such parts of the body are thus and thus beautiful, there is no necessity for our stopping and inquiring whether such beauty arises from this or the other ornaments adorning it, or whether there be indeed any ornament, unless it be specifically mentioned.

tributes little, if at all, to that spiritual understanding of the Song which is the ultimate end of its inspiration. The history of the interpretation of the Scriptures gives a pitiable exhibition of the workings of error in the human mind. There is hardly a passage without a variety of interpretations, opinions, and fancies engrafted on it; of these notions this book has received no ordinary share. So far from being able to discover divine truth by its unaided powers, how does the mind pervert these truths when revealed, and weave from them the most silly dreams. Ewald has truly remarked: "In connection with this little book we could make an instructive history of interpretation and false expositions, as a representation of the erroneous methods of dark exposition of the Scripture and the mistakes of human ingenuity; but also at the same time, as an encouraging proof how, from the light of impartial criticism, errors must finally vanish, which had for an indefinite period prevailed." It does not lie within the compass of the present introduction, to give a history of the opinions on this book, or even the names of its many commentators. Rosenmüller gives a catalogue of one hundred and twenty-five who have written commentaries on it; and there are many not not included in his list. The general opinion of the Jewish Church may perhaps be gathered from the Chaldee paraphrase, though this is possibly not earlier than the sixth century after Christ. It is accessible to English readers in the early edition of Gill's Commentary on the Song, and in the Commentary of Dr. Adam Clark; and represents the Song as illustrating the love of God towards his people in leading them through the wilderness into Caanan. Some of the Jewish writers advanced the opinion afterwards adopted by Rosenmüller, that the spouse is the wisdom which Solomon asked and received from heaven. This was the sentiment of Abarbenel in the sixteenth century. Origen, whose love of allegory this book perfectly suited, wrote ten books of commentaries on the Song, of which two homilies translated from the Greek are found in Latin in the works of Jerome; and four books of commentaries in the version of Rufinus, the contemporary of Jerome, by whom several of the works of Origen were translated. Jerome says, "Origen having in his other writings exceeded all others, has in his work on the Song of songs, exceeded himself. In this work, extended to great length, he has discoursed so grandly and lucidly, that he seems to have fulfilled that which is written, 'The king has brought me into his chambers.'" He gives it an allegorical interpretation as showing the communion of the soul of the saint or the church with the Redeemer. Epiphanius, Philo, Theodoret, Cassiodorus, and most of the fathers, follow in the track of Origen. Gregory of Nyssa wrote fifteen homilies containing an allegorical exposition to the end of the sixth chapter. Augustin says, "The Song of songs is a spiritual delight of holy minds, in the nuptial union of that king and queen of the heavenly kingdom, which is Christ and the Church. But this pleasure is wrapped up in folds of allegory that it may be more ardently desired and may be unfolded with greater delight."* Theodoret states that Cyprian, Eusebius, and others nearer the time of the apostles, recognized this as a spiritual book, though, as at present, there were some who denied it. Theodore of Mopsuestia opposed the allegorical interpretation, and supposed this book written for gaining the affection of an Ethiopian princess. He was condemned by the council of Constantinople for disparaging the Song as an impure book, though Lardner observes this

---

* De Civ. Dei, lib. 17, 20.

accusation was probably untrue and had been made by his enemies. In a fragment of his that has come down to us, he says that this book should not be looked on as immoral, nor yet commended as fit for the spiritual edification of the Church, but is, like the Banquet of Plato, a nuptial song of Solomon. Theodoret and Theodore were the leading expositors of their age; and to the latter, the former seems to refer when speaking of some who calumniate the Song of songs and do not believe it a spiritual book. Theodore was possibly led to disparage the book by his opposition to the allegorical mode of exposition carried to such extent by Origen, against whom and concerning allegories he wrote a treatise. It is worthy of consideration, that while Theodore of Mopsuestia was a man of learning, a great expositor of the Scriptures, of celebrated piety, and died in the communion of the Church, he was considered to have given a start to the Pelagian and Nestorian heresies. His view of the Song seems to have been in accordance with the views taken of it at the present day by some pious and eminent interpreters holding sentiments verging towards Pelagianism.

As in other domains of theology, the various opinions concerning this book in modern times are to some extent the resurrection and reproduction of the notions of the early ages. That the Song is a continuous and coherent whole, was never doubted till the time of Richard Simon, who supposed that this book was made up of the productions of different authors, who cannot however be now known, as they have left no distinguishing marks for recognizing them. With him agreed Le Clerc; and the opinion has since been maintained by Eichhorn, Jahn, Pareau, and others. Kleuker, Hufnagel, and others, hold that the book consists of separate erotic Songs which were gathered into one collection by some person, like the Psalms and Proverbs. Bossuet, followed by Bishop Percy, Calmet, Taylor, and Williams, supposes it a kind of drama consisting of seven acts, each act occupying a day, and answering to the number of days during which wedding services were celebrated. Lowth adopts this with some reservation, viewing it as a nuptial dialogue or song of loves, as Psalm xlv., and in the chorus of virgins, bearing some resemblance to the Greek drama. Milton calls it "a divine pastoral drama, consisting of two persons and a double chorus, as Origen rightly judges." Delitzsch makes it a drama of six acts, and divides each act into two scenes. From the likeness here discovered to the cassides or idyls of the Arabian poets, Sir William Jones thinks this book consists of a collection of Hebrew idyls. In this he is followed by Bauer, Jahn who makes it consist of eight idyls, Melesegenio an Italian translator of this poem, John Mason Good, and after him Fry, who make it consist of twelve idyls. In his work, the "*Eclogæ regis Salomonis*, Leipzig, 1777," Lessing views them as pastorals like the eclogues of Virgil and Theocritus.

From the age of Theodore of Mopsuestia, the allegorical interpretation of the Song prevailed till the time of Erasmus, who is said to be the first among the moderns who took ground against it. The modern Romish interpreters have generally followed Origen and Jerome in their expositions; some of them make Christ the beloved and Mary the bride. St. Bernard wrote eighty-six sermons on the first two chapters, which are highly commended by Erasmus. Genebrand, a Benedictine, in the latter part of the sixteenth century wrote a larger and a smaller commentary, in which great use is made of copious quotations from the Rabbins. Cocceius holds it to be a prophetical representation of the destiny of the Christian Church. This notion has been entertained by others, as Brightman and Cotton. Some have even gone so far as to point out the several periods to which the different parts of the Song may be referred, answering to the states of the seven churches of Asia, in the book of Revelation, and making these last also prophetical. Robinson of Cambridge supposes it a topographical essay, descriptive of some beautiful places in the estates of Solomon; and particularly that the description of the beloved, in chap. v., means nothing but a mountain ornamented with copses, and enriched with quarries of marble, and a mine of gold. John Gerhard, who is commended by Glassius* in the highest terms for the line of interpretation adopted in his *Postilla Salomonea*, teaches that it sets forth the reciprocal love of Christ and his Church. Luther, in his commentary on the Song, following somewhat the track of Augustin, views it as a kind of encomium on the government of Solomon, making God the beloved and the Jewish Church the bride; though in another treatise he takes the bride to mean the Christian Church. Hug understands by the bride the ten tribes of Israel, of whom a meagre remnant being left in their country after the destruction of the kingdom of Samaria, wished to unite with the kingdom of Judah; but the citizens of Judah, who are represented by the brothers of Shulamith, oppose this, because the citizens of Israel were not suitable for such union. This notion has been opposed and refuted by Bertholdt. Kaiser takes it as historico-allegorical, and celebrating the restoration of the Mosaic worship by Zerubbabel, Ezra, and Nehemiah. In 1764 appeared an anonymous translation, with notes, since

---

* Philologia Sacra, 1959.

known to have been made by Bishop Percy, which, though professing to go no farther than an explanation of the literal meaning, and seeming really to appreciate some of its beauties, does nevertheless make many suggestions untrue, unnecessary, and degrading to the Scriptures. In 1768, Harmer published his "Outlines of a New Commentary on the Song of Solomon." Viewing the Song not as a pastoral, nor as an epithalamium, he considered it as describing a royal marriage, that of Solomon with an Egyptian princess, yet an allegory illustrating the love of God, in admitting the Gentiles to equal privileges with the Jews. He divides his work into three parts:—1. Remarks on the general nature of the Song; 2. Observations on detached places of it; 3. Queries concerning the rest of this poem. The work of Jacobi in 1771, found many followers; still more that of Herder, in 1778, who, treating the Song as different erotic idyls, carried through his design with such judgment and taste as to find general acceptance. While confining his exposition entirely to the verbal meaning, Rosenmüller views the Song as an allegory; and though, in a treatise published in 1813, he explained it after the Chaldee paraphrase and Sol. Jarchi, as representing the mutual love of Christ and his Church, he afterwards changed his opinion, and supposed it to set forth the mutual loves of Solomon and wisdom. Making it a drama in four acts, Ewald supposes that when abroad in his chariot, Solomon fell in with a beautiful country girl near Engedi, and having had her forcibly carried off, tries to gain her love by this poetry. Michaelis thinks it is for recommending conjugal love; he has been opposed by Eichhorn, Jahn, and Rosenmüller, who suppose the love of two young unmarried persons is here represented. Umbreit, Lindeman, Velthusen, and Ammon, think it consists of love epistles addressed by Solomon to a shepherdess, who nevertheless remains faithful to her husband. The gross views of Grotius need not be repeated, of whom Doderlein said: *Grotii turpem ac obscenam interpretationem ex eo genere existimo quod turpitudinis occasionem rapit.* Nor need we mention those of Whiston, who held it to be a dissolute love song. Hence, Semler, without any reason, but on the mere strength of his fancy, refuses to take any notice of this book, as a production beyond all question spurious. Adam Clark treats this Song with disrespect, while making it an occasion for showing some oriental learning, and thinks it impossible to bring any reasons for an allegorical meaning. Professor Stuart has not written a commentary on this book, but in his work on the Old Testament, when giving "Conscientious scruples to a part of the Old Testament," utters sentiments which could excite no surprise in one not receiving this book as canonical, but which, in a man of his position, piety and influence, cannot do otherwise than cause deep regret. Some men, like Good and Rosenmüller, who have gone no further than the illustration of the literal meaning, have yet held to an allegorical sense.

Amid this chaos of notions and fantasies, there has always been among orthodox Christians as much general unanimity concerning the meaning of this book, as that of any other book of the Bible; amply sufficient to justify the language of Munster, the eminent follower of Luther: "The general Church of Christ hold that in this divine Song are contained the mysteries of the love of Christ and the Church." This is the scope of the exposition of John Gerhard; of the homilies of Beza on the first three chapters; of the excellent discourses on some passages of this book by Romaine; and of the commentary on the Song by Lady Guyon. With these President Edwards agrees, who views it as "representing the high and glorious relation, and union, and love, that are between Christ and his redeemed Church." The same view is taken by Henry and Scott, in their Commentaries; and by Owen, in his treatise "On Communion with God," and in other parts of his writings, where many passages of this book are incidentally expounded. To Gill's volume may be applied what Robert Hall said unjustly of Owen's works, "a continent of mud." We may well wonder that, with apparently the best intentions, and a regard for the Scriptures, many good men, instead of trying to soften down and accommodate to present views some peculiar oriental expressions in the Song, seem to have exerted their ingenuity for getting from it as many amatory ideas as possible. What we mean may be seen by referring to Bishop Percy's annotations and introduction. We are free to say, that after reading, studying, and meditating on the Song for years, we had never entertained the faintest suspicion that some passages are to be understood in their literal sense, according to his gross and offensive explanations. Let any person who is disposed to find fault with this portion of Scripture, take it and read it as it appears to an unprejudiced mind, unoccupied with any theories; and then let him read what has been made out of it by some commentators; and we are confident he will feel that the Holy Spirit has woven the allegory of a beautiful and delicate texture, and that the offensiveness imputed to it arises from the perversion of man. We are unable to understand what good can possibly arise from such representations as those of Bishop Percy and others. But they do positive injury. They degrade the Scriptures in the estimation of the irreligious; and they infest the pious mind with associations of which it can be with difficulty divested, and which might never have arisen without this foreign aid. Even in the commentaries of such men as Gill and Durham, amid so much that is spiritual and edifying, there are interpretations offensive to everything like good taste, and the more to be regretted, because irrelevant, unnecessary, and incorrect. Like the miracles of the fabulous gospels, in contrast with the narrative of the Evangelists, many of the efforts of the human mind on this Song, in comparison with the simplicity of the language, not in the English version, but in the original Hebrew, show with what superiority the Holy Spirit manages so delicate a subject.

We have spent no time on the inquiry, whether the Song has any of the characteristics of the Greek drama; whether it contains, according to regular divisions, the actions of the seven distinct days allotted to the celebration of the Jewish nuptials; or whether, according to Dr. Good, it consists of twelve sacred idyls. The fact that so many commentators have tried to divide this book, whether into seven parts answering to the seven days necessary for celebrating a Jewish marriage, or into separate idyls, or into a drama, shows there must be ground for a division of some kind. Taking the Song as designed to illustrate the operations of holy love, under various circumstances, we feel that the grouping together of the incidents to elucidate the different periods of growth in grace, must make changes in the thread of the story, and those changes often abrupt. The summary and analysis we have attempted, will show the reason there is for those changes of scene, and account for them fully, without any resort to the attempt at finding out idyls, or the different scenes of a drama.* Nor is it necessary to spend time in determining the truth or falsity of the opinions, that it was written to celebrate the marriage of Solomon—that the bride was the daughter of Pharaoh—or even that the circumstances here recorded are undoubted facts. Were these points settled beyond all cavil, they could not throw a single ray of light on the spiritual meaning of the allegory. The truths intended to be taught remain the same, whether the incidents had existence in reality or in imagination. What benefit could be derived from our knowing there was a specific individual designated in the parable of the sower, who he was, what was his name? The truths and duties inculcated by our Lord, in Luke xix. 12—27, receive no additional force from knowing that the nobleman mentioned was the son of Herod, and the far country to which he went was the city of Rome. The beauty and instructiveness of the allegory in Spenser's Faery Queen, are no more delight-

---

* The following are some of the divisions adopted by different commentators:

Delitzsch.

Act I.	chap. i. 2—ii. 17.	Scene 1, chap. i. 2—17.	Scene 2, chap. ii. 1—7.
II.	ii. 8—iii. 5.	ii. 8—ii. 17.	iii. 1—iii. 5.
III.	iii. 6—v. 1.	iii. 6—iii. 11.	iv. 1—v. 1.
IV.	v 2—vi. 9.	v. 2—vi. 2.	vi. 3—vi. 9.
V.	vi. 10—viii. 4.	vi. 10—vii. 5.	vii. 6—viii. 4.
VI.	viii. 5—14.	viii. 5—7.	viii. 8—14.

Bossuet.		*Good.*		*Jahn.*	
Day 1,	chap. i. ii. 1—6.	Idyl 1,	chap. i. 1—8.	Song 1,	chap. i. to ii. 7.
2,	ii. 7—17.	2,	i. 9 to ii. 7.	2,	ii. 8 to iii. 5.
3,	iii. iv. v. 1.	3,	ii. 8—17.	3,	iii. 6 to v. 1.
4,	v. 2 to vi. 9.	4,	iii. 1—5.	4,	v. 2 to vi. 9.
5,	vi. 10 to vii 11.	5,	iii. 6 to iv. 7.	5,	vi. 10 to viii. 3.
6,	vii. 12 to viii. 3.	6,	iv. 8 to v. 1.	6,	viii. 4—7.
Sab. 7,	viii. 4—14.	7,	v. 2 to vi. 10.	7,	viii. 8—12.
		8,	vi. 11—13.	8,	viii. 13—14.
		9,	vii. 1—9.		
		10,	vii. 10 to viii. 4.		
		11,	viii. 5—7.		
		12,	viii. 8—14.		

ful and profitable to him who sees in the different sketches portraits of Queen Elizabeth, Sir Philip Sidney, and others, than it is to him who may happily read the same poetry, ignorant of any historical allusions. The very nature of an allegory renders it perfectly unimportant whether the incidents be real or imaginary.

Taking, therefore, this Song as an allegory, whose imagery has been drawn from the court of Solomon, for illustrating the mutual love of Christ and the Church, we cannot understand it fully, without viewing that love as exercised in the case of individual believers. Taking the Church as a whole, its love becomes a generality of the vaguest kind, intangible and unsatisfactory. But when we take the exercises of an individual heart, all is intelligible and interesting. Jesus loves the Church, by loving every single member of the Church; and manifests his love to the Church, by a special manifestation made to every member of the Church.

> "Sees all, as if that all were one,
> Loves one, as if that one were all."

The Song was given to illustrate that love; and hence it must be interpreted by looking at the manifestations of the love of Jesus towards every believer, and at the corresponding exercises of every believer towards Jesus.

In the glorious temple of revelation, a place which the Lord our God has chosen to cause his name to dwell there, even in brighter glory than in the temple of the material world, does this book stand, like one of the apartments in the temple on Mount Zion, small indeed, but exquisitely finished, the walls and ceiling of something richer than cedar, richer than bright ivory overlaid with sapphires, and filled with specimens of truth brought down from heaven by the Holy Spirit, and here deposited for the comfort and delight of those who love the habitation of God's house, and the place where his glory dwelleth. As the man skilled in geology will take a bone of fossil remains from a bygone world, and from this alone restore the whole fabric of the creature to which it belonged, with a knowledge of its nature and instincts; so may we take the germs of truth, the heavenly fossils laid up for us with such care in the spiritual treasury of this Song, and, taught by the Holy Spirit, our souls may develope the system of heavenly love, the mutual affection of Jesus and his saints—a love not native to our earth in its present fallen state, but existing in all the vigour and fulness of an immortal life, in yonder heavenly world. In the Banquet, Plato puts into the mouth of Alcibiades sentiments which show that the principles contended for in the Song are recognized in other great productions of antiquity. "Should any one be willing to hear the discourses of Socrates, they will appear to be very ridiculous at first; so that every man who has neither skill nor sense, will laugh at his words. But he who beholds his discourses when opened, and gets within them, will in the first place find that they alone of all other discourses possess an internal meaning; and in the next place, that they are most divine, and hold the most numerous images of virtue, and extend to the farthest point, or rather to everything which is fitting for him to consider who intends to become a man, both morally beautiful and good."*

* Banquet, p. 247.

SUMMARY OF THE SONG.

This Book consists of three parts: The first includes chapter i. verse 1; chapter ii. verse 7. The second extends from chapter ii. verse 8, to chapter vii. verse 9. The third includes the remainder of the book, chapter vii. verse 10, to chapter viii. verse 14.

I. The way in which the soul longing for the manifestation of the love of Christ is led along in the gratification of that desire, from one degree to another of pious enjoyment, until attaining the greatest delight possible for the saint in the present world. Chap. i. 1; chap. ii. 7.

These periods of enjoyment are separated by vicissitudes of fortune and diversity of feeling, through which the believer is brought to those more cheering scenes in his progress to heaven. These seasons may be repeated in our experience, some of them more than once, before we attain those which succeed. 1. We enjoy the love of Jesus, as manifested in private communion, in "his chambers." Chap. i. 4. 2. In the way of duty and self-denial. Chap. i. 7—11. 3. In sitting with the King in the circle of his friends, and enjoying, as one of them, the delights of social communion with him. Chap. i. 12—14. 4. In delightful repose with him amid enlarged prospects of spiritual beauty. Chap. i. 15—17. 5. In the protection and delights set forth in chap. ii. 1—3. 6. And in enjoying, at last, the pleasures mentioned in chap. ii. 4—7, the greatest possible on earth.

II. An exhibition of motives by which the Lord Jesus would allure such soul away from the present world, for being with him in glory. Chap. ii. 8; chap. vii. 9.

As we are treated throughout our redemption and discipline here, like beings possessing a will, the spiritual decays and sluggishness into which we are liable to fall must be counteracted by the presentation of powerful motives to the mind; and our faith can be best matured by strengthening the soul, as is done in these periods of great enjoyment, and then leaving us in that strength, without such sensible pleasures, to manifest our steadfastness by struggling against difficulty and the absence of Jesus, by dependence on his word and promises and love. Hence our Lord allures us—

1. By the beauty of heaven, as a place he has prepared for us, and where he is awaiting us. Chap. ii. 8—17.

2. By the splendour of the reception awaiting us there, no less than by the security and grandeur of our conveyance towards glory. Chap. iii. 1—11.

3. By his great love for us—an affection so intense as to be incapable of being fully expressed by the strongest illustrations, and so strong as to remain constant even amid our neglect. Chap. iv. 1; chap. vii. 9.

III. The effect produced on the heart of the saint by these manifestations of love, and by these motives. Chap.

SUMMARY.

vii. 10; chap. viii. 14. 1. Assurance of hope. Chap. vii. 10. 2. Desire to be much alone in communion with Christ. Chap. vii. 11. 3. Willingness to engage in labours of holiness and love. Verse 12. 4. Consecration to him of our best and most valued gifts and possessions. Verse 13. 5. Desire that everything hindering the full interchange of affection between Jesus and our soul may be removed. Chap. viii. 1—2. 6. The desire to guard against every sin and every act at all likely to cause the withdrawal of Jesus' love. Verses 3, 4. 7. The pleasing consciousness of leaning on Jesus, and of being upheld by his everlasting arms. Verse 5. 8. Desire to lie continually near the heart of Jesus, and to be sustained by his power. Verse 6. 9. Willingness to sacrifice every thing coming between us and Christ. Verse 6. 10. A conviction of the meanness of everything the world could offer for bribing us to renounce Christ. Verse 7. 11. An interest for the salvation of the impenitent. Verses 8—10. 12. A sense of our accountability as stewards of God, holding our property and our all in trust. Verse 12. 13. The privilege of access continually to the throne of grace, with full encouragement from our Lord for addressing to him our voices in prayer and praise. Verse 13. 14. The desire for the completion of our redemption, and for the perfecting of his love to us and of our love to him, by the second coming of our Lord. Verse 14.

TRANSLATION.

CHAPTER I.

Ver. 1. The Song of songs which is Solomon's.

SPOUSE.

2. O that he would give me kisses of his love:
    For thy love is more delicious than wine.
3. Thy perfumes are rich in fragrance;
    Thy name is perfume poured forth;
    Therefore the virgins love thee.
4. Draw me; we will run after thee:
    The king hath brought me into his apartments:
    We will be glad and rejoice in thee;
    We will cherish a more pleasing remembrance of thy love than wine;
    They love thee sincerely.
5. Dark am I but lovely, O ye daughters of Jerusalem,
    As the tents of Kedar, as the pavilions of Solomon.
6. Look not on me, I am dark,
    Because the sun hath browned me;
    My mother's children were ill-disposed towards me;
    They made me the keeper of the vineyards;
    My own vineyard have I not kept.
7. Tell me, O thou whom my soul loveth,
    Where thou feedest? where thou makest thy flock to rest at noon?
    For why should I be as one veiled,*
    Among the flocks of thy companions?

BELOVED.

8. If thou know not, O thou fairest among women,
    Go forth in the footsteps of the flock,
    And feed thy kids beside the shepherds' tents.

* Regarded as a harlot.

CHAPTER II.

9. I compare thee, O my love,
   To my chariot-steed from Pharaoh.
10. Thy cheeks are beautiful with rows of jewels:
    Thy neck with strings of pearls,
11. Gold chains will we make for thee,
    Adorned with studs of silver.

Spouse.

12. While the king sitteth in the circle of his friends,
    My spikenard diffuses its fragrance.
13. An amulet of myrrh is my beloved to me,
    Which shall continually abide in my bosom.
14. A boquet of cypress flowers is my beloved to me,
    From the garden fields of Engedi.

Beloved.

15. Behold, thou art beautiful, my love,
    Behold, thou art beautiful; thine eyes are doves'.

Spouse.

16. Behold, thou art beautiful, my beloved, yea attractive;
    And the green flowery turf is our place of repose.
17. The roof of our summer-house is cedars,
    Our carved ceiling firs.

CHAPTER II.

1. I am the rose of Sharon,
   A lily of the valleys.

Beloved.

2. As a lily among the thorns,
   So is my love among the daughters.

Spouse.

3. As a citron tree among trees of the forest,
   So is my beloved among the sons.
   In his shade I delight to sit,
   And his fruit is sweet to my taste.

4. He brings me into the banqueting-house,
   And his banner over me is love.
5. Revive me with cordials,
   Refresh me with citrons,
   For I am sick of love.
6. His left hand is under my head,
   And his right hand doth embrace me:
7. I charge you, O ye daughters of Jerusalem,
   By the gazelles and by the hinds of the field,
   That ye rouse not and disturb not
   My love, till he please.
8. Hark! my beloved: behold, there he comes
   Leaping over the mountains, bounding over the hills.
9. My beloved is like a gazelle, or a beauteous fawn.
   See! he is standing behind our wall;
   He is looking in through the window;
   He is throwing sparkling glances from behind the lattice.
10. My beloved begins to speak, and says to me;
    Arise, my companion, my beautiful one, and come away.
11. For, lo, the the winter is past,
    The rain is over and gone.
12. The flowers appear on the earth,
    The time of singing of birds has come,
    And the voice of the turtle-dove is heard in our land.
13. The fig-tree is distilling aromatic juice into its green figs;
    And the vines in blossom are sending forth fragrance:
    Arise, come, my companion, my beautiful one, come away.
14. O my dove, in refuges of the rock,
    In a hiding-place of the precipice,
    Let me see thy countenance,
    Let me hear thy voice;
    For sweet is thy voice,
    And thy countenance lovely.
15. Take for us the foxes,
    The little foxes which destroy the vines;
    For our vineyard is in bloom.
16. My beloved is mine, and I am his;
    He feeds among the lilies.
17. Until the day break, and the shadows flee away,
    Return my beloved,
    Like a gazelle, or a beauteous fawn,
    Over the craggy mountains.

CHAPTER III.

1. On my couch, in the night,
    I seek him whom my soul loveth,
    I seek him but find him not.
2. I will arise now, and I will go about in the city;
    In the streets and in the public squares,
    I will seek him whom my soul loveth:
    I seek him and I find him not.
3. The watchmen who go around in the city found me;
    "Saw ye him whom my soul loveth?"
4. Hardly had I passed them,
    When I found him whom my soul loveth.
    I laid hold on him and would not let him go,
    Till I had brought him to the house of my mother,
    Into the apartment of her that bore me.
5. I charge you, O ye daughters of Jerusalem,
    By the gazelles and by the hinds of the field,
    That ye rouse not and disturb not
    My love, till he please.

DAUGHTERS OF JERUSALEM.

6. Who is this coming up from the wilderness,
    Like pillars of smoke,
    Surrounded with the perfume of myrrh, and frankincense,
    And all kinds of aromatic dust from the perfumer?
7. Lo, it is the palanquin of Solomon:
    Around it are threescore valiant men,
    The most valiant of Israel;
8. All of them with sword in hand, experienced in war,
    Each with his sword girded on, against peril in the night.
9. A palanquin Solomon the king made for himself
    Of the wood of Lebanon:
10. Its pillars he made of silver,
    Its railing of gold, its seat purple,
    The midst of it being tessellated with love,
    For the daughters of Jerusalem.
11. Go forth, ye daughters of Zion,
    And behold king Solomon,
    With the crown with which his mother crowned him
    On the day of his espousals,
    On the day of gladness of his heart.

CHAPTER IV.

BELOVED.

1. Behold thou art beautiful, my companion, thou art beautiful:
Doves are thine eyes within thy locks;
Thy hair is as a flock of goats
Which lie along downwards from mount Gilead.
2. Thy teeth as a flock of the same size,
Which come up from the washing-pool,
All of them bearing twins,
And none of them without its young.
3. Thy lips are like a thread of scarlet;
And thy mouth beautiful.
Like a piece of pomegranate,
Are thy cheeks within thy tresses.
4. Thy neck is like the tower of David
Built for an armory;
A thousand shields are hanging on it,
All bucklers of the mighty.
5. Thy two breasts are like two fawns,
Twins of a gazelle, feeding among the lilies.
6. Until the day break and the shadows flee away,
I will betake me to the mountain of myrrh and to the hill of frankincense.
7. Thou art all beautiful, my companion;
And no spot is there in thee.
8. Come with me from Lebanon, my spouse,
With me from Lebanon;
Look from the top of Amana,
From the top of Shenir and Hermon,
From the dens of lions, from the mountains of leopards.
9. Thou hast ravished my heart, my sister-spouse,
Thou hast ravished my heart with one of thine eyes,
With one fold of thy necklace.
10. How beautifully delightful is thy love, my sister-spouse;
How much more delicious is thy love than wine,
And the fragrance of thy perfumes than all spices.
11. Thy lips drop as the honey-comb, my spouse:
Honey and milk are under thy tongue;
And the fragrance of thy garments is as the fragrance of Lebanon.

CHAPTER V.

12. A garden enclosed is my sister-spouse;
 A spring shut up, a fountain sealed.
13. Thy productions are a paradise of pomegranates,
 With delicious fruits, cypresses with spikenards,
14. Spikenard and crocus, calamus and cinnamon,
 With all trees of frankincense;
 Myrrh and aloes with all chief spices;
15. A fountain of gardens, a well of living waters,
 And streams from Lebanon.

SPOUSE.

16. Arise, O north wind; and come thou south;
 Blow upon my garden that its perfumes may flow forth.
 Let my beloved come into his garden,
 And enjoy its delicious fruits.

CHAPTER V.

BELOVED.

1. I have come into my garden, my sister-spouse;
 I am gathering my myrrh with my spice;
 I am eating my honey-comb with my honey;
 I am drinking my wine with my milk:
 Eat, O friends, drink,
 Yea, beloved companions, drink abundantly.

SPOUSE.

2. I was sleeping, but my heart was awake:
 Hark! the voice of my beloved! he is knocking:
 "Open to me, my sister, my companion,
 My dove, my perfect one;*
 For my head is filled with dew,—
 My locks with drops of the night."
3. I have put off my dress,
 How shall I put it on?
 I have washed my feet.
 How shall I soil them?

* Equivalent to our expression, "My angel."

4. My beloved withdrew his hand from the aperture in the door;
And my heart was moved towards him.
5. I arose for opening to my beloved,
And my hands dropped myrrh,
And my fingers liquid myrrh,
On the handles of the bolt.
6. I opened to my beloved;
But my beloved had turned and gone away.
My heart sunk in consequence of what he had said;
I sought him, and found him not:
I called him, and he answered me not.
7. The watchmen who go around in the city found me,
They smote me, they wounded me;
The guards of the walls stripped my veil from me.
8. I charge you, O ye daughters of Jerusalem,
If ye shall find my beloved—
What shall ye tell him?
That I am sick of love.

DAUGHTERS OF JERUSALEM.

9. What is thy beloved more than another beloved,
Thou most beautiful of women?
What is thy beloved more than another beloved,
That thou dost thus charge us?

SPOUSE.

10. My beloved is white and ruddy,
Conspicuous among a host.
11. His head is finest choice gold;
His locks young waving palm branches, black as the raven:
12. His eyes as doves by valley rills of water,
Washed in milk, reposing by the full water springs:
13. His cheeks as banks of fragrant flowers,
As towering trellises covered with aromatic blooms;
His lips lilies distilling liquid myrrh:
14. His hands rollers of gold, set with the beryl;
His body wrought ivory overlaid with sapphires.
15. His legs pillars of white marble
Fixed on pedestals of fine gold;
His appearance is as Lebanon,
Pre-eminently noble as the cedars:
16. His voice is exquisitely sweet;
His whole being is constituted of delightful attractions:
This is my beloved, and this is my friend,
O daughters of Jerusalem.

CHAPTER VI.

Daughters of Jerusalem.

1. Whither has thy beloved gone, thou most beautiful of women?
   Whither has thy beloved turned away?
   Tell, that we may seek him with thee.

Spouse.

2. My beloved has gone down to his garden,
   To the banks of fragrant flowers,
   To feed in the gardens, and to gather lilies.
3. I am my beloved's, and my beloved is mine,
   Who feeds among the lilies.

Beloved.

4. Beautiful as Tirzah art thou, my companion;
   Elegant as Jerusalem;
   Imposing as a military host with banners.
5. Turn away thine eyes from me,
   For they are taking me by storm.
   Thy hair is as a flock of goats
   Which lie along downwards from mount Gilead.
6. Thy teeth as a flock of sheep,
   Which come up from the washing-pool,
   All of them bearing twins,
   And none of them without its young.
7. As a piece of pomegranate,
   Are thy cheeks within thy tresses.
8. There are threescore queens,
   And fourscore concubines,
   And virgins without number:
9. My dove, my perfect one, she is the favourite;
   The darling is she of her mother,
   The delight of her who bore her.
   The virgins beheld her, and called her blessed;
   The queens and concubines also praised her.
10. Who is this that looks forth as the dawn,
    Beautiful as the moon,
    Of purest brightness as the sun,
    Imposing as bannered hosts?
11. I went down to the fruit garden,
    To behold the green growths of the valley,

      To see whether the vine was putting forth buds,
      Whether the pomegranates were in bloom:
12. E'er I was aware, my soul made me
      As the chariots of Amminadib.
13. Return, return, O Shulamith;
      Return, return, that we may behold in thee,—
      What shall you behold in the Shulamith?
      As it were a festive choir of rejoicing hosts.

CHAPTER VII.

1. How beautiful are thy feet in sandals,
   O noble woman.
   The contour of thy person
   Is like the rounding of a necklace
   Wrought by the hands of a finished artist:
2. Thy waist is a round goblet
   Full of the rich spiced wine:
   Thy body is a heap of wheat
   Enclosed with lilies:
3. Thy two breasts as two fawns,
   Twins of a gazelle.
4. Thy neck as a tower of ivory;
   Thine eyes pools in Heshbon,
   By the gate of Bath-rabbim;
   Thy nose as a tower on Lebanon,
   Looking towards Damascus.
5. Thy head crowning thee is as Carmel,
   And the full flowing hair of thy head rich as purple:
   The king is captivated by the tresses.
6. How beautiful and how charming,
   O my love, art thou in fascinating graces
7. Thy stature is like a palm-tree:
   And thy breasts to its clusters.
8. I said I will go to the palm-tree:
   I will clasp its waving branches;
   And thy bosom shall now be as clusters of the vine;
   And thy breath sweet as citrons;
9. And thy voice as the delicious wine
   Which flows pure to my best loved friend,
   Which makes the lips of the slumbering move gently.

CHAPTER VIII.

Spouse.

10. I am my beloved's,
And his ardent affection is towards me.
11. Come, my beloved, let us go forth into the country;
Let us abide in the villages;
12. Let us be early in the morning in the vineyards;
Let us see whether the vine is budding, its blossom unfolding;
Whether the pomegranates are in bloom:
There will I give thee my loves.
13. The choicest flowers are giving forth their fragrance,
And at the entrance of our summer-houses are all kinds of delicious fruits,
Both new and old, which I have treasured up, my beloved, for thee.

CHAPTER VIII.

1. O that thou wert as a brother to me,
Nourished in the bosom of my mother!
Should I find thee abroad, then would I kiss thee,
Nor should it be imputed to me as an impropriety.
2. I would lead thee, I would bring thee to the house of my mother;
Thou shalt teach me how to gratify thy wishes;
I will make thee drink of the spiced wine,
Of my fresh juice of the pomegranate.
3. His left hand shall be under my head,
And his right hand shall embrace me.
4. I charge you, O ye daughters of Jerusalem,
That ye rouse not and disturb not
My love, till he please.

Daughters of Jerusalem.

5. Who is this coming up from the wilderness,
Leaning on the beloved?

Beloved.

Under the citron tree I gained thine affection;
There thy mother pledged thee;
There she that bore thee betrothed thee.

Spouse.

6. Set me as a seal on thine heart;
   As a seal on thine arm:
   For love is strong as death;
   Devoted affection is unrelaxing as the realms of the dead:
   Its flames have the energy of lightning,
   Which have the fiercest blaze.
7. Many waters cannot quench love,
   And floods cannot overwhelm it:
   Should a man give all the wealth of his house for this love,
   It would be utterly despised.
8. We have a young sister,
   And she has not yet reached womanhood:
   What shall we do for our sister,
   With reference to the day when she shall be spoken for in marriage?

Beloved.

9. If she be a wall, we will build on it a turret of silver;
   And if she be a door, we will enclose it with boards of cedar.

Spouse.

10. I am a wall and my breasts as towers;
    Then am I in his eyes as one finding favour.
11. A vineyard has Solomon in Baal-hamon;
    He has let out the vineyard to keepers;
    Each shall yield him for its fruit
    A thousand pieces of silver.
12. My vineyard which belongs to me is under my own supervision;
    Thou, O Solomon, shalt have the thousand pieces of silver from it;
    And the keepers of its fruit two hundred.

Beloved.

13. O thou who dwellest in the gardens,
    The companions hearken to thy voice;
    Cause me to hear it.

Spouse.

14. Make haste, my beloved,
    And be thou like a gazelle, or a beauteous fawn,
    Over the mountains of spices.

ANALYSIS OF THE SONG.

CHAPTER I.

The desire which in the heart of the saint absorbs every other, is for the manifestation of the love of the Lord Jesus, through the influences of the Holy Spirit; and this love is thus ardently desired, because its effect is more reviving and exhilarating than any of the pleasures of sense, even of wine, the most refreshing of them all. Verse 2.

This desire is not a blind instinct or a fanatical impulse, but springs from an intelligent apprehension of the excellency of the nature of Christ, as transcending everything known to man, more than the holy anointing oil of the sanctuary surpassed any other perfume;—an excellence so rich, that the pure in heart, and they only, love him, and they cannot do otherwise than love him. Ver. 3.

The thought of the excellency of the character of Christ, and of the influences of the Holy Spirit shedding abroad his love in the heart, creates the desire of coming as near to him as possible, without any delay—of running to him; and as our own insufficiency and weakness are felt sensibly at such times, we pray for the attracting power of his grace and for the strength of his Spirit. This desire is never expressed in vain; with kingly majesty and condescension, he brings us into confidential communion with him apart from the world; this communion is attended with fulness of joy and a holy exultation in his superior grace; and these manifestations of his love thus made, only to the upright or pure, and by such sincerely appreciated, are followed by remembrances, not painful, like the pleasures of sense, but always refreshing and delightful. Ver. 4.

This love is a perfect regulator of the powers of the soul; and carrying with it true wisdom, gives us a correct knowledge of ourselves, as the offspring of the humility to which this divine love leads, and which consists in thinking of ourselves according to the whole truth, nothing more, nothing less, realizing that while, black like the tents of Kedar, we are darkened by native depravity, grace is working in us virtues more beautiful than the curtains of Solomon. Ver. 5.

The humility inseparable from this love makes us modest and retiring, and prompts us to shrink from courting admiration; because we are conscious of unworthiness; have been stripped of our spiritual beauty by sin; have suffered many evils and afflictions; have received ill treatment, not only from the ungodly world, but from brethren of the same household of faith; and have failed in many duties. Ver. 6.

This love so captivates the heart with the Lord Jesus, while keeping it thus humble, that we are anxious not only to enjoy his society in the blessedness of private communion, his chambers, ver. 4; but to follow the Lamb whithersoever he goeth, Rev. xiv. 4; to be with him in labours, fatigues, and dangers, no less than in the delights of his service—in the weariness of toil in the wilderness, no less than in the pleasures of the palace. It prompts us to inquire and seek, without waiting for commands, where we may labour with this gracious king

CHAPTER I.

as a shepherd, and enjoy his society;—where, in the discharge of duty, find his guidance and defence during the noontide heat of temptation, affliction, and sorrow; and makes us unwilling to be satisfied with any inferior love, or the company and teaching of any but Christ—unwilling to have any person or thing coming between us and Jesus. Ver. 7.

Such inquiries he answers, by assuring the soul thus humble in its own esteem, that while conscious of unworthiness, and misused by men, we are held by him in the highest admiration—"fairest among women;"—and that he may be always found by our following in the footsteps of those who through faith and patience have inherited the promises; and by activity in his service, by ministering to the saints, and by labouring to train up the young of the flock, "feed the kids," in co-operation with the ministers of the gospel—"beside the shepherds' tents." Ver. 8.

Having received these instructions, and going forth to carry them into practice, our soul is viewed with great interest by the Saviour, in our approaches to him. Seeing us, as it were, afar, he sets forth, by comparison to the horse, his impression of that character which is so despised by the world. In reference to its inherent vital energy, or principle imparted by the Holy Spirit, it is a character noble, adapted to impress us with respect and command admiration—possesses great energy and vigour, and inexhaustible powers of endurance—running without growing weary. Isa. xl. 31. Ver. 9.

Moreover, Jesus looks on those virtues which are superadded as ornaments to our character by grace, with a pleasure akin to what we feel in contemplating cheeks comely with rows of jewels, &c., viz. that golden chain with the pearls "love, joy, peace, meekness, &c.," Gal. v. 22. Ver. 10.

The principle is, "to him that hath shall be given," Matt. xxv. 29; and though so beautiful are these ornamental graces now overlaying the soul by the Holy Ghost, Christ will add unto these, others wrought by his own hands, too exquisite to be made even by angels, a spiritual body, &c. He will adorn us to the utmost possible that such wisdom and power as his can confer. Ver. 11.

Thus, following Jesus in the way of duty, under the impulse of this love, we are received by him with kingly majesty, and, as beloved friends, are entertained with princely magnificence at his table, spread with delicacies for the soul. This near approach to him, combined with his affectionate tenderness and great goodness, kindles the affections into a fervid glow, and draws from us the fragrance of the odoriferous graces—the spiritual spikenard—poured by the Holy Ghost into the alabaster of the pure heart. Ver. 12.

At such times, in near communion with Jesus, and with the affections in vigorous exercise, we feel our Lord amazingly precious. If asked, How precious is your Saviour? Tell me the impression thus made on your spiritual apprehensions? We can do no better than reply, Can you tell what is the sweet and refreshing influence of a bundle of myrrh, in the bosom, or of a cluster of camphire in bloom, such as is in the vineyards of Engedi? Ver. 14. The presence of Jesus produces an impression on my spiritual faculties, far more delightful than the effect of these perfumes on the bodily senses. Ver. 13.

Thus received by this friend and king, our beloved, and entertained by him, at the table of his confidential companions, with the marrow and fatness of his grace—while, under these manifestations of love, our heart is burning with affection, what is the nature of the language interchanged between him and us?—"We love him because he first loved us;" we presume to address to him the language of affection, because he first addresses us. He speaks to us in terms of the strongest and most tender affection—assures us that whatever may be thought of us by the world, we are beautiful in his eyes, and that love is the expression of soul which draws his admiration. Ver. 15.

The heart is glad to reciprocate this feeling; and calling him our beloved, the dearest object of our affection, we rejoice to give utterance to our sense of the beauty of his character, and the pleasantness of his society—together with the delightfulness of the repose he grants to those whom he so loves as thus to address—a peace sweet as repose on a bed of full-blown flowers of spring amid green pastures beside still waters, and at the same time, while open to all the fresh airs and balmy influences of the season, protected from the sun by day, the chill dews by night, and from the rain, by a richly wrought ceiling of cedar and cypress, shadowing forth the permanency and excellence of the defence from evil afforded by the divine righteousness of Christ, in a manner stronger, if possible, than the shadow of a rock, or than the pillar of cloud and of fire over the camp of Israel. Ver. 16.

CHAPTER II.

In verses 1—3, the spouse sets forth by beautiful comparisons, the character of herself and of the beloved, for putting before us the contrast between her humility and loveliness, and his majesty and beauty. The believer is as the rose of Sharon and the lily of the valleys;—Jesus is as the citron-tree among all other trees. The rose and the lily illustrate the Christian character, as possessing purity, beauty, loveliness; as being like the lily among thorns, in contrast with the general tone of character and feeling in the world. The words, "As the lily among thorns, &c.," ver. 2, are with propriety put into the mouth of Jesus, as a suggestion made immediately on mention of the features represented in ver. 1st, for reminding us that, as his people, our character must be the opposite of what it was by nature, and of what yet prevails among the ungodly,—as he also teaches in John xvi. 33; 2 Tim. iii. 12. He says that between earthly loveliness and the loveliness of the saint, there is as much contrast as between the lily and the surrounding thorns.

While, like the rose and the lily, the believer—the same who was seen in the foregoing chapter admitted to such delightful communion with the king at his table—is thus meek and lowly, beautiful in the modesty of humility;—Jesus towers on high in majesty and grandeur; the citron-tree is his emblem, and illustrates his character as combining majesty with beauty, as affording shelter and protection to his people, as capable of satisfying the wants of the soul. Ver. 3.

Such being the characteristics of Jesus and of the redeemed soul, the coming of such soul into fellowship with him must yield it great pleasure. Hence, when we come under the shadow of Christ, we have great delight, and find food for the hungering heart; his ways are ways of pleasantness and all his paths are peace. Though addressed by him in language of such endearment and equality, and permitted to tell him our love, we are not the less sensible that he towers above us in the majesty of his divinity, far more than the citron-tree above the humble rose; that this majesty is our protection; and that the surpassing greatness of our joy springs from the union in his character of such gracious condescension and such divine grandeur.

The Lord Jesus leads his people along to greater displays of the riches of his grace and of holy joy—as pleasures were found in the banqueting-house, richer and more varied than under the apple-tree. In chap. i. ver. 4, he is represented as bringing us into "his chambers," the place of his intimate friends;—in chap. i. ver. 12, as feasting us at his table, with a repast of holy joys; here, he is set forth as bringing us into the midst of means for securing the most abundant exhilaration and gladness of heart, where, like a person in the king's house of wine, we may be abundantly satisfied with the fatness of his house and may drink of the river of his pleasures. The foregoing passages show different stages of spiritual enjoyment, increasing in degree till they are the greatest possible. Ver. 4.

In all these manifestations to us, his banner over us is love. As the banner rallies for the defence of even the weakest citizen all the strength of the state—is his protection—so, the divine love is our defence against all evils, and secures for us all the aid that may be drawn from all the other attributes of God. As the banner shows the country of the soldier, it is by possessing love that we are seen to be citizens of heaven. As the soldier exults in the flag of his country, the saint glories in the consciousness of the divine love, and in having love shed abroad in the heart.

In the three following verses, viz. 5, 6, 7, is a representation of the state of the believer, when, thus overshadowed by divine love, he is in the banqueting-house, in the full enjoyment of these overflowing riches of heavenly grace, to the greatest degree possible for man. 1. The state of the soul at times of the greatest spiritual enjoyment, "sick of love," ver. 5—filled with communications of love almost beyond its power to bear. 2. The feelings had at such seasons, ver. 6; great contrition and humility—the head was sinking; the consciousness of being sweetly and powerfully sustained by the Lord Jesus, through his imputed righteousness and by his inward grace, "His left hand is under my head;" we feel ourselves drawn very near to Jesus, "His right hand doth embrace me." 3. The desires then had, are—to be stayed or sustained by the fruits of the tree, the doctrines and promises of the gospel, "Stay me with flagons, comfort me with apples," ver. 5, and—to guard against anything likely to make our beloved withdraw, "I charge you, O ye daughters of Jerusalem, &c." ver. 7.

As these overpowering manifestations of love cannot be expected to continue without interruption, and Jesus will for wise purposes withdraw from the soul, in verses 8 and 9 is set forth the way in which he returns and manifests himself after such withdrawal. In his approach, he makes us hear his voice, even when afar off, ver. 8, "The voice of my beloved, &c." He comes with perfect ease, over all obstacles intervening in consequence of sin, ver. 8; he comes unexpectedly, often surprising us by his grace, when we are looking not for it. Having thus returned, he cannot be enjoyed by us without much to hinder the full manifestations of his excellence and glory. Walls yet intervene between us and him; he is very near to us, but the vision of his glory is obscured, and the sound of his voice deadened by the barriers behind which he stands, the walls of the dungeon in which we are now confined, the walls of our earthly house of this tabernacle, of our present mortal state, ver. 8. At the utmost, we can now get nothing more than very partial glimpses of the glory of Christ, such as may be had of a person showing himself through the obscurity of a lattice. Ver. 9.

While in our present state, we are thus in the condition of persons in a dungeon with the doors thrown open, like Peter's, Acts xii. 7, and Jesus is standing without, in the invisible world, looking on us kindly through the lattice, and addressing us through the bars; he tries to allure us away from our darkness, loathsomeness, and chains, abroad into that bright and glorious world where he has gone to prepare a place for us—saying, "Rise up, my love, my fair one, and come away, &c." He addresses us in language of the tenderest love—"My love, my fair one." Loving us so strongly, he is even more desirous to have us with him where he is in glory, than we can be be to depart and be with him. As motives for alluring us away from earth to heaven, he says that in the world to which he would draw us—"the winter is past;" there the curse, which has fallen so heavily even on the ground as to cause the desolations of winter, is for ever done away—all is fresh and uninterrupted spring. "The rain is over and gone;" afflictions and sorrows, all the former things are passed away. "The flowers appear on the earth;" everything is there budding and bursting with beauty. "The time of the singing of birds is come;" there, all is vocal with enchanting melody, and even the inanimate creation are joining in the chorus. "And the voice of the turtle is heard in our land;" the burden of that music is love. "The fig-tree putteth forth her green figs;" there, everything is found that can gratify our capabilities of enjoyment. Hence, he says,

9*

"Come away" from the sin and sorrows, &c. &c. of earth, come away to the skies, &c. Ver. 10—13.

The saint who is thus loved and allured by the Lord Jesus, is often found in the rough, afflictive scenes of this life, and in seclusion from the world, "in the clefts of the rock;" but he encourages us not to be disheartened by a sense of unworthiness, or cast down by sorrow, for the voice of such persons, however broken by contrition, is sweet to him, and their countenance, though marked with tears of penitence, is pleasant in his sight. Ver. 14.

Those who would be pleasant to Jesus, and enjoy frequent visits, such as mentioned in the foregoing verses, viz. 8—13, must be careful to guard against sin, and especially little sins; "the little foxes" will spoil the vines with tender grapes. Ver. 15.

Those who thus watch, and act, and love—who enjoy these manifestations of the beloved—may use the language of full assurance, and feel the amazing richness of the inheritance they have in Jesus. 1 Cor. iii. 22—23; John xvii. 10. The friendship and union existing between Jesus and his people, is of the most intimate and confidential kind; and as the feeding-place of the young hart is the place of the strongest desire, and though he may withdraw for a time from his pasture grounds, to them he must return; so, Jesus loves the dwelling-place among his saints, Ps. lxxvii. 2; lxxviii. 68; and though he seems to withdraw at seasons, he will not forsake us utterly, but will come back in his own good time, and make his abode with us. Ver. 16.

As these delightful visits of the beloved, the times when he comes over the hills and feeds among the lilies, must be interrupted, the saint here prays that he would repeat them as often as possible, until the day of eternal blessedness break, and the shadows now closing around us, for ever flee away. Ver. 17.

CHAPTER III.

This chapter consists of two parts, verses 1—5, showing the earnestness with which the believing soul seeks its absent Lord; and verses 6—11, illustrating the magnificence of the mode in which the saint is carried onward to glory.

The first verse, together with those following to the fifth, is connected with the last verse of the foregoing chapter. The prayer there offered for the repetition, as often as possible, of those precious interviews with Jesus, during the dark and lonely scenes of this life, is a prayer which prompts to activity in seeking him. This activity springs from a vehement desire kindled in the heart by our experience of the excellence of our Lord. Having been overpowered with his loveliness, and feeling, by his withdrawal, how precious his presence and how great the loss sustained by his absence, we have longings so intense for him as to be unsatisfied with earnest prayers; as to rise above and keep down the strongest cravings of our bodily nature. Nothing is more importunate and necessary than sleep; but the hungering and thirsting for righteousness, felt when the manifestations of Jesus are withheld, are stronger than the claims of even sleep, and cause us to seek him on our bed, during hours belonging to repose.

But it does not stop in desires, however intense. It incites to exertion for coming to him, though by great efforts and self-denial, making us even leave our bed and go out amid the chill dews and dangers of the night. Ver 2.

Animated by the fervent emotion which makes us feel Jesus to be him whom our soul loveth, we avail ourselves of every aid in finding our Lord, and inquire especially of those appointed as watchmen in Zion, the ministers of the word, concerning our spiritual state and the means of being restored to the joy of his salvation. Ver. 3.

Under these circumstances the promise is fulfilled, "They that seek shall find;" and efforts showing such earnestness and sincerity of purpose, are rewarded by the return of Jesus to our longing hearts. Ver. 4.

Having found him, we are anxious to enjoy the blessedness of his society, where there can be no restraint, and we may commune with him in secret, of all that is in our heart; we desire to be alone with Jesus, and the influences of his Spirit are laid hold of with the greatest eagerness.

The desire before expressed, is again felt, to avoid everything at all likely to make him withdraw from us. Ver. 5.

These manifestations of the loveliness of Christ on earth, lead to the glorious displays of his love in heaven; and our finding him, as just noticed, is the preparatory step to finding him in the splendour of his throne at the right hand of God. She who was allured by the motives in chap. ii. 10—13, to arise and come away, having embraced the invitation, finds on coming out from the walls of her dungeon, the royal palanquin waiting for her, under escort of a powerful guard; and the angels who desire to look into these things, view with admiration this imposing procession, as coming up from the wilderness lying between this world and heaven, the cortege is overshadowed by the reality represented in the pillar of cloud and of fire, by the cloud and smoke by day, and the shining of a flaming fire by night; while around is ascending the perfume of those odoriferous graces which are fed by the oil of gladness, and kindled by the flame of the Holy Ghost. In this manner, is the soul of him who is so humble in his own eyes, and neglected by the world, carried by the angels to Jesus' bosom. Luke xvi. 22.

In this progress to glory, the soul is overshadowed by the glorious covering or protection of the divine nature of Christ, our righteousness, like pillars of smoke or cloud, breaking the force of the rays of divine justice, and surrounded by the incense of prayer and all other graces, more pleasing than the perfumes burned in golden censers around the eastern bride. Ver. 6.

The soul is resting in a palanquin guarded by the angels who minister to the heirs of salvation; and who, in consequence of the dangers besetting us, are fully armed, and competent for every emergency. Ps. xxxiv. 7. Ver. 7, 8.

This conveyance is one of royal magnificence, belonging to Jesus, and made by the hands of him who did by himself purge our sins. Heb. i. 3. Ver. 9.

It has been built of the most precious and costly materials imaginable; materials so costly as to be obtainable not with corruptible things, as silver and gold, but with the precious blood of Christ. The conveyance in which we are borne onward to heaven, is so rich and precious, that the lining of it is love; and however heavy the storms and rough the scenes around us, we are in a litter, or portable pavilion, where the soul is o'ercanopied with love, where it is reclining on love, where the head is pillowed on love, and where everything its eyes rest on, is curiously wrought with the emblems of love. Ver. 10.

The meeting of Jesus with a redeemed soul clothed upon with a spiritual body, in the last day, at our entrance into heaven, is represented as the day of our espousals with him. He is waiting to receive us, in his kingly robes and crowned with many crowns; and those who have been on earth "a spectacle unto the world, and to angels, and to men," 1 Cor. iv. 9, shall then be viewed with admiration by all the holy angels and heavenly host. Ver. 11.

CHAPTER IV.

In this chapter, with ver. 1 of chap. v., we have, 1. The estimation of the beauty of holiness in the saint, as it appears in the eyes of Jesus. Ver. 1—5. 2. His gracious designation of a place where he wishes such souls to meet with him even now, until the day of glory in heaven cause our shades to flee away. Ver. 6. 3. The reasons given by him for alluring us to meet with him where he has appointed. Ver. 7—15. 4. The effect of these truths and reasons on the heart, to make us seek in prayer those influences of the Holy Spirit, which alone can prepare the soul for these meetings with our Lord. Ver. 16. 5. The consequence of thus hearkening to his voice and seeking the Holy Spirit, is that Jesus comes into our souls, and, by his presence sensibly felt, manifests his acceptance of us, and with the light of his smiles, fosters our pious virtues, chap. v. 1;—while the angels who rejoice over the soul first repenting, gather around it with no less joy, when our Lord comes again to visit and revive his garden.

The soul thus on the road to this glorious destiny, is humbled with the growing sense of its unworthiness, and feels more deeply that in our flesh dwells no good thing—sees nothing in us that we can suppose Jesus will love. The growing conviction of our sinfulness, attending growth in grace, would create despondency, did not our Lord give us assurances of his esteem; and those who are thus humble may be safely entrusted with these assurances, without danger of being exalted above measure. We must observe how much of this book, especially henceforward, is occupied with these expressions of Jesus' love to the saint, and how small, in comparison, the space given, viz. chap. v. 9—16, to our expressions of the beauty of Christ.

The proper meaning of the words in verses 1—5, and indeed of the subsequent addresses of the same kind, must be got by gathering together all the different impressions of beauty felt when we gaze on the eyes of doves, the flock of goats feeding on mount Gilead, the flock of sheep coming up from the washing, the thread of scarlet, the tower of David, covered with its thousand shields, the two young roes feeding among the lilies; each one of these separately, is viewed with great pleasure, but when we sum up the feelings of satisfaction had in contemplating them all unitedly, then may we have a representation of the delight with which Jesus dwells on the soul of the believer in process of sanctification.

While in this world, and in preparation for the day of our espousals, we are not cut off from communication with Jesus. His love makes him wish to have us with him even now, though it must be in a different way from that in which we shall be with him hereafter. In this world, he comes and manifests himself to us. John xiv. 21, 23.

He has appointed a place for such interviews, where he may always be found. He appointed the mountain of the Lord's house of old, where the Shechinah dwelt, as the place where he would meet with his people, and dwell among them, and commune with them, obscurely indeed, but really;—the place where he has now recorded his name to dwell there, is the mountain of myrrh and the hill of frankincense; the hill where the mercy-seat is established; where the cloud of the Holy Spirit's influences abides in dews richer and more refreshing than the dews on the mountains of spices. Ver. 6.

That we may have no hesitation in coming to meet him on the hill of frankincense, till the day break and the shadows flee away, he gives us eight reasons for our encouragement:

1. Thou art to me all beautiful, without spot or any such blemish. Eph. v. 27. Ver. 7.

2. Here only canst thou be safe; the choicest spots of this world, though beautiful as the top of Amana, or Shenir, or Hermon, or that goodly mountain, even Lebanon, are full of peril—lions' dens and leopards; therefore come away with me from all these, however inviting; come away to the mount where I meet with my loved ones, under the bright cloud of the Holy Ghost, dropping on their souls the myrrh and frankincense of the heavenly world. Ver. 8.

3. Come away with me to this mount; because my heart is enraptured—is taken away—with only the partial development of thy loveliness that as yet appears; with one of thine eyes unveiled to me, with one chain of thy neck: thy graces are not yet perfected, sanctification is not yet completed, nor thy spiritual body prepared; but even the little now seen in thee of the glory that shall be revealed, enraptures my heart. Ver. 9.

4. He wishes us with him there, because our love, wrought by the Spirit, is beautiful in his eyes; this is

what is especially delightful to him, and in the absence of any other excellence, commends us; and this love is more pleasing to him than wine to our taste. Not only is the affection of love thus grateful to him, but equally so are all those graces of the heart which are the fruit of the Spirit, Gal. v. 22—23, Eph. v. 9, and are the perfume of the soul—better even than the holy oil shed over the head of Aaron. Ver. 10.

5. The language of the heart thus filled with love as the consequence of being anointed with our glorious Head, with the oil of gladness—distils in accents as pleasant to him as drops of the honey-comb to our tongues. He sees within the heart a fountain of this loveliness, not soon exhausted, because springing from a source no deeper than the lips, but springing up into everlasting life—"honey and milk are under thy tongue." Ver. 11.

6. The presence of the saint is altogether pleasant to our Lord, as much so as the fragrance of Lebanon to us. Ver. 11.

7. For showing why he wishes us to come away with him, he states that his delight in the soul of the believer is as great and pleasing as what is felt by us in enjoying the most beautiful garden. Verses 12—15.

This garden is enclosed, abounds in all pleasant fruits, is full of trees of frankincense and all the chief spices, and is watered, not only from an unfailing spring in its midst, but also with cool, refreshing streams from the snowy tops of Lebanon. Thus precious in the eyes of our Lord is the soul which Jehovah has set apart for himself, Ps. iv. 3; which yields the peaceable fruit of righteousness; which sends up its desires as incense; which enjoys those copious streams issuing from the fountain of the Holy Spirit within the heart, and coming with the refreshing influence of waters from a more glorious than Lebanon in the skies.

The effect of such impressions of Jesus' love, creates the desire that he may come into our hearts and make his abode with us; that he may sup with us, and we with him. Rev. iii. 20. We wish, however, to prepare the way of the Lord, and therefore address ourselves to prayer for the influences of the Holy Spirit to revive our graces; "Awake, O north wind! and come, thou south," &c. Then, when the soul has been thus prepared by the Holy Ghost, we rejoice in finding Jesus coming into our hearts and enjoying the pleasant fruits of our sanctified graces. Ver. 16.

8. And if we thus come to him with preparation of heart, he will come down into our souls by his Spirit, and spread around us a host of angels rejoicing to be our guard. Chap. v. 1. Prayers thus offered under the intercession of the Spirit, are answered, without delay, by Jesus coming and dwelling in our hearts, Eph. iii. 17, ii. 22, and manifesting his acceptance of our services and graces; the great acceptableness of which to him is illustrated by the combination of gratifications had in a pleasant garden, where we are regaled with pleasant odours, beautiful scenes and flowers, and delightful fruits. Nor does Jesus enjoy these by himself. He who is anointed with the oil of gladness above his fellows, desires those associates—anxious as they are to look into the mysteries of redemption—to come and enjoy with him the beauties and delights of this new creation, over which, while he rejoices as a bridegroom over his bride, they, the sons of God, may sing together and shout for joy.

CHAPTER V.

In chapters v. vi. and vii. we have, 1. The effect of sluggishness and indifference when the Lord Jesus draws near to the soul; viz. the loss of his presence and favour: ver. 2—6. 2. The anxiety, labour, and trouble to which this neglect gives rise, in our efforts for seeking him: ver. 7, 8. 3. The answers given to the questions put by those who witness our anxiety and sorrow at such times—viz. What is the character of him who is so anxiously sought? ver. 9, and, Where has he gone, where may he be found? chap. vi. 1. 4. The willingness of Jesus, even when he has been forced from us by our own sins, to receive his people who seek him in sincerity and truth, as shown by the address of the beloved to the spouse, chap. vi. 4; vii. 9. 5. The feelings towards our Lord by the soul thus kindly received into his love, expressed in the wish to enjoy retirement with him, and to offer him our best gifts, chap. vii. 10—13, and to the end of chap. viii.

After the most glorious displays to us of the love of Jesus, we may soon sink into indifference, entangled and overcome through weakness of the flesh, Matt. xxvi. 41, by the necessary duties of life running out into temptations; our perceptions being allowed to close against these manifestations of grace, through our own apathy and sluggishness. But while at such time, the flesh may be weak, the spirit remains willing—we sleep, but our heart waketh; though there is a law in our members, warring against the law of our mind and bringing us into captivity to the law of sin, we do yet delight in the law of God, after the inward man, Rom. vii. 22: though the outward evidences of love to Christ have very much disappeared under the pressure of spiritual sloth and decay, grace is still in the heart with its glimmerings; the heart is awake, but not in sufficient strength to counteract the pressure of carnality and control the doings of the body. So far from fulfilling his wishes and coming away from Lebanon, &c., chap. iv. 8, to the mountain of myrrh, there to meet with him, we prefer the indulgence of our fleshly, carnal inclinations—sleep—to all the attractions of his loveliness and society. Ver. 2.

But so strong is his love, that when he does not find us meeting him at the appointed place, he graciously comes to seek us, even in our sloth, and tries to allure us away, by considerations the most endearing and affecting: "Open to me, &c.," Rev. iii. 20. Unmoved by these, we content ourselves in our apathy, by excuses the most frivolous. The love of our Lord does then prompt him to go further than entreaty, to use exertions, for finding his way into our heart: "My beloved, &c." Ver. 4.

At length, moved by his tender addresses to us, and by the measures of mercy used by him for reviving our love, the affections begin to move, and we arise to meet him. Instead however, of running at once to meet him, and opening our soul to him, just as it is, we delay in order to prepare ourselves to see him; and the consequence of this delay is, that although we bring with us the best of our acts and endeavours, our hands dropping with myrrh, &c., he is gone. Nothing of our own, however costly, as duty and self-denial, and mortification, can excuse us for hesitating to rush into his arms; and as many a repenting sinner loses all interest in him, and also the soul, by delaying in order to make himself fit to come, so does many a saint often lose precious interviews with the Lord. Ver. 5—6.

Her soul has been deeply moved under the language of the beloved standing at the door; and thus moved, does now impel her to seek him. While the withdrawals of Jesus are a just recompense for our sluggishness, they give occasion for calling into exercise our love, and for showing its strength. What was lost by indifference, can now be got only by great exertion; we seek him; we call on him without receiving an answer; we have to suffer reproach and ill-treatment from the watchmen of Zion, who, instead of helping us in our zeal, view our love and devotion as fanaticism, and both misuse and expose us to shame; "Took away my vail, &c." The sympathy that is often denied to the devoted heart by those high in office in the Church, may be found among our pious equals; and seeking an interest in their prayers, Eph. vi. 19; 2 Thess. iii. 1, we entreat their aid, serving, seeking, and following our Lord. Ver. 7—8.

This earnestness and zeal is not without its effect on others before whom the light of the believer is thus made to shine. Seeing the manifestations in various ways, of such intense love to Christ, a love that will be satisfied with nothing short of himself, and which is willing, for the enjoyment of his presence, to incur any self-denial and any humiliation, they naturally inquire, What there is in Christ above others, that so strongly affects us? The illustration that follows in verses 10—16, is unequalled for beauty and richness. It is the Holy Spirit, by the mouth of an inspired saint, illustrating the beauty of Christ by language, through the same means used in creation, drawn from the beauties of the world. The most fine gold, the raven's blackness, the eyes of doves, the beds of spices, the lilies dropping sweet-smelling myrrh, &c.; all these, as works of Christ, show his excellence. But when we would understand the loveliness of that human person through which the Son of God, the eternal Creator, manifests himself as our Redeemer, these separate clusters, radiant with his glory, and scattered at large in his works, must be gathered into a form of the man Christ Jesus; and we are told that, just as beautiful as a person must be, whose appearance would impress us with all the ideas of loveliness got from the most fine gold, the beds of spices, the majesty of Lebanon, &c. &c., so beautiful is Christ. Yes, though even in a case like this, there would still be something wanting; in Jesus there is everything that can be desired; he is altogether lovely. This person, combining beauties beyond what man may possess, or the mind of man, in the farthest stretch of his imagination, unaided by the Spirit of God, could conceive—"this is my beloved, and this is my friend." Ver. 9—16.

CHAPTER VI.

Such a representation of the excellence of our Lord, creates in those hearing it a desire to see him for themselves; and they inquire where he may be found, "Whither has thy beloved gone? that we may seek him with thee?" Ver. 1.

The reply is, that he may always be found and seen in "his garden," in his church, which is in the midst of this world, a sacred enclosure, beloved by him, Ps. lxxx. 12; Isa. v. 1—where is his strongest desire, Matt. xxviii. 20; there does he dwell among his people, to enjoy the fragrance of the beds of spices, the grateful incense of desires arising from sanctified hearts, and "to gather lilies,"—to take to his bosom, transfer to heaven those ripe for change. Though Jesus may be withdrawn from the heart of one and another of his saints, he is never absent from his Church; he is always in some part or another of it, among the beds of spices; and those who have estranged him from them by neglect, must seek for him there. Ver. 2.

The bright manifestations of Jesus' love may be withdrawn from us, without unsettling our hope; the absence of joy, and of such views as represented in chap. ii. 5, iv. 1—15, &c., does by no means imply the absence of piety or faith. Faith reposes on Jesus when the light of his countenance is withheld; and, as we follow him, though amid gloom and trial, makes us still feel and say, in the absence of all spiritual comforts—even in the deadly gloom of the greatest spiritual darkness—"I am my beloved's, and my beloved is mine;" though his presence is not manifested now to my soul, I know that "he feedeth among the lilies," that his nature constrains him to dwell among his saints; and there, by keeping within his garden, under the influence of the means of grace, I shall again soon find the joy of his salvation, in the fulness of his presence. Ps. xlii. 1, 5, 11. Ver. 3.

A faith thus steadfast is never disappointed. The soul, thus following hard after Christ, and seeking him, perhaps with tears, finds him. The gracious Friend who had been so misused, chap. v. 2—6, though he had forsaken the soul for a season, rejoices to receive us when we show our sorrow by seeking him, Ps. ciii. 9; Isa. lx. 10; lxiv. 5. He comes to meet us as he sees and hears us following him through the paths of his garden; and he assures us his love is unchanged; he encourages us to come to him, by such language as is used in verses 4—13, &c. This passage, down to chap. vii. 9, is the language of Jesus to the believing soul when restored from the estrangement caused by neglect of his love, as stated in chap. v. 2—6. At such times, humbled by our unworthy conduct towards such a friend, we hesitate until reassured of his unabated love. As Tirzah, situated on Judea's beautiful hills, and Jerusalem, "beautiful for situation," and a bannered host, were objects impressing the mind with sensations of beauty, and of commanding dignity and majesty; so appears the soul of the saint advancing towards Jesus awaiting us amid the beauties and fragrance of his garden. Ver. 4.

In accommodation to human modes of speaking, he says the impression is the greatest possible, is overpowering. Ver. 5.

Then, as though to reassure us that, after our unworthy conduct, his love is still the same, he uses the same language previously addressed to us, chap. iv. 1—3. Ver. 7.

Around the Lord Jesus, God the Son, there are innumerable lovely and glorious beings, "queens, and virgins without number," on whom he might bestow his love; but among these the soul of the believer stands preeminent; this is the *one* amid that host, whom he loves above all others, and loves as devotedly as though there were no other to love. Moreover, that soul thus sanctified, thus beautified with the beauty of holiness, is the object of universal admiration; all that saw her praised her; the redeemed, fully perfected, are the admiration of the heavenly host. Ver. 8, 9.

And as he sees the estranged soul of his saint hastening towards him, impressed with her beauty and dignity of bearing, he exclaims, Who is this approaching, covered with the blush of beauty and glow of health, more pleasing than the dawn of the morning; beautiful as the moon in her silvery brightness; pure and impressive in loveliness as the brilliancy of the sun; grand and imposing in her demeanour as hosts with streaming banners? Numb.

CHAPTER VI.

xxiii. 21. This is even my ransomed one, new created through the Holy Spirit. Ver. 10.

Receiving the returning saint with this cordiality and love, our Lord proceeds to tell his feelings during his withdrawal. He withdraws not in anger, but in love; he feels, without ceasing, the strongest desire to return to us; he earnestly invites us to return; he continues still to view us with unabated love, with even greater pleasure than he views the angels, the hosts seen by Jacob at Mahanaim. Though leaving the individual soul, he went into other portions of his garden, God's husbandry, 1 Cor. iii. 9, the Church, for exercising over it his care. But the strength of his love towards us, unkind though we had been to him, would not allow him to forget us; his mind, his heart, was on us, even though he was withdrawn, and his countenance hid; and spontaneously, almost before he was aware, his nature being love, he found himself inclined to us with tender compassion, and returning to meet us, with the rapidity of the chariots of Amminadib. Though we grieve Jesus by our neglect, and compel him to leave us, he departs in sorrow and in love, drawn towards us still by the strongest affection, and not only willing to receive us if we seek him again, but coming with the greatest rapidity to meet us, Song ii. 8; Luke xv. 20. Ver. 11, 12.

With tenderness and emphasis, he encourages us not to hesitate, but to come on, "Return, return, &c.," assuring us that his heart had been with us, and that he is not only willing, but desirous, to look upon us. And does any one ask, what he sees in this sanctified soul, that so captivates? He replies by summing up the whole in one expression—the festive chorus of two hosts. He has as much pleasure in contemplating this redeemed spirit, as we could have, were we permitted to gaze on hosts mingling in the festal dances and rejoicing of a day of triumph—such hosts as were seen by Jacob at Mahanaim, and exulting in such rejoicings as were seen when, over the first creation, "the morning stars sang together, and all the sons of God shouted for joy." Job xxxviii. 7. Ver. 13.

CHAPTER VII.

The commendation of the beauty of the pious soul, for the purpose of encouraging it to trust in Jesus, notwithstanding past neglect and estrangement, is continued without interruption to verse 9. The same principles of interpretation apply here that have been used for interpreting the other similer passages, chap. iv. 1—5; v. 10—16. Having set forth this beauty, he is represented as held enchained by it, ver. 5, "the king is captivated by those locks;" and expresses that his most delicate and pleasing delight is had in the company and contemplation of the new creation going forward in the soul of the saint. Ver. 1—6.

As a consequence, he wishes to gather us in his arms, and carry us in his bosom, Isa. xl. 11, and to hearken to our voices engaged in thankfulness and praise; the agreeableness of which to our Lord is as great as to ourselves would be such wine as mentioned in verse 9. Ver. 8, 9.

With the 10th verse, begins the third part of the book, which contains a statement of the effects produced on the heart by the manifestations of love, and by the motives before mentioned.

1. The effect is the full assurance of hope, "I am my beloved's, and his desire is towards me." Ver. 10.

2. We wish to be much alone with Jesus in retirement, "Let us go forth into the field, &c." Ver. 11.

3. We engage spontaneously in labours of holiness and love, such as enjoined by our Lord, "Let us get up early to the vineyards, let us see if the vine flourish, &c.," ver. 12. In such ways and duties as these do we give Jesus our love.

4. For him do we lay up, and to him do we consecrate our best gifts, as well as our diligent services, under the influence, of this love: "All manner of pleasant fruits, which I have laid up for thee, O my beloved." Ver. 13.

CHAPTER VIII.

The next effect mentioned, is a desire that everything hindering the full and perfect interchange of affection between Jesus and our soul, might be removed, and that it were possible to enjoy his love to us, and express our love to him, as we shall be able to do in heaven. Much as we may now long for stronger displays of his love, and to give stronger evidence of our love to him, we acquiesce in the present state of things, because we feel there would be an impropriety, no less than impossibility, in those overpowering exhibitions of love that belong to heaven. But this does not preclude us from feeling that, were it seen best by him, we would rejoice, even now, in those raptures which belong to heaven, where we shall be able to speak of his love in the strongest language, and give expression to it in the most exalted praise, without danger of exposing ourselves to the contempt of the ungodly. Ver. 1. There shall our fellowship and communion with him be far more intimate and endearing than ever on earth. Ver. 2.

6. Yet though this desire, of ver. 1 and 2, cannot be granted, we wish to have as much as can now be enjoyed of Jesus, even such seasons as are here mentioned, and

had been enjoyed in chap. ii. 6, 7, and with it, the desire, as there expressed, that nothing be done to interrupt it. This seems mentioned as though it was viewed by the soul as a blessed and satisfying foretaste of what may be expected hereafter, and as much as is best or possible for us in this world. Ver. 3, 4.

7. But though we cannot now enjoy what we could desire, and what shall be enjoyed in heaven; though the delightful scenes now had must be interrupted, yet we are permitted to go up from this wilderness, leaning on the beloved; we feel that underneath us are the everlasting arms; in all circumstances he sustains us; and throughout our pilgrimage we are thus upheld by him who first found us, raised us up, and took us into covenant relation "under the apple-tree," as in chap. ii. 3, under the shadow of Christ. Ver. 5.

8. Another result of this love is the desire to be continually near to the heart of Jesus, to be perpetually in his remembrance, and sustained by his Almighty power; that like the stones engraved with the names of Israel on Aaron's breastplate, and like the stones on the shoulder of the high priest, we may be set as a seal on his heart, as a seal on his arm. Ver. 6.

9. This love sacrifices everything that would come between us and Christ. Death cannot arrest us—we love Jesus better than life, "for love is strong as death." Matt. xvi. 24, 25. The delights of it being such as have been represented in the foregoing verses, 1—4, and other parts of this book, we desire to abide on the heart of Jesus, and run to embrace even death, if necessary, sooner than loose his love. As there is nothing which jealousy will not sacrifice, so there is nothing which this love will not sacrifice for the full enjoyment of Christ.

10. Everything that the world can offer for bribing or

CHAPTER VIII. 117

enticing us away from our Lord, is rejected; as this love cannot be got from Jesus with silver and gold, neither can the heart which feels it in the fulness here described, be induced to part with it for the world. Ver. 7. It is felt to be more precious than rubies, and all the things thou canst desire are not to be compared unto it. Ps. iii. 15; Phil. iii. 8.

11. While thus enjoying the love of Christ in such fulness and power, we are not unmindful of the impenitent among our friends, &c., feeling them a kindred to us by the flesh, Luke x. 29, Rom. ix. 3, and anxious for them to obtain like precious faith. As a younger sister not yet of marriageable age was thought of by her who was exalted to be the queen of even Solomon in all his glory, and had a care exercised over her for raising her in due time to an eligible position of dignity, wealth, and splendour—so the impenitent are not forgotten by those who are already enjoying the pledges of the love of Christ; these watch for souls as those who must give account, that we may present them with us in the day of the Lord. Ver. 8.

The change that will then be wrought in the condition of souls thus brought forth from their estrangement, nigh unto Christ, is illustrated in ver. 9. Though in their natural condition they are like an ordinary wall without ornamental work, they shall be made beautiful as a palace of silver built on such a foundation, or as a door of ordinary materials encased in cedar, the most polished, and costly, and beautiful, of all wood. The Holy Spirit takes our nature, dark and unseemly as a wall, and is raising thereon, and from the midst of these dilapidated and ruined materials, that which shall be more beautiful than a palace of silver, a spiritual temple, an habitation of God through the Spirit. Eph. ii. 12. In this world we are to glorify God, by seeking our own holiness, and the salvation of others; to show forth his praise by being a wall on which shall be built the silver palace of our holiness, and by being a door, which, encased in the most precious materials of its kind, shall stand in beauty worthy of admiration while opening to others the way of life.

Though, like the spouse's sister then unfitted for her exalted destiny, the impenitent are in a state giving no promise whatever of the glory just stated, and attainable only by the workmanship of the same Spirit who is the builder and maker of the heavenly Jerusalem, Heb. ix. 10, the saint feels that by nature such were we, 1 Cor. vi. 11—"I am a wall"—and that the grace which so changed us, made us fit, gave us power, John i. 12, to become the sons of God, to find favour in his eyes—can, will change them from sin to holiness, so that though they have lien among the pots, they shall be as the wings of a dove covered with silver, and her feathers with yellow gold. Ps. lxviii. 13. Ver. 10.

12. This love makes us feel and labour for the souls of the impenitent, by making us sensible of our accountability as the stewards of God, 1 Cor. iv. 1; Luke xii. 42; Matt. xxi. 33; xxv. 15; Luke xix. 13. All our property, gifts of intellect, influence, &c., are entrusted to us by God, are things held in trust from the Lord, who will require of us an account of our stewardship. Ver. 11.

This responsibility is felt by him whose heart is alive with love to Christ, while others refuse to acknowledge it; and in view of his obligations, the saint cheerfully consecrates to his Lord the due portion of his services, his income, his all. Ver. 12.

CHAPTER VIII.   119

13. Thus constrained by the love of Christ in the way of duty, the soul enjoys the privilege continually of audience with the King of kings through Christ the Saviour, and is encouraged in the exercise of prayer and praise, not only by a sense of our need and by the delights of holy worship, but by the assurance that our voice thus heard is pleasant to Jesus, chap. ii. 14;—that these expressions of holy emotions so agreeable to our companions in the kingdom and patience of Jesus, Rev. i. 9, abiding with us here in the gardens of his grace, are heard with still greater pleasure by him who now dwells in these gardens by the Shechinah of the Holy Spirit, chap. v. 1, as he shall hereafter dwell among us in the paradise of God, its light and glory. Rev. vii. 15—17; xxi. 23. Ver. 13.

14. Thus encouraged to dwell at the mercy-seat in confidential and constant communion with our Lord on earth, we are becoming fitted for being with him in heaven; and this fitness, combined with the displays of his love before mentioned, carries with it a stronger and stronger desire for the enjoyment of his glory as it shall be revealed when the Lord perfects that which concerneth us—at his second coming when the day breaks and the shadows flee away. To this, as the ultimate, absorbing desire of the soul, do all these assurances of the love of Jesus lead. As the book begins with a burst of desire for the love of Christ as that love can be enjoyed only by his intimate friends, chap. i. 2, it ends with a prayer for the hastening of the time when we shall no longer see him through a glass darkly, but face to face— when there shall be nothing to interfere with the manifestation of his love to us, and the expression of our love to him: this desire is expressed, and its intenseness

shown by the prayer, that he would hasten that happy day, and come with the celerity of a roe or a young hart bounding over the mountains of spices, and at every step shaking fragrance from the dewy boughs. Rev. xxii. 7, 12, 20. Ver. 14.

COMMENTARY

ON THE

SONG OF SOLOMON.

CHAPTER I.

VERSE 1. *The Song of songs, which is Solomon's.*

THESE words are as unmistakenly given by inspiration as any succeeding portion of this book, and show the estimation in which the Song is held by the Holy Spirit. It is called the Song of songs, or the most excellent Song. For the purpose of meeting the numerous objections brought against this portion of Scripture, the divine wisdom writes on the front of it an attestation of its superior excellence, not only to the thousand and five songs by Solomon, but to all the songs ever produced by all other poets. He who cannot err, tells us, in language of no doubtful meaning, that this Song is unrivalled.

Poetry is the expression of the best and most beautiful thoughts, of exalted emotions, in the best and most beautiful language. The language of poetry is the language of excited feeling. The best poetry must have the noblest theme, deal with the purest emotions, and be adorned with the richest ideas. God has garnished his works of every kind with beauty, and formed us with a capability of receiving pleasure from that beauty. Hence, in conveying to us important truth, he does throughout the

Scriptures make it attractive, by adapting it to this love within us of the beautiful. Now, love is the very excellence of God; for God is love. Love is the purest, deepest, and most powerful emotion known to man. Nothing can, therefore, be better or more beautiful than the subject of this Song; and being a song, a poetical composition, it must be in the best and most beautiful language. A translation gives no idea of the excellence of Homer; and beautiful as is this Song, in our English version, we must remember that it is the poetry of an age more remote than the earliest Greek poets, in a modern language of very different structure and idiom.

The fact that this Song is so much rejected, is a proof of its excellence. How many persons can see no excellence in the best productions of genius, even when there is about them no allegory, as is here the case, to be interpreted by the Holy Spirit. "A work of genius, designed in a lofty spirit, and executed with a fine sense of the noblest functions of poetry, is assuredly not worthily appreciated, unless by those who have in some measure apprehended that world of suggestive thought which the poet aims at embodying in his imaginative scenes and figures; and, if a series of poetic images suggest, to diverse minds, diversified trains of reflection and emotion, this is perhaps the clearest evidence of their poetical intensity and truth."* The better the poetry, the more profound the ideas embodied in it, the farther is it above the range of the common mind, and the more likely to be appreciated only by the cultivated few whose taste has been carefully refined. This being the Song of songs, the same thing must be expected here, and to a much greater degree, because there is need of a taste

* Ed. Review, No. 181, Art. 7.

which cannot be attained without the supernatural aid of divine grace. Even when the highest beauty and excellence was personified in Jesus Christ, how perfectly was all this above the comprehension of man. They saw in him no beauty that they should desire him. Isa. liii. 2. His beauty cannot be seen and understood without a taste imparted by the Holy Spirit. "No man can say that Jesus is the Lord, but by the Holy Ghost." 1 Cor. xii. 3. Much is said about the Beautiful, the Good, and the True. Jesus was the personification of them all. In him did God represent unto us these abstract, spiritual excellences, in a sensible, bodily form. In its loftiest flights, the imagination of man never had so glorious a conception as that which is given in the union of the divine and human natures in the person of Jesus Christ. The object of this Song is the celebration of the love which led to that union—its beauty, its attractiveness, and its glorious results. Others of the divine songs of Scripture celebrate some particular consequences flowing from this love; the song of Moses at the Red Sea, speaks the praise of Jehovah for their deliverance; the Psalms are utterances of pious feeling, for various mercies; this Song goes to the spring of all that is beautiful, good, and true, and celebrates the love which is the fountain of all blessedness. Homer, generally received as the prince of poets, sings of the malignant passions, the wrath of his hero, the cause of woes unnumbered; this book sings of the wondrous love of God, which is the spring, not of desolation, misery, and tears, but of the new creation, the deliverance from guilt, the consolation, the heavenly anticipations that are abroad in our world of woe. It sings of the same love which is the burden of the new song in heaven. How glorious was the chorus when, at the completion of creation, "the morning stars sang together, and all the sons of God shouted for joy." Will not that be the Song of songs which shall be heard amid the new heavens and the new earth wherein dwelleth righteousness, when the innumerable company of the redeemed and the angels join to celebrate the love of the Lamb that was slain. The theme of this Song is the same redeeming love; and those whose hearts are here brought by grace to feel the excellence of this portion of Scripture, are already learning that Song which no man could learn but those redeemed from the earth.

God can express to us inward spiritual beauty, only through the means of outward sensible beauty; and in this Song he makes use of this outward beauty for impressing on us that which is inwardly beautiful, true, and good. What beauty is comparable to the beauty of holiness? This is the source of all other beauty. All the deformity, ugliness, and filthiness in this world, are owing to the want of holiness. In the sky or heavens, where no stain of sin has fallen, there is nothing but beauty. This beauty of holiness is that which the Psalmist so earnestly desired to behold. Ps. xxvii. 4. And the celebration of that beauty in this divine poetry, renders it the Song of songs. A few years ago, on a clear winter's night, there burst forth a northern light that suffused the whole heavens with a rosy tinge, and threw over the snow and landscape the same unearthly hues, different from anything previously seen, and causing emotions of inexpressible pleasure in those who beheld this transient burst of heavenly splendour: this Song, is, as it were, a rosy burst of the divine love, which, through the Lamb, is the Shechinah of heaven; and those whose souls have the spiritual perception for seeing the divine light here beaming, feel their hearts thrill with the beauty of the tinge it throws over our blighted and wintry world. Elsewhere there can be seen nothing of equal or like beauty.

It was proper that such a Song should be written by Solomon. Aaron having prefigured Christ as a priest, and Moses foreshadowing him as a prophet, Solomon prefigured him as a king. And while David represents Jesus as suffering persecution and subduing the enemies of his people, Solomon represents him as the triumphant Prince of peace. Under Solomon, the kingdom of Israel was perfectly established by the conquest of all their enemies, and by the building of the temple in Jerusalem; and as the camp in the wilderness may represent the Church in this world, the reign of Solomon may be a representation of the Church in heaven. While, therefore, David sung, in the Psalms, of the various conflicts of the Christian life, Solomon here sings of that which is the end of all our conflicts, the consummation of the love of Christ and his Church. His mental endowments were as glorious as his position. Not only did he surpass all others in wealth and splendour, the most kingly of kings; before him there was none like him for wisdom, neither after him shall any arise like unto him, 1 Kings iii. 12; and he possessed noble poetic powers. A man combining these rare qualifications, was very properly selected by the Holy Spirit as the means for conveying to the saints this divine allegory, this unequalled Song of love.

VER. 2.—Let him kiss me with the kisses of his mouth; for thy love is better than wine.

In the opening scene of this poem, as in this verse, the king had probably gone forth, according to oriental customs, to meet the bride, and was awaiting her, with his princely retinue, in an encampment where his rich pavilion stood pre-eminent. The spouse, looking forward with great interest to this meeting, on coming in sight of those kingly tents, almost involuntarily, as it were, gives utterance to the strong emotions of her heart, in these words.* Kitto remarks: "There are few acts bearing more diversified and contrasted significations than the kiss. It denotes as well the tenderest affection, as the most profound and even adoring reverence." The words "kisses of his mouth," are not merely a redundant expression, like "words of my mouth," Ps. xix. 14, and "with their mouth they speak," Ps. xvii. 10; but a mode of distinguishing the kiss which was evidence of the tenderest affection, from the kiss which was the expression of submission, reverence, and obedience. In the East the kiss was impressed on the mouth, the hands, the feet, the garments, and even the ground where the feet had trodden—the difference being caused by the greater or less intimacy between the individuals. Permission to kiss the hand of a sovereign is considered an honour; but for that sovereign to give another the kisses of his mouth, is evidence of the tenderest affection, and is the highest possible honour. This metaphor is common to all oriental poets: "O suffer me to quaff the liquid bliss of those lips! Restore thy slave with their water of life." Thus again: "Thou who sippest nectar from the radiant lips of Pedmá, as the flattering Chacóra drinks the moonbeams!"†

The language of the spouse is, therefore, a desire that

---

* Reiske, as quoted by Dopke, says: "It is a fundamental principle of the Arabic language, without which we cannot understand their best writers, and by ignorance or neglect of which we get into inextricable perplexity, that very frequently poets do not name that which they designate, because the reader or hearer may easily gather the sense from the thread of the discourse and character of the epithets used."

† From the Gitagovinda.

the beloved would give her those evidences of affection which none but the most cherished friends can have right to receive. They express the desire of the pious heart, that the Lord Jesus would give us manifestations of the love which none but his dearest friends can receive, or have reason to expect. Jesus says to his people, "I have called you friends," John xv. 15; "He that loveth me, shall be loved of my Father, and I will love him, and will manifest myself to him." John xiv. 21. The persons to whom these words were spoken, understood them as referring to manifestations very different from anything the world could receive: "Lord, how is it that thou wilt manifest thyself unto us, and not unto the world?"

What are those manifestations of Jesus' love which none but his friends can receive? He explains them to consist in the influences of the Holy Spirit. As the burst of feeling which in the bosom of the spouse swallowed up all others, was for these expressions of affection; so the predominating, absorbing desire of the believer, is for the full communications of the Holy Ghost. It is a point of the greatest importance for a man to know, what is the one thing which should be the leading principle of his life, to be pursued with oneness of view and indivisibility of purpose. Every person has some such aim; and if the object thus selected be a wrong one, here is a radical error which must throw everything else astray. The influences of the Holy Spirit are that primary, essential object. It is much for the impenitent to know that his nature can be renewed only by God's Spirit; and much has been done towards making us Christians of more than ordinary growth, when we feel more than ordinarily the necessity of being filled with the Spirit according to the full capacity of our souls. Great advances in holiness must be made by seeking eminent measures of the Spirit. Those will be most holy, will feel most deeply the love of Jesus, who seek the greatest degrees of the communications of the Spirit. Preparation for heaven does not consist in rising to any imaginary standard of piety, in being as holy as we may consider some illustrious saints, in rising to certain frames of which we have heard and which we have desired; but in being filled as full of the Holy Spirit as our capacities can bear. Do you ask, How can I attain eminent holiness? Seek with undeviating and self-sacrificing purpose, eminent measures of the Holy Ghost.

There are various ways in which God may show his love, even to the saints. The multiplied comforts of life, home, family, friends; the continuance of health, reason, eyesight; the exercise of our faculties of body; exemption from calamity; prosperity in ordinary duties; enjoyment of spiritual privileges; all these are ways in which God may manifest love to his people. But while thankful for these, as tokens of divine love, the saint fixes his eye far above and beyond them—on the influences of the Holy Spirit. In his view of life, the principal thing is held to be not wealth, not honour, not popularity, not power, but the riches of this heavenly grace. His ruling passion is to amass the durable riches and righteousness of the Holy Ghost. He views the Spirit as the strongest pledge of the love of Jesus—a gift so important that God can now confer on us no other gift of equal value. Jesus did not promise his disciples crowns, or riches, or honour, or ease in this world; but he did promise them affliction, with the Holy Ghost. John xvi. 33; xiv. 16. And as the Spirit touches our soul in the communication of his grace, how delightful the sensations. When they told Jacob "all the words of Joseph which he had said unto them, and when he saw the wagons which Joseph had sent to carry him, the spirit of Jacob their father revived, Gen. xlv. 27: how much richer the feelings of the patriarch, when that long lost son presented himself unto him, and he fell on his neck, and wept on his neck a good while. Gen. xlvi. 29. The gift of the best robe and the costly ring was not to the prodigal so precious a proof of his father's love, as that given when the father fell on his neck and kissed him. Luke xv. 20. While the common gifts of Providence are received with thankfulness, as evidences of God's love, and our spirit may revive in meeting with the conveyances loaded with blessings, that have been sent to encourage and refresh us, by Jesus our brother, exalted to more than a second place in the heavenly kingdom; no proof of his affection is so much coveted, is so delightful, as when, coming through the person of the Holy Spirit, he gathers us, the lambs of his fold, with his arms, and carries us in his bosom, Isa. xl. 11,—manifests himself unto us not as unto the world. Refreshing as are good news from a far country; more pleasing is the letter written by the well known hand; more so the sight of the absent friend; best of all the return, when we press him again to the bosom: and refreshing as are the words of Jesus, written to us in the Scriptures; blessed as is the ministry of his angels, who, like Jacob's sons with the wagons from Egypt, come to us laden with mercies ministered to the heirs of salvation; pleasing as are the daily gifts of his providence; our greatest happiness is enjoyed, when he impresses on our hearts his love through the Holy Spirit.

In the latter clause of this verse, the reason is given why those influences of the Spirit are so ardently desired: "Thy love is better than wine;" that is, thy love is more reviving and exhilarating than the effects of wine, the most delightful of the pleasures of sense. In Eden, the most precious of the trees, even where was everything that is pleasant to the sight and good for food, was the tree of life which stood in the midst of the garden. Jesus, the true wisdom, is the tree of life to them that lay hold on him, Ps. iii. 18; his love shed abroad in our hearts by the Holy Spirit, is the fruit of this tree of life; and who will tell how much better was the fruit of the tree of life in Paradise, than the fruit of Canaan's richest vines?

The love of Christ is reviving, and counteracts the debilitating effects of sin, felt so painfully through body and soul.

> "The stream that feeds the well-spring of the heart,
> Not more invigorates life's noblest part,
> Than virtue quickens with a warmth divine
> The powers that sin has brought to a decline!"*

A more powerful stimulant than the love of kindred, the love of money, or the love of fame, it so revolutionizes the heart as to make the ambitious man sacrifice his vanity, the proud man his reputation, the vindictive man his vengeance, the drunkard his drunkenness, the sensualist his lust, the miser his gold, for the name of Jesus Christ. It changes the parched ground of the selfish soul into a limpid pool of beneficence, and the thirsty land of the sensual heart into water-springs of holy affections. Unlike the pleasures of sense, this love is more than a temporary stimulant. As satisfying as it is pure, this is the antidote of spiritual death, the principle of eternal life; and when age enfeebles the body, palsies the hand, and makes cold the heart, this love, so powerful, so reviving, keeps the spirit vigorous, the mind active, the affections warm; renews our youth like the eagle's; until

---

* Cowper's Table Talk.

at last, from the very ashes of this bodily frame, it makes the spirit emerge, like the angels from the tomb of Jesus, with the vigour of youth and immortality in its wings.*

This love is exhilarating, raises the spirits, gives cheerfulness to the soul. "Wine maketh glad the heart of man." Ps. civ. 15. "Give wine unto those that be of heavy hearts." Prov. xxxi. 6. And religion maketh glad the heart of man; give the love of Jesus unto those that be of heavy hearts. Religion is not the gloomy thing so frequently supposed by the votaries of worldly pleasure. Purifying the heart for seeing God, it clarifies our enjoyments. The amusements of the irreligious world are inventions for recruiting the tone of the spirits, which impiety depresses and corrodes. The glitter and revelry of the ball-room, the excitement of the theatre, the ten thousand little trickeries of dress and artifices of manners for drawing applause, the empty novel, the table of hazard, all are efforts by man for doing what religion would do for him in a noble and effective mode; not by convulsions, but by opening in the heart a well of water

* "There is this difference between my poetship and the generality of them—they have been ignorant how much they stood indebted to an Almighty power, for the exercise of those talents they have supposed their own; whereas I know, and know most perfectly, and am perhaps to be taught it to the last, that my power to think, whatever it be, and consequently my power to compose, is, as much as my outward form, afforded to me by the same hand that makes me in any respect to differ from a brute."—Cowper to the Rev. John Newton.—*Southey's Edition of Cowper's Works*, vol. iv. 186.

Such was the experience of Madame Guyon: "When God gave back to me that love which I had supposed to be lost, he restored the powers of perception and thought also. That intellect, which I once thought I had lost in a strange stupidity, was restored to me with inconceivable avdautages. I was astonished at myself. The understanding, as well as the heart, seemed to have received an increased capacity from God; so much so, that others noticed it, and spoke of its greatly increased power."—*Life by Upham*, i. 258.

springing up into everlasting life. Those who have never known the elation of soul springing from the love of Christ, have yet to learn what is meant by exhilaration of spirits. How much better than wine is the love of country? the love of family? the love of friends? How much better than all these is the love of Jesus? The joys of sight and sound, combine them all, and yet there is no comparison.

> "Nor rural sights alone, but rural sounds,
> Exhilarate the spirits and restore
> The tone of languid nature."

If these utterances, speaking of the divine wisdom and goodness through the heavy medium of material things, do, as we well know, thus enliven and recruit the soul, how delightful and life-giving must be those spiritual visions unfolded to our minds by grace, and those sounds conveyed directly to our heart by the Holy Spirit—expressions of power and goodness, but expressions of power and goodness as the means of filling our souls with emanations of mercy and love.

VER. 3.—Because of the savour of thy good ointments, thy name is as ointment poured forth, therefore do the virgins love thee.

This verse would be better translated, Thy perfumes are rich in fragrance; thy name is perfume poured forth, therefore the virgins love thee. The universal use of rich and costly oils and perfumes among the orientals, for health and beauty, and at public entertainments, especially on nuptial occasions, as well as in common domestic life,* renders this language appropriate, and made such a

---

* "The custom of anointing the body is usual in hot climates, and contributes greatly to comfort. Even the Greeks, Romans, and others, whose limbs were mostly protected by clothes from the dryness of the air, found the advantage of its use. In going to entertainments, it is probable, that like the Greeks, the Egyptians anointed themselves comparison not unusual; as in Eccl. vii. 1, "A good name is better than precious ointment."

"The name of God is used as a compendious formula to denote his whole moral greatness, the sum of his whole attributes and character. And it is in Jesus that we have the full exhibition of this moral and spiritual excellency."* The nature of Christ is here illustrated by the richness and pleasantness of the best perfume; and as the very best known to men was not good enough to represent the character of him who was fairer than the

---

before they left home; but still it was customary for a servant to attend every guest, as he seated himself, and to anoint his head; and this was one of the principal tokens of welcome. The ointment was contained sometimes in an alabaster, sometimes in an elegant porcelain vase; and so strong was the odour, and so perfectly were the different component substances amalgamated, that some of this ancient ointment in one of the alabaster vases in the museum at Alnwick Castle, yet retains its scent, though between two and three thousand years old."— Wilkinson's Ancient Egyptians, vol. iii. 379. "To what extent the luxury of using fragrant oils and the like was carried on, may be inferred from Seneca, Epist. 86, who says, that people anointed themselves twice or even three times a day, in order that the delicious fragrance might never diminish. The wealthy Greeks and Romans carried their ointments and perfumes with them, in small boxes of costly materials and beautiful workmanship."—*Smith's Dict. Antiquities.*

* Russell on the Covenants, p. 310. "The name of the Lord is the Lord in the richness of his deeds." Hengstenberg on Ps. cxxiv. 8. "One name would serve as well as ten thousand, if we had but one relation to, or one idea of God. For instance, could we, being perfect creatures as angels, only depend on him as our great Creator, that name would have been sufficient for us to declare him: but being sinful creatures, yet creatures to be redeemed, our Creator stood immediately in many relations to us, according to our several conditions of sinfulness, recovery, redemption, and salvation, which it was necessary for us to know, that we might apply to him under these relations, and receive every benefit and blessing we need. He hath, therefore, suited himself, as it were, to us, in the revelation of his names."—*Serle's Hor. Sol.* 444.

sons of men, God had a perfume compounded for the express purpose of showing the divine riches of our great High Priest, the holy anointing oil of the Jewish sanctuary. The whole nature of Christ is as this fragrant oil, so pure, so delightful, and so excellently divine. The loveliness of Jesus consists in this divinity, this fountain of liquid perfume which is continually pouring forth in deeds of kindness to his creatures; and these acts of goodness are the means of showing forth his glory, and developing his excellence. The comparison in the second verse sets forth the pleasantness of the love of Christ in its effects on our hearts, as there shed abroad by the Holy Ghost; the third verse exhibits the richness of that love in its own inherent nature, as it exists in the divine excellences of the man Christ Jesus.

The three chief means of purification under the law were blood, water, and oil: the last was the type of the Holy Spirit, as the source of healing and of life. Nothing capable of notice by the senses, could be more precious and fragrant than the holy oil; hence the Holy Spirit* is called "the oil of gladness," Heb. i. 9; and in the passages where mention is made of pouring out the Spirit, reference is had to this emblem. The pouring of the precious oil upon Aaron's head in such profusion that it ran down even to the skirts of his garments, had its fulfilment, when at his baptism Jesus was anointed with the oil of gladness above his fellows, by the Shechinah settling on him, even the Holy Spirit, symbolized by the dove. Hence, the Redeemer never received any public official unction of this priestly oil from the hand of man. "The Spirit of the Lord God is upon me, because the Lord hath anointed me." Isa. lxi. 1. When Jesus is said

---

* See Serle's Essay on the Oil of Gladness, in his Horæ Solitariæ; Leighton's Sermons on this verse, and on 1 Pet. ii. 9.

to be anointed, more is meant than merely setting him apart to office; the idea is that of his receiving the Holy Ghost without measure, John iii. 34, as Aaron received the holy oil without measure—a divine nature into union with the human nature. The shedding of the Spirit on our Lord constitutes his designation to office, and his fitness for that office. A body was prepared for him, Heb. x. 5, that it might be the dwelling-place of the Spirit, and the means of pouring this oil of gladness forth among men for healing the soul from the corruption of sin, and adorning it with the beauty of holiness. In him dwelt all the fulness of the Godhead bodily, or really, and not merely symbolically, as it dwelt in the cloud over the mercy-seat, Col. ii. 9. This holy perfume of the divine nature, as exuberant and infinite as it is excellent, fills the precious alabaster of his human nature full, and running over on every side, like a golden vessel of the sanctuary overflowing with the fulness of the sea. In this immeasurable fulness of the Spirit of holiness, is the difference between Jesus and his fellows. They are anointed as the leper, when a drop of oil was put on his ear, and his hand, &c., Lev. xiv. 17: Jesus was anointed with the Holy Spirit as with an illimitable sea of liquid perfume. His superior excellency to his fellows, the angels, the prophets, and the saints, associated with him in the work of redemption, consists in his having all the infinite riches of the Godhead.

He has by inheritance, by partaking of the nature of God as a son partakes of the nature of a father, and by possessing a right to all things, not through donation or conquest, but through his right as a son, a more excellent name or cluster of perfections than the angels, thereby being made so much better than they. Heb. i. 4. The unfolding of these excellences to us, is as the pouring forth of the precious oil of the sanctuary. The precious oil of the heavenly sanctuary is the divine nature of Jesus Christ. All his garments smell of myrrh, aloes, and cassia, as he came out of the ivory palaces of the heavenly glory, Ps. xlv. 8; and this is because God has anointed him with the oil of gladness above his fellows. The object in filling his human nature to so overflowing a degree with the precious perfume of the Holy Spirit, was that this oil of gladness might be poured forth among men. There was no way of sending it down to us, but through this human nature of the Lord Jesus. Before this, the emblem of God towards us sinners was a consuming fire, such as was placed at the east of Eden, and was seen on the top of Sinai. How great the contrast between the fire which on the mountain burned into the midst of heaven, Deut. iv. 11, and the holy oil poured forth in rich perfume under the shadow of the peaceful cloud over the mercy-seat: the former consuming with terrible vigour, and shooting forth lightning and death, if even a beast, much less a sinful man, touch the mountain, represents God as he must ever be towards the guilty; the latter, delicious in its fragrance, soft in its richness, and healing in its efficacy, shows the loveliness and grace of God as reconciled through Christ. As the woman broke the alabaster box, and poured the pure spikenard, very precious, on the head of Jesus, and the house was filled with the odour of the perfume; so, through his broken body, are those excellences of the divine nature, mercy, love, grace, truth, forgiveness, and sanctification, unsealed to ruined man. And though his name was poured forth in so many ways, under the Old Testament, by prophecy, by providence, and by types; all these were through his broken body, and in connection with the shedding of his blood. His crucifixion was the breaking of the alabaster containing the precious oil; and then did the fragrance of his name begin to spread abroad for filling the world. Even as in the operations of nature, using means for sending the knowledge of his excellence into all the earth by the gospel preached to every creature, he who brought from heaven this sacred treasure of healing truth, deposited it not in vessels of gold, found in the palaces of Herod and Cæsar, but in men of humbler mould, in earthen vessels gathered at random on the shores of Galilee, that the excellency of the power might be of God.

His name is poured forth by the shedding abroad of the Holy Spirit in our hearts. The truth, the sacraments, the ordinances, are means subserving the end of the Spirit; and ministers of the gospel "are unto God a sweet savour of Christ, in them that are saved, and in them that perish," because they are vessels through which the Spirit pours out the holy oil on the perishing. 2 Cor. ii. 15. From Jesus as the head, the Holy Ghost is shed down on all the members of his spiritual body. As thus poured forth, how precious is his name, in the hour of repentance, in trouble, in affliction, in temptation, in sickness, in death! As the Holy Spirit pours the healing oil of grace into the heart, how can these truths be felt sinking down through the soul! There is something peculiar and inexplicable in the sweetness and attractiveness of the name of Jesus to the saint, soothing, delightful, refreshing, life-giving; and when we begin to open up any one of his perfections, there seems to rise around the soul something richer than "a steam of rich-distilled perfumes."

The persons that love him whose name is thus precious, are "the virgins," the pure in heart. As the purity of

Jesus, or his holiness, is his great attractiveness, and as in love there must be an adaptation of our affections to the virtues of the loved one, those only can love Jesus, who purify themselves even as he is pure. 1 John iii. 3. Those by whom he is despised and rejected, are they to whose spiritual leprosy the oil of gladness has never been applied, and whose constitution is filled with all unrighteousness, as sadly pointed out in Rom. i. 29—31, and in Gal. v. 19—21. Those whose souls have been made pure by the fruit of the Spirit, as in Gal. v. 22, whose hearts have been fed by heavenly grace, like the candlestick all of gold, with the two olive trees by its side, which through the two golden pipes emptied the golden oil out of themselves, Zech. iv. 2, are continually ascending to Jesus in the purity of flames of love, nourished by the Holy Ghost. Their love is rendered thus ardent, not so much because he is the means of their escape from hell and suffering, as by their perception of his inherent purity, excellence, and loveliness.

While, therefore, the first desire of the saint, as here expressed, is for the influences of the Holy Spirit, we are led, in the next place, to the infinite excellence of Christ. These two grand truths are the proper introduction to such a book as the Song; like the two pillars at the entrance of the temple, Jachin and Boaz, firmness or foundation and strength, the doctrines of the righteousness of Christ as our corner-stone, and of the grace of the Spirit as our strength, are never lost sight of by the believer, and become more precious to us as we grow in holiness. We cannot behold the beauty of the Lord, and inquire in his temple for the utterances of his love, without having on our right hand and left, these grand and sustaining truths.

Ver. 4.—Draw me, we will run after thee. The king hath brought me into his chambers: we will be glad and rejoice in thee; we will remember thy love more than wine: the upright love thee.

The imagery of the allegory in this verse, and indeed in the greater part of the first chapter, seems based on the supposition that Solomon had, according to oriental custom, gone forth in kingly state to meet his bride on the road. Hence the tents of the king and of his attending nobles would be set up with royal magnificence, at the place where he was to meet the spouse. It is now customary in the East for persons of distinction to lodge in their own costly tents on a journey. Van Egmont and Heyman state that the festivities attending an occasion of great public rejoicing, when they were at Constantinople, were held in a camp pitched for that purpose in the neighbourhood of the city.* In this place, we may suppose that the bride, in her progress towards the royal city, comes in sight of these tents of the kingly party awaiting her, and gives expression to her feeling in the

* "It must be owned, that the Turks spare for nothing in rendering their tents convenient and magnificent. Those belonging to the Grand Signior were exceeding splendid, and covered entirely with silk; and one of them lined with a rich silk stuff, the right side of which was the apartment for the eunuchs. But even this was exceeded by another, which I was informed cost twenty-five thousand piastres. It was made in Persia, and intended as a present to the Grand Signior, and was not finished in less than three or four years. The inside of this tent was lined with a single piece made of camel's hair, and beautifully decorated with festoons and sentences in the Turkish language."—*Van Egmont and Heyman*, vol. i. 212.

"Maillet states that the Beys of Egypt are wont to be attended by large bodies of servants, magnificently dressed; that one of them did, on days of ceremony, appear with a train of three hundred horsemen, all his slaves, mounted on horses of value, whose harness was of silver gilt, and with saddle-cloths embroidered with gold and silver, hanging down to the ground. The sight of the different Beys, with their attendants, riding in troops in the neighbourhood of Cairo, had a very magnificent and imposing effect."—*Harmer*, 200.

language of these verses. The conveyance seems hardly swift enough for the ardour of her love, and she gives utterance to her deep emotion in the words, "Draw me," &c.

The perfections of Christ are transcendent in excellence, and infinite in variety and extent, for they are nothing less than the excellences of the Godhead. The glories and delights centring in Jehovah as the fountain of life and beauty, are an illimitable treasury, an ocean of light, resplendent with greater riches than gold and gems, into which we are permitted to gaze, through the person of the man Christ Jesus; he is the door, John x. 7, Eph. ii. 18, the central aperture of light, through which, during eternity, we shall be seeing and hearing things impossible for man to utter—so glorious as to have merely a foreshadowing in what was beheld by the apostle when a door was opened in heaven, Rev. iv. 1, and he saw the wonders and heard the chorus of the heavenly host. Every glimpse of the beauty of Christ increases our desire to know more of his loveliness, and strengthens the ardour of our affections. Expanding and growing more intense, through ages of ages, with the enlargement of our view of the perfections of God unfolded to us through Christ, our love towards him will increase with a progression, and to a degree, now incomprehensible, and will draw us to him with a gentle power and wondrous pleasantness, of which the mind cannot now even remotely conceive.

As those precious perfumes or excellences of character were the cause of attraction or love, the first words of this verse are a prayer that he would unfold his loveliness, and thereby draw the soul to himself. The character of Christ, as opened to the heart by the Holy Spirit, is the corrective of our natural sluggishness, and kindles within us the desire of following him with all our energy, of running after him; but as our weakness is more sensibly felt as this desire strengthens, we pray that his strength may be made perfect in our weakness, and we may be constrained by the influence of his grace. "The love of Christ constraineth us." 2 Cor. v. 14. "All my springs are in thee." Ps. lxxxvii. 7. Nothing is more attractive than a lovely character, to those capable of relishing its beauties. The Creator has made us susceptible of this attraction, as naturally as matter is susceptible of attraction by gravitation. When the Holy Spirit unfolds the loveliness of Christ, and restores the perceptive powers of the heart, we are spontaneously drawn towards Jesus.

When we are inclined towards our Lord with animated affections—running after him—he receives us, and brings us into his apartments, the place into which none are admitted but his confidential friends. There was the court of the garden of the king's palace, where the king made a feast unto all the people, Esther i. 5; and there was the inner court of the king's house, where none were permitted to enter but invited guests, Esther iv. 11, v. 2, and there were the apartments here called chambers, where he saw only those whom he intimately cherished and loved. These apartments are what is meant by the words, "In the secret of his tabernacle shall he hide me," Ps. xxvii. 5; "He that dwelleth in the secret place of the Most High shall abide under the shadow of the Almighty." Ps. xci. 1. How beautiful was the holy of holies with its sides overlaid with gold, its veil of blue and purple and scarlet, and the mercy-seat of pure gold, overshadowed by the two cherubim of gold beaten out of one piece, while the cloud of glory was its only light; this was the representation of the spiritual chambers in which the king who dwelleth between the cherubim receives his faithful friends, and of those mansions prepared in heaven, where, when he comes again, he will receive us unto himself. The Psalmist says of one thus favoured, "his soul shall dwell at ease," or lodge in goodness, the divine goodness forming the walls of the dwelling in which he passes the night of his sojourn on earth. The secret of the Lord is with such, Ps. xxv. 14; he treats them as confidential friends. And as he revealed to Noah the secret of the flood, and to Abraham the secret of the destruction of Sodom, Gen. xviii. 17, and to Daniel the secret of the king's dream, Dan. ii. 19, so does he show unto us his covenant, speaking to our hearts in the still small voice of his Spirit; and, while giving unto us the white stone, in which is a new name written that no man knoweth saving he that receiveth it, feeding us on better than angel's food, even the hidden manna of the riches of his grace. How can we utter the blessedness of having such an intimate friend? Do we need wisdom? Our confidential friend is Christ, the wisdom of God. Do we need protection? Our dearest friend is Christ, the power of God, able to save to the uttermost, even from the grave, and from hell. His is a friendship that no change of circumstances can alienate. Unlike the heartless friends of the world, he does not forsake us when riches flee away; he gathers us more closely to him in the hour of sorrow. Touched with the feeling of our infirmities, he binds up the broken-hearted, and pouring the oil of gladness and the wine of grace into the bruised spirit, from which even the priest and Levite had turned away, he says, "I will never leave thee nor forsake thee." In him are hid all the treasures of wisdom and knowledge; with him are durable riches and righteousness; he holds for us, in his right hand, a crown of glory that fadeth not away. No friendship is so intimate, reliable, honourable, and confidential, as that existing between Jesus and the soul of the saint. No secret entrusted to him will ever be dishonourably divulged. When father and mother forsake, he remains faithful still. To him may we go with our secret griefs; to him may we unburden our heaviest sorrows, with the confidence of being never received with coldness, of being welcomed with the tenderest sympathy and most compassionate love. Though we have forsaken him like Peter, he remembers our iniquities no more, and receives us with no heavier rebuke than the look he turned upon that weeping disciple. Happy are they who know how to value such a friend.

The words, "We would be glad and rejoice in thee," show the results of this communion with Christ, great joy and exultation. The Psalmist sings, "How good and how pleasant it is for brethren to dwell together in unity;" much greater is the pleasure had in dwelling with Jesus as our confidential friend. In his presence is fulness of joy. With him is the fountain of life; and as our joy must increase in purity and intensity with every step of approach towards him, when we rest with him at the throne of grace, our joy must be full. Unlike the pleasures of the world, these gratifications are attended with no painful remembrances: "We will remember thy love more than wine." Here, with Jesus, we have great peace in present possession, glorious hopes for the future, sweet recollections of the past. What are the remembrances continually gathering around an irreligious life? Hopes blasted, expectations disappointed, a sense of having never realized what was anticipated from any source, the enfeebling effects of dissipation, apprehensiveness of detection and exposure in unrighteous gratifications, and forebodings uttered by conscience of judgment to come; these are the best fruits that memory can gather from the past, wherein there have been no visions of Jesus. How empty is the recollection of even the temperate and allowable enjoyments of the irreligious! But how sweet is the remembrance of God's grace! These memories are as a luminous stream of living waters,—unlike the seas whose waves follow the track of the ship with light at midnight,—winding amid the deepening gloom and ruins of the past. How tender the recollection of the times and places where first this precious Friend met us with the assurance of forgiveness, where his Sprit melted down the soul in deep contrition, where we had brightening views of heaven, where Jesus showed us his glory and gave us his love! Could any pleasures of wine, of sense, of the world, be remembered as fondly as the disciples cherished the recollection of the farewell words of their Lord, of the discourse on the road to Emmaus, of the scene at the transfiguration? And as the tide of time will not allow us to make tabernacles and dwell where thus our Lord met us, memory delights to build her shrines there, and linger fondly on those consecrated hills.

The last clause, we would read, They love thee sincerely, rather than, "The upright love thee."* In verse 3, it is said, the virgins, or the pure in heart, love him for the excellences of his character. Here, the same

---

* Following the Latin Vulgate, the English translators have thus rendered this clause. The version here given is more correct. Something must be supplied in the Hebrew, in order to make out the sense in the English version. In Ps. lxxv. 3, the same word here translated "the upright," is rendered "uprightly." There is no reason why it

persons are said to love him with sincerity, with a love they have good reason to indulge—a love pure, deep, and intense, separated from all interested motives, and stronger for being thus pure. These words are the natural expression of a heart occupied with such love. And when our precious Lord has drawn us by his grace, so that the soul rises towards him with the energy of eagles' wings; when he has taken us apart into chambers filled with visions more glorious than those had by Moses in the mount, where he saw the God of Israel, and under his feet as it were a paved work of a sapphire stone, and as it were the body of heaven in its clearness; then, how deep, how reasonable, how sincere is felt our love! As Satan accused Job of serving God from selfish motives, and as a bad man will not admit that others can be actuated by pure, disinterested principle; we feel, on the other hand, that, like ourselves, our brethren are controlled by simplicity and godly sincerity in their devotion and love to Jesus.

VER. 5.—I am black, but comely, O ye daughters of Jerusalem, as the tents of Kedar, as the curtains of Solomon.

Received in these tents with royal magnificence, and seeing around her a company of female attendants on the king, here called the daughters of Jerusalem, the spouse notices the contrast between the freshness of their complexion, always shielded at home from exposure, and her own dusky hue, contracted from being abroad under the

should not be thus rendered here. With the Hebrew word used adverbially, rather than as a substantive, the connection of the clause with the foregoing part of the verse is obvious; and the meaning is, They, that is, the virgins, love thee sincerely. The import of the words then is, that they who love Jesus, love him sincerely, with an affection lawful, deep, and pure.

scorching sun; she accordingly expresses her feelings by saying that though dark, she was beautiful, and illustrates her meaning by a comparison drawn naturally from the surrounding encampment. Even now the Arabs generally make use of tents covered with black haircloth; those of Kedar especially are thus covered, and being generally low and of flat appearance, cause a camp of such tents at a distance, to look like a number of black spots. The curtains of Solomon are here most probably put for a splendid state-tent of that monarch, something like those even yet known among oriental monarchs. "History has recorded, that at the famous marriage feast held by Tamerlane at Ranighul, the royal tents were gilded, and adorned with precious stones. Each tent had twelve columns of silver, inlaid with gold; the outside was scarlet and seven other colours, and the inside was lined with satin of all colours. The curtains were of velvet and the ropes of silk. At the encampment of the same conqueror in the plain of Ourtaupa, the pavilions were richly ornamented, and hung with curtains of brocade covered with golden flowers. At other times, we read of tents 'covered with tartaries full nobly:' and at the great encampment at Mineegheul the tent of Timur himself was under a canopy supported by forty pillars, and was as spacious as a palace. In the middle of it was a throne, so ornamented with precious stones that it resembled a sun. The contrast between such glorious pavilions as these, and the sombre tents of the pastoral tribes, is great indeed."*

Love and communion with Jesus is the means of imparting to us a more correct knowledge of ourselves—"I am black, but comely, O ye daughters of Jerusalem."

* Kitto's Daily Bible Readings, on the Song. See notes on ver. 4.

The daughters of Jerusalem mentioned in Luke xxiii. 28, were the native women of Jerusalem; and by these words are here meant those companions of the spouse, the saint, in the spiritual Jerusalem, with whom we, though strangers and foreigners, are brought into association by conversion. To these pious brethren are these words addressed, as those who love the Lord speak often to one another, and the Lord hearkens and hears. Mal. iii. 16. The spouse was aware of her deficiency in point of beauty, and was yet conscious of an excellence that had been imparted to her. There is no correct knowledge of our nature, without the prior knowledge of Christ. The maxim of the ancient sage, "Know thyself," was an impossibility without the gospel and the Holy Spirit. Man may feel the want of things, without being able to attain the knowledge for relieving such want. The unpretending disclosures in the Scriptures give a deeper view into the nature of man, than all the philosophy of all ages. They give us all the knowledge of our nature now necessary, and lead to the Holy Spirit as the means of enlightening the mind. Our condition by nature is one of atheism, Eph. ii. 12, without God as well as without Christ. Atheism is well defined, "an invincible ingnorance, fancying itself the highest knowledge;"* it might be added, an ignorance of self, originating in ignorance of God. The spring of our being is in God; in him is the source of our knowledge no less than our pleasures. In the study of every science or subject, there are elementary truths which cannot be disregarded without affecting all our subsequent investigations with more or less error. The first principles of the knowledge of ourselves, for which metaphysics is but another name,

* Plato against the Atheists. The Laws, book x. 1.

are found in the Scriptures, must be studied at the feet of Jesus, and can be read only in the light diffused by the Holy Spirit. Such branches as mathematics and physics may be pursued without any material tendency to error, arising from want of religious knowledge; the metaphysician must, however, begin by being a pious man. The fine theories woven by the most acute minds and dignified as transcendentalism, show the importance of building all such structures on the foundation of the apostles and prophets, with Jesus Christ as the cornerstone.

The Holy Spirit does not give us distorted views of our nature, but shows that nature as it is; its deficiencies and its virtues. Like the dark tents of Kedar, a wandering tribe of the desert descended from the second son of Ishmael, the spouse was of a swarthy colour; the original beauty of the human soul has been thus clouded and blackened by sin, yet through grace, there is gathering around it a drapery of holy virtues, beautiful as the curtains adorning the pavilion of Solomon. 1 Kings x. 28; Ezek. xxvii. 7. While our earthly house of this tabernacle is, without, black as the tents of Kedar, uncomely to mortal eyes; the redeemed soul, the king's daughter, is all glorious within, as there adorned with curtains of pious graces, wrought in heaven by a greater than Solomon, and hung around the sanctuary of this spiritual temple by the hands of angels under the eye of God the Spirit. The beauty and glory of the believer are now very much hidden from the world. Our life is a hidden life. There is a fulness of "glory which shall be revealed in us" at "the manifestation of the sons of God." Rom. viii. 19. When the apostle, speaking of heaven, says, "I saw no temple therein," Rev. xxi. 22, he would intimate that the outer covering of the tabernacle, with its golden walls and all its costly appendages, had fallen away, that nothing had been left but the holy of holies, with the cloud of glory, and this holy place had been expanded into the dimensions of the paradise of God: thus when Christ, who is our life, shall appear, we also shall appear with him in glory; the secrets of all hearts shall be revealed; the image of Christ within us the hope of glory, shall be manifested; our earthly house of this tabernacle shall be dissolved, and the soul emerge from it like the most holy place of the heavenly sanctuary, pure, spiritual, luminous with the divine glory. Of the existence of holy graces within us, we cannot be unconscious, if we are the sons of God; yet will we be painfully sensible of our depravity and corruption. Humility consists in a true knowledge of our character, without being insensible of what grace has done for us, while aware of our extreme unworthiness. How useless and unnecessary would it have been to put such fine and costly curtains on the outside for the covering of a tent exposed to the sun, wind, and rain. The tabernacle was covered with coarse skins; the costly vail was within, screened from the eyes of the multitude; so the beauteous, transparent drapery of holiness, which the Spirit of God is hanging around the soul, is within, concealed from the gaze of the world, while the outer covering of this habitation of God through the Spirit, Eph. ii. 22, is the coarse fabric of this dark and weather-beaten body. The crystal palace reared in London has been justly the admiration of the world; like it, there has been nothing seen in any age; an unlettered savage could hardly be made to understand how a building could be formed so beautiful, so transparent, and how there could be gathered in it such choice products of skill, into the beauties of which even kings and nobles naturally desire to look. In the heavenly Jerusalem will be reared a spiritual palace which shall be the admiration and ornament of that world of light and glory; nothing will there be known more splendid; it will rise on those heavenly hills a new and astonishing creation, of materials clearer and more beautiful than a fabric of glass and gold, open on every side to the rays of the Sun of Righteousness, stored with those choice products of the Holy Spirit's wisdom and power, the graces of the sanctified heart—into which things the angels desire to look. That crystal palace is the redeemed Church; even a more glorious temple is every sanctified soul.

VER. 6.—Look not upon me, because I am black, because the sun hath looked upon me: my mother's children were angry with me; they made me the keeper of the vineyards; but mine own vineyard have I not kept.

Having acknowledged the whole truth concerning herself, dark but comely, the spouse seems here to say, that she was not worthy of the high regard with which the daughters of Jerusalem beheld her; for she was of a tanned or swarthy colour, and this had been caused by exposure to the sun, in the discharge of menial services, to which she had been compelled by her kindred.* She shrinks from their admiration, by a consciousness of unworthiness. She had beauty, as travellers even now speak of Arab women met with in Syria, who, though swarthy, have good features. Zenobia, the celebrated

---

* D'Arvieux observes of the Arabs of the Holy Land, that though the ordinary women are extremely tawny, yet the princesses are not so, but of a very fair complexion, being always kept from the sun. Shaw made a like observation as to the women of Barbary. Thevenot states that when he travelled into Mesopotamia, though he wore on his head a great black handkerchief, like a woman's hood, which sort of handkerchiefs the Turks commonly use upon the road, yet his forehead was scorched many times, and his hands continually.

queen of Palmyra, is described by historians as a woman of remarkable beauty, possessing a dark brown complexion, eyes black, sparkling, and of an uncommon fire, a countenance highly animated and sprightly, a person surpassingly graceful and genteel, with teeth white as pearl, and a voice strong and musical. But though thus beautiful, the spouse does not encourage them to admire her for her beauty; she rather entreats them to turn away from her their gaze, because she felt that over her beauty had been thrown a shade.

Communion with Jesus leads the soul enjoying it to shrink from courting the attention and admiration of men, even of our fellow Christians: "Look not upon me, because I am black." The desire of applause is deeply rooted in the natural heart, and is as universal and strong as the love of gold. Pursuit of this seems the business for which many irreligious persons are living. From the frail beauty fluttering in the ball-room, to the politician with his wily schemes, and the soldier seeking "the bubble reputation at the cannon's mouth"—all are trying to push themselves into notoriety, and their feeling, though policy keeps it unuttered, is, Look on me, see how worthy I am of admiration.

> "Fame is the spur that the clear spirit doth raise,—
> That last infirmity of noble minds,—
> To scorn delights, and live laborious days."*

This principle, springing from vanity, is seen in weak minds no less than in the highest genius, in poor as well as in rich, in the obscure no less than in the most exalted. Hard is it for the believer to get this propensity eradicated; and often does it injure, even destroy, the ambassador of Christ. Grace crucifies us to the world, makes us see through the speciousness of "the things of the

* Milton's Lycidas.

world," abates our desire for them, and absorbs the soul in a passion for the honour that is from God. It makes us see our vileness and weakness, so as to feel unworthy of any commendation, and realize how dangerous is praise to the good of the soul. Hence those whom Jesus loves are often subjected to humiliation and mortification from the world, for training them to a renunciation of the pride which is the root of ambition, and for obliging them to cultivate lowliness of heart. So far from seeking worldly honour and applause, He who is our example, when he perceived that they would come and take him by force to make him a king, departed again into a mountain himself alone. John vi. 15. In Ps. cxxi. 5, "The Lord is thy shade upon thy right hand; the sun shall not smite thee by day, nor the moon by night; the Lord shall preserve thee from all evil, he shall preserve thy soul;" the sun is represented as the source of the evils from which we need to be screened, and Jehovah as our protection and shade. Thus the words "the sun hath looked upon me," express the cause of this injury to the beauty once natural to the soul, the withering and darkening effects of sin, of the divine justice blazing forth towards us as a consuming fire. This sense of inward depravity, of the hateful effects of sin on the heart, better known to ourselves than any others through the illumination of the Spirit, makes us shrink from the applause of men, and feel unworthy of the favour of God. Far from the desire of climbing to the conspicuous eminence of worldly fame, we seek to withdraw in quietness to the calm retreats found in the "shadow of the great Rock in a weary land." With Moses, we prefer the solitude of Horeb to the splendour of the court of Egypt. The cause of the comeliness or beauty of the soul is not noticed in this verse, as it springs so evidently from communion with our Lord, "in his chambers," at the throne of grace, where "we all with open face beholding as in a glass the glory of the Lord, are changed into the same image from glory to glory, even as by the Spirit of the Lord."

Love to the Lord Jesus, special tokens of his favour, meekness, and lowliness of heart, are no security against hatred and ill-treatment from the world, and even from followers of Christ. Such was the case of Jesus on earth; we must expect the same. "My mother's children were angry with me,* they made me the keeper of the vineyards."† This was a work laborious and menial. Those whom Nebuzaradan left for vine-dressers and husbandmen were the poor of the land. 2 Kings xxv. 12. The blessings promised to his people by the coming of the Messiah, are represented by freedom from this service. "The sons of the alien shall be your ploughmen and your vinedressers." Isa. lxi. 5. Well is it that the saints have been made to feel that the Saviour's kingdom is not of this world. Temporal power is as prone to ruin the Church, as riches and ease are to ruin individual Christians. Feeling the uncongenial and hostile

---

* "In the East, the husband is a stern and unfeeling despot: his harem, a group of trembling slaves. The children espouse with ardour, unknown to those who are placed in other circumstances, the cause of their own mother, while they regard their common father with indifference or terror. It greatly aggravated the affliction of David, that he had become an alien to his mother's children, Ps. lxix. 8; the enmity of his brethren, the relations of his father's other wives, or his more distant relatives, gave him less concern."—*Stackhouse's History of the Bible*, book viii. chap. 4.

† "Great care was taken to preserve the clusters of the vine from the intrusion of birds; and boys were constantly employed, about the season of the vintage, to frighten them with a sling and the sound of the voice."—*Wilkinson's Ancient Egyptians*, vol. ii. 149.

spirit of the world, the young believer fondly trusts to find among his fellow Christians the sanctuary of a brotherhood, unclouded by envy, undisturbed by a jar. Experience shows how fallacious was his expectation. The remains of corruption in the hearts of good men prove elements of dissension, discord, and collision. The love of power, desire of prominence, jealousy of rivals in ability and influence, frequently excite to efforts for keeping down brethren whose offence is that they are apparently superior in learning, piety, or usefulness. "Whence come wars and fightings among you? come they not hence, even of your lusts?" Jas. iv. 1. While sanctification remains imperfect, these tendencies to discord will more or less frequently rise above the control of grace, as well as surmount the influence of natural affection. Members of irreligious families are yet exposed to persecution on becoming pious; and the believer often finds a man's foes are they of his own household of faith. The same unhallowed principle, not yet entirely uprooted by grace, is the cause of the ill treatment and ill feeling received by the humble saint from the wicked world, from other religious denominations, and from members of the same church. How common for different sects, even of evangelical Christians, to endeavour to injure, if not destroy, each other's influence, when their energies combined against the enemies of all religion, would produce little enough impression; when there is more than a sufficiency for them all to do in converting the world; and when each is designed by the Head of the Church to exert an influence, and occupy a position the other is not adapted to fill. The spirit of detraction and selfishness, so rife in the world, will never be entirely banished from the Church, till we reach the spirits of just men made perfect. Among those of the same sect, how common for such as live near to Christ to be envied, maligned, and ill treated by their brethren. Speaking to him that is poor and of a contrite spirit, and trembleth at his word, the Holy Spirit says: "Your brethren that hated you, that cast you out for my name's sake, said, Let the Lord be glorified: but he shall appear to your joy, and they shall be ashamed." Isa. lxvi. 5. In his last affecting address to them, Jesus insists strongly on his disciples loving one another, because, among other reasons therefor, they would be hated by the world, John xv. 17; and though the intolerance among rival sects, and the envy often apparent in Christian brethren, may be overruled for good, just as other sin may be, Ps. lxxvi. 10, those show themselves to have departed most from the temper of the world, and come nearest to Jesus, who strive not to pull down others, but cultivate love to Christ's people wherever found, manifesting kindness and forbearance towards the persecuting spirit yet hanging around them, as well as towards the malice of the impenitent.

The soul thus blessed with Jesus' love, feels and confesses its omissions, short-comings, and neglect of duty; "my own vineyard have I not kept." A sense of unworthiness increases with growth in grace. As advancement in learning makes us more sensible how little we know, so the more we increase in Christian activity, the more active do we wish to be, and the more painfully are we conscious of deficiencies. No man feels so acutely how far he falls below the full measure of holy duties, pious zeal, and heavenly love, as he who is growing up nearest to the stature of a perfect one in Christ. He who has done most for the Redeemer feels himself to have done least. Our obligations to Jesus are seen to be so great, love to him would so constrain us, that after stretching our powers to the utmost, we are ready to weep that we do no more. Though the trust committed to us has been kept, we are humbled with the consciousness that in many respects it might have been kept with greater faithfulness. Duties have been neglected, opportunities of usefulness misimproved, watchfulness unheeded, prayer offered with coldness, temptation tampered with, self-denial too little exercised, everything, indeed, however laborious our piety, bearing traces of the imperfection inseparable from earth, and filling us with deep humiliation. With contrition and tears, we acquiesce in the words of Jesus, "When ye shall have done all those things which are commanded you, say, We are unprofitable servants." Luke xvii. 10. The moral man will look with complacency on some trifling deeds done for religion, thinking he is conferring an honour on Christ, and is showing a praiseworthy condescension in such a work of supererogation: our feeling is, "in many things we come short all." Many duties have been crowded out of place by selfish desires; and with those which have been done are mingled many imperfections, and much of an improper spirit. Sensible of these things, we feel the uprightness of God in his chastisements, even when from the hands of brethren, rather than of the wicked; and instead of fretting against our Father in heaven, or complaining of those who misuse and oppress, we find in our own unworthiness more than sufficient reason for all these ills, and are filled with wonder that our blessings are yet so numerous, and our sorrows so few, that while we deserve a sea of troubles, God has sent only a surge. Grace makes the believer feel painfully how much more closely he might have walked with God, how much more his privileges might have been improved.

Ver. 7.—Tell me, O thou whom my soul loveth, where thou feedest, where thou makest thy flock to rest at noon: for why should I be as one that turneth aside by the flocks of thy companions?

For carrying out the design of the allegory, this regal encampment is here represented as moving from place to place, in search of green pastures, cooling shades, and still waters, under the guidance of their shepherd-king. The spouse having been received so kindly and feeling increased ardour of affection, wishes to follow the beloved, not merely as one among the mixed multitude, but enjoying, as she had already, the pleasure of his pavilion and society.*

The first burst of desire from the pious heart is for the fulness of the Holy Spirit, as in verse 2; this creates the

---

* "It would be difficult to describe the appearance of a large tribe, like that we now met, when migrating to new pastures. We found ourselves in the midst of wide-spreading flocks of sheep and camels. As far as the eye could reach, to the right, to the left, and in front, still the same moving crowd. Long lines of asses and bullocks laden with black tents and variegated carpets; boys driving flocks of lambs; horsemen armed with their long tufted spears, scouring the plain on their fleet mares; riders urging their dromedaries with their short hooked sticks, and leading their high-bred steeds by the halter; colts galloping among the throng; high-born ladies seated in the centre of huge wings, which extended like those of a butterfly from each side of the camel's hump, and are no less gaudy and variegated. Such was the motley crowd through which we had to wend our way for several hours. When we reached the encampment, our horses, as well as ourselves, were exhausted by the heat of the sun, and the length of the day's journey. The tents were pitched on a broad lawn in a deep ravine; they were scattered in every direction, and amongst them rose the white pavilions of the Turkish irregular cavalry."—*Layard's Nineveh*, vol. i. 91. "Looking to the east, flocks and herds were seen spreading through the undulating valleys. In one place, we saw many of them gathered together under a shady tree, waiting till the excessive heat of noon should be abated. At other times, the shepherds gather the flocks beside a well, as we afterwards saw at Lebonah, where many hundreds were lying down around the well's mouth."—*Mission of Inquiry to the Jews*, p. 109.

anxious wish to run after Jesus, ver. 4; and this feeling receives its gratification in being brought to intimate communion with our Lord, ver. 4. The soul thus blessed desires to follow Jesus whithersoever he goeth, Rev. xiv. 4; John x. 27; and when this Shepherd-king goes abroad to take charge of his flock, we would go with him, anxious to be with him in difficulty, fatigue, and danger, no less than amid the luxuries of his palace. The formalist and lukewarm have their view occupied with the difficulties and self-denial likely to be encountered; the spiritual Christian has his attention so engrossed with the loveliness of Christ, as to overlook, or encounter with alacrity, all obstructions in reaching the presence of his Lord.

This results from the intensity and energy of his love—a love such that his whole soul seems melted down into this one affection, and its delighted expression is, "O thou whom my soul loveth." When love to Jesus is compared with love felt for anything that may be a man's ruling passion, such as the love of fame, of power, of money, we are far from doing it justice. These are strong; but far stronger is love to Jesus. In these cases there is but one solitary thing, and that an inferior one, to satisfy all the cravings of all the powers of the soul; the one propensity is only partially satisfied, and the other affections are still more restless. But in Christ, love taking the lead, as its most exalted exercise is in cleaving to an object as far above every other as the Creator is above the thing created, all the faculties find in him the richest field for activity; and the Holy Ghost does in the meantime, open to us his loveliness, and brace up every fibre of the soul for beholding, adoring, and loving him; so that all our energies are concentrated on this one point of love to Christ, and thus drawn to a focus, burn with a heavenly radiance, a consuming fervour. Love to Christ thus becomes the strongest passion which can take possession of the soul of man. Husband, wife, children, father, mother, life, however fondly cherished, are so much less loved, that in comparison with Jesus they may be said to be hated. Matt. x. 37; Luke xiv. 26. By the power of the Spirit, who makes us partakers of the divine nature, we are through this love so absorbed in Jesus as to be one with him; so that as Christ thus dwells in our hearts, and being thus rooted and grounded in love, we know his love which passeth knowledge, we are filled with all the fulness of God, and approximate to the feeling enjoined in the command, "Thou shalt love the Lord thy God with all thy heart, and with all thy soul, and with all thy strength, and with all thy mind." Luke x. 27. With what depth of blessedness does the soul then look earnestly towards Jesus, and say: "O thou whom my soul loveth!"

"Tell me, where thou feedest;"—where thou dost watch over thy flock as a shepherd;—where I may be under thy care as my shepherd. The word "feed" in this verse, as well as in Isa. xl. 11, Rev. vii. 17, means to discharge the office of a shepherd. As in the services of the law, a variety of sacrifices and purifications was necessary, because no one type could prefigure everything necessary to be known about Jesus Christ in the work of purchasing redemption; so, various illustrations are used for showing the different relations he sustains to the saints, in applying the benefits of his purchase. The blessedness of the seasons when we are favoured with delightful communications of the Holy Spirit, is set forth by communion with the king in his chambers; but as our course is long and lies through difficulties, trials, and dangers, wherein we are of ourselves helpless and need the superintending care of an all-powerful hand. Jesus is represented as a shepherd. Ps. xxiii. 1: as the Shepherd and Bishop of souls, 1 Pet. ii. 25; as the chief Shepherd, 1 Pet. v. 4: as the great Shepherd of the sheep. Heb. xiii. 20. This includes protection, guidance, provision for the soul, pastures and waters, and company with our Lord. There are places where Jesus may be thus found; and as the sheep that wanders from the shepherd loses these benefits, we must be careful to keep near him, among his flock. He has a variety of pastures into which he leads his flock, all increasing in richness and luxuriance, as we draw nearer to the limits of this wilderness and the borders of the promised land in heaven. At first, under his pastoral care, these green pastures and still waters of the spiritual life are found at intervals, like the green spots in the desert, wells of water and palm-trees, with many a weary journey between; but as we draw nearer to heaven, more frequent evidences are met of our approaching a better country; the desert tracts are less desolate and less extensive; the verdure grows richer, as lying more nearly under the influence of a more refreshing than Hermon's dews; until at length we pass over into that good land, where the Lamb, which is in the midst of the throne, shall feed us, and shall lead us into living fountains of waters. In the illimitable wilderness around us, how can we find these precious spots, without his guidance? If we rest in green pastures, it is he that makes us lie down there; if we repose beside the still waters, it is he that leads us thither. The world has many alluring scenes for drawing us away from Christ; but we wish to come away even from Lebanon and Hermon. Song iv. 8. to leave Egypt itself, and Goshen, for Horeb, desolate as it may seem, if there we may, like Moses, find the good Shepherd, in the attractive manifestations of his glory. Exod. iii. 2. Tell me—make me to know by the inward voice of thy Spirit, and by the outward guidings of thy providence, where and what are those situations and occupations in life, and those seasons pervaded by more than usual influences of the Holy Spirit, in which I may dwell, not by my own choice, but by thine appointment, and there enjoy unceasing thy gracious presence and thy shepherd-care.

"Where thou makest thy flock to rest at noon."* At noon, they led their flocks aside into the shade, and by wells or streams, that they might be sheltered from the oppressive heat, and enjoy the refreshment of cool waters. Gen. xxix. 7. "They shall feed in the ways, and their pastures shall be in all high places. They shall not hunger nor thirst; neither shall the heat nor sun smite

---

* "'Tis raging noon: and, vertical, the sun
  Darts on the head direct his forceful rays.
  Welcome, ye shades! ye bowery thickets, hail!
  Around th' adjoining brook that purls along
  The vocal grove, now jutting o'er a rock,
  Now scarcely moving through a reedy pool,
  Now starting to a sudden stream, and now
  Gently diffused into a limpid plain;
  A various group the herds and flocks compose."
  —*Thompson's Summer.*

We might further mention in illustration the Culex of Virgil, ver. 110.

  "Now at the shepherd's call, the kids once more
  Seek the deep shade, their devious rambles o'er,
  Where murmuring waters wash th' o'erhanging moss
  And limpid steal along the blue-tinged fosse.
  While from his mid-day course the sunbeams beat,
  To shades the shepherd and his flock retreat."

And again, Georg. iii. 331.

  "When noon-tide flames, down cool sequestered glades,
  Lead where some giant oak the dell o'ershades,
  Or where the gloom of many an ilex throws
  The sacred darkness that invites repose."

them: for he that hath mercy on them shall lead them, even by the springs of water shall he guide them." Isa. xlix. 10, Ezek. xxxiv. 13. The day has not more certainly its noon, a time when in the East all are glad to seek repose in the shade, by springs, to slake their consuming thirst, than has the life of the believer its period of trial and sorrow. In following our Lord, we must expect not only to enjoy seasons when everything in the spiritual life is calm, dewy, and refreshing, like the morning; but also to encounter times when all things conspire to weary, discourage, and exhaust the spirit with the withering power of an oriental noon. But there are at such times, wells and fountains in this wilderness, like those which were concealed in the desert, and to which the wearied hosts of Israel were led by "the Shepherd of his flock." They are known to our good Shepherd, and he will so guide us, that, like Jesus, wearied with his journey, and sitting on Jacob's well at noon, John iv. 6, we may, when worn with the difficulties of our pilgrimage, sit there, and drink, and with joy draw water out of the wells of salvation. There is an "hour of temptation," Rev. iii. 10, and an hour of affliction. These are sure to follow any remarkable communication of grace to us. It was directly after the baptism of the Holy Spirit, that Jesus was tempted by the devil. In all these times, when the soul is ready to wither under the power of trials and sorrows, Jesus has provided "a tabernacle for a shadow in the day-time from the heat." Isa. iv. 5. To this refuge will he lead his chosen ones; and there, in time of trouble, he will hide us in his pavilion, in the secret of his tabernacle will he hide us. Wearied with the assaults of Satan; worn with toil; oppressed with grief; with the cherished objects that requited our affection, gone by death; and those from whom we have a right to expect better things, treating us with neglect, ingratitude, and scorn, how anxiously does the soul, feeling there is but the one object, even Jesus, left for it to love, seek his hand to guide us where there is shelter from evil, and where on his bosom the weary are at rest. "And the sheep hear his voice, and he calleth his own sheep by name, and leadeth them out; and when he putteth forth his own sheep, he goeth before them, and the sheep follow him, for they know his voice." John x. 3, 4.

"For why should I be as one that turneth aside by the flocks of thy companions?"* The divine love which constrains us to follow Jesus with earnest self-denial wherever he may see best to lead, whether through dark

---

* Concerning the precise import of the word here rendered "turneth aside," interpreters are divided. It properly means "to cover;" and the feminine participle "covered, veiled;" that is, Why should I be as one veiled among the flocks of thy companions,—Why should I, as a faithless harlot, turn away from thee with an unsteady, erring love, and seek among those connected with the flocks of thy companions some new and improper object of affection. Thus, Gen. xxxviii. 15, "He thought her to be an harlot, because she had covered her face." Not only did she wish to seek no other love; she wished to avoid even a suspicion of not being entirely devoted to him; and consequently desired to know precisely where she might find him, without having to make the inquiries, and to incur the treatment afterwards met with from the watchmen. Chap. v. 7. Hence, Mercerus happily remarks, "The spouse wishes to create the impression of her devoted affection, as though there were danger, while she wanders about inquiring for him, that she be taken for a harlot," According to Kitto, "it is customary for all the women inhabiting towns to go about closely veiled; while all the women of the different pastoral people who live in tents do not commonly wear veils, or at most only so far as to cover their foreheads and lower parts of the face, leaving the countenance exposed, from the eyebrows to below the nose. It is evident, that although the use of complete coverings was known, the women of the pastoral patriarchs did not conceal their faces completely, except on extraordinary occasions."—*Illustrated Commentary*, Gen. xx. 16.

and rough valleys, or into the most refreshing pastures; which makes us seek his direction in trouble, and rest in the covert in which he would then have us to abide, does equally incline us to dread any liability of being led astray from him, and to avoid following any but Jesus. Companions of Jesus are mentioned in Acts i. 21, John xv. 27, Luke i. 2; they were the Apostles. Sin consists in apostasy from God. It creates in the heart a repulsion to God, and a disposition to occupy the powers of the soul with anything in preference to the Creator. Whatever the manifestations of God, however attractive and glorious, depravity so changes our constitution as to carry us away from Jehovah by its natural opposition to holiness. It is the nature of a sinful being to fall away from God. Such cannot be drawn and kept near the Fountain of light and life, the Sun of Righteousness, without the restraining influences of the Holy Spirit. From God, as manifested in Paradise, in the flood, on Sinai, sinful man turned spontaneously away; and when at last he disclosed himself to us in the fulness of grace and truth in the Lord Jesus, the same native propensity towards evil and darkness inclines us to adopt the teachings of others rather than of Christ; to worship and serve the creature more than the Creator thus incarnate; to turn aside from the Redeemer, even though no farther than after his companions. From the first there was a disposition to say, "I am of Paul, and I of Apollos, and I of Cephas." 1 Cor. i. 12. And ever since, much of the divisions among Christians has sprung from the disposition to turn away from God even in Christ, and cleave to men, to church organizations or forms of doctrine, to anything, indeed, though an idol or a crucifix, if thereby the Author of our being, the Spirit of holiness, may be displaced from the heart. Even when holding firmly to Christ, we find within us a propensity to model our religious life after the example of our pious associates, without thinking of rising above the general tone of feeling around us, and to take as the pattern to which our ambition and efforts for holiness aspire, the life of some eminent saint, rather than the glorious righteousness of Christ. This love, as here expressed, desires to follow Jesus only, to take his example. Unsatisfied with being led by any other, we feel, with Bunyan's Pilgrim, "Wherever I have seen the print of his shoe in the earth, there I have coveted to set my foot too." Taking his truth as the first rule of duty, and his life as the only perfect representation of what ours should be, we study to be not so much like any development of piety in any saint however eminent, as to be like Christ. While valuing church organizations, this love puts them in their proper place, without letting them come between the soul and Christ, and rejoices in the prosperity of religion among undoubted Christians, even though not of its own sect. Phil. i. 18. While these means of grace, creeds, and denominations, are seen necessary in the present state of man, we are able to feel they are trivial things in comparison with Jesus, to be done away in heaven. 1 Cor. xiii. 10. Through this divine love absorbing the soul, we are able in a measure to rise in our desires above everything else, however closely allied to him, and feel Christ to be all in all. Like many things and associations viewed as very important during childhood, but lost sight of under weightier considerations in riper years, these earthly things, even those essentially connected with religion, will be seen in their true proportions, and sink down into their proper place, when that which is perfect shall come, and that which is in part shall be done away in heaven.

Ver. 8.—If thou know not, O thou fairest among women, go thy way forth by the footsteps of the flock, and feed thy kids beside the shepherd's tents.

These words are an answer to the inquiry in the foregoing verse. It is necessary for the good of those having too high an opinion of themselves, that they be reproved and humbled: there are pious spirits so borne down by humbleness of heart, as to need encouragement. Some must be held in with bit and bridle; others are so lowly they may be guided by the good Shepherd's eye, Ps. xxxii. 9, and need encouragement by his speaking to their heart. Among the latter, are those having the state of mind expressed in verses 5 and 6, "I am black, but comely, &c." Jesus seeing the lowliness of such, and unwilling to break the bruised reed, comforts them, and says, "O thou fairest among women." While the pious are despised by the world, as possessing nothing of loveliness, Jesus looking on the heart, beyond the mere accomplishments of person and manners, beholds the saint as the fairest among the sons of men. Heart has very little, if anything, to do with beauty among the fashionable world. The most accomplished there, is most heartless. Speaking of the court of Louis XV. a writer observes, "Generations of luxury had given to the manners of court-minions the polish of steel, and its hardness to their hearts." All is outward polish and grace, while inward, deformity and corruption. The devotee of fashion is at best but a whited sepulchre, beautifully garnished to the eye, but full of all uncleanness; his courtly bearing an embroidered pall, which it has been the whole business of his life to weave, covering from the view of men, perhaps of himself, spiritual loathsomeness and death. God, who is love, begins his estimate of beauty, by taking into consideration, first of all the heart, and the heart purified by love. Whatever our outward circumstances, even though unfavourable in appearance as those of Lazarus, we are beautiful in his eyes, if the heart be filled with the limpid and life-giving influences of the Holy Spirit.

Having thus received encouragement, so that by knowing the opinion had of her by the beloved, the spouse might be cheered onward in following him, she was prepared to hear the duty that is enjoined in reply to her inquiry: If thou know not, if you are at any time in doubt, go thy way forth by the footsteps of the flock, follow the example of those gone before you to glory. The same direction is given in Heb. vi. 10—12. They are exhorted to "be not slothful, but followers of them who through faith and patience inherit the promises." This is to be done with a diligence continued to full assurance of hope, and on to the end. The state of heart thus acceptable with God, and inclining us to those ways where are the footsteps of the flock, shows itself in works and labours of love, manifested towards the name of Jesus, by ministering to his saints. Christ is given as our example: "Leaving us an example that ye should follow his steps." 1 Peter ii. 21. We are to follow the saints as they follow Christ. 1 Cor. xi. 1. It is necessary to have the examples of both constantly before us. If the Scriptures had given nothing but doctrines in a didactic form, we must have had difficulty in comprehending and obeying them. We require something sensible and tangible; we must see the thing not only described, but done before our eyes. There is in the mind a propensity to personify abstract things, arising from the extreme difficulty of making them otherwise intelligible to beings, who, like us, derive their knowledge mainly through the senses. When the poets would make their instructions attractive and impressive, they resort to personification; and try to represent abstract truths as nearly as they can be represented, by allegorical forms. With this, the ancient mythology abounds. The Jewish ritual was formed on this principle. In making to the Jews promises and threatenings, God often had them symbolized by both acts and things. Thus the truths of religion brought down from time to time into the darkness of our world, like rays of glory from heaven, were not left to shoot afar at random, but have been concentrated, embodied, clothed with a living form, in the person of Jesus Christ; and of him may be said with truth, what was said of a heathen god;

> "Each conception was a heavenly guest,
> A ray of immortality, and stood
> Star-like around until they gathered to a God."*

There is danger of overlooking Christ as our exemplar, while receiving him as our teacher. It is required in an instructor that himself should do what he teaches others. This was eminently done by Jesus when sojourning on earth. While receiving his teachings, we must study to find how he carried out the spirit of such instructions, in his actions. The artist who seeks perfection in painting or statuary, devotes himself to the study of the works of the best masters and the models of antiquity. God has set forth, in the incarnation of Christ, a perfect model for those who would attain moral perfection. As ancient temples were ornamented with statues and sculpture, so in the temple of our God in heaven, there will be pillars, Rev. iii. 12, living statues, wrought out from the living stones here found in the horrible pit, of which the cherubim and palm-trees carved in the golden walls of the

---

* Childe Harold, Canto 4, clxii.

earthly temple were the foreshadowing, 1 Kings vi. 29, Ezek. xli. 18; and those of us who are co-workers with God in forming our souls for that position of glory, can accomplish our trust, can, under the co-operating influences of the Holy Spirit, have our whole man reduced to the beauty of holiness, only by taking as our model, Him in whom, when on earth in human form, did all the fulness of the Godhead dwell. It has ever been a device of Satan, to draw attention away from Jesus to his saints— first from his example, and then from his instructions— to the lives of martyrs and the teachings of the fathers, as they are called. When he cannot succeed in doing both, he will be satisfied in turning our view from the example of Christ, while we retain our hold on his word. He knows that in proportion to the degree he can thus turn the eye from Jesus, the only perfect teacher and perfect model, will be his success in introducing error; because no man is infallible, either in doctrine or practice, and accordingly, those who are content with human guides, may be more easily corrupted by imbibing their errors. The coldness of many Protestants springs from losing sight of the living example of Christ, while his word may be retained and perhaps studied; the errors of Popery arise from displacing both the word and the example of Jesus, and giving the attention to the doctrines and lives of the so-called saints.

But the example of the followers of Christ, is nevertheless of great value. In many things, Jesus cannot be imitated. While found in fashion as a man, there are things which he could not have in common with our nature. He was a man, but a man who did no evil, who was sinless. In devotion to the will of God, in bearing reproach, in all things pertaining to holy living, he is a

15*

perfect model. But there are spiritual exercises arising from our being fallen sinners, and in a course of sanctification, that Jesus could never know. Regeneration, repentance, contrition, conversion, temptations to sin caused by corruptions of the heart, are things he could not have personally experienced: these things modify the whole tenor of our spiritual exercises; and, consequently, if we are to enjoy on this ground the advantage of any who has been before us, this must be found, not in the history of Jesus, but in the lives of his people. The fall of David, his recovery and the feeling attending this recovery, as given in the Scriptures, is necessary for the encouragement of the saint under discipline: the same is true of the exercises of Paul, mentioned in Rom. vii. 15—25, and 2 Cor. xii. 7—9. Nothing in the life of Christ could furnish features of an example for our encouragement in cases like these. We need doctrinal statements, such as our Lord has given, of what we should be, and of the means by which we can become such; the example of a perfect model like Jesus, towards which to be conformed; and the example of fallen men in process of restoration by grace to the image of Christ, that through the knowledge of their exercises we may have warning, consolation, and hope. Great encouragement is derived from studying the lives of those who have been among us, and have passed through like difficulties and conflicts to glory. Good biographies are valuable to the saint as an exhibition of the operations of the Holy Spirit, and of God's gracious dealings with those in course of deliverance from the dominion of sin. With these marks so numerous—thus compassed about with so great a cloud of witnesses—we need not wander, as did Joseph, and get bewildered when seeking his brethren with their father's flock in Dothan, Gen. xxxvii. 15; but are enabled to ask for the old paths, where is the good way, and find rest for our souls. Jer. vi. 16.

"And feed thy kids beside the shepherds' tents!" While Jacob was waiting at the well, Rachel came with her father's sheep, for she kept them, Gen. xxix. 9; and the daughters of the priest of Midian came and watered their father's flock. Exod. ii. 16. The direction to the spouse is, In feeding thy kids, keep near to the shepherds' tents, and thou shalt find me at noon in the midst of my sheep. Jesus said unto Peter, "Feed my lambs," John xxi. 15; and our Lord "shall feed his flock like a shepherd; he shall gather the lambs with his arms, and carry them in his bosom." His ministers are the under-shepherds. Jesus is to be sought by following in the footsteps marked out for his people; and by waiting for him near the shepherds' tents, in the use of the means of a regular ministry, and by "feeding the kids," that is, in the discharge of duties of usefulness to the souls of others, particularly the young. Christ is not to be found in retirement only, "in his chambers:" by following these directions, we may enjoy his presence amid the active duties of life. While religion requires us to be much alone with God, it also requires us to be much with man, especially the brethren and the ministry. They are appointed by Jesus in his stead, and must be esteemed highly for his sake. In the exercise of his sovereignty, God may renew and save souls without the regular means of grace; but this is the exception, not the rule. Grain, fruit, and choice flowers, may be found on remote islands, where no hand has sown or tilled; yet this does not show it is not our duty to labour, if we expect to live. These words include the duty of keeping ourselves under the influence of all the means of the sanctuary, at the head of which stands the ministry of the word. With this, must be joined active usefulness. While bound to offer the sacrifice of praise continually, we must not forget to do good, and to communicate. Heb. xiii. 15. The deepest spirit of love, and of acquaintance with the glory of Jesus, is not found in seclusion, nor in action alone, but in the two combined. Activity, to a certain extent, is the life of our whole being; without this, the body shrivels, the mind withers; nor are we more certainly broken down by overtaxing the powers, than by continuance of sluggish repose. The development of our spiritual life follows the same law. Like the seasons of rest and sleep for the body, times of withdrawal from the world, and of seclusion with our Lord, are essential for recruiting our spiritual energies; but those energies, when thus renewed, will not expand into their full vigour, unless we use them for running without weariness, and walking without faintness, in the ways and duties of the Lord. There is something which every Christian may do, and must do, in feeding the Church of God, which he hath purchased with his own blood. "Feeding the kids" requires that we be careful in training our household in the ways of the Redeemer; that we do good to those whom we may find, by seeking opportunity, in our daily walk; and that in the Sabbath-school, we labour according to our situation, in training the young to follow Jesus. The spirit of these words has its perfect fulfilment in the faithful instruction of their children by parents, and in the unobtrusive but important duties of the teacher in the Sabbath-school. There, are the young of the flock gathered under the shadow of the shepherds' tents, and happy are those servants who are found thus employed when the good Shepherd appears in the midst of his fold. "Blessed is that servant whom his Lord, when he cometh, shall find so doing." Matt.

CHAPTER I. 9.   173

VER. 9.—I have compared thee, O my love, to a company of horses in Pharaoh's chariots.

In this encampment, where the bridal company are now supposed to be, the king would have his most splendid equipage; the Egyptian horses were celebrated for their beauty, "they were even exported to the neighbouring countries, and Solomon bought them at a hundred and fifty shekels of silver, from the merchants who traded with Egypt by the Syrian desert."* In modern, as well as in ancient times, the mares are considered in all respects most beautiful, valuable, and desirable. Such a steed in a chariot, like that which Solomon had brought out of Egypt by his agents, for six hundred shekels of silver, was an object of great beauty to the eye, especially when adorned with the costly trappings then usual. The beloved does therefore naturally compare the bride to such a horse in these words, which would be more correctly rendered, "I compare, thee, my

---

* Wilkinson's Anc. Egyptians, vol. iii. 35. "It was mid-day before we found a small party that had stopped and were pitching their tents. A young chestnut mare, belonging to the sheik, was one of the most beautiful creatures I ever beheld. As she struggled to free herself from the spear to which she was tied, she showed the lightness and elegance of the gazelle. Her limbs were in perfect symmetry; her ears long, slender, and transparent; her nostrils high, dilated, and deep red; her neck gracefully arched, and her mane and tail of the texture of silk. . . . . Two sheiks rode into the encampment, and hearing that the chief was with us, they fastened their high-bred mares at the door of our tent, and seated themselves on our carpets. . . . . . Sofuk was the owner of a mare of matchless beauty, called, as if the property of the tribe, Shammeriyah. . . . No one can look at the horses of the early Assyrian sculptures without being convinced that they were drawn from the finest models."—*Layard's Nineveh*, vol. i. 91.

The superiority of the mares at the Olympic games is repeatedly referred to in the classic authors.

love, to my chariot-steed, or mare, from Pharaoh;" or to my Egyptian chariot-steed. Though unusual in the present age, this comparison will appear beautifully appropriate, when we call to mind still further the affectionate adoration and tenderness with which these animals are regarded by the orientals. Theocritus has adopted the same illustration:

> As towers the cypress mid the garden's bloom,
> Or in the chariot proud Thessalian steed,
> Thus graceful rose-complexioned Helen moves.*

Having called the spouse "fairest among women," in reply to her inquiry after him in ver. 8, the Holy Spirit proceeds to express the impression had by our Lord, of the beauty of the saint, by the endearing words, "my

---

* The words of Horace are well known. Odes, lib. iii. 11. Thus Sophocles:

> E'en as a high-bred steed, though old, retains
> His mettle still in danger, and his ears
> Pricks upright; so thou us dost onward urge
> And art the first to follow.—*Electra*, 25.

And Homer says Paris went forth to battle,

> "As some stalled horse high-fed, his stable-cord
> Snapt short, beats under foot the sounding plain,
> Accustomed in smooth sliding streams to lave
> Exulting; high he bears his head, his mane
> Undulates o'er his shoulders, pleased he eyes
> His glossy sides, and borne on pliant knees,
> Shoots to the meadow where his fellows graze."—*Iliad*, vi. 506.

See also the same simile applied to Hector, *Iliad*, xv. 265.

The epithet "magnanimus" is often applied to the horse by the ancients, as in Virgil, Æn. iii. 704, who speaks of "noble spirited horses," produced in the country of the Agrigentines, who were famous for sending superior horses to the Olympic games. We need hardly add that the same word is very commonly applied to heroes.

love." This shows the deep, devoted, pre-eminent, and tender love of Jesus for his people. Among all his creatures there can be none for whom he has a stronger affection than for the redeemed. Towards these he bears a three-fold love. To the original affection felt for them as for the holy angels and all his creatures, is superadded the tenderness necessarily arising towards those for whom he has thus suffered, and the love arising from forming them a second time as new creatures. His love for the unfallen inmates of heaven, is the love felt by him as their Creator: his love to the saints has the three-fold strength resulting from creation, redemption, and sanctification.

In Rev. iv. 8, and Ezek. i. 10, the living creatures had faces like different animals, emblematic of various qualities of the mind. The horse is here referred to as the emblem of the saint; and as the best horses came from Egypt, and of these the finest were in the chariot of the king, so whatever excellences this emblem expresses, must exist in the greatest perfection in the believer. Contemplating the saint as following him through the difficulties of pilgrimage in the wilderness, with self-denial, energy, and perseverance, Jesus would intimate by this comparison, that there is in the Christian character something noble, adapted to impress us with respect, and to command our admiration.* The feeling of unrenewed men towards religion is still the same—"Can

---

* "These Arabian horses are noble animals, and are no less remarkable for their chivalrous disposition, than for their strength and endurance: gallant, yet docile; fiery, yet gentle; full of mettle, yet patient as a camel. The head is beautiful: the expansive forehead, the brilliant, prominent eye, and the delicately shaped ear, would testify to nobleness in any animal."—*Warburton's Travels.*

any good thing come out of Nazereth?" With them piety is in disrepute, as fitted for base and ignoble minds, as incompatible with true honour. As war was the favourite and most honourable employment of the Romans, virtue was in their language synonymous with courage. And the word *honour* will have, among different classes of men, a meaning varying according to the traits of character which, in their view, show the highest excellence. Thus, with some persons, truth is made almost the sole test of honour; and the honourable man, in their judgment, is the man who, whatever other vices he has, will not lie. With others, honour consists in promptitude and severity in avenging an insult.

True honour lies in the possession and practice of the most exalted virtues. Among the irreligious in Christendom, public sentiment has been so affected by religion, that the word *honour* is brought nearer to its true meaning than among even the most refined heathen; yet how glaring and palpable are the vices which the world cherish and associate with what they call honour. That man makes the nearest approach to honour, and has the true claim on our admiration, who has concentrated in his heart, and embodies in his actions, most of the purest moral virtues. He shows something better than the ragged and meretricious excellence in which "gallantry atones for every vice." The trait which has in every age been assumed as the basis of honour, whatever else might be its aspect, is the principle which prompts to exposure of comfort and life to peril for the good of others. This is the principle which stands pre-eminent in the character of Christ. He exhibits the noblest magnanimity, honour unallied with any imperfection. His people must be like him in self-denying benevolence, and expose themselves for the welfare of enemies no less than friends.

> "Honest courtesy,
> Which oft is sooner found in lowly sheds
> With smoky rafters, than in tap'stry halls
> And courts of princes, where it first was named,
> And yet is most pretended."*

There is nothing on which men of the world pride themselves, that religion does not give in the full measure of absolute perfection to the saints. Nobleness of soul, courtesy, excellence of heart, beauty of appearance, objects of such desire to the fashionable, are gifts dispensed at the foot of the cross, not to many rich, not to many wise, not to many noble, but to the poor of this world, and will be enjoyed at last in greater perfection by Lazarus than by the proudest princes. All the excellences that have adorned all the great and noble of the world, and made their character the admiration of ages, would not form a single cluster so rich as the many found in the bosom of the humblest saint.† The

---

* Milton's Comus, 322.—Thus, the following from Æschylus:
> Integrity burns a lamp with brilliant beams,
>   In smoky cottages,
> And crowns with honour purity of life.
> But turning with averted eyes away
> From gilded prosperity with polluted hands,
>   Draws nigh to goodness;
> Not honouring wealth stamp'd with a counterfeit impression
>   By false applause of men.—*Agamemnon*, 709.

† Sir Walter Scott says: "I have read books enough, and observed and conversed with enough of eminent and splendidly cultivated minds, too, in my time; but I assure you, I have heard higher sentiments from the lips of poor uneducated men and women, when exerting the spirit of severe yet gentle heroism under difficulties and afflictions, or speaking their simple thoughts as to circumstances in the lot of friends and neighbours, than I ever yet met with out of the pages of the Bible. We shall never learn to feel and respect our real calling and destiny

world despise religion as overlooking what is honourable, because they judge of piety by what they see in the actions of professing Christians, rather than by the words of Scripture and the example of Christ. And in their judgment of pious men, they overlook their virtues, through eagerness to contemplate their failings. Should the heroes of the world's idolatry be estimated according to the same rule, by neglecting their little excellence and summing up the many vices with which this single good trait is in union, worldly honour would appear a very beggarly and worthless thing. Piety, as seen in God's people here, is at best a conflict of grace with corruption, a yearning and struggling after perfection. Because dishonourable doings are found in those called by Christ's name, it by no means follows these are integral elements of pure religion. Whatever meanness may be seen in God's people, is owing not to their religion, but to their remaining corruptions. If a real Christian exhibit anything of meanness, notwithstanding sanctification is begun, much more of this would be visible were he entirely without grace. Charity doth not behave itself unseemly, 1 Cor. xiii. 5; that is, avoids all conduct which may be indecorous, or, in common estimation, unbecoming a follower of Christ.

> "The best of men
> That e'er wore earth about him was a sufferer,
> A mild, meek, patient, humble, tranquil spirit,
> The first true gentleman that ever breathed."*

Grace elevates the fallen soul of man; and giving it a

unless we have taught ourselves to consider everything as moonshine, compared with the education of the heart."—*Lockhart's Life of Scott*, vol. ii. 412.

* Decker.

heavenly nobleness, imparts an honour which, like its courage, is above fear and above reproach. In their idolatry of heroism the world are willing to overlook the many defects, even vices, of the hero, in admiration of his gallant bearing; and to deify one who has but the single virtue of courage to redeem a character marked by almost all other imaginable vices. Let them judge of the nobleness inseparable from piety, by looking not at the imperfections of the man, but at his virtues; not at the dark and corrupt soil, but at the stateliness of the growth and beauty of the flowers, which the creative energy of the Spirit is evolving from that mass of corruption.*

Homer gives a majestic portrait of his hero on appearing again to his foes, when Minerva threw over his shoulders her terrific ægis, and crowned his head with a golden cloud from which burned an all-brilliant flame. And when God sends forth to the good fight of faith, to wrestle with wicked spirits in high places, no less than with flesh and blood, the soul of the believer weeping for sin; covered with the shield and buckler of those divine truths more precious and adorned with richer sculpture than all the gold and silver of all the shields of the earth; and with that brilliancy of which the cloud over the mercy-seat was the emblem, burning on his brow; even the hosts of enemies of such soul, whether evil spirits or evil men, are compelled to gaze on such

---

* "There is not any kind of spirit in the world so noble as that spirit that is in a Christian, the very Spirit of Jesus Christ, that great King, the Spirit of glory, as the Apostle calls it, 1 Pet. iv. 14. This is a sure way to ennoble the basest and poorest among us; this royalty takes away all attainders, and leaves nothing of all that is past to be laid to our charge, or to dishonour us."—*Leighton* on 1 Pet. ii. 9.

a character with reverence, even while using every exertion to destroy it:

> "So spake the Cherub, and his grave rebuke,
> Severe in youthful beauty, added grace,
> Invincible: abashed the devil stood,
> And felt how awful goodness is, and saw
> Virtue in her shape how lovely."

A low and sordid disposition is the offspring of man's corruption, and must vanish as he rises in purity and fitness for heaven. By the grace which is carrying our fallen nature back to the perfection of Paradise, we cannot but be ennobled.

The horse is here mentioned as the emblem of the energy belonging to piety. Sloth, lack of energy, indolence, detract from any character. We look for energy in what we would admire; not the energy of feverish irregularity, but that which results from the calm, harmonious movement of well-balanced powers. The faculties of the maniac may be vigorous, but are destitute of harmony. There is an energy peculiar to the nature of different beings, and this only can we admire in them. Grace diffuses through the soul the energy which belongs to creatures like ourselves in perfection, but of which we have been despoiled through sin. A healthy mind, of good endowments, is always active, perhaps more or less so, even in hours of sleep. Perfect inactivity is a feature of perfect death; and as the soul sinks down under the influence of spiritual death, the faculties become more enfeebled, and activity becomes a greater effort. Counteracting this tendency, the Holy Spirit opens in the heart a fountain of water springing up into everlasting life; and makes us, while not slothful in business, fervent in spirit; a divine energy rising in the soul, like the waters boiling up in a perennial spring, and flowing with greater fulness as we draw nearer to him with whom is the fountain of life. Indolence is one of the many infirmities from which sanctification sets us free. Industry and perseverance in our calling, whatever that calling may be, prove a duty and a pleasure to the Christian. How are the flagging energies of the soul roused into new life by the presentation of a new motive, like the hope of fame; and the body recruited by the application of a healthful stimulant. The means provided for arresting the decay of the soul, and restoring a perfect vigour, are the influences of the Holy Spirit. Compared with these, how weak, how temporary, are all the stimulants which the power of man can bring to bear on the sinking body or the failing mind. Those who are filled with the Spirit will be active according to their capability; and even when the flesh may be weak, the spirit may be willing. Besides the direct operation of the Holy Ghost feeding the powers with heavenly strength, there are combined in action on the heart the noblest motives from without, heaven, eternal life; and the purest, strongest love within, affection to the dying Redeemer; the greatest of works to be done under the strongest of motives, and with the most encouraging aid. What a calm yet steady energy appears in the example of Christ! From the workshop of Nazareth, and from the wilderness, from nights spent alone in the mountains in prayer, did he go forth on his ministry, to heal the sick and preach in their cities. How abundant in labours was Paul! in all these the love of Christ constrained him.

The horse may be the symbol of an activity that does not tire. The idea of beauty includes that of an elastic vigour of the frame, light, free from heaviness, and with power of enduring fatigue and exposure.* These characteristics are imparted in perfection to the body and soul, by grace. So light, elastic, and airy, shall be the tread of the spiritual body, so different from the care-worn footsteps with which we now drag along this body of corruption, that we shall at last be like the angels, not liable to death any more, being the children of the resurrection. Luke xx. 36. While other pursuits bring weariness and satiety, the Christian life grows more interesting and pleasing. Retirement from business, with an independence and full honours, grows burdensome, though desired and laboured for through a long life. After a degree of success, wealth, and reputation, the soldier becomes weary of his triumphs, and longs for repose. But the man who is filled with the Holy Spirit, and cultivates the habits of contemplation and action excited by grace, will find the service of Jesus more and more delightful: every act of duty exhausts not, but renews his strength; and though the infirmity of the flesh, the dulness creeping through the bodily frame, from age, and ardent desire to enjoy the glory of his Lord, may make him anxious to flee away to the rest in

---

* "Thus I set my printless feet
  On the cowslip's velvet head,
    That bends not as I tread."—*Comus*, 897.

"E'en the light hare-bell raised its head,
  Elastic from her airy tread."—*Lady of the Lake.*

"Unwearied as in the morning, my gallant mare dashed away over the rocky valley, exulting in her strength and speed. She pressed against the powerful Mameluke bit, as if its curb were but a challenge, and it was only by slackening the rein that she could be induced to pause over some precipitous descent, or tangled copse; then, tossing her proud head, she would burst away again like a greyhound from the leash."—*Warburton's Travels.*

heaven, no weariness with the work of holiness and benevolence is felt; he is sensible that as his outward man perishes, his inward man is renewed day by day, he mounts up on wings as eagles, and never is he more willing to remain at the post of duty, never more active in every good work, than when the time of his departure is at hand.

VER. 10.—Thy cheeks are comely with rows of jewels, thy neck with chains of gold.

The chariot-horses were in ancient times more richly adorned than those used for riding; "the harness and trappings of such were extremely elegant; plumes waved over their heads, or fanciful crests rose gracefully in an arch above the ears, and descended in front to the nostrils; round the neck, immediately at the head, was an embroidered collar, ending in a rich tassel, or bell; the bit, as well as many ornaments of the bridle and trappings, were of gold, and other precious materials."* A drawing given by Layard of the head of an Assyrian horse, thus ornamented, is certainly very beautiful. The mention of the Egyptian steed in ver. 9, naturally sug-

---

* Layard's Nineveh, vol. ii. 272. "On grand occasions the Egyptian horses were decked with fancy ornaments; a rich striped or checkered housing, trimmed with a broad border, and large pendent tassels, covered the whole body; and two or more feathers, inserted in lion's heads, or some other device of gold, formed a crest upon the summit of the head-stall. But this display was confined to the chariots of the monarch, or the military chiefs."—*Wilkinson*, vol. i. 335. Thus when Latinus ordered the ambassadors sent by Æneas to have horses given them on which to return,—in Virgil—

> "At his command
> The steeds caparisoned with purple stand
> With golden trappings glorious to behold;
> And champ betwixt their teeth the foaming gold."

gested the reference here made to the beautiful head-dress of the spouse. Olearius tells us, that "all the head-dress that the Persian ladies make use of, are two or three rows of pearls, which are not worn there about the neck, as in other places, but around the head, beginning on the forehead, and descending down the cheeks, and under the chin, so that their faces seem to be set in pearls. This coiffure seems to be very ancient among the eastern people." Royal brides are represented by oriental authors as dressed after this manner. So, when the Caliph Al Mamon went to receive Touran-Dokht, that prince found her seated on a throne, her head loaded with a thousand pearls, every one of them as big as a pigeon's egg, or a large nut, which rich coiffure the caliph resolved should be assigned her for her dowry. D'Arvieux, who describes the Arab women as wearing pieces of gold coin hanging down by the sides of the face, adds, that they have chains of gold about their necks, which hang down their breasts.*

* Harmer, 206. Females in the East wear an ornament on the forehead, which is made of thin gold, and is studded with precious stones. Tyerman and Bennet say of a bride they saw in China, "Her head-dress sparkled with jewels, and was most elegantly beaded with rows of pearls encircling it like a coronet; from which a brilliant angular ornament hung over her forehead, and between her eyebrows." Curzon, in his "Visits to Monasteries in the Levant," referring to the Jews of Palestine, says, "The women are covered with gold, and dressed in brocades stiff with embroidery. Some of them are beautiful; and a girl of about twelve years old, who was betrothed to the son of a rich old rabbi, was the prettiest little creature I ever saw; her skin was whiter than ivory, and her hair, which was black as jet and was plaited with strings of sequins, fell in tresses nearly to the ground." P. 186. The sufa of the modern Egyptian females is a head-dress of beautiful network, hanging down the back, and filled with jewels of various kinds. This ornament is generally made by dividing the hair into a number of tresses, and attaching to each tress three silken threads. These threads have jewels attached to them, and at

The words of this verse do, therefore, refer to the rows or strings of pearls and jewels ladies were in the habit of wearing as part of the head-dress, and to the rich necklaces with golden chains over the bosom. Speaking to the Jewish church by Ezekiel, chap. xvi. 11, the Holy Spirit says, "I decked thee also with ornaments, and I put bracelets upon thy hands, and a chain on thy neck. And I put a jewel on thy forehead, and ear-rings in thine ears, and a beautiful crown upon thine head. Thus wast thou decked with gold and silver." The comparison of the horse refers to what may be called the vital energy or principle of the Christian life: this verse expresses the virtues which may be superadded by grace. Such allusions are frequent. "They shall be an ornament of grace unto thy head, and chains about thy neck." Prov. i. 9. Wisdom "shall give to thine head an ornament of grace, a crown of glory shall she deliver to thee." Prov. iv. 9. "In like manner, also, that women adorn themselves in modest apparel, with shamefacedness, and sobriety; not with broidered hair, or gold, or pearls, or costly array, but with good works." 1 Tim. ii. 9. "Whose adorning, let it not be that outward adorning of plaiting the hair, and of wearing of gold, or of putting on of apparel; but let it be the hidden man of the heart, in that which is not corruptible, even the ornament of a meek and quiet spirit, which is in the sight of God of great price."

When Pharaoh would honour Joseph, he took off his ring from his hand and put it on Joseph's hand, and arrayed him in vestures of fine linen, and put a gold chain about his neck. Gen. xli. 42. Thus, by the king's com-

---

the end a small gold coin. Mr. Lane remarks, "The sufa appears to me the prettiest, as well as the most singular of the ornaments worn by Egyptian ladies. The glittering of the burck, and their clinking together as the wearer walks, have a peculiarly lively effect."

mand, they put a chain of gold about the neck of Daniel. Dan. v. 29. And when, like Joseph, we are drawn from the horrible pit of our natural condition, and raised by adoption to the second rank in God's glorious kingdom, even to be the sons of God, how pure and rich the robe he throws around us, the same in texture with that worn by Jesus, even his resplendent righteousness; how beautiful those pearls of virtue and chains of heavenly graces, conferred by him, clustered together by the invisible thread of divine influence, while kept steadfast and illumined by the golden clasp of love. These the topaz of Ethiopia shall not equal, neither shall they be valued with pure gold; ornaments so priceless as to be brought down to us by the hands of the Holy Spirit from that world where so excellent are all things, that the very pavement of the streets is pure gold, as it were transparent glass. The Apostle enumerates some of the jewels thus grouped together; "Add to your faith, virtue; and to virtue, knowledge; and to knowledge, temperance; and to temperance, patience; and to patience, godliness; and to godliness, brotherly kindness; and to brotherly kindness, love." 2 Peter i. 5. So beautiful and valuable are these, that a single one of the number is above all price. "If a man would give all the substance of his house for love, it would utterly be contemned." Song viii. 7.

These virtues, the ornament of the saint, are something distinct from his character by nature, and are superadded by grace. There are not in our hearts the germs of graces, lying like seeds in an ungenial soil, awaiting the beams of the summer sun for warming them into life: our sanctification, as well as our regeneration, is not the development of latent goodness of heart, but the creation of those excellences which constitute holiness. No new faculties are added by the work of the Spirit. He does not take of the intellectual powers belonging to a superior order of beings, and ingraft them into our soul. He gives life to the withered hand, strength to the palsied limbs, and sight to the blinded eye of the soul. Like the author of our spiritual being, rising as a branch from the stem or stump of the decayed tree of Jesse, there comes forth, by the energy of grace, from the roots of the fallen trunk of our ruined soul, a shoot that grows by sanctification into a tree of righteousness. By the Holy Ghost, the soul darkened and changed to stone through sin, is inlaid with eyes pure as the seven eyes upon the stone laid before Joshua, Zech. iii. 9; pure as those seven eyes of the Lamb, Rev. v. 6; and is inlaid with sensibilities alive to the faintest beams of divine goodness; and with ears that gather home to the very core of our being the tones of the melting voice of our God; and with affections which, unfolding more beauteous than Sharon's rose, exhale a perfume grateful even amid the odours of heaven, and gather in their bosom the rays of the Father's love, the drops of the Spirit's dews. What jewels of the spouse, so beautiful as those endowments! What chains of gold, so comely as these clusters of heavenly graces!

Ver. 11.—We will make thee borders of gold with studs of silver.

The Hebrew word here rendered "borders," is the same with that rendered "rows," in ver. 10; and would seem to refer here to the same kind of ornaments.* The

* In the Odyssey, lib. xv., there is much said that refers to the pursuits and skill of the Sidonians, whose intercourse with the Jews in the time of Solomon is well known. Among other things, there is a reference which seems to illustrate this text:

"A man of theirs, subtle and shrewd, produced
A splendid collar, gold with amber strung.
With deep delight, my mother and her maids
Gazed on it."—*Lib.* xv. 459.

queen was, however, distinguished by a crown,* Jer. xiii. 18; Ezek. xvi. 12; Esth. ii. 17; and to the crown these words may refer. Struck with her beauty, as adorned with rows of jewels, the king wishes to give the finish to her head-attire, by placing on her a crown of gold, variegated with studs of silver. As in Ps. xxi. 3: "Thou settest a crown of pure gold on his head." There is laid up for every saint a crown of righteousness, which the Lord shall give at that day unto all them that love his appearing. Whatever the exact ornaments here mentioned, the idea is that the beloved would add to the beautiful ornaments already worn by the bride, others of the most precious kind, devised and made by himself. While the graces considered under the foregoing verse, are developing in this life, there are in reserve in the treasury of heaven, crowning glories which shall be received when the chief Shepherd shall appear. "Unto every one that hath shall be given." Those who are faithful to their trust, even though by making their pound gain five pounds, shall be made rulers over cities, kings unto God. Were we presented by some kingly friend with costly jewels, the same in appearance with those worn by himself, he would be little likely to follow those gifts with others equally valuable, did we receive them with eagerness but afterwards appear without them, and allow them to lie neglected, unworn, and bedimmed. Neglect of the ring and gold chain by Joseph, would have certainly drawn on him the displeasure of Pharaoh. By guarding faithfully the treasures committed to our heart by the Holy Spirit, we shall find him constantly adding

---

* The Hebrew word rendered "spouse," in Song iv. 8, 9, 10, 11, 12, means a crowned one, derived from a root signifying to make perfect; and then used to express a bride, from the completion put to her attire by the bridal chaplet or crown

to them, changing us from glory to glory, till the soul, all glorious within, with clothing of wrought gold, emerges from its probation on earth into the unending bridal festivities of heaven, fairer than the woman clothed with the sun, and the moon under her feet, and on her head a crown of stars. Success in amassing wealth depends on keeping and using properly the amounts acquired from time to time; no reasonable expectation can be indulged of its being otherwise in our efforts for gathering the riches of God's grace.

How much more glorious and desirable must be the ornaments thus conferred by Jesus, than those which man elaborates for himself. Desire of personal independence is a besetting sin of our fallen nature. Among men of the world much is heard about self-reliance as the spring of success in life: with such persons the glorification of self is the chief thing; and they wish the impression made that this fabric of fortune is the work of their own wisdom and power; they hate the idea of dependence even on Him who formed the machinery of their intellect, even of their whole being, and without the stream of whose living influence that machinery must instantly cease to move. With the nature of the characters thus formed, we are familiar. Their portraits are recorded in colours of selfishness, pride, ambition, and blood. However ill-disguised by vanity and policy, the smothered sentiments of such hearts, on viewing their doings, position, and success, are, "Is not this great Babylon that I have built by the might of my power, and for the honour of my majesty." Dan. iv. 30. Reputation, influence, riches, everything thus relying on self as its foundation, must be unsubstantial as a fabric resting on the vapour that appeareth for a little time and then vanisheth away. All such hopes and structures of pride are so fragile and unreal, that a breath of air may blast them, and reduce their possessors to a condition as friendless and pitiable as that to which the haughty king of Babylon was brought down by a voice that fell from heaven while yet the word was in his mouth. Like the palace of ice, fairy-like in appearance yet repulsively cold, built on a foundation underneath which was a hidden river ready to swallow it up at the return of spring, all the labours of human pride and self-reliance, for rearing a fabric of happiness and renown, must issue in results equally unsubstantial, and destined to be perfectly lost when the scenes of this wintry world are displaced in heaven by the beauties of an unbounded spring. How much superior the character which is formed by the virtues made for us by God the Father, the Son, and the Spirit! Casting aside this self-reliance, which is another name for pride, let us substitute therefor reliance on the Holy Ghost; so that to us the words may be addressed, "Ye are his workmanship, created in Christ Jesus unto good works." The results of the artistic skill of this boasted self-reliance are enumerated by one who best knows the heart; which are these—"adultery, fornication, uncleanness, lasciviousness, idolatry, witchcraft, hatred, variance, emulation, wrath, strife, seditions, heresies, envyings, murders, drunkenness, revellings, and such like." Gal. v. 19. The borders of gold, with studs of silver, made for those who depend on the Spirit, include such jewels as, "love, joy, peace, long-suffering, gentleness, goodness, faith, meekness, temperance."

How much honour is conferred on the spouse, and how strong the proof of his love, when the beloved, the king, condescends to make these ornaments himself.

He does not say, "We will give," but "We will make, &c." There were two reasons for this; none but himself could finish those things in a manner sufficiently royal and splendid; and it is a gratification for him to be thus occupied in labours for the souls he loves. The virtues adorning the redeemed, the beauties of their souls, their spiritual bodies, can be the workmanship of none less than Jesus Christ. Growing unto an holy temple in the Lord, we are builded together for an habitation of God through the Spirit; and he by whom we, as living stones, are built up a spiritual house—is one who has been filled to an infinitely greater degree than Bezaleel, the architect of the tabernacle, with the Spirit of God, in wisdom, and in understanding, and in knowledge, and in all manner of workmanship, Exod. xxxi. 3—is Christ the wisdom of God, and Christ the power of God. He cleanses us from sin; he overlays the refined gold of the sanctified heart, with engraving more beautiful than was ever wrought in the gems worn on Aaron's breast; his hands alone set this priceless jewel of a transparent soul in the pellucid shrine of a spiritual body; and deposits it among the peculiar treasure of the King of kings, in the secret of the Most High, under the shadow of the Almighty. And this is to him a labour of love. His affection for us forbids the idea of entrusting this work to other hands, even could any be found equal to the task. The heart of Jesus delights to anticipate our wants, to labour for our good, though in bearing the burden of a cross. He is the artificer of our fortune; he carves out our whole destiny; he makes all that is valuable and beautiful about us; and our only pride is in the consciousness of having nothing which we have not received.

VER. 12.—While the king sitteth at his table, my spikenard sendeth forth the smell thereof.

According to oriental customs the encampment moving from place to place is here supposed to have stopped, and the king to have seated himself for enjoying the society of his friends. Thus Layard says: "When they reached the tents, the chiefs placed themselves on the divan, whilst the others seated themselves in a circle on the green-sward. An abundant repast had been prepared for them. The meaning of the verse is this—My perfume is most fragrant, and while the beloved is enjoying his repast in the circle of his friends, delights him with the richness of it odour.* According to Good, the phrase "gracing the banquet," is in common use among the Persian poets, to delineate an elegant woman. Mary showed her regard for our Lord by bringing very costly spikenard, and anointing Jesus while at table, so that the house was filled with the odour of the ointment. John xii. 3. In the same spirit does the spouse here desire to show her affection for the beloved.

After the manifestations of Jesus' love alluded to, in being brought into his chambers, ver. 4, the soul longing

---

* See notes on ver. 3. The spikenard was a very precious and costly unguent, obtained in Judea by foreign commerce from the eastern coast of Africa and from India. The ointment of spikenard used by Mary, John xii. 3, was "very costly;" and Horace, who lived in the same age, promises Virgil a whole cadus, about nine gallons, of wine, for a small onyx-box full of spikenard. "The composition of this unguent is given by Dioscorides, who describes it as being made with nut oil, and having as ingredients malabathrum, schœnus, costus, amomum, nardus, myrrha, and balsamum, that is almost all the most valued perfumes of antiquity." Dr. Royle, when in India, near the foot of the Himalaya mountains, found this plant brought down in considerable quantities as an article of commerce; and shows that the Jewish spikenard was most probably derived from these regions.—*Kitto's Cyc. Bib. Lit.*

for his presence follows hard after him by pilgrimage in the paths of duty, "by the footsteps of the flock." Having found him whom her soul loved, and being brought again into his presence on terms of affectionate friendship by receiving the reviving power of the Holy Spirit under different circumstances from those before noticed, she here expresses, in ver. 12, the effect produced by his presence, in kindling the affections into a lively glow. The presence of Jesus as felt by the divine light beaming in the effulgent cloud of the Spirit's influences continually around him, is unfolded to us at different times, and in various ways. Now, we are revived by entering into that cloud alone in our closet, more retired perhaps, than the three chosen disciples amid the glory on Tabor; again, we feel ourselves with him by our hearts burning within us when journeying by the way; and then, we meet with him by grace showered on the soul in the enjoyment of public ordinances, especially the sacrament of the supper. Here, his society is enjoyed not in private communion, his chambers, but in public, at his table, in the circle of his friends.

At this banquet, he presides in person, with kingly majesty. In the Psalms, especially the forty-fifth and seventy-second, to which this Song is allied, the epithet "the king," was held by the Jews to designate, in all cases, except where the context directs otherwise, the Messiah. As here used, this title seems to refer less to what is technically called his kingly office, than to his divine nature. He who receives us into reconciliation and communion, is the King, the most exalted personage in the government of God, is divine, is God. When, after especial blessedness in the private duties of religion, at times when there may be nothing unusual in the Church as a body, we have been cleaving to Christ by patient labours, without any uncommon enjoyment, we find not unfrequently, on coming to the sacramental table, the King of saints there refreshing us with the hidden manna for the hungry soul, with the water of life for the thirsting spirit, and with golden censers alive with holy fire and heavenly incense for kindling anew the smouldering affections of the heart. At these seasons of reviving love, we dwell much on the grandeur and divinity of our Lord; and love to feel, "Thou art fairer than the children of men; grace is poured into thy lips."

Sitting together at table was evidence of reconciliation and friendship: "If any man hear my voice, and open the door, I will come in to him, and will sup with him, and he with me." Rev. iii. 20. There is in preparation in heaven a marriage-supper of the Lamb, at which he and those who having been once enemies are reconciled, shall sit down in affectionate fellowship and unbroken peace. Just as, previous to the coming of Christ, the nature of his death was represented by the Jewish sacrifices; so, the nature of that feast of love on high, for which all things in this world are a preparation, is illustrated to us by the services of the Lord's supper. In every sacrifice, the part consumed by fire was considered as God's; and the offerer ate a portion to show his restoration to fellowship with his offended king; while the altar was God's table, at which he and the sinner thus met in reconciliation. In the Lord's supper we are partaking, in the only way now possible, of the sacrifice once for all offered on Calvary; and while doing this, show forth the Lord's death, till he come and drink the fruit of the vine anew with us in his Father's kingdom; till the reconciliation through his death, now shadowed dimly through these emblems, shall be perfectly consummated in both body and soul, by sitting with him at table in the New Jerusalem. This feast of love will be enjoyed in perfection in heaven; and all things connected with this sacrament on earth are pledges and foretastes of the fulness enjoyed above. All the sacrificial appointments of the tabernacle were shadows of the blessings we now enjoy; and shadows of them as the beginning of the manifestation of God to his redeemed, and their attending joy in heaven. In the camp of Israel, God was in the circle of his friends by the Shechinah; at the supper, he was thus present in the bodily form of Jesus; now at the communion table, in the congregation, and where two or three are gathered in his name, he is there in the influences of the Holy Spirit; and in heaven, he that sitteth on the throne, even the Lamb, shall for ever dwell among them. The covenant made with Israel at the foot of Sinai, was not completed until, after the shedding of blood and its application by sprinkling, the elders, as representatives of the people, went up into the mount, and there seeing the God of Israel, did eat and drink in his presence. In like manner, the new covenant, established on better promises, will not receive its perfect ratification until all those on whom has been shed the blood of sprinkling, are gathered up into the most holy mount on which rests the purity of the eternal clearness of heaven; and there, led on by a greater than Moses, even by the Lamb slain, drink the new wine at the table where presides the King of kings in the fulness of his glory.

"My spikenard sendeth forth the smell thereof."*

* The following, from Chardin's Voyages, illustrates this—mentioned by him for showing how prodigal the oriental females are in the use of perfumes. "I remember that at the solemnization of the nuptials of the three princesses royal of Golconda, whom the king, their father, who had no other children, married in one day, in the year 1679, per-

This was the oil of spikenard, the most costly, precious, and grateful perfume, with which the spouse was anointed according to the practice of using such things profusely at entertainments. In this communion with Christ, our presence is as agreeable to him as the fragrance of spikenard, and his society is delightful to us as a bundle of myrrh or cluster of camphire. With these perfumes of the oil of gladness, the great governor of the feast is anointed without measure; and as the virgins love him because of the savour of his good ointments, so his delight is with none among the sons of men but those who have received an unction from the Holy one. The use of fragrant oils was not a more necessary preparation for the society of friends at a feast, than is the anointing of the Spirit requisite to fit us for seeing God. This unction comes from himself. Hence the Psalmist says, "Thou anointest my head with oil." The graces of the holy heart, so acceptable to God, are the work of the Spirit. He makes us partakers of the excellency of the fulness of Christ, even grace for grace. He brings to us, in this wilderness, from the hills of frankincense on high, those graces of liquid perfume which arise from the alabaster of a heart broken in contrition, in odours of prayers,

fumes were lavished on every invited guest as he arrived. They sprinkled them on those who were clad in white, but gave them into the hands of those who wore coloured raiment, because their garments would have been spoiled by throwing it over them, which was done in the following manner. They threw over the body a bottle of rose-water, containing about half a pint, and then a large bottle of water tinted with saffron, in such a manner that the clothes would have been stained with it. After this, they rubbed the arms and the body with a liquid perfume of laudanum and amerbgris, and they put around the throat a thick cord of jasmine. I was thus perfumed with saffron in many great houses of this country, and in other places. This attention and honour is a universal custom among the women who have the means of obtaining this luxury."

desires, and affections, most grateful to this kingly friend. Love, holiness, all the desires unfolding purity of heart, are the things well pleasing to our Redeemer. The unction of the Holy Spirit diffuses around us a refreshing perfume, by enlivening and developing our graces. As the Spirit is inseparable from the presence of Jesus, every approach of our Lord brings with it an influence which, by enlivening the affections, draws forth the precious exhalations of the spikenard of the heart. Thus does the sun of spring fill the calm, pure air, with fragrance from the landscape's blooms, the garden's flowers, by pouring around their roots the genial unction of his reviving glow. In the sacrament of the supper we are merely expressing by ceremonies that which it is our privilege and duty continually to enjoy. Not the communion service only, but our whole life, is a continual sacramental feast. As such, this feast may preserve our affections always in a glow, by keeping us near to Christ; and when our fervour may have manifestly declined, we shall find that it is not because Jesus has left the circle of his friends, but because we have gone out from among them, like Judas, led by love of gain or some kindred desire, when, had we, like the beloved disciple, lingered fondly near our Lord, we might have enjoyed a like fervour of affection.

VER. 13.—A bundle of myrrh is my well-beloved unto me; he shall lie all night betwixt my breasts.

The twelfth verse having expressed the agreeableness of the holy heart to Jesus, the thirteenth and fourteenth verses set forth the pleasantness of the society of Christ to the saint. This passage has been much misrepresented. We would read it, My beloved is unto me as an amulet, (a bag, or delicate vessel,) filled with liquid myrrh, that is borne continually in the bosom.* Myrrh was one of the most costly and fragrant perfumes. The shrub was beautiful, with smooth leaves of a dark green on the upper, and a whitish colour on the under surface, with flowers of a reddish purple, and a remarkable odour in the root, branches, leaf, and bloom; so that a cluster gathered therefrom was beautiful and fragrant; yet the liquid obtained by exudation gave the tree its chief value, and is most probably what is here mentioned. Nothing of the kind could be more delightful to the senses, than myrrh thus worn in the bosom. Rich perfume very appropriately represents the influences of the Holy Spirit; and what can illustrate more beautifully than this, those divine influences distilled as dew from the mountain of myrrh and hill of frankincense, and lying with

* "The eastern women, among other ornaments, used little perfume-boxes, or vessels filled with perfumes, to smell at. These were worn suspended from the neck, and hanging down on the breast. Such smelling-boxes are still in use among the Persian women, to whose necklaces, which fall below the bosom, is fastened a large box of sweets; some of these boxes are as big as one's hand; the common ones are of gold, the others are covered with jewels. They are all bored through, and filled with a black paste, very light, made of musk and amber, but of very strong smell."—*Burder*. Among the Egyptians, "Small boxes, made of wood or ivory, were very numerous, offering, like the vases, a multiplicity of forms; and some, which contained cosmetics of divers kinds, served to deck the dressing-table, or a lady's boudoir. They were carved in various ways, and loaded with ornamental devices in relief; sometimes representing the favourite lotus-flower, with its buds and stalks, a goose, gazelle, fox, or other animal."
—*Wilkinson*, vol. ii. 356, where may be found much that is interesting on this subject. He gives also, (vol. iii. 107,) an account and drawings of some curious Chinese bottles, which have been found in various tombs, and were evidently brought to Egypt through India at a very remote period. They are about two inches in height; one side presents a flower, and the other this inscription: "The flower opens, and lo! another year." They must have been filled with some precious ingredient, whose value may be inferred from the size of the vase.

an embalming power and exhilarating fragrance in the very bosom of the soul, the centre of the spiritual heart. This language is not stronger than those passages of Scripture which speak of Christ dwelling in us by his Spirit—"Christ in you the hope of glory," Col. i. 27; "Filled with all the fulness of God," Eph. iii. 19. Jesus says that his Spirit shall be in us "a well of water springing up into everlasting life," John iv. 14. Here, the illustration is varied for showing still further the loveliness and benefit of his presence, by saying that through his Spirit he is in the pure heart, as distillations of liquid myrrh. Lodged at the bottom of the heart, like a cluster of liquid or pulverized myrrh, the love of Jesus, the truths, thoughts, consolations, and influences of the Holy Spirit, exhale and roll through all the channels of the soul, with a soothing exhilarating power, and diffuse there as much as is now possible to be enjoyed of heaven.

Ver. 14.—My beloved is unto me as a cluster of camphire in the vineyards of Engedi.

The idea of the foregoing verse is presented in another form; My beloved is like a cluster, or bouquet, of camphire blooms from the gardens of Engedi.* By

---

* "After the ceremony of anointing was over, and in some cases at the time of entering the saloon, a lotus-flower was presented to each guest, who held it in his hand during the entertainment. Servants then brought necklaces of flowers, composed chiefly of the lotus; a garland was put round the head, and a single lotus bud, or a full-blown flower, was so attached as to hang over the forehead. Many of them, made up into wreathes and other devices, were suspended upon stands placed in the room, to be in readiness for immediate use, and servants were constantly employed to bring other fresh flowers from the garden, in order to supply the guests as their bouquets faded; and, to prevent their withering, they were generally put close to jars of water, into which their stalks were probably immersed. The stands that served

the camphire is most probably meant the *hennah,* a plant growing to the height of eight or ten feet, beautiful to the eye and grateful to the smell. " The dark colour of its bark, the light green of its foliage, the softened mixture of white and yellow, with which the flowers, collected into long clusters like the lilac, are coloured; the red tint of the ramifications which support them, form a combination the effect of which is highly agreeable. The flowers whose shades are so delicate, diffuse around the most grateful odours, and embalm with their strong fragrance the gardens in which they grow, and the apartments which they adorn. The women take pleasure in decking their persons and apartments with these delightful blossoms." The best of these flowers grew in Engedi, a part of the fertile plain of Jericho, abounding not only in vineyards, but also in gardens for aromatic shrubs, in the gums and balsams of which the Jews carried on a traffic. In the days of Jerome, this region was remarkable for the balm of Gilead. To persons thus familiar with these beautiful and fragrant clusters, nothing could be more expressive of the loveliness of the presence of another, even of the Lord Jesus Christ. How could we express otherwise, or more intelligibly, than by these emblems, the apprehension had of Jesus as lodged in our hearts by his love, and of that love as hoarded by us, and the source of inexpressible pleasure; as grateful, not

for holding the flowers and garlands, were similar to those for the vases, and varied in size according to circumstances. The Greeks and Romans had the same custom; and their guests were, in like manner, decked with flowers and garlands. They not only adorned their heads, necks, and breasts, like the Egyptians, but often bestrewed the couches on which they lay, and all parts of the room, with flowers. They also perfumed the apartment with myrrh, frankincense, and other choice odours, which they obtained from Syria."—*Wilkinson*, vol. ii. 215.

merely in public, like the incense burning on the altar, but in private, withdrawn from society. The love of Christ, his consolations and joys, are to us not unstable and evanescent, like fragrance floating on a passing breeze; but are, in the depths of the soul, a perpetual fountain of exhilarating perfumes, refreshing as myrrh, beautiful as the clusters of camphire. And when we are most alone, his presence makes us realize something delightful and delicately beauteous to our spiritual perception, and inseparable from us, as the bundle of myrrh or camphire, which may attend us with an influence pleasant to others, no less than ourselves, in the public assembly, in our closet retirement, or in our private walks.

By our precious Lord there is given to us something better than the golden vial full of odours; the heart of the pure in spirit is a richer vial, and the love of Christ imbedded there in the myrrh of Scripture truth, holy desires, and heavenly anticipations, is a more precious incense. The promises and Scripture truths gathered from time to time, from different parts of the word of God, and borne in our bosom, in clusters, as we need them, are the clusters of camphire, flowering and fragrant with the love of Jesus:

> "A flower which once
> In Paradise, fast by the tree of Life,
> Began to bloom; but soon for man's offence
> To heaven removed, where first it grew, there grows;
> And flowers aloft, shading the fount of life,
> And where the river of bliss through midst of heaven
> Rolls o'er Elysian flowers her amber stream."

In the fragrance of this divine love thus diffused around us, we are breathing sweeter odours than known by Adam in Eden, such as are even now reviving those who are

* Paradise Lost, book iii. 353.

under the shadow of the tree of life in the midst of the Paradise of God. There is in the love of Christ something refined and ethereal, to which the most sublimated extracts from the most elegant things of earth cannot approximate; very different from the gross pleasures of sense, better than wine; and as the wind is the best emblem of the Holy Spirit, John iii. 8, so the wind loaded with such fragrance as the myrrh and camphire blooms, is the best illustration of the Holy Spirit in his office of conveying to the soul the exhilarating love of our Lord. In what perfect contrast are the enjoyments of the glutton, and the drunkard, and "all that wallow in the sensual sty," to the pleasures inhaled from a cluster of myrrh or camphire blooms. While the presence of Christ diffuses a pure and elevating influence through the soul, from the influences of the Holy Spirit gathered like liquid myrrh at our heart, it does also gratify the sight by visions more delicately exquisite than the flowers of the camphire. How fragrant does this presence render our retirement, and cause us to linger fondly there while the world are pitying our loneliness. The Scriptures, this precious volume, the visible means of our communion with Christ, with the exquisite net-work of its literary materials and style, filled with words fitly spoken, is more beautiful and valuable than a basket of silver filled with apples of gold; and no golden vase on a centre-table of the purest marble, containing clusters of camphire mingling their fragrance with the odour of distilled myrrh, can diffuse so pleasant an incense as that filling the retired room of the believer, in which the central ornament is this book of life, this golden urn of salvation, filled with the pure water of life, with clusters gathered in the heavenly Paradise, and fragrant with truths in unfading bloom.

Ver. 15.—Behold, thou art fair, my love; behold, thou art fair; thou hast doves' eyes.

While thus entertained by Jesus, what is the language addressed by him to the believer? No tenderer epithet could be used, "My love;" or, as the Hebrew word strictly means, a female friend, a companion—the import of the language is, thou art indeed beautiful, my friend, my companion; my love, thou art beautiful. So literally true are the words, "As the bridegroom rejoiceth over the bride, so shall thy God rejoice over thee," Isa. lxii. 5. There are among his creatures none that he loves better than the redeemed. He who is altogether lovely, who is love, shall he not know what is lovely? and shall not his love be of great worth? He that planted the ear, shall he not hear? He that wove the texture of Sharon's rose, shall he not know what is beautiful? Yet, he says to us, "My love, behold thou art fair." Feeling our depravity and knowing our shortcomings, we wonder what there can be in us to admire; but he whose all-present eye sees pure gems in the deep caves of ocean, and delicate flowers in secluded retreats of the wilderness, penetrates beyond the outward appearance, and notices what is beautiful in the heart, which may still be too much like the troubled sea when it cannot rest. An unseemly shoot ingrafted into a tree grows more beautiful by growing into the tree, till at length it bursts into bloom. We are ingrafted into Christ; and as we become more and more one with him, our beauty increases by his beauty becoming ours. The parent looks on the infant as beautiful according to the likeness to himself, though there is much weakness and infirmity in the child, and very much beauty remains to be developed. In his created works, God does not wait until they are perfectly finished, before he can see beauty in them; he traces it in all things, from the first, as there forming; and the unfolding of beauty in the several stages of its progress towards maturity cannot be less interesting to him than the view of its full perfection. There is pleasure in training the tender plant; in watching the bursting bud and fragrant bloom of spring, as well as in enjoying the golden fruits of autumn. As soon as born again, the soul begins an assimilation to Christ, which is scarcely seen in the body, and must be much hidden from those who see the body only, while the lineaments of this loveliness must be apparent to those who can behold the soul. We are made one with Christ by justification; and sanctification then transfers to our soul the excellences existing in Jesus. Beauty is inseparable from holiness, as deformity is inseparable from sin. Jesus is making us what he pleases, with none to interfere; and he certainly cannot wish to make us otherwise than beautiful.

"Thou hast doves' eyes," or literally, Thine eyes are doves. The doves of Syria have eyes remarkably large and beautiful. The eye, as here mentioned, seems to combine the beauty of the brilliant light-blue eye of Minerva, with that of the tender, melting, languishing eye of Venus, to represent which her statues have the lower eyelid drawn up a little over the eye. All poets dwell on the eye as a most expressive feature. Every one is familiar with the varied epithets on this point in Homer, and the description of a beauty in Anacreon, Ode 28:

> And paint her eye Minerva's blue,
> With Venus' melting, languid hue.

The eyes of Agamemnon enraged, "were like blazing fire;" those of Minerva, a mild, sparkling, animated blue; Juno's, large, round, and full, "ox-eyed." The countenance has been called "the living telegraph of all that is felt within;"* especially may this be said of the eye. As in Milton's Penseroso,

> "Thy rapt soul sitting in thine eyes."

And an oriental poet, "All his soul sparkled in his eyes." As the soul of the saint is the shrine wherein lies the sacred fountain of divine love, the eyes of doves, the emblem of affection, are the best expression to others of this inward emotion. The eyes are transparencies through which the soul may look out on surrounding things; and as through these we do, as it were, come nearer than in any other way, getting glimpses of the soul, the expression of the eye is an index of the passions within, as of anger, envy, guilt, innocence, or love. Hence the language, "An evil eye," Matt. xx. 15; "Eyes full of adultery," 2 Pet. ii. 14; "An high look and a proud heart," Ps. ci. 5. The dove is an emblem of gentleness, innocence, and love; and has been chosen by the Holy Ghost for representing his divine nature and offices towards man. As the Spirit changes us to his own likeness, and makes us harmless, guileless, or pure, as doves, Matt. x. 16, the eyes must acquire an expression like the eyes of doves. Not the haughty air of the devotee of fashion, not the proud bearing of the soldier, not the selfish cast of the miser, not the fierce glare of malice, not the ill-concealed vanity, betokening, under the guise of feigned humility, a hungering and thirsting for admira-

---

* The Body and the Mind, by Dr. Moore, p. 85.—"The sagacious traveller, Nicolai, states that he saw the most divinely beautiful female countenances among women who were most devout. The calm contemplation of loveliness where affection blends with adoration, seems to act most powerfully in tranquilizing and exalting the features. Doubtless the apprehension of spiritual truth being absolute, the reflex of the divine mind would possess the mind with a more heavenly idea, and correspondingly transform the whole being." P. 86.

tion; but the eye bespeaking gentleness, purity, and love, is the expression of countenance agreeable to our Lord. As the man, who is the head of the woman, 1 Cor. xi. 3, does everything requiring energy, defence, danger, and resistance, while the woman in her sphere acts, but confides and loves; so we must do all things in love, feeling that the head of every man is Christ; and not avenging ourselves, but committing our cause to him in well doing, and sensible that with this well doing our business now is, as the spouse of Christ, to confide and love.

> "They tell of things which no gross ear can hear,
> Till oft converse with heavenly habitants
> Begin to cast a beam on th' outward shape,
> The unpolluted temple of the mind,
> And turns it by degrees to the soul's essence,
> Till all be made immortal."*

VER. 16, 17.—Behold, thou art fair, my beloved, yea, pleasant: also our bed is green. The beams of our house are cedar, and our rafters are fir.

We love him because he first loved us; we presume to call him our beloved, because he first calls us his love. It is much for such unworthy creatures to have the right of saying this; much to have the feelings and desires which prompt this language. When Jesus speaks to our heart, as in the 15th verse, there arises the trepidation of warm affection; and we would gladly give utterance to the strongest expressions of love; but we are so overwhelmed with his grandeur, and our unworthiness, as to hesitate in using words our emotions would justify. Hence the Holy Spirit has indited this language, and assures us we cannot do wrong in thus speaking of our Lord. Jesus is well pleased to have us call him our beloved.

"Thou art fair." How fair? Fairer than the sons of

---

* Milton's Comus.

men; adorned with greater beauty than any of our fallen race; fairer too than the angels. Heb. i. "Grace is poured into thy lips;" and when, in consequence of this, we wonder at the gracious words which proceed out of his mouth, we delight to add, "Yea, pleasant." The pleasures of refined society, of society ennobled by intellectual culture and polished manners, in combination with the grace which purifies the heart for seeing God, are the most delightful possible for man. The society of Jesus, far from being gloomy and irksome, is captivating and delightful. In him are united all conceivable charms, princely dignity, mind of infinite compass, illimitable influence, beauty, knowledge, and wisdom divine, a nature that is itself love. When in the form of a slave, in the flesh, emptied of his glory, there was a wondrous charm about his person, his presence, his conversation. "Never man spake like this man." What, therefore, must be the charm investing him now in glory. Those who have been admitted to the gatherings in which the hospitality of high rank loved to assemble the courtly, the powerful, the learned, and the influential, delighted in those privileges as their happiest hours, and cherish the remembrance of them fondly in declining age.* Of such privileges the humble saint may be deprived; but he mingles intimately in a more refined, more intellectual, more fascinating society—a gathering wherein he who presides is the king in the circle of his friends. How pleasant is the society of Jesus, when he unfolds to us the way of salvation, opens the promises, encourages in difficulty, comforts in trouble, and speaks of the blessedness of heaven! How rich the influence around his presence! In his presence is fulness of joy. When on

---

* Final Memorials of Charles Lamb, p. 238.

earth, he must have possessed great attractions, to draw multitudes after him into the wilderness, and retain them there for days without food. The indifference of the believer to the highest society among the irreligious, is the result of a deep and intelligent conviction of the superiority of the society of Christ. Entranced with his pleasantness, enchained with his wisdom, and rapt by the glorious visions of the ideal world unfolded by his promises, we exclaim, "This is my rest for ever; here will I dwell. Whom have I in heaven but thee? and there is none upon earth that I desire beside thee."

"Also our bed is green," or, the green flowery turf is our place of repose. The scene in which these words, and possibly all from verse 12 are used, seems to be laid in the kiosk or summer-house in the royal garden.*

* "The next day we went to visit the gardens, and to spend a day there. The place was about a mile out of town. It afforded us a very pleasant summer-house, having a plentiful stream of water running through it. The garden was thick set with fruit-trees, but without any art or order. Such as this are all the gardens hereabouts: only with this odds, that some of them have their summer-houses more splendid than others, and their waters improved into greater variety of fountains."—*Maundrell*, p. 130. In Kitto's Illustrated Commentary, Deut. iii. 11, is a drawing of what he calls "a garden bedstead," which is in fact a kiosk, and illustrates precisely what is meant in these two verses. "The Egyptians spent much time in the cool and shady retirement of their gardens, where, like the Romans, they entertained their friends during the summer-season, as we may judge from the size of some of the kiosks which occur in the paintings of the tombs."—*Wilkinson*, vol. ii. 187. Thus the following from Plato: "How beautiful a retreat! For this plane-tree is very wide-spreading and lofty, and the height and shadiness of this agnus castus are very beautiful; and being now in full bloom, in makes the place exceedingly fragrant. Moreover, there flows under this plane-tree a delightful fountain of very cold water, to judge from its effect on the foot. It appears from these images and statues, to be sacred to certain nymphs, and to Achelous. Observe again the freshness of the spot, how charming and delightful it is, and

Oriental gardens were without the city, and from half a mile to a mile distant from the houses of the persons to whom they belonged. "In the gardens around Aleppo, commodious villas are built, for the use of the inhabitants, to which they retire during the oppressive heats of summer. Here, amid the wild and almost impervious thickets of pomegranate, and other fruit-bearing trees, the languid native and exhausted traveller find a delightful retreat from the scorching beams of the sun. A similar custom of retiring into the country, and taking shelter in the gardens, at that season, appears to have been followed in Palestine, in ages very remote. The exquisite pleasure which an oriental feels, while he reclines under the deep shade of the pomegranates, the apple, and other fruitful trees, in the Syrian gardens, which, uniting their branches over his head, defend him from the glowing firmament, is well described by Russel: "Revived by the freshening breeze, the purling of the brooks, and the verdure of the groves, his ear will catch

how summer-like and shrill it sounds from the choir of grasshoppers. But the most delightful of all is the grass, which, sloping gently, gives an easy support to the head as we recline."—*Phædrus*, 5.

In the bower of Nehushta,
"With fragrant moss the floor
Was planted, to the foot a carpet rich,
Or, for the languid limbs a downy couch
Inviting slumber."

Milton mentions,
"Beds of hyacinth and roses,
Where young Adonis oft reposes."

And Theocritus,
"On soft beds recline,
Of lentisk and young branches of the vine."

"My tent was pitched on a carpet of soft, green sward, under the wide-spread arms of one of the old cedars."—*Warburton's Travels*.

the melody of the nightingale, delightful beyond what is heard in England; with conscious gratitude to heaven, he will recline on the simple mat, and bless the hospitable shelter." Lady Montague writes, "In the midst of the garden is the kiosk, that is, a large room, commonly beautified with a fine fountain in the midst of it. It is raised nine or ten steps, and enclosed with gilded lattices, round which vines, jessamines, and honeysuckles, make a sort of green wall. Large trees are planted round this place, which is the scene of their greatest pleasures." Speaking of the plain of Sharon, a traveller remarks, "The fields were decked with thousands of gay flowers, forming an enamelled carpet, that perfumed the air, and offered a scene replete with everything that could gratify the eye, or charm the imagination." In such a place, and on such a couch, are the beloved and the spouse here represented as reposing. This picture is common in poetry. Thus Thompson:

> "There on the verdant turf and flowery bed,
> By gelid founts and careless rills to muse."

And Homer:

> "Beneath them earth
> With sudden herbage teemed; at once upsprang
> The crocus soft, the lotus bathed in dew,
> And the crisp hyacinth with clustering bells;
> Thick was their growth, and high above the ground
> Upbore them. On that flowery couch they lay,
> Invested with a golden cloud that shed
> Bright dew-drops all around."*

From such scenes does the Holy Spirit draw the means of illustrating the loveliness of the society of Jesus. His presence can make the desert itself delightful. When he

* Iliad, book xiv. 347.

brings his beloved into the wilderness for speaking to her heart, Hos. ii. 14, he makes the wilderness and the solitary place glad, and the desert rejoice and blossom as the rose. To the charm of his society is added the beauty of the place in which it is enjoyed. The word *bed*, here expresses the place where, in a pastoral scene, the two friends may recline on the verdure, and share the pleasures of each other's company. We would read, Our couch or place of repose is spread with the verdure and flowers of spring; the roof, the ceiling of our summer-house or kiosk, our canopy, is cedar interspersed with fir, richly carved. As if it were said, The place where I rest and enjoy the society of this beloved friend, is invested with the freshness and richness of vernal beauty, amid green grass and blooming flowers. The same idea is expressed, in different words, in Ps. xxiii. 2, "He maketh me to lie down in green pastures;" and in Isa. xi. 10, "His rest, or place of rest, shall be glorious." And when the same prophet would show that the dwelling-place of God among men shall be adorned with the most attractive beauty, he says, "The glory of Lebanon shall come unto thee, the fir-tree, the pine-tree, and the box together, to beautify the place of my sanctuary; and I will make the place of my feet glorious." Chap. lx. 13. Into the oriental gardens, many of which were very extensive, the owner delighted to go with a few friends, and sitting down in some shady place, most commonly a small open structure or summer-house, elegantly made, there enjoy the cool shade, the refreshing breeze, the foliage of the groves, the fragrance of the flowers, and the golden luxuriousness of the ripening fruits, while the ear was pleased with the murmuring of the rills and the melodies of the nightingale. By such scenes as this, would the Holy Spirit represent that in our communion with Jesus we are surrounded with pleasantness and peace.* There are many barren tracts and wilds in our pilgrimage; but he who comforts Zion, "will make her wilderness like Eden, and her desert like the garden of the Lord; joy and gladness shall be found therein, thanksgiving and the voice of melody." Isa. li. 3. The curse cannot encroach on the spot where the Lamb slain reposes with his redeemed;† the earth, cursed for the disobedience of the first Adam, receives through the righteousness of the second Adam, a deliverance from the bondage of corruption; the first fruits of which we now feel clustering around us in hours of communion with Jesus. Like the early violets, the harbingers of spring, these incipient joys of holiness bespeak the vernal glories of heaven nigh. Heavenly pleasures can no more be separated from the presence of Jesus, than flowers can be separated from the spring.

* Plato says, "Love does not settle on any spot where flowers are not, or where they have fallen off; but wherever is a spot flowery and fragrant, there he settles and fixes his abode."

In the same spirit, Lucretius, speaking of Love, says,—

Thee flee the winds; the fleecy clouds of heaven
Thy coming flee; for thee th' embroidered earth
Pours fragrant flowers forth; before thee smiles
Old ocean boundless; and from tempests freed,
With radiant light suffused, heaven tranquil smiles.
De Rer. Nat. 1: 6.

† "When the conscience discovers the favourable sentence of God concerning man, and intimates the same to itself, and at the same time bears testimony of its unfeigned piety towards God, it spreads a surprising serenity and calm over the whole soul. Consequently, the peace of God necessarily brings with it peace of conscience, and much confidence in God. The soul nowhere reposes itself more comfortably, than in that bed of tranquillity, and in the bosom of Jesus, its loving, lovely spouse, singing at that time to its adversaries, 'Know that the Lord hath set apart him that is godly for himself. I will both lay me down in peace and sleep, for thou, Lord, only makest me dwell in safety.'"—*Witsius on Spiritual Peace, Cov.*, book iii. 9. 13.

He is to this blighted world, what spring is to the dreariness of winter, the resurrection and the life. Feeling already the first fruits of that better order of things when

> "The storms of wintry time will quickly pass.
> And one unbounded spring encircle all;"

we read in these earthly beauties, the patterns of things in the heavens; and with the eye of faith resting on the blessedness of the second Eden, exclaim with triumphant exultation,

> "Come, gentle spring! ethereal mildness! come;
> And from the bosom of yon dropping cloud
> Of balm of Paradise and heavenly dews,
> While music wakes around, veil'd in a shower
> Of shadowing roses, on our plains descend."

From the presence of Jesus, however manifested, nothing can be separated that is delightful. He makes all things work together for good. How sweet is our repose when we sit down with him in the hour of repentance, in times of refreshing, in seasons of prayer, amid his gracious providences, in the ordinances of the sanctuary. He makes even the valley of Baca a well; he sheds down divine blessings, as the rain that filleth the pools. Around his footsteps, around the place of his rest, the desert blossoms abundantly, and rejoices even with joy and singing. The heavenly host still attend him with more of glory and of melody than at his appearance on the plains of Bethlehem; and when we are thus with Jesus, "the angels with their silver wings, o'ershade the ground thus sacred by his presence made." They yet delight to praise God for every display of his good will to man; their music spreads around us a sea of harmonious undulations; so that

> "The place is full of noises,
> Sounds, and sweet airs, that give delight and hurt not;

> Sometimes a thousand instruments melodious
> Will murmur round our ears; and sometimes voices,
> That if we then had waked after long sleep,
> Will make us sleep again; and then in dreaming,
> The clouds will seem to open and show riches
> Ready to drop upon us."*

And though shut out from these airs by "this muddy vesture of decay," there are frequently effects produced on the soul, which force on us the impression that we are in the midst of such a chorus; and that these harmonies are quivering faintly through the flesh, and trilling in upon the heart. No couch of flowers, not even of Sharon's roses, can excite sensations of pleasantness at all equalling those felt by the soul thus reposing in the society of Jesus. All, all is peace, love, harmony; with the surrounding harmonies our disordered soul grows more in unison.

> "We lay the head
> In golden slumber on a bed
> Of heaped Elysian flowers, and hear
> Such strains as sweetly win the ear
> Of spirits from the flesh set free."†

"The beams of our house are cedar,‡ and our rafters of fir."§ Our place of repose, while thus beautiful, is

---

* Tempest, Act. 3, Scene 2.

† Milton's Allegro.

‡ "Hardly any kind of wood unites so many good qualities for building as the cedar: its wood not only pleases the eye by its reddish stripes, and exhales an agreeable smell, but it is hard and without knots, and is never eaten by worms, and lasts so long, that some persons consider it imperishable. Hence it was used for rafters and boards, either to cover the houses or floors."—*Burder.*

§ The Hebrew word here used, seems to be only the Aramæan pronunciation of the word which, in most passages where it occurs, is translated cypress in the old Greek and Syriac versions. "The wood of the cypress is hard, fragrant, and of a remarkably fine, close grain, very durable, and of a beautiful reddish hue, which Pliny says it never not open to the rays of the sun, nor to the rain, but is protected by a shelter, a roof with rafters of cedar, and a ceiling of fir or cypress, adorned with exquisite carved work.* These were materials used in the temple; in their nature rich and enduring. The ceilings of oriental houses, in the present day, as well as in the time of Solomon, are beautified with carvings and arabesques, with highly coloured paintings. According to Josephus, the roof of the temple was of cedar; and that part of the roof that was under the beams, was made of the same materials, and had ornaments proper for roofs; also the royal palace of Solomon was supported by fluted, quadrangular pillars of cedar, and adorned with sculptures, whereby were represented trees and all sorts of plants, with the shades that arose from their branches, and leaves that hung down from them; the leaves were

---

loses. According to this author, 'The statue of Jupiter in the Capitol, which was formed of cypress, had existed above six hundred years, without showing the least symptom of decay; and the doors of the temple of Diana at Ephesus, which were also of cypress, and were four hundred years old, had the appearance of being quite new.' This wood was used for a variety of purposes, as for wine-presses, rafters, and joists."—*Kitto's Cyclopedia*.

* "The ceiling was slightly arched, and clustered with stalactites of purple and gold, that appeared to have oozed out from some rich treasury above. The walls were of panelled cedar, or some such dark and fragrant wood, exquisitely carved; and curtains of Damascus silk were gathered into thick folds between pilasters of cedars, polished, yet rugged with rich carving."—*Warburton's Travels*. "The ceilings were divided into square compartments, painted with flowers, or with the figures of animals. Some were inlaid with ivory, each compartment being surrounded with elegant borders and mouldings. The beams, as well as the sides of the chambers, may have been gilded, or even plated with gold and silver; and the rarest woods, in which the cedar was conspicuous, were used for the wood work."—*Layard's Nineveh*, ii. 208. There are some beautiful "patterns from Egyptian ceilings," in Wilkinson, vol. ii. 125.

wrought so thin and subtle, that you would think them in motion. He made the whole building entirely of white stone, and cedar wood, and gold, and silver: he also adorned the roofs and walls with stones set in gold. The idea then seems to be, that the spouse was enjoying this pleasant society of the beloved, reclining on a bed of grass and vernal flowers, over which was spread the protection of a ceiling of durable materials and exquisite carving, and open on every side to the pleasing prospects and balmy airs. One emblem, or set of emblems, was not enough; the Holy Spirit, in a kind of anxiety to set forth our privileges, brings together whatever is most beautiful in nature and in art—beds of flowers, rural beauty, the shelter of a palace without the confinement of its walls. The true conception of happiness, as connected with our restoration from the curse, is that of being amid such scenes as those in Eden, and sheltered from the smiting of the sun by day, and of the moon by night. Ps. cxxi. 6. This protection is set forth as a cloud and smoke by day, and the shining of a flaming fire by night; as a shadow from the heat; as a shade; as a shadow of a great rock; as a covering of us with his wings; here, by the figure of a durable, beauteous, costly ceiling.

That protection is nothing less than the divine nature of Jesus Christ. Nothing can harm us beneath this heavenly shade. Evil, Satan, affliction, death, the chill dews of sin, cannot strike us there. Homer represents the god of the sun coming down gloomy as night, and by his arrows scattering death through the Grecian camp; from which protection was sought in vain: in the cloud lowering with wrath over our guilty world, the angel of death, the minister of divine justice, has his stand; but from his arrows of death, our pardoned spirits are more secure than she, who reposed with the beloved beneath this ceiling, was from the withering rays of the sun. As on the ceiling of ancient temples might sometimes be seen beautiful paintings, and in the roof of this summer-house was curious carving; so, in this overshadowing defence of the divine nature of Jesus, are all the excellences of the Godhead. The arch spread over us at midnight, with its stars, nebulæ, and constellations, does not present to the eye, assisted by the best telescope, anything comparable with the overshadowing divinity of Christ. While, like the roof, it is our shelter; like the evening sky, it sheds down dews on the thirsting soul, refreshing airs on the fainting heart, guiding light on the bewildered spirit; and reveals to our enraptured contemplation, transcendent and inexhaustible glories. As God inhabited a pillar of cloud and of fire, that was the protection of the camp of Israel, and did at the same time commune with them through the form of a man supposed to be seen between the cherubim; so, while the divine nature of Christ is our glorious covering, he in whom dwells all the fulness of the Godhead bodily, communes with us through the human nature of Jesus Christ. In the quaint language of Francis Quarles,

> "Hath thy all-glorious Deity no shade,
>   Where I may sit and vengeance never eye me?
> See, here's a shadow found: the human nature
>   Is made th' umbrella to the Deity.

This shelter can never decay: He is the same yesterday, to-day, and for ever. We may wander to the verge of creation, without being beyond the limit of this defence. The temples and palaces of earth are crumbling; its fortresses, even the tower of David, and the stronghold of Zion, are in ruins; the temple of Solomon, with its marbles, its cedars, and gold, is in the dust; but this spiritual covert of the soul, reared for us hard by the tree of life in the paradise of God, stands, and shall stand, through ages of ages, pure, fresh, and undecaying: and when the heavens shall have passed away with a great noise, and the earth, with all that is in it, be consumed, this refuge, the place of repose of the Beloved and his redeemed, shall be seen emerging from the ruins, towering on the Rock of Ages in imposing grandeur, and crowned with that cloud of glory which is the light of the upper world.

CHAPTER II.

Ver. 1.—I am the rose of Sharon, and the lily of the valleys.*

Reclining thus on a bed of grass and flowers, and beneath such a shade, with the beauties and odours of an oriental paradise spreading around, the beloved and the

---

* Patrick, Henry, and Scott, take this verse as the language of the beloved, and consequently the rose and lily as the emblems of Christ. We interpret these as the words of the spouse, for several reasons. 1. The scope of the passage requires this view; because the evident design is to put the spouse in contrast with the beloved, by comparison of the rose and lily with the majesty of the citron-tree. 2. The lily is in the next verse expressly applied to the spouse; and these two verses are parts of the same continuous sentence; so that it is unreasonable to apply the lily as the emblem of Jesus in the former clause, and then find it restricted to the saint in the latter. 3. The Jewish interpreters in general are of this opinion. 4. With us also agree the best Christian expositors, such as Rosenmüller, Delitzsch, Dopke, Cocceius, Michaelis, Vatablus, Ainsworth, Harmer, Percy, Fry, Good, &c.

The Septuagint and Vulgate render the Hebrew word "rose," by "flower;" and Sharon they translate, not as a proper name, but "a plain," making the words together mean "a flower of the field." Hence Bishop Percy reads, " I am a mere rose of the field." Kitto, however, bride naturally speak of each other in language drawn from the beautiful objects under their notice. The plain of Sharon was particularly rich in flowers. The orientals have ever been fond of images derived from the rose. The Great Mogul, in a letter to James I. of England, compliments him by comparing him to this flower. A modern eastern poet has the same thought, when speaking of Nischabur, the city in which he resided: he says, "I, like Atthar, that famous poet, came out of the garden of Nischabur; but Atthar was the rose of that garden, and I am only a bramble." Pliny reckons the lily the next plant in excellence to the rose. In the East, as with us, it is the emblem of purity and moral excellence. So the Persian poet Sadi compares an amiable youth to "the white lily in a bed of narcissuses;" because he surpassed all the young shepherds in piety, goodness, and vigilance. The spouse is evidently speaking of herself in a modest, humble manner; and the emblems of the rose and lily do, therefore, illustrate the Christian character as possessing a beauty in which delicacy, lowliness, and purity, are leading characteristics.

Nothing could be more delicate than the texture, hues,

---

truly remarks, "There can be little doubt that the rose is really intended by the Hebrew word. Even if in the general sense it should mean but a flower, we should still infer that when applied in a particular sense, it means a rose; for this would be according to the usage of the East. Thus the Persian word *gul* describes a flower in general, and the rose *par excellence;* and the Arabic term *ward* is employed in the same acceptations." In the East, still more than with us, the rose is the queen of flowers. In May, the hills towards Rama and Joppa, as going from Jerusalem, were found covered with pink and white roses; the gardens of Rama were filled with roses of a powerful fragrance. Mariti states that in the hamlet of St. John, in the desert of that name, "the rose-plants form small forests in the gardens." Burckhardt was struck with the number of rose-trees he found among the ruins of Bozra, beyond the Jordan.

and fragrance of the rose and lily. When even Sharon's vale was filled with such beauteous flowers, so soon to fade and wither under the wintry frosts of the curse, shall the same creative power form with less delicacy those souls which are to flourish in the freshness of immortality, as the spiritual roses and lilies by the river of life, in the heavenly paradise? Piety refines our whole nature. It is a cleansing from the coarseness and defilement of sin. It purifies the heart, the motives, the views, the aspirations, the soul; and so completely does it bring the body into subjection to this spiritual purity, that we are at last invested with a corporeal frame so pure that its nature can be expressed only by calling it a spiritual body. This purity sheds through all our powers, and all our actions, an increasing and delightful delicacy of sentiment, thought, and feeling. The import of the word "reverence," in Heb. xii. 28, is the spiritual modesty, the delicate sensibility, diffused through the soul, by the pervading influence of the Holy Spirit, which brings spontaneously a blush over the heart, at the very appearance, or mention, or thought of sin, without our taking time to think of the consequences of the act, or its hatefulness in the sight of God. Coarseness of feeling, as well as of language and of action, is the offspring of the impurity of sin, and must disappear under the purifying energy of divine grace. The human eye, which is the bodily organ attempered to the various degrees and shades of light, the most subtile form of matter known to us, is the most delicate of the faculties of sense, and would be unfitted for its office, were it less exquisite in its texture; but the splendour of the stars, the grandeur of the sun, the tints of the rainbow, are merely representations of the excellence of him who points to light as the best emblem of his spiritual purity; and as the pure in heart shall see God, not through the drapery thrown around him when he clothes himself with light as with a garment, but in his unveiled glory; who can tell the delicate sensibility requisite in a soul for beholding such visions; for thus contemplating the beauty of holiness; a sensibility which the Holy Ghost is now diffusing through the whole fabric of our being by sanctification, as the preparation for our dwelling evermore under the shadow of the Almighty, and enjoying the unutterable beauties there unfolding to the view.

Like Jesus, whose yoke we bear, the believer finds rest for his soul in meekness and lowliness of heart.* Love is not more certainly the distinguishing virtue of the pious character, than is humility its vital grace. Love being the fruit which holiness bears in the heart, humility is the root by which it is nourished. When the righteous flourish like the palm-tree and grow like a cedar in Lebanon; when he grows as the lily and casts forth his roots as Lebanon; when his branches spread and his beauty is as the olive-tree; then is humility the root which spreading beneath, as the branches develope above, supplies life and nourishment to all the graces of godliness. Our piety may ever be judged by our humility. When Jesus would cause holiness to grow, he places us in situations where humility may expand. The rose and the lily could hardly be expected to grow with vigour, or, if growing at all, to put forth the fulness of their beauty, in a public

---

* "The soul of a true Christian, as I then wrote my meditations, appeared like such a little white flower as we see in the spring of the year; low and humble on the ground, opening its bosom to receive the pleasant beams of the sun's glory; rejoicing, as it were, in a calm rapture; diffusing around a sweet fragrancy; standing peacefully and lovingly, in the midst of other flowers round about; all in like manner opening their bosoms to drink in the light of the sun."—*Edwards's Works*, vol. i. p. 21.

thoroughfare, the streets of a city, or the halls of fashionable life: in secluded retreats of the country, in lowly meadows, they find a genial soil. In scenes withdrawn from the world and depressed, unthronged with the crowds who seek and bestow the honours coming from man, scenes kindred in lowliness to those so loved by him who was meek and lowly in heart, does the Lord of the vineyard place those whose holiness he would have to blossom as the rose; whom he would have to spread out their root by the water, and the dew to lie all night on their branch.

> "He sprang from a stock of lowly parentage
> Among the wilds of Scotland, in a tract
> Where many a sheltered and well-tended plant
> Bears, on the humblest ground of social life,
> Blossoms of piety and innocence."*

Before honour is humility. When God is about to exalt to honour or usefulness one on whom his love is placed, he prepares him therefor by humiliation; and when the blessings of the Holy Spirit are poured on the soul in an unusual degree, we find the way was prepared for them by humility, and by humility are they attended. The richest crowns are beautified with gems, gathered in untrodden regions; the freshest chaplets are woven of flowers bathed in the dews of secluded meadows:

> "Like virtue, thriving most where little seen."

So calm is the prospect, so bracing the airs of the valley of Humiliation; the believer says with Mercy, "The place, methinks, suits with my spirit. I love to be in such places, where there is no rattling with coaches, nor rumbling with wheels: methinks, here one may, without

---

* Wordsworth's Excursion, book ii.

much molestation, be thinking what he is, whence he came, what he has done, and to what the King has called him: here one may think, and break at heart, and melt in one's spirit, until one's eyes become as the fish-pools of Heshbon. Behold how green this valley is; also how beautiful with lilies."

Like the lily of the valleys, the pious soul is invested with a loveliness combining purity with delicacy and lowliness.

> "Our thoughts
> Pleasant as roses in the thickets blown,
> And pure as dew bathing their crimson leaves."*

Purity and holiness are inseparable. Perhaps we may say holiness is immaterial purity, the moral spotlessness of spiritual beings. Holiness works purity; sin works corruption. Taking the sinner in the midst of his pollution, with a body tending to corruption, because the dwelling-place of a soul under the dominion of guilt, the Holy Spirit unfolds by degrees that newness of life which swells at last into the perfect holiness and dazzling glory of both body and soul in heaven. A person who might possibly be unacquainted with the growth of plants, would hardly believe that the unsightly root of a lily, or even the stalk in its greenness, could be developed into so rich and fragrant a flower. The same Almighty energy whose Spirit causes the seed or root to grow amid earth and corruption itself, into the flower no less pure and beautiful than the lily or the rose, is even now carrying forward, amid our corruption of soul and body, a growth of holiness which shall ripen into the purity and beauty of heaven. Like the flower of the lily full-blown, perfect sanctification, with a spiritual body, is the consummation of our redemption. The lilies that shall

---

* Wordsworth's Excursion, book ii.

adorn the meadows amid which winds the pure river of water of life, are the souls of an innumerable multitude "without spot or wrinkle, or any such thing," who have washed their robes and made them white in the blood of the Lamb. When the Holy Spirit first dawns on the heart at the new birth, we are surprised at the degree of our impurity. Often will it seem as though our prayers and struggles against the tide of impure thoughts and desires were in vain; yet, "shall we know, if we follow on to know the Lord; his going forth is prepared as the morning." Over the soul thus clouded with darkness and sin, the day shall break, and the shadows flee away. By nature, in a state of darkness, like that of the night laden with chilling mists and noxious vapours, the soul receives the influences of the Holy Spirit, at first faint and gradual, as the early dawn: like the morning light which goes on and shines not only to sunrise, but to high noon; (more literally, the fixed part of the day, when the sun seems to stand immovable in the zenith;) and then, every vapour sunk, every cloud vanished away, lights up all the atmosphere with purity, and rains down brilliancy on earth and heaven; the faint streaks of light and holiness shooting over the darkened soul in the new birth, go on increasing to the brightness of mid-day splendour in heaven, where all will be purity and glory, as the Sun of Righteousness from the zenith showers on the heart his soft, enlivening rays.

VER. 2.—As a lily among the thorns, so is my love among the daughters.

While combining these excellences, the disposition of the believer is very different from that of the world. As the lily among thorns, so is the believer, during his probation, "among them that are set on fire, even the sons of men, whose teeth are spears and arrows, and their tongue a sharp sword." Ps. lvii. 4. The wind bloweth where it listeth, and bears on its bosom seeds scattered at random, and springing up unnoticed in desolate places; even as the Holy Spirit, according to his sovereign will, causes the seed of the word to take root in souls scattered far and wide among the nations, to grow here, as in their nursery, until fit for transplanting to heaven. The saint must expect to find himself, while in this world, among uncongenial and hostile spirits. Holiness, however perfected, will not alter this state of things. Spotless though he may be, as the lily, he is yet the lily among thorns. Through his first disciples, the Lord Jesus said to his servants in all ages, "Behold, I send you forth as sheep in the midst of wolves." Matt. x. 16. Still is the carnal mind enmity against God, and against the sons of God; still the wicked watcheth the righteous, and seeketh to slay him. Our position is surrounded with those whose evil passions, pride, haughtiness, envy, malice, avarice, sensuality, vindictiveness, bristling from their hearts on every side, make it difficult for us to move without encountering something keener than thorns or drawn swords, by which deep and excruciating wounds are inflicted on the delicate sensibility of the heavenward spirit. We cannot move through the world without feeling more or less of these lacerations. Because of the voice of the enemy, because of the oppression of the wicked, how often does the bleeding heart feel, " O that I had wings like a dove, for then would I fly away and be at rest." As much care is necessary in dealing with the wicked, as in handling a thorn bush; yet will those who use the greatest prudence, frequently find themselves wounded. With the best wishes, offences cannot be always avoided: "As far as in you lies, live peaceably with all men." Those whose souls are brought by grace nearest to the delicacy of holiness set forth by the lily, and who move with most of steady, undeviating Christian energy through the world, are made to feel most sensibly that the believer is here a lily among thorns. Even in Christian countries, the hearts of the wicked are armed with as fierce passions against piety and the pious, as at any former age; and though they may be kept out of view by the civilities of life, change of circumstances often brings us in contact with them where we had hoped they did not exist. Accordingly, our Lord warns us that in becoming his disciples, we must take up the cross, must prepare for suffering. Ignorant of the true state of things here, we expect too much of the world, and thereby injure our peace. Deceived in men thought worthy of confidence, and finding those who are under the greatest debt of gratitude treating us with persecution the most bitter, we would not think our lot singular and hard, did we feel that ingratitude is an inseparable feature of sin, and that as Jesus was a man of sorrows, the disciple cannot be above his Lord. As we are liable to do even good deeds from improper motives, God has kindly placed us in a world where we are thus repelled in our disinterested acts; and are laid under the necessity of doing good and following after holiness, not from any recompense likely to be got from men, but from principle, from love to God. And the believer who examines carefully his infirmities, and the peculiar discomforts and afflictions meeting him, will most probably find that these ills are just what was necessary for counteracting his besetting sins, for weakening his propensities which are unduly strong, and for strengthening those which are disproportionately weak; so that his life, however checkered and painful, may constitute a course of discipline most wisely adapted for bringing his soul into the perfect balancing of all its powers, which is perfect holiness. Hence, one course of life, one series of sorrows, which may be the best possible for the chastisement and discipline of a heart with one class of infirmities, would not be at all applicable to the spiritual wants of another with failings very different. One man on whom God has set his love, may be of such a disposition that riches would ruin him; and it is necessary for his preparation for heaven that these be denied him, and he be tried with something of a different kind. Another may be so constituted that praise would foster vanity and pride; and he can be kept humble most safely by being depreciated and maligned; while another may pass through the fiery ordeal of worldly applause with less danger of injury. Hence those who are called to greatest holiness are called to greatest mortifications; and the apostle exhorts his son Timothy no less than ten or twelve times in his second Epistle, to bear with evil, to endure hardness. Too often, alas, is this hardness to be borne from brethren from whose hearts the remains of sin have not been removed by grace. Well did Luther say, "If thou art the lily and the rose of Christ, know that thy dwelling-place is among thorns. Only take heed lest by impatience, rash judgments, and pride, thou thyself become a thorn."

VER. 3.—As the apple-tree among the trees of the wood, so is my beloved among the sons. I sat down under his shadow with great delight, and his fruit was sweet to my taste.

Having given in the two foregoing verses the character of the believer as represented by the rose and the lily, the Song sets forth in these words the charms of him, who is the object of the believer's love. These illustrations, the rose, the lily, and the apple-tree, are such as would naturally fall under the view of persons reposing on a bed of flowers in an oriental garden, as seen in chap. i. 16. Comparisons drawn from the tree are not unfrequently applied to Jesus in the Scriptures. Isaiah says, "There shall come forth a shoot from the stem of Jesse, and a branch shall grow out of his roots; and the Spirit of the Lord shall rest upon him." The promised Messiah was called the Branch, for showing that like a shoot or twig springing from the stump of a tree, he should spring from the stock of Judah, through the family of Jesse. The two natures of the Lord Jesus are here pointed out —his coming forth as a branch, representing him to be the Son of man, while the Spirit of the Lord resting on him shows him to be the Son of God. He is here represented under the figure of that shoot or branch full grown, of a tree. The citron-tree seems to be the one here intended. The name is derived from the fragrance it exhales. The foliage is perpetual; there is no time, not even mid-winter, when there may not be seen on it a profusion of flowers; there is throughout the year a continual succession of blossoms, young fruit, and ripe fruit, at the same time; the fruit was of the colour of gold, very pleasant to the taste, very fragrant, and and reviving to those who were ready to faint; the leaves are studded with small glands, to which the tree owes its rich fragrance. The shade of this tree is deep and refreshing.* Maun-

* Shade is an article of oriental luxury. "In this fairy-like garden, there were very few flowers; but shade and greenery are everything in this glaring climate; and it was passing pleasant to stroll along these paths, all shadowy with orange-trees, whose fruit, 'like lamps in a night of green,' hung temptingly over our heads. The fragrance of large beds of roses mingled with that of the orange-flower, and seemed to repose on the quiet airs of the calm evening. In the midst of the garden we came to a vast pavilion, glittering like porcelain, and supported on light pillars, which formed cloisters surrounding an immense

drell speaks of the very great beauty of the orange garden or citron grove, at Beroot, attached to the emir's palace. The walks were shaded with orange-trees of a large spreading size, and all of so fine a growth that nothing could be imagined more perfect, and "gilded with fruit hanging thick upon them. Around were booths, and summer-houses, and other apartments, very delightful." The difference between citron and orange-trees is hardly discernible except by the fruit, which in both is of the same golden colour. Such a tree, therefore, as the citron, standing among the trees of the forest, must be an object of pre-eminent beauty and strong attraction. Thus is Jesus distinguished "among the sons." Him hath God anointed with the oil of gladness above his fellows, Heb. i. 9; that is, through the Holy Spirit given without measure to Christ, God has conferred on him a nature more excellent than that of his fellows, those associated with him in the work of redemption, whether angels, or prophets, or saints. As the citron-tree stood in an atmos-

---

marble basin, in the centre of which sparkling waters gushed from a picturesque fountain. Through the clear depths of the waters gleamed shoals of gold and silver fish."—*Warburton*. "That variety of fragrant lemon called the 'citron,' attains its highest perfection in Palestine, and is very abundant; and by the consent of the Jewish writers themselves, as well as from the probability of the case, we apprehend that 'citron' is always to be understood by the word translated 'apple' in the common version. That the citron was well known to the Hebrews, we learn from Josephus, who mentions that on one occasion, at the feast of tabernacles, King Alexander Jannaeus was pelted in the temple with citrons, which the Jews had in their hands—for which he assigns the reason, that the law required that at that feast every one should have bunches of the palm-tree and the citron-tree. The fruit of the citron-tree is much used by the oriental ladies to smell to, for which purpose, they often have it in their hands, or within reach, and, as its fragrance is considered most reviving, it is employed for much the same purpose as a scent-bottle in this country."—*Kitto*.

20*

phere of perfume rising in continual freshness from its perennial bloom, the human nature of Jesus dwells in the midst of the spiritual fragrance breathing in his divine nature, and encompassing him for evermore on every side in the infinity of the fulness of the Godhead. Modern poetry has adopted the spirit of this illustration:

> "The mountain ash,
> No eye can yet overlook, when 'mid a grove
> Of yet unfaded trees she lifts her head
> Deck'd with autumnal berries, that outshine
> Spring's richest blossoms; and ye may have marked
> By a brook side or solitary tarn,
> How she her station doth adorn. The pool
> Glows at her feet, and all the gloomy rocks
> Are brightened round her. In his native vale,
> Such and so glorious did this youth appear;
> A sight that kindled pleasure in all hearts
> By his ingenuous beauty."*

And the meaning of the passage has been well expressed in the words,

> "From Jesse's root behold a branch arise,
> Whose sacred flower with fragrance fills the skies;
> The ethereal spirit o'er its leaves shall move,
> And on its top descends the mystic Dove."†

While the pious spirit is lowly, though beautiful like the lily, with the beauty and majesty of the citron-tree, Jesus towers above all others, in the infinite grandeur of his

---

* Wordsworth's Excursion, book vii.
† Pope's Messiah. Thus Homer,
> "So falls a poplar, that in watery ground
> Raised high the head with stately branches crowned;
> Cut down it lies, tall, smooth, and largely spread,
> With all its beauteous honours on its head;
> There left a subject to the wind and rain,
> And scorched by suns, it withers on the plain.
> Thus pierced by Ajax, Simoisius lies."
>
> *Iliad*, iv. 482, and xiv. 414.

divinity, as the Son of God. The crown of glory and honour resting on him who was made a little lower than the angels, is the glorious crown of his eternal divinity.

He is the shade of his people. The Lord is thy shade on thy right hand. A shade does not deprive of the light of the sun. It so breaks and tempers the force of the beams as to keep them from injuring us, and enables us to enjoy their brilliancy and warmth. Nothing does this more pleasingly than the stately spreading boughs of the citron-tree. What this shade did for the body, the Lord Jesus does for the soul. Exposed to the full blaze of the justice of him who is a consuming fire, we must be blasted and destroyed, did not Christ spread between us and him whose jealousy burns like fire, that which Israel's covering of cloud represented in the desert, his own divine nature. When the soul feels the agonies of conviction for sin, how sensible is the change, how reviving the shelter, as we pass under the shadow of the cross, and feel around us the refreshing influences of the righteousness of Christ. Within that sacred shelter, no evil spirit can enter, no affliction injure, no fiery dart fall.

The apple-tree yielded a profusion of the richest fruits in uninterrupted abundance. Its fruit was highly esteemed as sweet to the taste, of refreshing fragrance, and of the colour of gold. A word fitly spoken is compared to apples of gold, or the golden coloured fruit of the citron, in baskets of silver. Prov. xxv. 11. With richer fruits than these, does Jesus satisfy the soul that rests under his shadow. He is a tree of life to them that lay hold on him. Prov. iii. 18. He alone can satisfy the cravings of the heart. All attempts to pacify these restless desires, these surges of conscience, by any amount of property, or things of the world, is as unreasonable as to try to quiet the billows of the tempestuous sea, by pouring into its remorseless caverns treasures and gems. From the presence of him whose power was felt on the sea of Galilee, goes forth the influence which carries to the depths of the soul a great calm. Peace he gives unto us, that he may give unto us to eat of the tree of life, which is in the midst of the Paradise of God. This elder brother, a greater than Joseph, who has gone before us into heaven to preserve life, is a fruitful bough, even a fruitful bough by a well, whose branches run over the wall, separating us from the invisible world; and sweet indeed must be the fruits gathered therefrom, when their native soil is heaven, and they are the same which shall throughout eternity satisfy the redeemed.

The weary pilgrim, on coming to the citron-tree, would be delighted with the majesty of its appearance, the protection of its shade, the richness of its fragrance, and the delightfulness of its fruit.* As we come to Jesus, careworn with guilt and sorrow, he impresses us with the grandeur of his divinity, the excellence of his protecting righteousness, the blessedness shed around us by his Spirit, and the richness of the fruits of holiness found in the Scriptures, in the earnest of the Spirit in the practice of a heavenly temper, and in the anticipation of future glory in heaven. Here are richer than the golden fruits of the Hesperides; and this Angel of the covenant has destroyed the dragon that guarded them, that old

---

* "At the foot of each tree is a little circular carpet of verdure."—*Warburton.* "There is something peculiarly delightful in the shade of the fig-tree. It is far superior to the shelter of a tent, and perhaps even to the shadow of a rock; since not only does the mass of heavy foliage completely exclude the rays of the sun, but the traveller finds under it a peculiar coolness, arising from the air gently creeping through the branches."—*Mission of Inquiry,* p. 108.

serpent, which is the devil and Satan. In this shadow does the soul delight; here would we sit down in the fulness of joy, with the feeling, "This is my rest for ever, here will I dwell, for I have desired it;" here does God abundantly bless our provision and satisfy the poor with bread; here does he clothe his priests with salvation and his saints shout aloud for joy. Ps. cxxxii. 14.

The cool shadow of this lofty, beautiful, and fragrant tree, offered an asylum into which the spouse might well delight to retreat from the oppressive heat of noon. The exquisite perfume, the cooling shade, the beauty of the flowers, and the richness of the fruit, combined to make it a retreat the most delightful. In Jesus, the tree of life, we find the fragrance of the Holy Spirit, the shade of his divine righteousness, the beauties of his nature budding forth in infinite variety, and the precious fruits of his grace and truth—all uniting to render his shadow desirable and delightful. Hence do we sit down under his shadow with great pleasure: "In this shade I desire to sit down." While the desire of the worldling is towards the enjoyments spread around by riches, or fame, or flattery, or ease, looking unto Jesus, we say, "The desire of our soul is to thy name, and to the remembrance of thee." Isa. xxvi. 8. An intelligent traveller in the East could find no other refuge from the heat of summer than a recess cut into the bank of the river where it rose perpendicularly from the water's edge, and formed into a small room by screening the front with reeds and boughs of trees, and covering the whole with similar materials: such places, though infested with reptiles, were the best retreat that could be found.* In what contrast with this stands the shelter afforded by the citron-tree. More uncomfortable and miserable than the former, is the refuge found

---

* Layard's Nineveh, vol. i. 116.

by those who have their portion in this world; infinitely more delightful than the latter, is the sanctuary found by those whose resting-place is under the shadow of Christ. Around this place of repose the richest fruits continually fall. As entertainments under trees are common in the East, the soul that abides under the shadow of the Almighty Redeemer, feeds on those pleasant words which are as an honey-comb, sweet to the soul and health to the bones. Prov. xvi. 24. These truths do now excite in the depths of the soul sensations as delightful as those which shall be felt in heaven from eating the fruit of the tree of life.

VER. 4.—He brought me to the banqueting-house, and his banner over me was love.

Finding the spouse under the apple-tree, ch. viii. 5, he leads her to the banqueting-house, the house of wine, a place beautified with every ornament, and stored with everything refreshing and delightful. Among the apartments of his palace, Solomon built, according to Josephus, "a most glorious dining-room, for feastings and compotations, and full of gold and such other furniture as so fine a room ought to have for the conveniency of the guests; and where all the vessels were made of gold."* To this hall reference seems to be made, rather than to the places where their wine was stored. No pains were spared to

---

* Speaking of Solomon's palace, Josephus says: "It would be an endless task to give a particular survey of this mighty mass of building; so many courts and other contrivances; such a variety of chambers and offices, great and small; long and large galleries; vast rooms of state, and others for feasting and entertainment, set out as richly as could be with costly furniture and gildings; besides, that all the service for the king's table were of pure gold. In a word, the whole palace was, in a manner, made up, from the base to the coping, of white marble, cedar, gold, and silver, with precious stones here and there intermingled upon the walls and ceilings."—*Antiq.* viii. 5, 2.

make such rooms the splendid possible, as may be still seen in oriental palaces. In a hall of the Alhambra, "the eye is lost in contemplating the rich assemblage of ornaments which appear in every part of this noble hall. From the pavement to the beginning of the arches the walls are decorated with elegant mosaic; the panels between the arches are filled with a very delicate ornament, which, at a little distance, has the appearance of a plain mass; and the ceiling is composed of stalactites in stucco, and is finished in a style of equal elegance. The distribution of the various parts of this noble apartment is truly enchanting. The balconies above were occupied by musicians; below sat the women; while a jet of water in the centre diffused a refreshing coolness through the hall. The windows in the background are finished in a similar manner, and look into a little myrtle garden." Something like this must have been witnessed when the Queen of Sheba saw all Solomon's wisdom, and the house that he had built, and the meat of his table, and the sitting of his servants, and the attendance of his ministers, and their apparel, and his cup-bearers, and his ascent by which he went up into the house of the Lord; and there was no more spirit in her. Far more glorious is the place into which Jesus brings our souls, on that mountain where he has made unto all people a feast of fat things full of marrow, of wines on the lees well refined. Isa. xxv. 6. Here, our dwelling-place is amid walls formed of divine goodness, Ps. xxv. 13; our light is the Shechinah of the Spirit's presence; our food is the hidden manna; our cup salvation; our drink the new wine of the heavenly kingdom; our anointing the oil of gladness; our ministering attendants angels; and the banner over us is love.

Nothing can be so excellent as the influences of the Holy Spirit. How excellent the fragrance of the citron bloom, the effect of wine! no comparison can be drawn between these and the ethereal excellence of the Holy Ghost. When we feed on anything, it is so brought into contact with us as to nourish our life; and when the Spirit's influences are so diffused through the soul as to sustain its life, we may be said to feed on his grace. Hence it is written, "Man shall not live by bread alone, but by every word that proceedeth out of the mouth of God." Matt. iv. 4. There is literally such a thing as feeding on truth; and the place where these spiritual provisions are enjoyed in abundance, may well be called the banqueting house. How superior to every thing else in the world, is the banquet spread for us by Jesus! The truths and doctrines of Scripture, so rich, better than thousands of gold and silver, are the means, sacred vessels brought from heaven, for conveying to us this food of the Spirit. Here we banquet on the riches of redeeming love. The man who feeds on fame, flattery, riches, power, has nothing better than the husks of the dying prodigal; while those who are Christ's, share the luxuries of the marriage-supper of the Lamb.

"His banner over me was love." He brings us to this feast, with the exultation of a conqueror returning in triumph with a loved one wrested from the power of an enemy. Jesus is called the Captain of our salvation, Heb. ii. 10, a name which is applied in the New Testament to none but Christ, and signifies a chief or commander, one who leads a column and directs its movements. When Abraham heard that his brother was taken captive, he armed his trained servants, and pursued the enemy, smote them, and brought back Lot, and his goods, and the people: thus has Jesus come to our rescue, and delivered us from bondage to the powers of darkness. He is still "Captain of the host of the Lord," as when he appeared to Joshua before Jericho; and is leading the spiritual host, who, from a period earlier than that of Abraham, have been pressing onward towards the Canaan on high. The banner of this conqueror and king of glory has its inscription and symbol. Unlike the military nations of the world, whose lust has been for war, and whose emblems have been expressive of their character, as the eagle on the standards of Rome, he, as the Prince of Peace, has the dove as the symbol of his kingdom; and has a banner woven of the precious fabric of love. When combatants raise a red flag, it is for showing a determination to shed blood; the black flag is the signal that no quarter may be expected; a white banner bespeaks the desire for peace. With what propriety therefore is the banner of Jesus said to be love.

A banner rallies to the defence of the person over whom it floats, all the resources of the empire to which it belongs: wherever he wanders, this simple symbol calls up around him bulwarks invisible, but mighty with an empire's strength. Thus, under all circumstances in life, and in death, the love of Christ enlists all the perfections of the Godhead in behalf of his saint. As the flag shows to what country we belong, so by love we are shown to be citizens of heaven. As the banner of his country is an object of honourable pride to the good citizen, thus while the wise man glories in his wisdom, and the rich man in his riches, and the brave man in his valour, the saint glories only in the cross of Christ, and in possessing thereby the divine love. Poetry has delighted to portray the affection of the soldier for the flag of his country; and true to the feelings of human nature, is the dying patriot said to look upwards to its folds,

"And smile to see its splendours fly,
In triumph o'er his closing eye."

When he who has fought the good fight, and endured hardness as a good soldier of Jesus Christ, finds the dimness of death on his eye, and its coldness on his heart, how will his spirit revive on seeing over him this banner of love! And as a dying patriot requested that the flag under which he had fought and conquered might be placed under his head for a pillow, as life was ebbing away; then, with our sinking head pillowed on the divine love, while over us floats the banner of love, as paleness comes over the lips, and dimness over the eye, and coldness over the heart, shall the last beat of the heart send up to heaven the shout—Victory through Jesus Christ.

VER. 5, 6.—Stay me with flagons,* comfort me with apples: for I am sick of love. His left hand is under my head, and his right hand doth embrace me.

In these words the spouse expresses the impression made on her by the display of love in the banqueting house—"I am sick of love." From the beginning of the Song, we have had illustrations of the soul as led along from one degree to another of holy love, till reach-

---

* In Kitto's Cyc. Bib. Lit., art. *Wine*, 10, there is a dissertation on the Hebrew word here rendered "flagons." From it we extract the following, found in Olearius: "The Persians are permitted to make a sirrup of sweet wine, which they boyl till it be reduced to a sixth part, and be grown as thick as oyl. They call this drug *duschab*, and when they would take of it, they dissolve it with water. Sometimes they boyl the duschab so long that they reduce it into a paste, for the convenience of travellers, who cut it with a knife, and dissolve it in water. At Tabris they make a certain conserve of it, which they call *helwa*, mixing therewith beaten almonds, flour, &c. They put this mixture into a long and narrow bag, and having set it under the press, they make of it a paste, which grows so hard that a man must have a hatchet to cut it." This statement reconciles the version in the text with that which is preferred b· those who render the word "cakes—such as were prepared from dried grapes or raisins, pressed or compacted into a certain form."

ing here the highest degree of spiritual enjoyment possible in the present world. The Holy Spirit may so fill the heart with his influences as to make us literally "sick of love;" purifying our power of apprehension, and exciting irrepressible desires for seeing more of our Lord. As hope deferred maketh the heart sick, these longing desires run ahead of our enjoyment, and, indeed, of our capability of enjoying Jesus; and these desires, thus unsatisfied, make us sick of love. This state of heart is caused by ardour of affection, and inability to enjoy the society of the object of affection fully as we desire; by longings, sometimes so deep as to be expressed only in groanings that cannot be uttered, to behold Jesus in the fulness of his glory. With Moses, we pray without ceasing, "I beseech thee, show me thy glory." "There be some kind of assurances," says Leighton,* "that are more rare and extraordinary, some immediate glances or coruscations of the love of God upon the soul of a believer, a smile of his countenance, and this doth exceedingly refresh, yea, ravish the soul, and enables it mightily for duties and sufferings." This was the experience of Bunyan's Pilgrim, when towards the end of his course, "by reason of the natural glory of the city, and the reflection of the sunbeams upon it, Christian with desire fell sick." Rutherford's Letters abound in expressions of this state of heart. In the words of John Howe, "There will be a sickness at the heart by the delay of what I hope for, most of all, when the sum of my blessedness is the thing hoped for, and still deferred. They that never felt their hearts sick with the desire of heaven, and the blessedness of that state, cannot conceive of it a tree of life beforehand, nor ever know what

---

* Sermon on Rom. viii. 35.

patience in expecting it signifies in the meantime.* Even yet there are souls thus exercised, that are constrained to pray with an ancient saint, "Lord, withdraw a little, lest the brittle vial of my heart should burst by the rays of thy favour darting too strongly."

> "Then shall thy ravisht soul inspired bee
> With heavenly thoughts farre above humane skil;
> And thy bright radiant eyes shall planely see
> Th' idee of his pure glorie present still
> Before thy face; that all thy spirits shall fill
> With sweete enragement of celestiall love,
> Kindled through sight of those faire things above."†

In this state the predominating feeling of the soul is deep and melting contrition.‡ It is with the contrite

---

* Sermon on Heb. x. 36. An eminent divine now in glory, than whom no man understood theology better, either in a didactic or practical point of view, once remarked to us, in a conversation on this subject, that there were probably more of these exercises among scattered members of the Church, than was generally supposed. There can be no doubt this is the case. Nor are such instances as that recorded of Dr. Green confined always to the closing scene. "On the Sabbath but one before his death, after the family had returned from the morning service, it was observed on entering his room that his mind was burdened with meditations to which he wished to give utterance, and that his emotions were producing a restlessness and agitation that were inexplicable. The reading, by a friend, of the first chapter of the Gospel of John, not only allayed that distressing nervous excitement, but seemed to impart a sort of inspiration, by which his faculties were for the time emancipated: his tongue was loosed, and he burst out into an ecstasy of joy and thanksgiving. His voice was loud, his enunciation clear and distinct as it had been in the best days of his ministry; and this elevated strain of praise and holy exultation was continued until his strength was exhausted, and he sunk into a sweet and refreshing sleep."—*Dr. Jones's Life of Dr. Green*, p. 498.

† Spenser's Hymn of Heavenly Love.

‡ My gloom was very often relieved greatly by the highest exercises of a spiritual kind that I have ever experienced. I was made to feel that I could not command them at my own pleasure, and that Satanic influence could not account for their occurrence, without

and humble spirit that the high and lofty One that inhabiteth eternity dwells. The more intimately he dwells with us, the deeper will be our contrition. Like a blinded eye, the soul is insensible to the splendour of the divine glory and love shining around us with such brilliancy, until the touch of him who healed Bartimeus restores our spiritual sensibility; then the glory of the love of God is the light; and the sensations of the heart thus made pure, and acted on by these heavenly rays, are emotions of contrition and love. The happiest hours on earth, are those in which our contrition is deepest and most tender. In this exercise, there is a commingling in the heart of the two pellucid streams of humility and love: the nearer we come to heaven, the deeper, purer, and more tranquil is their flow. Our luxury is to prostrate ourselves at the mercy-seat, and there weep for sin; weep, not the tears that find vent when bemoaning some crushing sin, but the tears that well forth in the soul, dissolving in contrition when the Holy Spirit is within the heart as a fountain of water springing up into everlasting life. At such hours, we wish to do what was once done by a contrite heart, pour out before the blessed Saviour the precious perfume of the affections from the alabaster of a broken spirit; and as we lie prostrate before him, weeping, kiss those feet

making Satan hostile to his own interests; for their invariable effect was to humble to the very dust, and to exalt the Redeemer, and to fill my mind with love to God and man, in an eminent degree, and a desire to do all in my power to advance the interests of vital piety."— *Life of Dr. Green*, p. 302.

"Assurance of the love of God never produces self-complacency or pride; but always humility, self abasement, wonder, gratitude, and praise. The believer sees that the mysterious fountain of this love is in the divine mind; it is not in himself, who is ungodly and a sinner."—*Hodge on Romans*, v. 8—10.

which have been wounded for us, and bathe them with our tears. The sense of God's amazing goodness, of his tenderness to such unworthiness as ours, this it is that overcomes us, and makes us weep. We are thus sweetly subdued, because we are able in a clearer manner to "behold what manner of love the Father has bestowed upon us, that we should be called the sons of God." The predominating feeling is, "I am not worthy of the least of all the mercies, and of all the truth, which thou hast showed unto thy servant." We sink down in overpowering humility, because overcome with melting love. No wild or boisterous feeling, no nervous enthusiasm, no burst of passion, then disturbs the soul. All, all is perfect peace. Such were the exercises of Mrs. Graham, when on the borders of heaven, a few hours before her death, bathed in tears, she said: "I have no more doubt of going to my Saviour, than if I were already in his arms; my guilt is all transferred; he has cancelled all I owed. Yet I could weep for sins against so good a God: it seems to me as if there must be weeping even in heaven for sin." At a time of the deepest pious exercises, Edwards says: "There was no part of creature holiness, that I had so great a sense of its loveliness, as humility, brokenness of heart, and poverty of spirit; and there was nothing that I so earnestly longed for. My heart panted after this, to lie low before God, as in the dust; that I might be nothing, and that God might be ALL, that I might become as a little child."

"His left hand is under my head." We then feel sweetly sustained by the Lord Jesus, by his imputed righteousness, and by his inward grace. So far from wishing to rest on any merit of our own, we cast from us our righteousness as filthy rags, as a broken reed, on which if a man lean, it will go into his heart and pierce it, 2 Kings xviii. 21. His righteousness, like the pillars in the porch of the temple, Jachin and Boaz, firmness and strength; like the pillars of marble set upon sockets of fine gold, Song v. 15, with his human nature resting on the fine gold of his divine nature, is mighty to save even to the uttermost all who come to him, however great their unworthiness and guilt. By the grace of the Holy Spirit shed through the heart, the name of Jesus is as ointment poured forth, more refreshing than the cluster of camphire in the vineyards of Engedi, than the bundle of myrrh in the bosom; he is full of grace and truth. As he comes forth from the ivory palaces of the heavenly glory, his garments smell of myrrh, aloes, and cassia, the excellency of his divine nature sheds a divine influence around us; we rise gently above the din, the jar, the perplexities of earth; new vigour is imparted to our faith, new animation to our desires; the soul is filled with confidence, with joy, with peace; duty becomes pleasing, toils borne for Jesus seem delightful, for the love that we bear to him; sorrow ceases to distress, care no longer perplexes; the angel of the covenant makes us to ride on the high places of the earth, and drink of the pure blood of the grape of Israel's inheritance.

"His right hand doth embrace me." While thus sustaining us, Jesus draws us very near to himself. Onward, nearer to Jesus! is the ruling feeling of the saint. We may at times wish it had been our privilege to see Jesus, as the apostles saw him, with bodily eyes. But there is no evidence that their hearts experienced any more joy than may be now felt by the believer. The manifestations of the glory of his divine nature may be made to our hearts as vivid and as enchanting as they were to patriarchs and apostles. The glories of his glorified human nature we are not so unreasonable as now to expect to behold. The time will come for the body to have its share in ministering to our vision of the glory of God. Our happiness now consists not in seeing visions, and hearing sounds; not in bodily exhilaration and rapturous ecstasies; but in feeling God's love, and in being filled with his Spirit. There is no reason for supposing that the emotions of the multitude under the action of the Spirit on the day of Pentecost, were more delightful than the emotions now felt under the reviving power of the same Spirit. In the most glorious visions had by patriarchs and prophets, there was probably no more delight enjoyed than is now the portion of the contrite spirit. We may not see what they saw; but we may feel what they felt. It is doubtful that Jacob at Bethel, or at Penuel, or that the disciples at the transfiguration, had more real joy of heart than is now often experienced under the ministration of the Spirit. In the words of Witsius: "Hence it is, that while his saints are sometimes ravished on high by his Spirit, he surrounds them with the beams of his super-celestial light, gives them a view of his face, shining with the brightest love, kisses them with the kisses of his mouth, admits them to the most endearing, mutual intercourse of mystical love with himself; and, while he plentifully sheds abroad his love in their hearts, he gives them to drink of rivers of honey and butter; and that often in the greatest drought of the parched soul, when expecting no such thing. There are many more mysteries in this secret intercourse with our heavenly Father, which believers sometimes see, taste, and feel, and which no pen of the learned can represent as they deserve."*

"Stay me with flagons, comfort me with apples:" that

---

* Witsius on the Covenants, book iii. 11, 34.

is, give me support and refreshment with cups of wine from the banqueting-house, and with citrons from the tree whose shadow was so delightful. The fruits with which the soul sick of love desires to be refreshed, are the precious doctrines of the cross and the promises of the Scriptures. There is then a wonderful avidity for the word of God; we feel what it is to live not by bread alone, but by every word that proceedeth out of the mouth of God. The simple doctrines of the cross are sweeter than our daily food. Here at this fountain of life, where the doctrine of Jesus drops as the rain, and his speech distils as the dew, does the Holy Spirit give strong drink unto him that is ready to perish, and wine unto those that be of heavy heart—that best wine for the beloved, which goeth down sweetly, causing the lips of those that are asleep to speak; yea, here does the afflicted saint drink, and forget his poverty, and remember his misery no more.

VER. 7.—I charge you, O ye daughters of Jerusalem, by the roes and by the hinds of the field, that ye stir not up, nor awake my love, (the object of my affection,) till he please.*

As these animals were proverbially timorous, the greatest care must be taken not to disturb them; and the be-

---

* Some interpreters, among whom are Dopke, Rosenmüller, and Professor Stowe, in an article on the Song in the Biblical Repository, April, 1847, take these as the words of the beloved, applied to the spouse. The reason for this is, that the Hebrew word rendered "my love," is a feminine noun, and the following verb, "till he please," is also of the feminine form. The conclusion they draw from these facts is unnecessary and incorrect; and the meaning adopted in the English version seems the true one. 1. Because it harmonizes best with the scope of the passage. 2. It seems to be required also by the scope of the context in the other places, ch. iii. 5, viii. 4, where the same language occurs. 3. The beloved is compared to a gazelle, or a young hart, ch. ii. 9, and the immediate connection seems to restrict this verse accordliever enjoying the manifestations of heavenly love, will be as cautious in avoiding sin, as in watching the gazelle, which bounds away at the rustling of a leaf. Nothing could express more strongly with what carefulness the contrite heart seeks to retain those influences of the Spirit and the society of Jesus. Never have we such intense anxiety in guarding against sin, as when thus filled with intense love. Then do we watch and pray; then do we groan, being burdened; then do we moan for entire conformity to Jesus, that with Jesus we may for ever rest.

VER. 8, 9.—The voice of my beloved! behold, he cometh leaping upon the mountains, skipping upon the hills. My beloved is like a roe, or a young hart: behold, he standeth behind our wall, he looketh forth at the windows, showing himself through the lattice.

The Christian life is a series of visits and withdrawals of our Lord, of revivals of grace in the heart and expo-

ingly to the same, if it can be done without violence to the Hebrew. 4. This can be done. The Hebrew word "my love," means "love," then "an object of affection," whether male or female, precisely as the corresponding word is used in the English language. This noun, with this meaning, being thus feminine, the following verb would naturally take the same gender. In this very book, ch. v. 9, where the spouse is unquestionably addressing her female friends, the verb "if ye find," is the second person masculine instead of feminine. Moreover, the masculine form is used for the feminine, not only in the Future, as in Song viii. 4, Isa. lvii. 8, but also in the Præter, in Ruth i. 8; and in the Imperative, in Micah i. 13, and Isa. xxxii. 11. 5. Besides the English version, our view is that adopted by Delitzsch, Good, Fry, and Bishop Percy.

"Among the orientals it is considered barbarous in the extreme to awake a person out of his sleep. How often, in going to the house of a native, you are saluted with, "He sleeps." Ask them to arouse him: the reply is, "I cannot." Indeed, to request such a thing, shows at once that you are griffin, or new-comer. "Only think of that ignorant Englishman: he went to the house of our chief, and being told that he was asleep, he said he must see him, and actually made such a noise as to awake him; and then laughed at what he had done."—*Roberts.*

sure to trials. After the overpowering display of love in the foregoing verses, the beloved had left the spouse; these words describe his return. When we have been passing through a season of coldness and decline, how often have we been sweetly surprised by an influence coming over the heart, we could hardly tell whence, or how, warming the heart, drawing the attention back to the forgotten Saviour, inclining us to prayer, and giving evidence of the return of Jesus. We are taken by surprise; we look up with wondering love, and exclaim, "The voice of my beloved!"

At such times, the Saviour encourages us from a distance by his voice; gives tokens of his approach; makes us feel he is about to repeat his visits, and open to us fresh visions of his love. To the soul dead in sin, the idea of now hearing the voice of Jesus is visionary. But the good Shepherd says, the sheep know his voice. John x. 13. And if the friend of the bridegroom, which standeth and heareth him, rejoiceth greatly because of the bridegroom's voice; much more shall the bride rejoice when she heareth him. There is herein no visionary enthusiasm; no wonders ringing in the ear of the body. There is a something speaking to the soul; spirit whispering to spirit; tones from the lips of Jesus, adapted to the hearing ear of the renewed soul. Faith, "the evidence of things not seen," gives us the best kind of evidence, that this is indeed the voice of our Lord. Then, when his speech distils as the dew, as the small rain upon the tender herb, and as the showers upon the grass; the lonely soul feels him to be as the dew unto Israel, and that they that dwell under his shadow, shall return, they shall revive as the corn, and grow as the vine, Hos. xiv. 7; then is he to the reviving heart, like a serene heat after rain, like a cloud of dew in the heat of harvest. Isa. xviii. 4.

He comes over all difficulties to visit and revive us; on or over the mountains or hills, he comes leaping, surmounting all obstacles with ease. "Here, near the sea of Gallilee, we saw the gazelle bounding on before us, over shrubs and rocks and every obstacle, and felt the exquisite fulness of meaning in the Church's exclamation, 'Behold, he cometh leaping upon the mountains, skipping upon the hills. My beloved is like a roe or young hart.' It is the very nature of this lively animal to bound over the roughest heights with the greatest ease, it seems even to delight in doing so."* And it is the very nature of the Lord Jesus to come to the souls of his people, over all difficulties with perfect ease. Nothing, whether the inward sense of unworthiness and guilt, aggravated by numerous backslidings, or outward sorrows rising around us, dark and towering as the crags of the valley of the

---

corre.
this me Mission of Inquiry, p. 296. And thus Euripides puts these senti-
take the s into the mouth of the chorus:
unquestionab   With snowy foot, my marble neck
the second per   Shall mingle with the nightly choirs,
culine form is u Mid falling dews; as when the fawn
viii. 4, Isa. lvii. 8 porting upon the tender grass
perative, in Micah' joyous meadows, flees the snares,
version, our view is t hunters' shouts, and hounds' deep bay;
Percy.   quicker than the sweeping wind
"Among the orient do-winged o'erleaps the green
awake a person out of eland streams, and stretches far
a native, you are salute e wilds untrod by man,
the reply is, "I cannot, avy shades of pathless woods.—*Bacchæ*, 850.
once that you are griffin
Englishman: he went to
was asleep, he said he cut stand ye thus like fawns,
us to awake him; and th running through the spreading plain,
                          with senseless fear.—*Iliad*, iv. 243.

shadow of death, nothing can separate us from the love of Christ.

He comes to us speedily, unexpectedly. The roe was an emblem of swiftness: Asahel was as light of foot as a wild roe, 2 Sam. ii. 18; and certain of David's men were as swift as the roes upon the mountains. 1 Chron. xii. 8. The heart is surprised in an unexpected moment, by the appearance of the beloved. Though keeping afar off for a time, he comes speedily; his heart was turned; his repentings were kindled; and ere we were aware, his soul made him like the chariots of Ammi-nadib; he came as speedily as the angel came to Peter in prison asleep; as when he came to bless the Psalmist, and he rode on a cherub and did fly, yea, he did fly upon the wings of the wind; as speedily as on the first visit to the disciples after his ascension, when suddenly there came a sound from heaven, as of a rushing mighty wind, and they were all filled with the Holy Ghost. When churches long thirsting for the revival of his work have well nigh fainted under the thought that their sins and unworthiness were so great as to exclude them, perhaps for ever, from the blessing; he has been found among them, as a dew from the Lord, as the showers upon the grass, that tarrieth not for man, nor waiteth for the sons of men. Micah v. 7.

"Behold he standeth behind our wall." In the present life, we are in the condition of prisoners sentenced to hard labour. This world is our prison; the confinement of an inmate of a penitentiary is not more completely cut off from the community in the midst of which he is confined, and from association with the public, from knowledge of public affairs, from open landscapes and glorious skies, than are we, as offenders against God, cut off from all intercourse with the world of spirits, from knowledge of its realities, from views of its grandeurs and glories. After all the labours of science, we have no more acquaintance with the universe at large, than the prisoner is able to get of the world, through the bars of his dungeon. Like the fallen emperor of the French, we have lost our principality; the crown has fallen from our head, and we are confined on this earth, as a solitary, desolate island in the ocean of space; an impassable sea is around us, and we know but little, very little of the worlds and peoples lying beyond. Jesus, who has gone away to receive a kingdom for himself, and after preparing a place for us in that kingdom, to return and receive us to himself, does now kindly visit us in our confinement. But dark walls of our dungeon come between—the walls of our earthly house of this tabernacle, the walls that rise between us and the invisible world. How far is Jesus removed from me? He is standing behind this wall. This it is, and this only, which prevents us from having full view of him, from coming very near to him, from hearing distinctly his voice. When the Lord shall descend from heaven with a shout, with the voice of the archangel and with the trump of God; then shall these walls go down more perfectly than those of Jericho, and our souls, like liberated Rahab, be received into the host of the Lord, and into the presence of the Captain of our salvation.

"He looketh forth at the window, showing himself through the lattice,"*, than ore strictly, glancing through

* "I passed into a land streamed three sides of which the apartments ranged. A little wilds untrystal water lay enclosed by marble banks, and overshadowry shades utiful weeping-willows; little fountains leaped and spark   tirections, 'and shook their loosened silver in the sun.' Ar   ange, and lemon, and mimosa-trees, afforded a quivering sh   marble mosaic paths, and the parterres of flowers. At o   this court, or garden, was a lofty alcove, with a ceiling ric   d in gold and crimson fret-work; the

the lattice. The views now got of Jesus, are like the furtive glances which the spouse was able now and then to catch of the glistening eyes of the loved one through the lattice window. Vines, jessamines, roses, and honey-suckles, grew in luxuriance against and over the walls of the royal palace or summer-house, with their tendrils and bloom often flowering beautifully through the gilded lattices: to this there may be here an allusion, as though in this way, He who is the true vine, John xv. 1, does unfold to us, through the lattice in the walls separating us from the invisible world, some budding flowers of his glory. The ordinances, the sacraments, the scriptures, constitute the lattice through which we now get glimpses of the Beloved; and are enabled to see beauties unfolding, and breathe exhilarating fragrance, which thrill the soul with the assurance of the immeasurable fulness awaiting us amid the splendours of heaven.

VER. 10.—My beloved spake, and said unto me, Rise up, my love, my fair one, and come away.

To the spouse, confined within doors by the cold and rains of winter, the beloved having thus come from afar, addresses motives for alluring her away from her retreat, and abroad among the beauties of spring. Thus the Lord Jesus encourages us, by presenting to the mind the attractiveness of heaven as a place adorned with more than the beauties of Eden. And after the withdrawal of his presence, how kindly does he encourage the soul by

walls are ornamented with arabesques, and a wide divan runs round three sides of the apartment, which opens on the garden and its fountains. Next to this alcove is a beautiful drawing-room, with marble floor and arabesque roof, and carved niches, and softened light falling on delicately painted walls: in the midst is an alabaster basin, into which water falls from four fantastic little fountains."—*Warburton's Travels—The Crescent and the Cross.*

making us feel that he loves us none the less because he withdrew for a time; and how does the heart revive on hearing him still call us, "My love, my fair one!" We had thought that he left us because we had alienated his love by sin, and he was displeased by our many corruptions. His first words are, that he loves us as ever, and rejoices in our society as the bridegroom rejoices in the society of his loved one. Such being his love, he wishes to have us with him where he is, that there may be nothing to break the interchange of affection between him and our souls. Bunyan says, that when the summons came for Mr. Standfast to pass over Jordan, "the contents thereof were, that he must prepare for a change of life, for his master was not willing that he should be so far from him any longer." Much is said of the desire of the saint to depart and be with Jesus. We should think more of the desire of Jesus to have the believer depart and be with him in glory. The saint cannot be so desirous for being in heaven, as Jesus is for having us with him in heaven. "Father, I will that they also whom thou hast given me, be with me where I am, that they may behold my glory." John xvii. 24. He wishes us to be absent from the body and present with the Lord; to go forth from the walls of this prison-cell of the body, and walk with him by the living fountains of waters, in the vernal landscape of the heavenly world. How beautiful and attractive, as they are here shadowed forth, are the motives he addresses to the heart, as he says, "Rise, and come away." Never was there a more lovely description of spring, fit emblem of the time when we shall see

> "The various seasons woven into one,
> And that one season an eternal spring."

VER. 11.—For, lo! the winter is past, the rain is over and gone.

In the broad and open domains of that world which lies beyond the walls of our present condition, separating us from the Beloved, the winter is past: there, the reign of sin, the effect of man's guilt, as seen in the very ground, of which winter is so sad an evidence, is no more seen; in those realms of blessedness, there shall be no more curse. Rev. xxii. 3. St. Paul represents the whole creation as standing in earnest expectation of the time when the curse shall be removed. Rom. viii. 19. In those parts of this world most distinguished for the bodily and mental superiority of man, winter seems the order of nature; the warm genial weather of summer is confined to the smaller portion of the year, no more than sufficient for bringing from the bosom of the earth the productions necessary for the support of man; while cold storms and wintry blasts, chilling nights and gloomy days, fill up the greater part of the seasons, and invade with frequency even the few weeks of summer. In the present condition of the body and soul of man under the curse, this state of things is necessary. In those regions where uninterrupted summer reigns, the energies of the human mind and body wither, and the ills of the curse rage with greater power. In that world to which Jesus is drawing us, all these former things are passed away. There, the ground is no longer cursed for the sake of man; nor must he sustain life by the sweat of his brow; there, are no changing seasons, no days of labour, no tedious chilling nights, no pelting storms, no benumbing winds to breast even in works of mercy, no lightning and hail, snow and vapours, stormy blasts fulfilling the word of an angry God.* With imagery of this kind, has uninspired

* It will be seen that our interpretation of the passage, ver. 10–13, agrees essentially with the interpretation of those who take it as illus-

poetry, even among pagans, loved to invest the future abode of the blessed.

> "The blissful plains
> Where heavenly Justice in Elysium reigns;
> Joys ever young, unmixed with pain or fear,
> Fill the wide circle of th' eternal year;
> Spring ever smiles on that auspicious clime,
> The fields are flowery with unfading prime:
> From the bleak pole no winds inclement blow,
> Mould the round hail, or flake the fleecy snow;
> But from the breezy deep the blest inhale
> The fragrant murmurs of the western gale."*

In the same spirit, Pindar speaks of that state as realms where the virtuous enjoy the light of a sun that never sets, free from all toil, without sorrow, without tears; where ocean-breezes refresh the isles of the blessed; where flowers of gold cluster, some on the ground, others on beautiful trees, others bathed by the waters of pellucid streams; while entwining crowns and chaplets of these, the happy one follows a life of purity and justice; meads damasked with purple roses form the suburbs of their heavenly city, around which no evening throws its shades; peaceful plenty everywhere blooms; and over those lovely realms balmy fragrance is shed, as those heavenly meadows are shaded with groves of trees laden with gold and incense.†

---

trating the condition of the soul of the believer when passing from a state of sin to a state of holiness in regeneration. The new birth is the beginning with us of the blessings of the kingdom of heaven, which are brought to perfection in the "new heavens and new earth wherein dwelleth righteousness;" the pious graces first showing themselves in the heart in repentance, are the early violets of that eternal, celestial spring.

* Odyssey, iv. 564.
† Pindar, 2d Olymp. Ode.

The winter has thus passed away from the face of nature in that happy world, because the soul of man, on account of whose sin the curse fell on the ground, has been delivered from all his iniquity; his habitation is all pure and glorious, because his spiritual leprosy has been cleansed. No hurricanes of passion can there burst on the soul; no gusts of sin sweep over the heart; no thunderbolts of guilt shiver our peace; no mildew blight our hopes; no canker prey on the objects of our delight; no frosts chill the budding affections; no withering blasts spread desolation over our prospects, or freeze the currents of joy. Everything proclaims with a voice of gladness, there shall be no night there; they have no need of the sun, neither of the moon, for the glory of God and the Lamb is the light thereof; there shall be no more curse; "the winter is past."

"The rain is over and gone." About the close of winter in the land of Judea, the latter rains were frequent for many days; and while so necessary for ripening the harvest, and the forerunner of the serene sky of that joyous season were always unpleasant and chilly. The eastern winter is past by April; but all the showers were not over till May. The time referred to in these verses seems to be the period directly after the ceasing of these spring showers, when all nature was beautiful with a newborn freshness yet untouched by the withering drought of summer. Between the wintry rain of the curse over us in this world, and the bursting forth of the vernal beauties of that new earth wherein dwelleth righteousness, the believer must pass through many pelting storms of distress and affliction, which, though for the present not joyous but grievous, are necessary for ripening in our souls the peaceble fruit of righteousness. As the latter rain was the herald of spring and the forerunner of harvest, the divine chastisements are the closing evils connected with sin and the heralds of coming peace in heaven. These must be done away when we reach that world where "God shall wipe away all tears from their eyes, and there shall be no more death, neither sorrow, nor crying;" where the rain is over and gone; where the clouds return not after the rain, Eccl. xii. 2; and as a pledge that sorrow is over and gone, never to return, He who set his bow in the cloud, that the waters shall no more become a flood to cover the world, has placed a rainbow round about the throne, in sight like unto an emerald. Rev. iv. 3.

VER. 12.—The flowers appear on the earth; the time of the singing of birds is come, and the voice of the turtle is heard in our land.

At this time the fields were covered with beautiful flowers, which delighted the eye and filled the air with fragrance. Before the fall, the earth was robed in these vernal splendours, not merely during the few weeks of spring, and in a few spots scattered over its barren surface, but presented throughout the year a wilderness of sweets, rejoicing and blossoming as the rose, of which the glory of Lebanon, the excellency of Carmel and Sharon, is merely a shrivelled remnant. Equally glorious shall be the earth when the curse is done away, and all things are created new. The Paradise awaiting the just in heaven, shall not be less glorious than that Eden,

> "Where from that sapphire fount the crisped brooks
> Rolling on orient pearl and sands of gold,
> With mazy error under pendant shades
> Ran nectar, visiting each plant, and fed
> Flow'rs worthy of Paradise, which not nice art
> In beds and curious knots, but nature boon
> Poured forth profuse on hill, and dale, and plain,
> Flowers of all hue and without thorn the rose."

Spring is the living illustration to fallen man of the truth, that there shall be a like resurrection from the barrenness which the curse has spread over our world. Flowers are the most beauteous form that matter, as now known to us, assumes. And when told that in the future world the flowers appear in the earth as the attendants of an eternal spring, we feel nothing could represent to us more pleasingly that there the curse on the ground is repealed, and the face of nature invested with the attractive beauty of Paradise. There, Jesus as our Shepherd will make us to lie down in green pastures, and lead us beside the still waters; nor will the flowers there appearing in the earth soon wither under summer's heat, and fall under winter's frost; they will bloom unfading, undecaying, throughout a spring which shall fill the whole compass of a cycle boundless as eternal life.

"The time of the singing of birds is come." Thus, the following, translated by Sir W. Jones from a Turkish Ode by Meshi: "Thou hearest the tale of the nightingale, that the vernal season approaches. The spring has spread a bower of joy in every grove where the almond-tree sheds its silver blossoms. The roses and tulips are like the bright cheeks of beautiful maids, in whose ears the pearls hang like drops of dew. The time is passed in which the plants were sick, and the rose-bud hung its thoughtful head upon its bosom." Again, in a Turkish song given by Lady Montague: "The nightingale now wanders in the vines; her passion is to seek roses." Good remarks: "The bulbul, or Persian nightingale, is a far more beautiful bird than the European; and the vernal season, here referred to, is always a period of general hilarity among the inhabitants of this happy climate. Hence Hafiz sings—

"The charms of spring once more the fields salute:
Ope to the rose, ye nightingales! your suit:

> Ye Zephyrs, 'mid the meadow-youths that rove,
> Bear to the rose, the basil sweet, our love."

Thus the elegant Jami—

> "Though countless shrubs of balmiest breath
> Their fascinating forms disclose,
> The constant nightingale till death
> Still covets his beloved rose."

When Thevenot visited Jordan on the sixteenth of April, he found the little woods on the margin of the river filled with nightingales in full chorus; and Lady Montague, at the same time of the year, speaks of turtles as cooing on the cypress-trees of her garden from morning till night.* By reference to such things, would the Holy Spirit illustrate to us that in the world to which Jesus would allure us away, all is vocal with enchanting melody, and even the irrational creation are joining in the chorus.

Next to the pleasures of sight are those of sound; nor do we know that they are inferior. Man is not capable of richer pleasure than is felt in hearing delightful music. It has its foundation in the human soul. Both light and music seem to have the power of exciting the nervous energy of the human system, as though there were a more refined body imbedded in this physical frame. No one enjoys music with such exquisite delight as the sanctified believer. This delight keeps pace with our growing deliverance from the bondage of corruption, and our growing fitness for heaven.

> "Heard melodies are sweet, but those unheard
> Are sweeter."

"And thus the associations of a man familiar with holy

---

* Warburton says: "The air was the balmiest I ever breathed; myriads of birds were singing enthusiastically in the palm and olive-branches. The nightingales were thrilling the dark groves with their song."

truths, carry him away from the confused warfare of this world; the highest harmony belongs to another sphere, and in his estimation the best music of earth serves only to introduce us to that of heaven." Among the joys of heaven the Scriptures give this a very prominent place. In the Jewish temple, would their songs have been so sublime, and their choruses so grand, had they not foreshadowed the praise and chorus in which the worshippers shall join in that nobler temple, the heavenly Jerusalem? Well might the Holy Spirit therefore say, that in the world to which Jesus would allure us, "the time of singing is come;" the time of mourning and weeping has been done away; "violence shall no more be heard in thy land, wasting nor destruction within thy borders; but thou shalt call thy walls salvation, and thy gates praise." The mind can conceive of nothing more magnificent than the worship of the heavenly host as opened to us in the visions at Patmos. Rev. iv. v. vii. 9, 10; xiv. 3; xv. 3; xix. 1—6. The thoughts of hearing such deeds celebrated in such worship, of listening to such words set to appropriate harmonies, sung by such a chorus, under such circumstances; nay, of being one of the number who could learn and sing that song, may well-nigh overpower us; and no more of grandeur and of glory can be conceived, than the idea of being in the midst of that host, and helping to swell that burst of praise which is "as the voice of many waters, and as the voice of mighty thunderings, saying, Alleluia, for the Lord God omnipotent reigneth!" Rev. xix. 6. "Alleluia; salvation, and glory, and honour, and power, unto the Lord our God, and unto the Lamb! And again they said, Alleluia." Those who with souls most attuned to the worship of heaven, have heard the "Creation" and the "Messiah," have been made to feel how attractive and full of grandeur is this feature of heaven.

> "Such harmony is in immortal souls;
> But, whilst this muddy vesture of decay
> Doth grossly close it in, we cannot hear it."

With the melodies of the host who have lips and heart touched with the coal of the seraphim, will be mingled the voice of Jesus welcoming us to the service of that temple; some saints seem to have caught swells of those harmonies ere these walls of partition had yet gone entirely down in death; and they were enraptured with the sound. Who can imagine the overpowering feelings of the soul, when, in addition to the glorious visions bursting on the view, as the body is thrown aside, those deep-toned harmonies rise on the ear as the murmur of the tranquil ocean, as the sound of many waters; and as the spirit soars onward in the very midst of that chorus, we hear, as enriching and crowning all, tones from the lips of the glorified body of Jesus.

"The music of birds," as has been well observed, "was the first song of thanksgiving which was offered on earth before man was formed. All their sounds are different, but all harmonious, and all together composed a choir which we cannot imitate." In the words of Isaac Walton, "the nightingale breathes such sweet loud music out of her little instrumental throat, that it might make mankind to think miracles are not ceased. He that at midnight, when the very labourer sleeps securely, should hear, as I have very often, the clear airs, the sweet descants, the natural rising and falling, the doubling and redoubling of her voice, might well be lifted above earth, and say, Lord, what music hast thou provided for the saints in heaven, when thou affordest bad men such music on earth?"

> "Nature's sweet voices, always full of love
> And joyance! 'Tis the merry nightingale
> That crowds, and hurries, and precipitates
> With fast thick warble his delicious notes,
> As he were fearful that an April night
> Would be too short for him to utter forth
> His love-chaunt, and disburden his full soul
> Of all its music."*

"And the voice of the turtle is heard in our land." Even yet, in those regions, the time of the blossoming of the vines and blooming of flowers is the time of the singing of nightingales, of which the country may then be said to be full, and of the cooing of the turtle. The turtle is migratory. Jer. viii. 7. Aristotle says: "The ring-dove and pigeon are always to be seen, but the turtle in summer only; it does not make its appearance in winter." "The turtle and the crane and the swallow observe the time of their coming," which is about the end of April or beginning of May. The dove was the emblem of affection; and its mention here in preference to any other, is for showing that the key-note of the harmonies of that better land is love:

> "No war, or battle's sound
> Was heard the world around:
>   The idle spear and shield were high up hung,
> The hooked chariot stood
> Unstained with hostile blood,
>   The trumpet spake not to the armed throng:
> But peaceful was the night,
> Wherein the Prince of light
>   His reign of peace upon the earth began."

Much more shall all be peace, the result of universal love, when the reign then begun shall be consummated by the establishment of the Church triumphant in heaven.

---

* Coleridge's Nightingale.

The dove is here mentioned for the same reason that the dove was afterwards the symbol, to human eyes, of the Holy Spirit resting on Jesus by the Jordan. There, will be heard music, but not military sounds, making the soul frantic for horrors and blood; not the swells bursting from the heartless halls of revelry and dancing, but the harmonies rising from an innumerable multitude, which no man can number, of hearts perfect in love: "Unto him that loved us, and washed us from our sins in his own blood, and hath made us kings and priests unto God and his Father; to him be glory and dominion for ever and ever. Amen."

VER. 13.—The fig-tree putteth forth her green figs, and the vines with the tender grape give a good smell. Arise, my love, my fair one, and come away.

The fig-tree was now embalming or spicing its tender fruit, by filling it with aromatic juice. The vines were in bloom, with leaves of about two months growth, consequently very shady; and the buds bursting into full bloom, with the tender grape forming in the midst of the flower, yielded a delightful fragrance. This was at the time when the rose-trees were in bloom, and the gardens filled with nightingales.

The kiosk, the same meant by the word "bed," in ch. i. 16, stood in the midst of the garden, surrounded with large shady trees, and enclosed with gilded lattices, round which jessamines, honey-suckles, and vines, make a kind of green wall.* So sweet were the flowers of the vine, that the ancients had a practice of putting them, when dried, into new wine, for giving it a pure and delicious flavour, allowing two pounds of such flowers to every cadus or jar. As in Eden, "out of the ground made the

* See Notes on ch. i. 16, and ch. ii. 3, 8, 9.

Lord God to grow every tree that is pleasant to the sight and good for food;" the heavenly paradise is equally delightful, and there too grows the tree of life. All that can feast the eye and regale the senses is there spread forth. The new wine which Jesus wills to drink with the saints in his Father's kingdom, is even now awaiting us.

How attractive is heaven as thus represented. There, the curse is done away; no barren land is found in those realms of eternal spring; no clouded skies, no sorrows, no toil; the earth covered with unfading flowers, the air loaded with fragrance and with harmonious melodies, the tone of which is love; everything flourishing that can refresh and delight the powers of both body and soul. Hence, from that world of holiness and joy, does Jesus say to us, "Arise, my love, my fair one, and come away." Come away, from the sorrows, the afflictions, the infirmities, the trials, the bereavements, the toils, the chilling nights, the wintry blasts, of this vale of tears: Come away, to this world of endless spring, to the green pastures and living fountains of waters, to the innumerable company of angels, to the spirits of the just made perfect; come away to the skies, where Jesus, the beloved, awaits thee on the mountain of myrrh and hills of frankincense, over which the day breaks and the shadows flee away.

VER. 14.—O my dove, thou art in the clefts of the rock, in the secret places of the stairs, let me see thy countenance, let me hear thy voice; for sweet is thy voice, and thy countenance is is comely.

Doves in those countries take up their abodes in the hollow places of rocks and cliffs. Hence the words of the prophet, "O ye that dwell in Moab, leave the cities, and dwell in the rock, and be like the dove that maketh her nest in the sides of the hole's mouth." Jer. xlviii. 18.* And in Virgil we have a like comparison,

> As the affrighted dove, whose darling young
> And nest are in the covert of some rock.

And in the Iliad,

> She weeping fled,
> As to her cavern in some hollow rock
> The dove, not destined to his talons, flies
> The hawk's pursuit.

Thus, those whom Jesus would allure away to himself, are very frequently found in the rugged scenes of life, in situations of trial, affliction, and desolation, alone, away from the world. "Lo! the people shall dwell alone and shall not be reckoned among the nations." Num. xxiii. 9. And the prophet says, "Feed thy people with thy rod, watch over, as a shepherd with his staff, the flock of thine heritage, which dwells solitarily in the wood, in the midst of Carmel." Mic. vii. 14. As God took fallen man out of the garden of Eden, and placed him, for a check on his depravity, in a world blighted by the curse; so, those whom he would redeem, whose corruptions he would uproot, he cuts off from love of the world, by putting them in the clefts of the rock; he brings us, like Israel, "through the wilderness, through a land of deserts and of pits, through a land of drought and of the shadow of death," that we may desire a better country, that is, an heavenly; that we may hearken to the admonition of the still small voice from the holy oracle, the Spirit's dwelling-place in the sanctuary of

---

* "At such times of noon-day stillness and heat, the larger animals seek shelter in the recesses of the forest, and the birds hide themselves under the thick foliage of the trees, or in the clefts of the rocks."—*Humboldt's Aspects.*

our soul, "Arise ye, and depart, for this is not your rest." Mic. ii. 10. Affliction is the promised inheritance of the saints in this world. They have been left here an afflicted and poor people, whose trust is in the name of the Lord.

> "So virtue blooms, brought forth amid the storms
> Of chill adversity; in some lone walk
> Of life she rears her head,
> Obscure and unobserved."

The most remarkable displays of God's glory ever made to man, were made in scenes of loneliness and desolation. When the patriarch dreamed, and beheld a ladder set upon the earth, and the top of it reached to heaven, the emblem of the heavens opened and the angels of God ascending and descending upon the Son of man, he had taken the stones of that place and put them for his pillows, and thus lain down to sleep: The vision of the burning-bush was when Moses was a fugitive from his countrymen, and had led the flock to the back of the desert, to the mountain of God, even to Horeb, so named from its desolation; and when afterwards God would show this servant his glory, he put him in a cleft of the rock: On this Horeb, the mount of desolation, stood Elijah, when, unmoved by the wind, and the earthquake, and the fire, he wrapped his face in his mantle, as he heard the still small voice. The transfiguration was on a high mountain apart; the appointed place for the meeting of Jesus with his disciples, after the resurrection, and for appearing most probably to a body of above five hundred brethren at once, was a mountain in Galilee; the visions of John were on the rocky isle of Patmos; and when the angel would close those scenes by a view of that great city, the holy Jerusalem, he carried him away in the spirit to a great and high mountain. If now he withdraw us not from the world, he accomplishes the same end in spreading desolation around us, by bereavement, by loss of property, by affliction, by blasted hopes and bitter disappointments. "Of the eight beatitudes, five of them have temporal misery and meanness, or an afflicted condition for their subject. As long as the waters of affliction are upon the earth, so long we dwell in the ark; but when the land is dry, the dove itself will be tempted to a wandering course of life, and never to return to the house of her safety."*

The person thus addressed as in the cleft of the rock, was so affected with a sense of unworthiness, as to shrink back and stand in need of the exhortation to come forth to her Lord. To such trembling, timid souls, he says, Cut off though you may be from the riches, the honours, and even the comforts of this world, and feeling yourself most unworthy, there is One on whom you may cast all your care, for he careth for you, who speaks to you in language the most affectionate, My dove, my tender, timid one, the object of my deepest, most devoted love, "let me see thy countenance," for however the world may disregard and despise that expression of humility, in my eyes the countenance bespeaking contrition is beautiful. To the father of the prodigal, far more pleasing than the gayety of the company thronging his halls, was the careworn countenance of his humbled and repenting son. Let me hear thy voice, for it is sweet. The music and dancing were not so sweet to the father's heart, as the humbled tones of his lost son confessing his sin, acknowledging his transgressions, and giving utterance to his reviving love. No sounds are so delightful to Jesus, as the tones of the contrite spirit con-

---

* Jeremy Taylor's Sermons on 1 Pet. iv. 17, 18.

fessing sin, mourning the absence of his countenance, calling on him in trouble, and seeking advance in holiness.

VER. 15.—Take us the foxes, the little foxes, that spoil the vines; for our vines have tender grapes.

Foxes, jackals, little foxes, are very common in Palestine, and are particularly fond of grapes. They often burrow in holes in hedges round the gardens; and unless strictly watched, would destroy whole vineyards. Their flesh was sometimes eaten in autumn, when they were grown fat with feeding on grapes. Thus Theocritus says,

> I hate the foxes with their bushy tails,
> Which numerous spoil the grapes of Micon's vines
> When fall the evening shades.

And Aristophanes compares soldiers to foxes, because they consume the grapes of the countries through which they pass. They here represent anything which injures, by stealth and cunning, the graces of those who are the objects of divine love. Hence, as an enemy of God's people, Herod is called a fox by Jesus. Luke xiii. 32. This verse teaches that those who are favoured richly with grace, and whom our Lord is drawing towards heaven, will be careful to guard against sin, and especially against little sins. Heretofore we had to lament, in the words of ch. i. 6, "Mine own vineyard have I not kept;" now we are anxious to guard the vineyard of the heart against the inroad of anything, however trifling, that may corrode and destroy our graces. Too often we may have been like a boy represented by Theocritus, as set to watch a vineyard, but becoming so absorbed in weaving a chaplet of flowers as not to notice two foxes, one of which was stealthily plundering his food, while the other was making havoc with the grapes. Never is our carefulness in guarding against sin so great, as when most deeply filled with the love of Jesus; against the slightest sins we wish most carefully to guard. The services of the Jewish tabernacle taught the necessity of holiness, even in trivial things. By these little sins, Satan begins the most deadly temptations; he attacks us in an unexpected quarter, in an unlooked for way; and the time for resisting him, is at the very beginning of his insidious assaults. Indulgence in what may seem trifling departures from watchfulness and duty, blinds the mind to the truth of Scripture, corrodes and enfeebles our graces, and grieves the Holy Ghost. While watching with all diligence, our unceasing prayer will be, "Search me, O God, and know my heart; try me and know my thoughts; and see if there be any wicked way in me, and lead me in the way everlasting." Ps. cxxxix. 23.

VER. 16.—*My beloved is mine, and I am his; he feedeth among the lilies.*

The lily, on account of its beauty as well as fragrance, has been universally admired in all ages: the Greeks and Romans were no less fond of it than the orientals. The beloved, still compared to a gazelle, is here said to feed beside still waters, in green pastures abounding with lilies. A green meadow, in which the gazelle might be seen feeding and reposing, among the lilies, was a scene truly beautiful. Lilies grew wild in abundance in the fields. In early spring the plain of Sharon was seen covered with hyacinths and lilies, and the richest scarlet poppies strewed amid the verdant grass. On this grass the roes loved to pasture. Hence our Saviour says, "Consider the lilies of the field." And a Latin poet says,

> Lo, yonder noble stag, calmly at rest
> Mid the white lilies on the meadow's breast.

As in verses first and second of this chapter, the lilies are emblems of the pure in heart, the virgins surrounding the beloved. Thus Hengstenberg remarks on the title of the forty-fifth psalm: "This psalm employs itself on lilies, beautiful virgins, lovely brides. We take the lilies as a figurative description of the lovely virgins whose marriage with the king the Psalmist celebrates." The words "he feedeth among the lilies, do therefore mean, that as the instinct of the gazelle leads him back to his feeding-ground, and wherever he wanders, there is the place of his strongest desire, in which he loves to linger, loves to rest; so the place of our Lord's strongest desire is in the midst of his saints; and however he may withdraw, thither he will most certainly return. There is no place in which he loves to be, better than among his people.

In view of the assurances of love given in the foregoing verses, the spouse says, "My beloved is mine and I am his." Those who thus watch against sin, and are blessed with communications of heavenly love, enjoy the full assurance of hope, and rejoice to know that Christ is theirs, and they are his. It is not said, I am his and he is mine; but first, he is mine, and then, I am his; inasmuch as Christ's being ours is at the foundation of every blessing. While he is separated from us by the walls between this and the invisible world, unable to show us the fulness of his glory, and in the clefts of the rock, we are cut off from so many of the enjoyments of earth— we are permitted to feel that whatever else is wanting, Christ is ours. The whole of the covenant is simply this: Jesus says to us, give yourself to me, and I will give myself to you. On this principle does he act; and to the degree we surrender ourselves up to him, will we ever find him communicating to us his grace and causing us to receive of his fulness. This assurance is a blessing of unspeakable value. A deed is the legal security that an inheritance is ours and cannot be taken from us by law. This assurance, written in new characters on the white stone of the holy heart, by the finger which wrote on the tables of stone on Sinai, is the pledge that heaven, or what is better still, Christ is ours. This charter of our eternal hopes, this title to heaven, is thus laid up in the inner shrine of the heart, so secure, that we cannot be plundered of it even by the spoiler Death. We desire nothing more, as he says, "All mine are thine and thine are mine; and the glory which thou gavest me, I have given them." John xvii. 10. In the words of Quarles,

> "He is my altar; I his holy place;
> I am his guest; and he my living food;
> I'm his by penitence; he mine by grace;
> I'm his by purchase; he is mine by blood:
> He's my supporting helm; and I his vine:
> Thus I my best beloved's am; thus he is mine."

"He feedeth among the lilies." There is the place where he is drawn by the strongest desire. We may calculate unerringly on his returning at intervals, to manifest his presence in his Church; for the roe or young hart may forget his pasture grounds, but He can never forget the calm retreats of this world, where cluster his chosen ones robed in the purity of holiness. Yea, more, the mother may forget her infant child, "yet will I not forget thee." Isa. xlix. 15. Where would he be more likely to wish to dwell than among his redeemed ones? Hence his usual mode of expressing his relation to his people, is that of making his abode with them, John xiv. 23; of dwelling in their hearts by faith, Eph. iii. 17; and in heaven, God himself in his tabernacle shall dwell with them, and be their God. Rev. xxi. 3. In times of darkness and sorrow, let us therefore be comforted by the inward assurance, "My beloved is mine and I am his;" and by feeling that more certainly than the roe to his rich pastures among the lilies, will Jesus return to visit and abide with our longing hearts.

VER. 17.—Until the day break, and the shadows flee away, turn, my beloved, and be thou like a roe, or a young hart, upon the mountains of Bether.

While thus comforted during the withdrawal of our Lord, by the assurance of hope, and by the truth that he may be more certainly expected from time to time among the saints, than the roe may be expected in the pastures where he feeds, the desire of our heart is that Jesus would repeat those visits as often as possible, until the darkness now around us flee away. In those hot countries the dawn of day is attended with a fine refreshing breeze, much more grateful and desirable than the light itself, beautifully expressed by the words "the day breathe."* Thus, Milton—

> "And temperate vapours bland, which th' only sound
> Of leaves and fuming rills, Aurora's fan,
> Lightly dispersed."

As the Hebrew word *Bether* means a section or division, and as it occurs nowhere else as a proper name, we take

---

* Van Egmont and Heyman state that "the excessive heat on the coast, and in many places of the Holy Land, is very much lessened by a sea-breeze, which constantly blows every morning, and by its coolness renders the heats of summer very supportable." Dr. Robinson, of Cambridge, mentions that "every morning about sunrise, a fresh gale of wind blew from the sea across the land, which from its wholesomeness in clearing the infected air, is always called '*the doctor.*'

"At the approach of morning, the stir of life that seemed, like leaven, to ferment the surface of the world round, was very striking; first, the partridge's call joined chorus with the nightingale, and soon after their dusky forms were seen darting through the bushes, and then bird after bird joined the chorus; the lizards began to glance "mountains of Bether" here to mean mountains of division—spoken of a region cut up or divided by mountains and valleys, rough, craggy, and difficult to cross. Over these the spouse intreats the beloved to come like a roe or a young hart. See ver. 9. In the spirit of these words, Wordsworth says,

> "When like a roe,
> I bounded o'er the mountains, by the sides
> Of the deep rivers and the lonely streams."

As Jesus sees fit sometimes to withdraw, we pray for the repetition of his visits to the soul as often as possible. These visits are necessary for our advancement in holiness; they are both sunlight and shower. They give the greatest joys we can now have; they are foretastes of heaven. Jesus is the great attraction of heaven; and how comforting to know that although we cannot at present be with him amid the glories of heaven, he will come frequently, over all intervening obstacles, and visit us amid the darkness and ruins of earth, "until the day break and the shadows flee away." The ancient philosophers call this world the dark cavern of the imprisoned soul; and Plato* says, "Behold men, as if dwelling in a subterranean cavern." Our world is now involved in shadows dark as night; and well does the Apostle say, the "night is far spent, the day is at hand." Rom. xiii. 12.

upon the rocks, the insects on the ground and in the air; the jerboa peeping from its burrow, fish glancing in the stream, hares bounding over the dewy grass, and—as more light came—the airy form of the gazelle could be seen on almost every neighbouring hill. Then came sunrise, first flushing the light clouds above, then flashing over the Arabian mountains, and pouring down into the rich valley of the Jordan: the Dead Sea itself seemed to come to life under that blessed spell, and shone like molten gold among its purple hills."—*Warburton* —*The Crescent and the Cross.*

* Repub., book vii., chap. 1.

The morning star has long since risen; in the influences of the Holy Spirit, we feel the breathing of breezes from heaven, harbingers of an eternal day; in the increasing light of sanctification, we hail the brightening day-break of eternity. Like a person who might have been born in the depths of the Mammoth Cave, and wandering for years therein, without a sight of the glorious world above and around him—the impenitent are equally in darkness, living, wandering in caverns more desolate and gloomy to the soul, and with as little knowledge of the splendours of the invisible spiritual world. Should the poor offcast born in the cave, meet with some one from the outer world, penetrating with a torch into those chambers of death, with what interest would he listen to an account of the green earth, the morning sun, the starry heavens; with what feelings must he gaze on the brightening light, in his approach to the mouth of the cavern. How great the transition, when having left those labyrinths of darkness, he stands gazing on the morning star overhanging the brightening dawn of a day in spring, hears the singing of the birds, feels the refreshing breath of the pure breeze, and is exhilarated with the fragrance filling the air from the dewy flowers and trees in bloom. Far, far more delightful are our sensations, when our spiritual perception fixes on Christ the bright morning star, and on the dawning light of heavenly blessedness; and we hear swells of music from that better world, and feel the refreshing breezes of the Holy Spirit, laden with balm from the fields the Lord has blessed.

Then, our view of the boundless universe of God shall be enlarged, as is our view of the landscape under the rising sun; we shall mingle with an innumerable company of angels, with the spirits of just men made perfect; the truths now so precious, will be seen more clearly, and in wider relations; mysteries of Providence will be cleared up; God will be more fully known; Christ will be revealed in all his glory.

CHAPTER III.

VER. 1.—By night on my bed I sought him whom my soul loveth: I sought him, but I found him not.

THE portion of this book from chap. ii. 8 to chap. vii. 9, contains three leading motives addressed to the soul by Jesus for alluring us away from the world. Between these there are introduced, chap. iii. 1—5, and chap. v. 2—8, two seasons of spiritual desertion, differing from each other in this respect, that in the latter the beloved is repulsed by the neglect of cold indifference, while in the former, here under consideration, nothing of that kind seems mentioned. This verse is connected with the close of chapter second, and illustrates the earnestness of the soul in seeking Jesus during a time of his absence. God's way of carrying on our sanctification is by repeated visits and withdrawals, at seasons "put in his own power." When thus absent, he returns in different ways. Sometimes, as in chap. ii. 8, he surprises us with his grace, almost before he was expected, Isa. lxv. 1; then, as in this passage, he waits for us to seek him with earnestness. This verse expresses, that in the absence of Jesus, we seek him with desires so strong as to surmount the most necessary cravings of the body, even sleep.

No desire is so intense as the craving of a healthful soul after Christ. This is different from the thirst of the mind for intellectual pleasures. In the state of mind here set forth, there are as the basis of this craving—1. Foregoing manifestations of the love and loveliness of Jesus through the Holy Spirit; 2. A disclosure of the beauty and glory of heaven; 3. The assurance of hope; and, 4. Strong desires for beholding the glory of Christ. What was wanting, was a sense of the presence of Jesus. Now it is possible to have all these without the last. This is exceedingly desirable, and should be sought; but the want of it is no evidence God has cast us off, and is displeased. Many good people mistake at such time, by despairing and reproaching themselves, instead of seeking him. Through the disposition to walk by sense or sight, rather than by faith, they despond when the manifestations of the presence of Jesus are withheld. But they should feel the absence of these is no proof of want of acceptance; these withdrawals are for a wise end, and are essential in our preparation for heaven.* They test the strength of our faith and steadfastness of our love; they lead to deeper searchings for secret sins; they advance humility by making us feel our weakness and

---

* "Although it is not possible that any who is admitted into peace and friendship with God should altogether fall from it, yet the sense and relish thereof are often interrupted. For, 1. God doth not always show his pleasant countenance to his friends; sometimes he hides himself, Isa. viii. 17; standeth afar off, Ps. x. 1; admits them not into familiarity with him, nor fills them with the abundance of his consolations; he hears not when they call, Ps. xxii. 2, 3; as if he regarded them not. 2. Nay, he thrusts them from him with a kind of contempt; and 'is angry against their prayer.' Ps. lxxx. 4. 3. He terrifies them with many sorrows; not only by hiding his face, without which there is no joy, but by his fierce anger going over them. 4. He seems to deal with them as an adversary, and holdeth them for his enemies, and writes bitter things against them. 5. Gives them up sometimes to be vexed and buffeted by the devil. Job. ii. 6. After that the light of the divine countenance is set, immediately the beasts of the forest come forth against the soul, the young lions roaring after their prey."—*Witsius on Spiritual Peace, Cov.*, book iii. 9, 21.

our dependence on God. If this inward spring of divine influence flowed without intermission, in a current always full, we would be in danger of spiritual pride. Says Rutherford, "As nights and shadows are good for flowers, and moonlight and dews are better than a continual sun; so is Christ's absence of special use, and it hath some nourishing virtue in it, and giveth sap to humility, and putteth an edge on hunger, and furnisheth a fair field to faith to put forth itself."

How unreasonable to doubt the love of a friend when necessarily withdrawn: to love him only when under our eye betokens infant-like weakness. With love to Jesus, of a manly, vigorous cast, in seasons of spiritual desertion, far from despondency, with its attending inactivity, we will cherish a faithful, devoted affection, incapable of diversion from its cherished object by all the seductions of the tempter. How longs and seeks the soul for Christ, in times of temptation, of trial, of affliction, of spiritual desertion! How strong the feelings with which we think, at night on our bed, of those who are loved, but separated from us by distance or by death! When mourning the absence of him whom our soul loveth, how often have we made our bed to swim, and watered our couch with tears. After displays of his love, Christ gives us up to the power of the devil, within certain limits. In various ways, Satan will try to lead us into sin, if not against the moralities of the world, against the truth and faithfulness of God; failing in this, he will lead us as near as possible to sin, if perchance we may in an unguarded moment fall; repulsed in these attacks, he will then resort to slander, to worldly perplexity, to bodily affliction. Thus in his chapter on "the glory of Christ in the mysterious constitution of his person," Owen quotes this passage, and adds: "The Lord

Christ is pleased sometimes to withdraw himself from the spiritual experience of believers, as unto any refreshing sense of his love, or the fresh communications of consolatory graces. Those who never had experience of any such thing, who never had any refreshing communion with him, cannot be sensible of his absence; they never were so of his presence. But those whom he hath visited, to whom he hath given of his loves, with whom he hath made his abode, whom he hath refreshed, relieved, and comforted, in whom he hath lived in the power of his grace, they know what it is to be forsaken by him, though but for a moment. And their trouble is increased, when they seek him with diligence in the wonted ways of obtaining his presence, and cannot find him. Our duty in this case is, to persevere in our inquiries after him, in prayer, meditation, mourning, reading, and hearing of the word, in all ordinances of divine worship, private and public, in diligent obedience, until we find him, or he return unto us, as in former days."

Ver. 2.—I will rise now, and go about the city in the streets, and in the broad ways I will seek him whom my soul loveth; I sought him, but I found him not.

"The broad ways" seem to mean the broad open places at the gates of oriental cities, where the inhabitants were accustomed to assemble for public business. Not only in the streets, but in these public places, did the spouse seek her beloved. All the difficulties of this passage vanish when the Song is taken as an allegory for illustrating the love of the saint towards Christ. The heart warmed with thoughts of him, like a spring, boiling or bubbling up with deep emotions, Ps. xlv. 1, impels us to seek him in the way of self-denial. Time was when Jesus was sacrificed to the pursuit of worldly enjoyments, and pleasures of sense; now everything else is left, even sleep itself sacrificed, for finding the presence of Jesus. This verse is another way of setting forth the state of heart expressed in Ps. lxiii. 1, 2, and in Job xxiii. 8—10; more fully in the forty-second Psalm. This state is different from that noticed in chap. v. 3. The latter is a condition of spiritual sluggishness arising from absence of the Holy Spirit; here the affections are alive, the heart warm by the action of grace; but a sense of the presence of Christ is wanting. In such times of desertion and trial the soul seeks him with great earnestness; periods of conflict, peril, and sorrow, when we feel our best resolutions are nothing before the power of the devil, when the passions of the soul will struggle as though they would burst the cords of the heart asunder; and the fury with which they roll round through the chambers of the soul, reminds us of Virgil's description of the fury of the winds in the cavern of Æolus:

> Where struggling winds and roaring storms he rules
> With sway imperial; curbs with prison, chains.
> Impetuous rage they round their mountain-cave:
> Did he not check their wrath, forth would they burst;
> Land, sea and heav'n in a wild tempest sweep,
> Uptorn from their foundations, through the air.

Even more terrible than these, were the elements which burst so suddenly on the patriarch Job, and buried him under the ruin of his property, his family, his bodily comfort, his friendships, and his spiritual peace. In his passage onward to heaven, every believer has to pass through the valley of the shadow of death; some find it darker and more terrible than others, and have to encounter at its entrance Satan in fiercer mood. There are times of outward desolation and inward trial, when we say with Jacob, "All these things are against me;" and cry with the Psalmist, "Deep calleth unto deep at the noise of thy water-spouts, all thy waves and thy billows are gone over me." The most painful part of these struggles arises from the fiery darts of the devil. They seem at times to fall almost like hail; and attack is succeeded by attack, as though he was determined to weary us out by the very continuance of his assaults. Even struggling hard, with desperate determination, we may find ourselves giving ground; like Christian, we may be almost spent, almost pressed to death, so as to despair of life, and notwithstanding all we can do, be wounded in the head, hand, and foot; may get a dreadful fall; yet is his grace made sufficient for us. No battle can be so terrible as that which the believer does thus sustain against the powers of darkness. With thankfulness do we find hour after hour, and day after day, passing by, and our position yet held against this surging host of deadly foes. Now and then will there be a lull in the conflict, and grace will refresh us with cordials from heaven; but the battle will cease only with the setting of the sun, when around us gathers the nightfall of the grave. But though it be a hard fought day, the sun, like that of Waterloo, will go down on victory. Bunyan understood the spiritual conflict, and has in a few words sketched it with marvellous vigour and truth. When the world see the saint thus enduring "a great fight of afflictions;" see him under fire in the heat of the battle; they, and too often nominal Christians with them, are ready to judge hastily;" to censure him for his conduct; to impute to his own love of sin wounds he has got in his desperate and uncompromising resistance against sin; and congratulate themselves on being perhaps better than he, because they have escaped wounds incurred by him, when, had they been exposed in conflicts through which he has passed, their courage might have failed, and their souls perished.

Every believer who knows his own heart, will adopt the words of Mr. Great-heart concerning Christian's conflict with Apollyon: "No disparagement to Christian, more than to any others whose hap and lot it was. But we will leave the good man, he is at rest, he also had a brave victory over his enemy: let Him grant that dwelleth above, that we fare not worse, when we come to be tried, than he."

> "Through all stations human life abounds
> With mysteries;—for, if Faith were left untried,
> How could the might, that lurks within her, then
> Be shown? her glorious excellence—that ranks
> Among the first of powers and virtues—proved?"

So necessary are conflicts for ripening the excellences of character, and attaining noble rewards and enduring fame, that poetry has made the illustration of this the theme of some of its noblest efforts. Such is the tenor of Spenser's Faery Queen. And in the poem of King Arthur, "The hero thus purified and enlightened by sorrow, is ready to seek the sword, the possession of which confers immortal renown, and could not be won unless by a champion, who, through resistance of strong temptations, had been proved to possess noble moral endowments. The shield is next to be won by heroic valour shown in desperate combat against appalling enemies; not by the valour of the knight, but by the moral greatness of the man; not by warlike deeds, but by resistance to strong temptations, and by clear perception of the relative importance of conflicting duties."* Thus the Scriptures, "Blessed is the man that endureth temptation, for when he is tried he shall receive the crown of life, which the Lord hath promised to them that love him. Jas. i. 12.

* King Arthur, by Sir E. Bulwer Lytton. Ed. Rev. No. 181.

VER. 3.—The watchmen that go about the city found me, to whom I said, Saw ye him whom my soul loveth?

The loneliness and gloom of the spouse wandering at night through the streets, deserted by all save the watchmen, sets forth the darkness and desolation of the soul searching for Christ in these times of desertion and trial. The final state of the Church in glory is represented by the beauty of a city, as in Heb. xii. 22, and Rev. xxi. Now the Church is the city of the living God, but like Israel in the camp in the wilderness, rather than when established in the palaces on Mount Zion. The watchmen above are angels, Rev. xxi. 12; here they are men. Isa. lxii. 6. This class of men have the important trust of guarding the interests of the Church, warning of danger, instructing and comforting troubled souls. "They watch for souls as they that must give account." Heb. xiii. 17. They are stars in the right hand of Christ. Their aid must we seek in times of darkness and sorrow.*
They are expected to know more than others about experimental religion; their duty is to study this as the end of all their investigations. If it was necessary that Jesus should be made in all things like unto his brethren, ministers of the word should be led by the Holy Spirit

* "It is most advisable for tempted persons to consult some able, judicious minister, or compassionate and established Christian, whose counsel and prayers may be singularly useful in this case; observing the assistance which Great-heart gave to the Pilgrims, in passing through the valley. Sometimes temptations may be so multiplied and varied, that it may seem impossible to proceed any further; and the mind of the harassed believer is enveloped in confusion and dismay, as if an horrible pit were about to swallow him up, or the prince of darkness to seize upon him. But the counsel of some experienced friend or minister, exciting confidence in the power, mercy, and faithfulness of God, and encouraging him to 'pray without ceasing,' will at length make way for deliverance."—*Scott's Notes on the Pilgrim's Progress.*

through these exercises of the heart wherein they are to lead and comfort others.

VER. 4.—It was but a little that I passed from them, but I found him whom my soul loveth: I held him, and would not let him go, until I had brought him into my mother's house, and into the chamber of her that conceived me.

Very shortly after leaving them she finds the beloved. Jesus is always to be found near the watchmen, the ministry, the means of grace. How often when we have been seeking Jesus without any comforting sense of his presence, have some bright views of his glory burst upon the soul. Some truth shines forth adapted to our need, some promise precisely suited to our want, some warning that may arouse us from danger. He appears to us as unexpectedly as to the disciples on the way to Emmaus; and like the wise men from the East, on seeing the infant Jesus, we rejoice with exceeding great joy.

"I held him, and would not let him go." With eagerness does the soul then lay hold on our Lord. By night had those holy women been seeking Jesus, at early dawn while it was yet dark on the morning of his resurrection, sorrowful and in tears, when he "met them saying, All hail, and they came and held him by the feet and worshipped him:" this is the manifestation, in a different way, of the feeling now had by us on finding again our Lord. They did in form precisely what we now do by faith. Among the emblematical representations of truth in the Old Testament, this has its illustration in the wrestling of Jacob with the angel. It was night, he was alone, in a lonely place, and about to encounter a dangerous enemy in Esau. Convinced that this being in human form had power to deliver, he laid hold on him and refused to let him go without a blessing. His importunity prevailed, and in that person he found the Lord Jesus.

"I brought him into, &c." Speaking of oriental houses, Dr. Shaw says, "Their chambers are large and spacious, one of them frequently serving a whole family. At one end of each chamber there is a little gallery raised four or five feet, with a balustrade and doubtless a veil to draw in the front of it. Here they place their beds." Hence we have no difficulty in understanding why the bride speaks of her own apartment as connected with her mother's chambers. In this and in the other passage where reference is made to the mother and the mother's apartments, see chap. viii. 2, this is evidently for guarding against the idea of anything improper in this love. In the house and under the eye of a mother, a virgin must be supposed under the very best safeguard against anything like impropriety. The love here contemplated is that chaste, ideal affection, not entirely like anything known on earth, which combines the ardent affection of the marriage relation with the devotion of a brother's and sister's heart, without any unhallowed feeling associated therewith. Hence the expression so frequently used, "my sister-spouse."

Thus finding Jesus, we are anxious to commune with him in secret. In chap. i. 4, he is represented as bringing us into his chambers, drawing us into secret communion with him; here we are set forth as spontaneously drawing him into private communion, seeking intercourse with him by prayer. Though ever dependent on the Holy Spirit as our strength, and as the originating spring of every holy emotion and holy action, there are times when grace seems to visit, enliven, and draw us again to Christ, and there are periods when we feel that reviving grace cannot be expected without offering up supplications with strong cries and tears. Delightful as are ordinances and public duties, we wish, after deliverance from spiritual desertion, to have Jesus much to ourselves in study of the Scriptures, in meditation, in contrition, and in secret prayer. Seeking thus to enjoy confidential fellowship with Jesus where there may be no intrusion, the soul again expresses anxiety to guard against anything likely to make him withdraw: "I charge you, O ye daughters of Jerusalem, &c." ver 5. See chap. ii. 7.

VER. 6.—Who is this that cometh out of the wilderness like pillars of smoke, perfumed with myrrh and frankincense, with all powders of the merchant.

The first grand motive in the series here brought to bear on the heart, is the desirableness of heaven as a place. Chap. ii. 10. After a season of heavenly delight, and glimpses of heavenly glory, we are exposed to spiritual desertion and assaults of the devil, that the power of these motives may be put to test. When we are restored to the joy of his salvation, he allures by assurance of the security and grandeur of our conveyance thither. Dejected because he left us, as in ver. 1, we are told that however we may seem forsaken, we may be sure our souls are during the darkest hours in a chariot paved with love. As though he says to us, 1. Be not discouraged by these withdrawals of Jesus, for there is a state of glory awaiting you in heaven; 2. Do not despond under the heaviest trials, for you are on your road to glory in a conveyance guarded by angels, encompassed with the intercession of Christ, and made of materials precious as love; 3. Though Jesus may at times hide his face and expose us to trials, he loves us even more strongly than is shown in chap. iv.

The Scriptures speak of God's dwelling in heaven, yet coming down to us on earth; of his being continually around us, yet drawing near to us by his Spirit. Persons "absent in body but present in spirit," 1 Cor. v. 3;

may be near each other, yet effectually separated by difference of disposition and by enmity. Thus God may be near us in one sense and afar off in another. Hence there is a spiritual coming to Christ, and there is also a bodily coming to him. The former is by exercising the holy affections now wrought by the Spirit; the latter is by our having a spiritual body and going to be with him in glory. Phil. iii. 21; 1 John iii. 2. Redemption extends to both body and soul—first to the soul, then to the body. All the decay of our bodily system began with spiritual death working in the soul. The condition of the body is determined by the foregoing condition of the soul, of which it is the earthly tabernacle. Spiritual death, when not arrested by redemption, has its consummation in the dissolution of the body in the grave. Now spiritual life follows the same order; first a new life is imparted to the soul, as in regeneration and sanctification, and then, when the soul has been thus renewed, God gives us a new body, a body adapted to the nature of the soul thus restored to newness of spiritual life, and hence characterized as a spiritual body. These two things are here distinguished: the seeking of our Lord mentioned in the former part of this chapter, is the seeking of him with our spirits, but in the mean time we are in our way to meet him in his glorified body, when we shall be made like him by having a spiritual body.

In ver. 6—11, we have, 1. The splendid appearance, ver. 6. 2. What that cortege consists of, viz. his palanquin and its guard, ver. 7, 8. 3. A description of the palanquin, ver. 9, 10. 4. The king awaiting the arrival of this company, ver. 11.

As the leading of Israel through the wilderness was a representation of the progress of the saints towards glory, and as this book sets forth the love of Christ and his people, the words of ver. 6 may find their illustration in the camp in the desert. The object in bringing Balaam up to the high places, &c., Num. xxii. 41, was to have patriarchism pronounce an excommunication on the Jewish church. The patriarchal religion had been superseded by this; but it would not die without an effort, as was afterwards the case with Judaism in reference to Christianity. How imposing was the sight, when from one of the mountain-tops near Pisgah, he beheld the goodly tents of the host of Jacob and Israel coming up from the wilderness, Num. xxiv. 5, 6, beautiful as gardens by the river's side, as the trees of lign-aloes which the Lord hath planted, as cedar-trees beside the waters, the pillar of cloud and of fire overshadowing the whole, with the tabernacle in the midst, and with these, combined the idea of a nuptial procession, as in Homer—

> When from her halls through evening streets they lead
> The bride, with blazing torches, and the sound
> Of hymeneal gladness; rings of youth
> Dance to the melody of flutes and harps;
> And matrons standing in their doors, behold
> The joyous tumult with a wondering smile.*

The region lying between this world and the world where Jesus glorified is awaiting his saints, is as certainly a lonely wilderness as the desert lying between Egypt and Canaan. The angels standing at the gates and on the battlements of the New Jerusalem, see this procession coming up towards the Holy City, and are filled with wonder. As the metropolis of the universe, that city had been heretofore visited by various companies from different quarters of the dominions of the King of kings, but by none presenting an appearance so unusual. Those hitherto have come in a different way; these are drawing

---

* Iliad, book xviii.

near by "a new and living way." Hence the inquiry, "Who is this that cometh out of the wilderness?"

"Like pillars of smoke, &c."* There is not here one pillar, as in the Jewish camp, but pillars, many rising and towering on every side, and spreading into a canopy —or, according to the suggestions of the original word, going up like a palm-tree, straight upward for a distance, and then spreading out like the branches. Perfumes were used in great profusion at eastern marriages; the garments were made to smell richly of myrrh, aloes, and cassia; as they came forth from the ivory palaces, persons led the procession with silver-gilt pots of perfume, and the air was rendered fragrant by burning aromatics in the windows of all the houses in the streets through which the procession was to pass. Here these perfumes were burnt so freely, that they rose in pillars, and combined all possible richness capable of being furnished by the perfumer with all the variety of his spices. If one pillar was such a protection against the Egyptians, and

* "Oily liquids might be burnt as well as powdered gums, in their censers; and it is by no means impossible that the lamps that were carried before her, might be fed with odoriferous oils, and make an agreeable addition to the other precious smoke. So D'Herbelot tells us, the Eastern princes are wont to burn camphor, a precious and odoriferous gum, mingled with wax, to light their palaces in the night; and giving an account of the rich booty the Arabs found at Madain, in pillaging the palace of the Persian monarchs there, he tells us they found magazines of odoriferous camphor, which was wont to be burnt there, at once to light and perfume that palace: not to take notice of the frequent mention of tapers in the Arabian Nights Entertainments, mixed with aloes and ambergris, which gave an agreeable scent, as well as delicate light. As for the clause, "all the chief spices," it is visible that plants, whose flowers or leaves were fragrant, are meant by the word spices, as we may learn from the use of that word in the 16th verse; and the chief spices, therefore, must intend the principal aromatic plants that were known and esteemed in those days."—*Harmer*, 297.

such a glory to Israel in the desert, Exod. xiv. 20, what must be the grandeur and security of these many pillars of incense around the individuals of the host passing onward to glory. Those pillars are the righteousness of Christ, a righteousness glorious to the contemplation, mighty to save. In his righteousness is included all that he did and suffered for us in obtaining salvation; "his intercession is the continued efficacy of his expiatory merit, and has hence been spoken of by some as a perpetual oblation." We would understand by these pillars of incense, both what he did on earth, his righteousness, and what he is now doing in heaven, his intercession. The saint is passing onward to glory, encompassed and protected by both these. As the Jewish high-priest went into the most holy place, amid a cloud of incense from the golden censer, so did Jesus enter heaven, and thus does he there remain amid the cloud of glorious incense of his intercession; and thus must his saints enter there, encompassed with the incense of his prayers in our behalf. His intercession for us is continual in our progress through this world towards heaven. Hence we have always an answer in the heavenly sanctuary to the calumnies of Satan, and may be assured of acceptance with God through him whose offering is unto the Father of a sweet-smelling savour. As the phœnix was fabled to rise from the midst of the fires and sweet odours in which the parent bird had died in the temple of the sun in Egypt, and spread its wings toward heaven, as thus beginning an existence running through centuries; so do our renovated souls rise from amid the richer than aromatic fires and incense in which Jesus perished, and mount upward on wings as eagles, covered with feathers more beautiful than ruby and gold, on the cycle of a life running through ages of ages, carrying with us the memorials of the death of him through whom we live, and bearing them away with us to our eternal repose in the temple of the skies.

Ver. 7.—Behold his bed, which is Solomon's, &c.

These words are the answer to the question in the foregoing verse, "Lo, it is the palanquin of Solomon." The word "bed" here means a kind of sedan chair or open vehicle, in which persons in the East are carried on men's shoulders. Such was the means of conveying the bride to the house of the bridegroom. When Jesus was received up into heaven, it was by a cloud; when he appears the second time, "behold, he cometh with clouds;" "he maketh the clouds his chariot," and not to mention other places, the appearance in Ezek. i., was with a conveyance or chariot of glory beyond description. Thus, the saint is here represented as passing onward in a conveyance, chariot, or whatever called, towards heaven. When God would represent the glory of the way in which Elijah was taken up, he made visible a chariot and horses of fire—as light is the best symbol of what is pure and glorious. Every saint has a conveyance as real, though not visible to bodily eyes. As it is a chariot for the soul, this cannot be seen any more than the soul. In the case of Elijah, the conveyance was seen, because God was taking up body as well as soul. When by withdrawing at death the film of mortality now over them, our eyes are opened like those of the young man of the prophet, 2 Kings vi. 17, we shall find our souls in a bridal chariot, in which, from the moment of regeneration, we have been moving onward to the arms of our beloved Lord. While perfectly free in working out our salvation, on him we are dependent; "in him we live, and move, and have our being;" he gathers us in his arm, and carries us in his bosom; yet all this he does through means, by the chariot of salvation, and through the agency of those who are "ministering spirits." Heb. i. 14.

Hence, around this bed, litter, palanquin of the saint, "are threescore valiant men, of the valiant of Israel. They all hold swords, being expert in war; every man hath his sword on his thigh, because of fear in the night." ver. 8.* On account of the audacity of the Arabs, weddings were often turned into mourning by enemies lying in ambush. See 1 Maccabees ix. 37—41. "They went up and hid themselves under the covert of the mountain; where they lifted up their eyes and looked, and behold there was much ado and great carriage; and the bridegroom came forth and his friends and brethren to meet them, with drums and instruments of music and many weapons: Then Jonathan and those that were with him rose up against them from the place where they lay in ambush, and made a slaughter of them in such sort as many fell down dead, and the remnant fled into the mountains; and they took all their spoils. Thus was the marriage turned into mourning and their noise of their melody into lamentation."

> "It was the custom then to bring away
> The bride from home at blushing shut of day,
> Veiled, in a chariot, heralded along
> By strewn flowers, torches, and a marriage song
> With other pageants."

Around the saint are enemies lying in ambush amid the gloom shrouding from us the invisible world, and anxious to do us every possible injury. The holy angels are our guard against these. "The angel of the Lord encampeth

---

* "With the exception of occasional alarms in the night, caused by thieves attempting to steal our horses, we were not disturbed during our visit."—*Layard*, i. 105.

round about them that fear him." They are sent from heaven as a guard, an escort for us during our passage through this wilderness to heaven.

> "Millions of spiritual beings walk the earth
> Both when we wake and when we sleep; the soul
> Made in this wilderness the Spirit's shrine,
> A thousand liveried angels lacky her
> Driving for off each thing of sin amd guilt."*

And when at death the believer finds his eye opening on the mysteries of the unseen world, hitherto around him, but invisible to flesh, he sees battalions of angels waiting as a triumphant guard, and they close their shining ranks around the heir of heaven, and with the proud tread of victory, escort him safe through the regions of the dead; and the prince of darkness from afar looks with dismay on another soul wrested from his grasp; and the exulting band appproach the New Jerusalem with strains of triumphal music; and they enter in through the gates into the city. In the text, the number of sixty is mentioned, a definite for an indefinite number, a sufficiency for any possible emergencies; and they are called "the valiant of Israel," not a band of mercenaries who cannot be relied on, but native-born soldiers, faithful to their sovereign and his interests, from patriotic attachment; thus we may feel this angelic guard is sufficient for repelling any foes, and will ever be steadfast to us through their devotion to our king.

VER. 9, 10.—*King Solomon made himself a chariot of the wood of Lebanon. He made the pillars thereof of silver, the bottom thereof of gold, the covering of it of purple; the midst thereof being paved with love, for the daughters of Jerusalem.*

The word "chariot" here is explanatory of "bed" in ver. 7, and means a sedan, a portable couch, or palan-

---

* Milton.

quin. The object of these verses is to set before us the remarkable beauty and excellence of the conveyance provided by Solomon for his bride. Such vehicles are even yet in use in the East, and are of equal magnificence. In the year 1796, the British government presented the Nabob of the Carnatic with a carriage of this kind, thus described at the time: "The beams are solid gold, the inside beautifully decorated with silver lining and fringe throughout: the panels are painted in the highest style of finishing, and represent various groups and heads of animals, after the manner of Asia, beaded with gold richly raised above the surface, and engraved. The stays and different other ornaments are f embossed silver." Such litters were in use among the Egyptians. Wilkinson gives a copy of a representation of a person of distinction carried in an open palanquin by four bearers, followed by an attendant with a sort of parasol. Those yet in use in the East are couches with a canopy supported by pillars at the four corners, and hung round with curtains, to protect the person within from the sun, and carried on men's shoulders, or in their hands, by means of poles by which they are supported. They are long enough for the rider to lie down at length, and about three feet broad, though varying in size and richness according to the wealth of the owner.* In this

---

* Robert Fitch, in his voyage to the kingdom of Pegu, in 1591, speaking of its sovereign, says, "The king keepeth great state. When he rideth abroad, he rideth with a great guard, and many noblemen; oftentimes upon an elephant with a fine castle upon him, very fairly gilded with gold; and sometimes upon a great frame like a horse-litter, which hath a little house upon it, covered overhead, but open on the sides, which is all gilded with gold, and set with many rubies and sapphires, whereof he hath infinite store in his country, and is carried upon sixteen or eighteen men's shoulders."

of Solomon, "the pillars" were silver; "the bottom" as in our version, or more correctly, "the railing" around it, was gold; the seat—English version, "covering"—was purple; the midst thereof being checkered or tesselated with love, "for the daughters of Jerusalem." Among the different interpretations of these words, this seems the best, and in accordance with the Hebrew; this chariot was made thus rich and beautiful for their benefit; the last clause being thus understood as referring not merely to the midst paved with love, but to the whole structure of the vehicle.

It seems no part of the mind of the Spirit that we should take this description to pieces, and try to allegorize the several parts. The intention is to represent to us the fact that the believer is carried onward to heaven in a conveyance as costly and glorious as that here described; that the materials are of the richest, choicest, most durable character; that the midst is paved or tesselated with love. The provision made, the means provided for bringing us to glory, are of a rare and splendid nature. After exhausting the things most valuable among men, making the pillars silver, the railing gold, the seat or couch purple, he adopts a feature in the description entirely new, and says the midst is curiously wrought with something more precious than silver or gold, even with love itself—showing that the saint, while thus passing through the wilderness between this world and heaven, between our state of guilt and our state of glory, is in a palanquin of the most costly make, borne up in the hands of angels, surrounded by an armed angelic guard, and reclining on a soft couch beautiful as purple, the most costly colour, with the midst of the litter formed of love—the many acts of divine love from Father, Son, and Holy Spirit, there combining underneath us like the different pieces in a beautiful mosaic, tesselated pavement. In the spirit of this passage, those who wait on the Lord are said to renew their strength; and he will give his angels charge concerning such, to bear them up in their hands, lest at any time they dash their foot against a stone. Isa. xl. 31, Ps. xci. 12. With the author of our faith finishing his temptation in the wilderness, it may be said of every saint passed away to glory:

> "A fiery globe
> Of angels on full sail of wing flew nigh,
> Who on their plumy vans received him soft
> From his uneasy station, and upbore
> As on a floating couch through the blithe air;
> Then in a flowery valley set him down
> On a green bank, and set before him spread
> A table of celestial food, divine
> Ambrosial fruits, fetch'd from the tree of life,
> And from the fount of life ambrosial drink."*

The redeemed soul is a "peculiar treasure," Ps. cxxxv. 4; this litter is the casket, the conveyance, in which it is carried towards heaven by the hands of angels, sent by Jesus, our elder brother, gone away to prepare a place for us in a better land than Egypt, and more fitted to cheer our fainting spirits than the wagons sent by Joseph, which so revived the heart of Jacob.† To

---

* Paradise Regained, book iv. 581.

† With this representation we may compare the following from Pindar, where, in the ninth Pythian Ode, he is speaking of Cyrene: "Whom the long-haired son of Latona snatched away from the recesses of Pelion echoing with the wind, and in his golden chariot brought the virgin huntress, where he constituted her sovereign of the realms teeming with flocks and transcendently fertile. And the silver-

human appearance, we are in the condition of the prophet who ran by the side, while Ahab was within the chariot; yet as the hand of the Lord was on Elijah for enabling him to glide along before the swift-rolling vehicle of the king; and to angels' eyes he was in a chariot far more glorious, unseen by flesh, of a spiritual fabric; thus are we in reality moving towards heaven, while around us, amid the darkness of our present state, angels and the spirits of just men made perfect see "the shining of a flaming fire," Isa. iv. 6, even the splendour of the righteousness of Jesus. The angel of the covenant who appeared to Manoah, when the flame of the sacrifice offered on the rock went up toward heaven, ascended in the flame of the altar, "as in a chariot," ὥσπερ ὀχήματος· says Josephus; and like him, the souls of the redeemed pass up towards glory in this precious chariot of salvation, pillowed on love, surrounded by an escort of angels, amid pillars of incense of the intercession of our divine Redeemer, and wrapped in the splendour of the righteousness of the sacrifice offered for us on the altar of the divine nature of Christ, even "the Rock of ages."

footed Venus, gently touching with her hand, received the Delian stranger, as he alighted from his heaven-built car."

Thus, in the Iliad, Dolon says of the chariot of Rhesus,

"With gold and silver all his chariot burns."

And the same poet thus describes the chariot of Juno:

"Hebe to the chariot roll'd
The brazen wheels, and joined them to the smooth
Steel axle; twice four spokes divided each,
Shot from the centre to the verge. The verge
Was gold, by fellies of eternal brass
Guarded, a dazzling show! The shining naves
Were silver; silver cords, and cords of gold,
The seat upbore: two crescents blazed in front.
The pole was argent all, to which she bound
The golden yoke with its appendant charge
Inserted braces, straps and bands of gold."—*Iliad*, v. 719.

Ver. 11.—Go forth, O ye daughters of Zion, and behold king Solomon with the crown wherewith his mother crowned him in the day of his espousals, and in the day of the gladness of his heart.

These words show the reception awaiting us on our arrival in heaven. While the magnificent cortege just noticed are coming up through the wilderness, that greater than Solomon, the Prince of Peace, is standing ready to receive us with all the gladness of a marriage festivity. The daughters of Zion, a general expression for the inmates of heaven, while gazing on this sight, are called on to behold the splendour of the appearance of Jesus and of his retinue as awaiting his redeemed in glory. The Jews knew nothing richer than the attire of a bridegroom; hence even of the sun, "He cometh forth as a bridegroom out of his chamber." It was here sufficient to mention merely the nuptial crown. The use of nuptial crowns was very ancient and very general.* Selden has gathered the information on this subject in his Uxor Heb. lib. 2. Among the Greeks and Romans, these crowns were usually chaplets of flowers. The Talmud states that

* "It was usual with many nations to put crowns or garlands on the heads of new-married persons. The Mishna informs us that this custom prevailed among the Jews; and it should seem from the passage before us, that the ceremony of putting it on was performed by one of the parents. Among the Greeks the bride was crowned by her mother, as appears from the instance of Iphigenia in Euripides, v. 903. Bochart supposes this the nuptial crown and other ornaments of a bride, alluded to in Ezekiel xvi. 8—12. Geogr. Sacr. p. 2, c. 25. The nuptial crowns used among the Greeks and Romans were only chaplets of leaves or flowers. Among the Hebrews they were not only of these, but also occasionally of richer materials, as gold or silver, according to the rank or wealth of the parties. The original word used in the text is the same used to express a kingly crown in 2 Sam. xii. 30; 1 Chron. xxii. 2; and is often described to be of gold, Esth. viii. 15; Ps. xxi. 4; but appears to have been worn by those who were no kings, Job xix. 9, and was probably often composed of less valuable materials; as of enamelled work, also of roses, myrtle, and olive-leaves."—*Bishop Percy.*

the crown of the bridegroom was of gold or silver, or else a wreath of roses, olives, or myrtle; that the bride's crown was of gold or silver, in the shape of a tower, like those represented on the head of the heathen goddess Cybele. Jesus is crowned with many crowns. Rev. xix. 12. There was no crown given by the ancients for distinguished conduct, which is not merited by our Lord. But on the reception of his ransomed ones, here referred to, there is peculiar propriety in mentioning only the nuptial crown.

We naturally inquire, How will Jesus receive me on my approach to heaven? The answer is here. He is awaiting us, not as he appeared when discoursing on the mount, when sitting at Jacob's well, when weeping over Jerusalem, when ascending from Olivet, or even as when appearing to John at Patmos; but invested with all the glory of heaven, and with the affection of the bridegroom receiving the bride. For "as the bridegroom rejoiceth over the bride, so shall thy God rejoice over thee." Isa. lxii. 5. That time will be a day not of trouble and war, but of marriage festivity; the conflict over; his soul not exceeding sorrowful unto death, as in Gethsemane, but exulting in having finished the work of redemption by the destruction of even the last enemy death, and in having nothing henceforth, but the uninterrupted enjoyment of the society of the bride, the wife of the Lamb. To this period had he reference continually in his humiliation. "For the joy that was set before him, he endured the cross, despising the shame, and is set down at the right hand of the throne of God." Heb. xii. 2. "The Lord shall rejoice in his works." Ps. civ. 31; especially shall he rejoice in the completion of redemption, and in the finishing stroke of the bringing of many sons unto glory. Amid the discouragements, the conflicts, the gloom of earth, with our souls passing onward to heaven in a chariot paved with love, borne in the hands of angels, and with Jesus crowned with glory and honour, crowned with a nuptial crown, awaiting us, well may we rejoice even in tribulation, and sing, "I will greatly rejoice in the Lord, my soul shall be joyful in my God; for he hath clothed me with the garments of salvation, he hath covered me with the robe of righteousness, as a bridegroom decketh himself with ornaments, and as a bride adorneth herself with her jewels." Isa. lxi. 10.

CHAPTER IV.

THE soul, thus conveyed to the bosom of Jesus, is oppressed with a deepening sense of unworthiness, and finds difficulty in believing there can be so glorious a destiny awaiting us; conscious of our corruptions and short-comings, we cannot understand how the pure eyes of Jesus can see anything in us attractive. Hence, he takes special pains to enlarge on this point, and assure us how greatly he delights in beholding our ripening graces. This is the portion of the Scriptures which sets forth what is thought by Christ, the King of glory, concerning those who are despised and offcast by the world.

When Zeuxis would paint Helen the most beautiful of women, he copied the beauties from several different persons, and by concentrating these in an individual, represented a beau ideal of feminine grace.* In these following

---

* These principles have been laid down by Cicero for elucidating another subject. "We can conceive of something more beautiful than even the statues of Phidias and the pictures I have mentioned, than descriptions of both the bride and the beloved, the same course is pursued by the Holy Spirit, save that the beauties are here embodied in words instead of colours, and are represented by comparisons drawn from the beauties of nature. Yet it is entirely according to the rules of poetry and the laws of nature, that the beauty of a person be illustrated by the beauty of natural objects. Lord Jeffrey says, "Our sense of beauty depends entirely on our previous experience of simpler pleasures or emotions, and consists in the suggestion of agreeable or interesting sensations with which we had formerly been made familiar by the direct and intelligible agency of our common sensibilities; and that vast variety of objects to which we give the common name of beautiful, become entitled to that appellation, merely because they all possess the power of recalling or reflecting those sensations of which they have been the accompaniments, or with which they have been associated in our imagination by any other more casual bond of connection." The same, or very similar effects may be produced on the mind from different sources and by different causes. A picture may make impressions of beauty very like those raised by a landscape of which it is the copy; music may be so composed as to start feelings of the same kind; a relic, a memento, may be the occasion of reviving a whole cloud of remembrances; things very unlike in point of fact may awaken the same sensations in the breast, by suggesting analogies: as when Ossian says, "The music of Carryl was like the

---

which we can think of nothing more perfect in their kind. Yet that artist when about to make the statue of Jupiter and of Minerva, did not draw his representation from any visible thing, but there was abiding in his mind an imaginary form of beauty, and studying this attentively, he fashioned his representations after this image."—*Cicero, Orator,* 2.

memory of joys that are past, pleasant and mournful to the soul." The grounds or causes of beauty, while the result or internal emotion is always identical in its nature, are multiplied and various. In other words, beauty in the mind is one, while outward beauty, or rather the causes of beauty in outward objects, is many."

Now, in these descriptions, Jesus wishes to give us an idea of the impressions of beauty and pleasure he has in contemplating the souls of the saints. Hence, he must use resemblances, and those of things we can see and enjoy. He might have used comparisons drawn from the angelic host and superior beings; but such illustrations could not have done us any good, for they could not convey to us any idea. Nor would it answer to use references to others of the human race; for there is no perfection on earth, and the Scriptures are for the benefit of mankind at large in all ages; so that the reference should be to things which may be essentially lasting. Here we find an unbounded field opened in the beauties of nature. The resemblance in these comparisons consists not in any outward likeness, but lies in the views and effects produced in the views and sensations of the soul, in the pleasure had in contemplating these natural objects. Here is light combining seven different colours; how would the philosopher represent what he sees in it, to an ignorant man? He would say, one of these is like the violet, another blue like the sky, a third like the verdure, another like the rose. In these comparisons, the only resemblance is in the effect produced on the mind by the colours. These natural objects and the rainbow, so unlike in other respects, agree in this—in making certain impressions on us which are expressed by our words for those colours. Now the pure in heart are growing like God, who is light; and Jesus, in pointing out what hidden beauty he sees in the soul, says, those graces of the Christian life produce on him impressions more pleasing than those made on us by the lovely objects there specified in nature. And the mode of some interpreters in explaining these, is as unreasonable as it would be to run the parallel farther than the mere colour, out into the most minute particulars; between the tints of the rainbow and the objects by which they might be illustrated.

This is exactly what might be expected in cases like the present. Christ is a spiritual being; and though invested with a body, that is a spiritual body. There can therefore be no outward resemblance between him and these material objects; nor between these and the renewed soul as it appears in his eyes. That likeness must therefore exist in the emotions and impressions made on the soul.

VER. 1.—Behold, thou art fair, my love; behold, thou art fair; thou hast doves' eyes within thy locks.

See notes on chap. i. 15.* The large beautiful eye of

---

* "It was pleasant, now and then, to look up from one's book, as the window was darkened by a slight turban from which rich tresses hung over the shoulder, and dark but gentle eyes shone beneath it. The bosom was generally open, or but partially enclosed by the crape garment within; a light turban, or a handkerchief of Damascus silk, covered the head, from which the rich hair flowed free, or was plaited into two long braids. Suddenly the door opened, the tapestry that hung over it was moved aside by a beautifully rounded arm, on which jewels gleamed, and there stepped forth a female form which fascinated my attention as if it had been a vision. She had a light gauzy turban, with a glittering fringe falling gracefully over the shoulder; masses of black and shining hair, that made the forehead and delicately browned cheek look as fair as a Circassian's; if a thought of luxury hovered upon the richly rosy mouth, it was awed into admiration by the large dark eyes, so fearless, yet so modest, glancing round as if they read a meaning in everything, and everywhere, yet calm and self-possessed in their consciousness of power."—*Warburton's Crescent and Cross*, ii. 132.

the Syrian dove appears even more beautiful when seen amid its native groves of noble trees and rich foliage; and hence the eyes of the saint are spoken of as embowered within her locks.* The point of the words does therefore seem to be this, that Jesus contemplates the expression of love beaming from the soul of the pure in heart, with a pleasure greater than what is felt by us in gazing on the large, sparkling, melting eyes of the Syrian dove, amid the wild beauty of its native groves.

Thy hair is as a flock of goats that appear from mount Gilead.

The Hebrew here reads, "Thy hair is as a flock of goats that lie down from mount Gilead;" that is, like a flock of goats lying along the sides of mount Gilead from the top towards the bottom, so that they seem to hang from it. The hair of the oriental goat has the fineness of silk, and is observed by an ancient naturalist to bear a great resemblance to the fine ringlets of a woman's hair. The Angora species of goat is probably meant here. The country of Gilead was most beautiful and fertile, and abounding in rich pastures and aromatic growths, among which was the celebrated balsam. The whole region is covered with groups of limestone mountains, intersected by fertile valleys, and includes the territory east of Jordan, as far south as the Jabbok. Hills rising behind hills in pleasing elevations, clothed with luxuriant verdure; the finest trees and noblest oaks; lovely slopes opening in the forest, and affording the best pastures and most lovely flowers; valleys murmuring with

---

* We retain the rendering "within thy locks," rather than "within thy veil." 1. The same Hebrew word is translated "locks," in Isa. xlvii. 2. 2. The Arabic root, as given in Gesenius and Winer, favours this. 3. The connection requires this meaning. 4. Locks adds to the consistency of the portrait; and the Jewish females carefully cultivated a luxuriant growth of hair.

limpid rills; and the romantic wildness softened by lovely park-like scenes; all combined to form a landscape so delightful that the beholder could hardly persuade himself it was real. Such mountain scenes were more beautiful when on their slopes might have been seen a flock of these beautiful goats lying down. The comparison of a fine head of hair to the long, silk-like fleece of such goats in such a scene, was natural. Few things could be more beautiful than the sight of such a flock reclining on the verdant, balmy slopes of Gilead, on a clear, calm day. Now in conveying to us an idea of the satisfaction Jesus has in dwelling on his saints, he here gives an additional particular, and says, that in contemplating us, another group of delightful impressions is gathered into his heart, like that felt in gazing on a flock of those goats, with long, silky hair, amid the richness, beauty, and grandeur of Gilead.

VER. 2.—Thy teeth are like a flock of sheep that are even shorn,* which came up from the washing; whereof every one bear twins, and none is barren among them.

Rather, "thy teeth are like a flock of sheep all of the same size." The word rendered "bear twins" is in

* The word "even shorn," means of an equal size. 1. This is not the common word for shorn in the Hebrew. 2. The word, in other places, has a meaning in accordance with what we here give. 1 Kings vi. 25, "were of one size;" also, 1 Kings vii. 37, "one size." "This expression," says Rosenmüller, "embodies the idea, that two or more things, whether of wood or stone, had been so wrought that the same relative proportion was preserved among them. By a metaphor thence derived, this Hebrew word is applied to sheep, for showing that throughout the flock they were as much alike as if they had been fashioned from wood or metal, after the same pattern." 3. The design of the comparison requires it, as applying to the teeth, to mean they were of equal size. 4. The idea of perfection is intended; this is not associated with sheep shorn; their being of equal size, and coming up from the washing-pool immediately before shearing, represents them as in all respects perfect.

Exod. xxvi. 24, "coupled together," speaking of the boards of the tabernacle, and may refer to the flocks standing close together; as "none is barren" expresses the perfection of the flock. Coming up from the place of washing, they had fleeces in perfection of growth as well as whiteness. The beauty of the teeth is spoken of by Lucian: "When laughing, she showed her teeth; in what way shall I express how white they are, how symmetrical, how perfectly fitted together? They are like a very beautiful necklace of pearls glistening and of the same size, thus ranged in regular order. They received additional beauty from the redness of the lips; for they appeared between them, like the cut ivory in Homer, not some broader, some larger than others, or separated, as is very frequently the case, but with a perfect uniformity of all in colour, size, and arrangement."* This is but another mode of illustrating the same idea, which, to a pastoral people like the Jews, was more beautifully represented in the comparison in the text. The illustration of this verse pours into the mind a flood of delightful ideas, and this goes a step farther in showing the aggregate of pleasing feelings had by Jesus in contemplating the saint.

Ver. 3.—Thy lips are like a thread of scarlet, and thy speech is comely.

The colour here meant seems to be a deep red, bright rich crimson: this was the meaning of the word "scarlet," in the time of James I. The colour now known as such, was then unknown. According to Wilkinson, the colour was imparted to the thread before woven into the cloth. The force of the comparison here lies in the

* Lucian, Imagines, vol. vi. p. 11.

colour; the lips were delicately free from undue thickness, and of the most beautiful deep red. The Jews knew no more beautiful red than the bright rich crimson here noticed as appearing in a skein of thread carefully dyed.

"Thy speech," or, as we should read, by a common figure of rhetoric, thy 'mouth is beautiful.'* While the colour of the lips is thus beautiful, the whole mouth is equally perfect.

Thy temples are like a piece of a pomegranate within thy locks.

This simile is still common in the East. Thus, in an anonymous Persian ode, cited by Sir William Jones, "The pomegranate brings to my mind the blushes of my beloved, when her cheeks are coloured with a modest resentment." The word *temples* is used for the upper part of the cheeks near them, and the design of this passage is to express the peculiar freshness, beauty, and ruddy colour of the cheeks. Some would make allusion here to the flower of the "pomegranate, rich with its bright green leaves, and its blossoms of that beautiful and vivid red which is excelled by few even of the most brilliant flowers of the East." We suppose the reference is however to a piece of the pomegranate, which is about the size of an orange, and contains within its hard, brown rind, a number of cells divided by membraneous partitions, in which lie in rows the seeds or grains, pellucid, tinged with red, and shining like crystal. When cut up, or bursting and displaying its seeds, this fruit

---

* "Both ancient and modern writers of the East agree in describing the mouth with simplicity, 'Her mouth small and vermilion,' says the writer of the Arabian Nights Entertainments. 'Her lips are like a thread of scarlet,' says the Jewish Poet."—*Harmer*, 289.

was of the richest vermilion. Hence the Portuguese poet, as quoted by Good,

> "The pomegranate of orange hue,
> Whose open heart a brighter red displays
> Than that which sparkles in the ruby's blaze."

Among the ladies of Persia the hair is still suffered to fall loosely over the forehead and cheeks, and is generally perfumed with the most exquisite essences. An oriental poet, quoted by Good, says, "O thou, whose lips, which outshine the grains of the pomegranate, are embellished, when thou speakest, by the brightness of thy teeth!" And in the spirit of the foregoing illustrations, is the following: "Thy lips, O thou most beautiful among women! are a bandhujiva flower; the lustre of the madhuca beams on thy cheek; thine eye outshines the blue lotos; thy nose is a bud of the tila; the cunda-blossom yields to thy teeth."

VER. 4.—Thy neck is like the tower of David, builded for an armoury, whereon there hang a thousand bucklers, all shields of mighty men.

This tower of David was probably the noblest of the towers built by him, of white marble, on a summit of Zion. Sandys says, "Aloft on the uttermost angle of mount Zion, stood the tower of David, whose ruins are yet extant, of a wonderful strength and admirable beauty, adorned with shields and the arms of the mighty." Speaking of Tyre, the prophet says, "They hang their shields upon thy walls round about; they have made thy beauty perfect." Ezek. xxvii. 11. Thus Pausanias, concerning the temple of Jupiter at Olympia: "On each corner of the roof is placed a gilded vase, and on the top of the pediment a statue of Victory, gilded likewise, under which is hung up a golden shield, with a figure of

the gorgon Medusa carved upon it. The inscription on
the shield imports it to have been a gift of the Tana-
greans for a victory gained over the Argives and
Athenians. On the cornice, which runs round the
temple on the outside over the columns, are hung one
and twenty gilt shields, a present from Mummius, the
Roman general, who took and destroyed Corinth."
According to Layard, "The castles of the maritime
people, whose conquest is recorded by the Kouyunjik
bas-reliefs, are distinguished by the shields hung round
the walls. Around the sides of the vessels were also
suspended the shields of the warriors."* The ancients
bestowed great care on their shields, adorning them with
precious metals and elaborate engraving, as may be seen
from the description of the shield of Achilles in the
Iliad. "King Solomon made two hundred targets of
beaten gold. And he made three hundred shields of
beaten gold; three pounds of gold went to one shield;
and the king put them in the house of the forest of
Lebanon." 1 Kings x. 16. When the text says, "all
shields of mighty men," it means simply all were shields
the most costly and beautiful. As the Jews built their
nobler edifices of white marble, a tower of this kind
rising on the summit of mount Zion, hung around with
shields of gold like those of Solomon, would furnish an
exquisite simile for illustrating the beauty of the graceful
neck of the bride, adorned with the rich ornaments and
necklace of those bygone ages. We can conceive of
nothing more appropriate and beautiful. The shields of
the warriors associate with the beauty of the tower the
recollection of the noble deeds and triumphs in which
those shields had been borne; as the pleasure had by

* Layard's Nineveh, vol. ii. 296.

Jesus in contemplating his saints is increased by the remembrance of his sufferings and victories in working out their salvation.

VER. 5.—Thy two breasts are like two young roes that are twins, which feed among the lilies.

All the monuments and pictures of ancient Egypt show us that the ancient oriental ladies dressed so as to leave the busts fully open to view, and of course there could then be no impropriety in alluding to, or describing that part of the person. It may be added, that this is the custom of modern oriental,* as well as of ancient oriental dress. Lilies abounded in their pasture-grounds; and the young twin roes, with eyes uncommonly black and large, creatures so exquisitely beautiful, that their name, as here used, signifies loveliness in general, would present a scene of the greatest pastoral beauty, while feeding in meadows overspread with those delightful flowers. In Proverbs there is a like allusion, " Rejoice with the wife of thy youth. Let her be as the loving hind and pleasant roe ; let her breasts satisfy thee at all times, and be thou ravished always with her love." Chap. v. 19.

Now, in the comparisons of the foregoing verses, the thing to be illustrated is the general beauty of the pious soul in the eyes of Jesus. The point around which they

---

* "The virgins wore their hair floating in exuberant curls over their shoulders; their dress is indescribable by male lips; all I can say of it is, that it is very graceful and pretty, and lavishly open at the bosom."—*Warburton.*

Theocritus puts the following into the mouth of Grecian virgins, on a nuptial occasion:

"While we, descending to the city gate,
Arrayed in decent robes that sweep the ground,
With naked bosoms, and with hair unbound."—*Idyl.* xv. 134.

are all clustered is stated in ver. 1, "Thou art fair;" this is repeated in ver. 7, "Thou art all fair." This is the golden thread which runs through this part of the allegory, and unites these poetical allusions in one string of unearthly pearls. Losing sight of this, most commentators have marred the passage by separating these emblems from one another, and appropriating them to other uses than the one intended by the Holy Spirit. What would be thought of a person who, under the plea of heightening the effect of a beautiful picture by a great artist, could cut out the several figures, the trees, the waters, the tinted clouds, and exhibit them apart in every imaginable variety of light and position? This would show something more than want of judgment. No argument would be necessary for making us feel such was never the mind of the artist. The common method of expounding this and the other kindred passages in the Song, seems no less unreasonable. The Apollo Belvidere can be appreciated, not by breaking off and examining severally an arm, a leg, or any other part detached, but by studying the whole, uninjured and untouched. These exquisite portraitures by the Holy Spirit must be viewed in the same way, as they are set constituting a group, a whole; and the various ideas of beauty radiating from them, must be gathered into a focus on the mind. How beautiful the scenes, how rich the pleasure, in contemplating the flock of silken-haired goats on beautiful, verdant Gilead; the even-sized, purely white, in all points perfect, flock of sheep coming up amid the beauties of early spring, from groves beside the pure waters; the deep, rich crimson of the scarlet thread; the vermilion blush of the slice of pomegranate; the tower of David, of white marble, hung round with costly shields, the mementos of noble achievements, rising in delicate majesty on mount Zion; the twin gazelles feeding among the fresh-blown lilies;—what a strong impression of beauty is made on the mind by viewing any one of those scenes at a time; how overpowering the sense of the beautiful, could the heart receive at the same time all the delightful impressions from these different sources, combined in one luxurious, glorious flood. Yet even that, however overwhelming and perhaps impossible for us, could give but a faint representation of the beauty seen by Jesus in the humblest of his saints, and the pleasure had by him in dwelling on their beauties of holiness. We are justified in saying, that the perfection of the nature of the redeemed will be the crowning beauty of all the works of God, the full-blown flower of which universal creation may be called the trunk and stem. Surely the glorified humanity of the Son of God, the nature which is taken into union with the Godhead, must surpass every other manifestation of creative power. That nature, when fully glorified, will differ infinitely more from the same nature seen in its germ in the babe of Bethlehem, than the beauteous flower differs from the humble seed. It is reasonable, it is right, that Jesus should thus honour the nature taken into oneness with his divinity, by making it the highest possible development of created beauty, splendour, and glory. But to this glorified nature of the man Christ Jesus, the nature of his redeemed people shall be made like. "Who shall change our vile body that it may be fashioned like unto his glorious body," Phil. iii. 21; "When he shall appear, we shall be like him," 1 John iii. 2. And with him there is no succession, all is present, so that he now sees in his saints all the glory which shall ever invest them, and which we may be years or ages in beholding; and thus contemplating it, he would give us an idea of his pleasure therein by such language as in the text, by referring us to our delight in gazing on whatever is most beautiful in the present world. The rich, the great, the noble of earth, look on the humble believer, only as Dives looked on Lazarus, to pity or despise; as the Jews looked on him who was in their eyes as a root out of a dry ground, with no form, nor comeliness, nor beauty, Isa. liii. 2; yet as certainly as the human nature of Jesus has been glorified and exalted far above all principality, and power, and might, and dominion, and every name that is named, not only in this world, but also in that which is to come, Eph. i. 21, so certainly shall these despised ones of Jesus be glorified with him, and be with him where he is, that they may behold his glory. John xvii. 24. Why should we heed the censure or praise of the world, when we are thus esteemed by the King of kings?

VER. 6.—Until the day break, and the shadows flee away, I will get me to the mountain of myrrh, and to the hill of frankincense.

While in this world preparing for the day of our espousals, we are not cut off from communication with Jesus. He who views us with the delight set forth in the foregoing verses, has appointed a place where he may always be found by us at present. That place is designated in this verse. For an explanation of the first clause, see chap. ii. 17. When passing over Lebanon and by Damascus, Pompey the Great is said to have passed through sweet smelling groves and woods of frankincense and balsam. "The approach to Lebanon is adorned with olive-plantations, vineyards, and luxuriant fields; and its lower regions, besides the olive and the vine, are beautified with the myrtle, the styrax, and other odoriferous shrubs; and the perfume which exhales from these plants is increased by the fragrance of the cedars which crown its summits, or garnish its declivities. The great rupture which runs a long way up into the mountain, and is on both sides exceedingly steep and high, is clothed from the top to the bottom with fragrant evergreens, and everywhere refreshed with streams descending from the rocks in beautiful cascades. The cedar-apples growing on the famous cedars must be classed with the scented fruits of the oriental regions; and have perhaps contributed greatly to the fragrance for which the sacred writers so frequently celebrate the mountains of Lebanon."*

The mountain of frankincense is the place where Jesus has established the mercy-seat. Zion, where our Lord dwelt amid the Shechinah, was a mountain of incense gushing from the censer and the golden altar; but the place where Jesus now dwells by his Spirit and meets with his saints, he would represent as fragrant with richer dews, so rich that here the odours come not from one altar or censer, but from groves crowded with trees of incense, every one of which is an altar, and with flowers every one of which is a censer, pouring upon the dewy air unearthly fragrance. Here, too, the point of the comparison is in the pleasing effect produced on the soul: the person who might go up into a hill of myrrh and frankincense at dewy eve, could not have emotions so pleasant as those arising in the heart drawing near unto the presence of Jesus and the sacred atmosphere spread by the Holy Spirit around the throne of grace. Fragrant odours are a favourite emblem in the Scriptures for expressing the gracious influences of the Spirit.

How delightful are the spiritual odours diffused around the heart at the mercy-seat, called a mountain, because apart from the busy scenes of the world; because the

* Paxton's Illustrations.

appointed place of God's meeting with his ancient people was on mount Moriah; and because, when Jesus wished to pray, he went apart into a mountain, Matt. xiv. 23; Luke ix. 2. As we come to the mercy-seat with our spiritual apprehensions enlivened by grace, we feel ourselves entering an atmosphere different from that of the world, and breathing an air so pure, so rich, so calm, that it must be a foretaste of heaven. At times of special manifestations of the Holy Spirit, the believer may sometimes feel as though in an atmosphere of calmness, purity, peace, and softened delight, around the soul, different from anything of this world—something which is to the heart what the air of heaven must be to the spiritual body, than which the air of the Holy City could hardly be more pure, refreshing, and pleasant. This is the Holy Spirit diffusing around us more and more of the amosphere which the soul will breathe in heaven; and at the same time making us feel how appropriately the place where such blessedness is enjoyed, is called the mountain of myrrh and hill of frankincense.

> "In the centre of a world whose soil
> Is rank with all unkindness, compassed round
> With such memorials, I have sometimes felt
> It was no momentary happiness
> To have *one* Enclosure where the voice that speaks
> In envy or detraction is not heard;
> Which malice may not enter; where the traces
> Of evil inclinations are unknown;
> Where love and pity tenderly unite
> With resignation; and no jarring tone
> Intrudes, the peaceful concert to disturb
> Of amity and gratitude."

To this place will Jesus get till the day break and the shadows flee away; till we pass into the final state of glory where all these former things are done away, and there shall be no night there. The mercy-seat is the appointed place of meeting with him till that time. Not only will he come to that place occasionally in answer to prayer, as in chap. ii. 17; he may always be found there. Whenever we wish to meet with Jesus, we have only to betake ourselves to the place of prayer. After the day breaks, he will be found by us in the heavenly Jerusalem, where we shall no longer enjoy his society dimly, as in a grove of frankincense, amid the shadows of night, but clearly, perfectly, knowing even as we are known. 1 Cor. xiii. 10.

VER. 7.—Thou art all fair, my love; there is no spot in thee.

This verse is the first of eight reasons he gives for encouraging us to meet him on the hill of frankincense, at the throne of grace. See chap. i. 15, 16. There, he speaks of the saint as being fair in his eyes; here, as being all fair, "without spot, or wrinkle, or any such thing." Eph. v. 27. How fair were Moses and Elijah when on the mount they appeared with Jesus in glory, being made like him; and his face did shine as the sun, and his raiment was white as the light. Luke ix. 29. Now, with Jesus there is no such thing as time; he inhabiteth eternity; with him there is no succession, all is present; and we are in his eyes attired with his glorious righteousness and luminous with the splendours of his Spirit; we are viewed by him precisely as we are when our sanctification is finished.

How kind, therefore, are these words, and how fitted for encouraging us to frequent the throne of grace. They express what is precisely the first encouragement necessary for us in coming to him in prayer. The more fervent our love, and the stronger our apprehension of his glory, the deeper is the sense of our vileness, unworthiness, and guilt, often so strong as to make us hesitate, under the impression that he cannot receive such sinners as ourselves. But he cheers us to come, assuring us that he has blotted out all our iniquities; that his blood cleanseth from all sin; that he will purge us with hyssop, and we shall be clean; he will wash us and make us whiter than snow. Ps. li. 7.

VER. 8.—Come with me from Lebanon, my spouse, with me from Lebanon: look from the top of Amana, from the top of Shenir and Hermon, from the lions' dens, from the mountains of the leopards.

Lebanon is well known as the noble range on the north of the land of promise, "that goodly mountain" which Moses so desired to visit. Amana was probably the southern part of Anti-Libanus, and was so named, perhaps, from the river which had its sources at its foot, called in 2 Kings v. 12, Abana, but in the margin, Amana. Shenir and Hermon were names for the same mountain; Hermon perhaps the name for the whole mountain; and Sirion the name for the part of it belonging to the Sidonians; Shenir for that belonging to the Amorites. All these lay in the same region in the northern borders of Palestine, and while abounding in the grandest and most attractive mountain scenery, were infested with leopards and lions, no less than with robbers, so that they might truly be called "the mountains of prey." Ps. lxxvi. 4. The view from these summits was extensive and unsurpassed.*

* "The lofty summits of Lebanon were the chosen haunts of various beasts of prey, the print of whose feet Maundrell and his party observed in the snow. But they are not confined to these situations; a recent traveller continued descending several hours, through varied scenery, presenting at every turn some new feature, distinguished either by its picturesque beauty or awful sublimity. On arriving at one of the lower swells, which form the base of the mountain, he and

Now these mountains, thus beautiful but dangerous, are put in contrast with the mountain of myrrh and hill of frankincense. The beloved would have his spouse leave the former, and seek his society in the retreats of the latter. The verse does then give a second reason for dwelling with Jesus at the mercy-seat. Those mountains are like the world, with its high places and pleasures, attractive but dangerous, beautiful to the eye, but filled with lurking places of the most stealthy and deadly foes. "The mountain of the Lord's house," Isa. ii. 2, Moriah, was more glorious and excellent, or, as it may better be read, brighter, more glorious, than the mountains of prey, Lebanon, Amana, Hermon, and Shenir; because, however rich the natural scenery of these latter, they were infested with beasts of prey, while the former was the place where Jehovah had in Salem his tabernacle, and his dwelling-place in Zion; where was the word of life, the emblems of heaven, the divine oracle, the cloud of glory overshadowing the mercy-seat.

The world is attractive and beautiful, but dangerous and deadly. Amid its specious scenes are lurking enemies, like the lion, powerful, 1 Pet. v. 8, and like the leopard, stealthy, Eph. vi. 11. In circumstances of the greatest prosperity, our adversary, the devil, with his agents, wicked men, "lieth in wait, secretly, as a lion in his den, that they may privily shoot at the upright in heart." From all these dangers and snares, the throne of grace is a refuge. This is established, not among the

---

his party broke rather abruptly into a deep and thick forest. As they traversed the bocage, the howlings of wild animals were distinctly heard from the recesses."—*Paxton.*

"We lodged this night on the very top of Libanus. We saw in the snow, prints of the feet of several wild beasts, which are the sole proprietors of these parts of the mountains."—*Maundrell,* 140.

mountains of prey, but on the hill of frankincense, on Zion, where is Jehovah's dwelling-place amid the innumerable company of angels: "No lion shall be there, nor any ravenous beast shall go up thereon; it shall not be found there; but the redeemed shall walk there." Isa. xxxv. 9. There, we do indeed dwell in the secret place of the Most High, and abide under the shadow of the Almighty. There is no place of safety on earth, save in that sacred refuge, under that heavenly shade. And while those who are enjoying the world are continually in greater danger than those wandering among dens of ravenous beasts; they who are in the company of Jesus have not only a perfect security against every possible evil, but are breathing an air richer than frankincense, and enjoying confidential friendship with the King of kings. Well may we, therefore, say with the Psalmist, "Because the Lord hath chosen Zion, because he hath desired it for his habitation; this is my rest for ever, here will I dwell, for I have desired it." Ps. cxxxii. 13.

VER. 9.—Thou hast ravished my heart, my sister, my spouse; thou hast ravished my heart with one of thine eyes, with one chain of thy neck.

After all the attempts to alter the shade of meaning by another translation and emendation of the text, the common version seems the best. The idea is, that even a partial glimpse of the beauties and ornaments of the bride, had so filled the heart of the beloved with intense affection, as to unheart, unman him; and the ardour of love thus felt, he gives as another reason for her coming away to meet him at the appointed place, on the mountain of myrrh. He calls her "my sister, my spouse," or, as it might be, "my sister-spouse." The word sister is applied to the wife in Tobit vii. 4, 16. Yet, keeping in mind this book is an allegory, as stated in the Introduction, we imagine the appellation of "sister" is here used for expressing more perfectly than "spouse" alone would do, the relation of Jesus and his people. Language can at best give us only a very imperfect expression of spiritual and heavenly things. Hence the necessity for multiplying types, illustrations, and epithets, in the Scriptures. So, while the relation between Jesus and the redeemed soul may in many respects be represented by that existing between husband and bride, it is in some essential points different; and that difference may be marked by the relation of brother and sister, for separating therefrom all unhallowed and carnal ideas. The union between Christ and his people is one combining the purest and noblest characteristics of both the unions just mentioned, separated from everything earthly and sensual, having the ardour of affection and the oneness of the marriage relation, with the purity and sacredness of a brother's and sister's love. This is a distinction of very great importance for understanding rightly the Song. Hence the Holy Spirit is so careful to repeat the appellation "my sister," as well as spouse. See chaps. iv. 12; v. 1, 2. This repetition has not been made without design by that pen of inspiration which never uses a superfluous word; and the many pitiable interpretations put by excellent men on some passages, show the necessity there was for closing the door against those unfortunate misapprehensions which this single word "sister" thus introduced and thus repeated was intended to prevent. The delicacy and emphasis with which this is here done by the Holy Spirit, is worthy of all admiration.

Like the Queen of Sheba, of whom it is recorded that on seeing the glory of Solomon "there was no more spirit in her," 1 Kings x. 5, the beloved says his heart was carried away with one of her eyes, with one chain of her neck—a most delicate and forcible way of expressing the very great intensity of his affection. It is not intimated that he was not acquainted with the full effect of all her charms; he seems to use this language as the best mode of setting forth the delight had in her beauty. The heart was ravished by merely a partial view of her loveliness; what shall then be said of the effect produced by the full disclosure of her beauty! Oriental poets often use the same language: "I meditate on the ravishing glances darted from her eye." And again, "Bring speedily to my presence her who has stolen the heart of Mejnún with a glance."* Theocritus speaks of "A most bitter wound inflicted on the breast by the dart of powerful Venus." And speaking of a beauty, Horace mentions the graceful turn of her neck. Wilkinson says of the Egyptians, "Handsome and richly ornamented necklaces were a principal part of the dress both of men and women. They consisted of gold, or of beads of various qualities and shapes, disposed according to fancy, generally with a large drop or figure in the centre. Some wore simple gold chains, in imitation of string, to which a stone scarabæus, set in the same precious metal, was appended. A set of small cups, or covered saucers, of bronze gilt, hanging from a chain of the same materials, were sometimes worn by women; a necklace of which has been found belonging to a Theban lady, offering a striking contrast in their simplicity to the gold leaves inlaid with lapis lazuli, red and green stones, of another she wore; which served, with many more in her possession, to excite the admiration of her friends."† Withdrawing from the

* A Persian poem quoted by Sir William Jones.
† Ancient Egyptians, vol. ii. p. 375. In the Hecuba of Euripides, the chorus speak of the daughter of Priam, slain at the tomb of Achilles, dyed in blood gushing in a dark stream from her neck adorned with

spouse for the mountain of myrrh, the beloved has a glimpse of her beautiful necklace and melting eye, as bidding him adieu; and then in this verse assures her she would not fail to meet him on the hill of frankincense, did she know the ardour and intensity of his love. After the farewell spoken, while casting a longing, lingering look behind, he found a single glance of her eye and view of the golden chain of her neck causing his affection to burst forth afresh, in a vehement flame; from this she might judge with what delight he would receive her in the balmy retreats of their appointed place of meeting.

And from this we may understand with what a heart-warm welcome Jesus will gather us to his bosom, when we withdraw to meet him at the throne of grace. In coming to the mercy-seat we are apt to draw near rather with a feeling that our Lord permits it, than with the impression he is deeply anxious to receive us, and meets us with delight. Through lingering unbelief, the sense of unworthiness makes us think he can hardly rejoice to meet us. But, "Thou meetest him that rejoiceth and worketh righteousness, those that remember thee in thy ways." Isa. lxiv. 5. Our besetting sin, the desire for merit, makes us hesitate. Jesus will love us no better in heaven than he loves us now. Merit in us, personal excellence, has nothing to do with his love. This will be no stronger towards us when invested with the spiritual body in glory,

---

gold. And Homer mentions Amphimachus coming, like a girl, to the war, arrayed in gold. And in the Homeric Hymns we have the same idea,—

"When he the goddess viewed without disguise,
Her shining neck beheld, and radiant eyes,—
Awed and abashed, he turned his head aside,
Attempting with his robe his face to hide,
Confused with wonder and with fear oppressed."

Hymn to Venus, 182.

See also notes on chap. vii. 2.

than it is at present, amid our infirmities and imperfect sanctification. The spring and strength of his affection is entirely apart from us, and independent of anything like goodness in ourselves. His love cannot know increase nor diminution. He cannot welcome us with any stronger affection to heaven, than that with which he now welcomes us to the throne of grace. The words of this verse are but another mode of expressing the greatness of the love of Christ, and his readiness to receive us, as a motive for our coming with "boldness to the throne of grace, that we may obtain mercy and find grace to help in time of need." Heb. iv. 16. That love is represented as passing knowledge. Eph. iii. 19. If it passeth knowledge, it must pass expression; and therefore such language as this must be viewed as an effort for conveying, though yet in a very dim way, all that can now be known of this glorious and incomprehensible truth. The person whose heart has been completely carried away with the loveliness of a loved one, cannot be so delighted to welcome her, as Jesus is to welcome us to his bosom in prayer. He would therefore have us to leave the attractions of this dangerous and ensnaring world, for enjoying his society at the mercy-seat; and to come not with the hesitancy of Esther, but with the feeling that he loves us thus intensely.

VER. 10.—How fair is thy love, my sister, my spouse! how much better is thy love than wine! and the smell of thine ointments than all spices!

The words give a fourth reason for encouraging us to come to Jesus in prayer—the beauty and delightfulness to him of the graces of piety in the believer's heart. Among these excellences, the first mentioned is love. The reason of this may be readily understood from 1 Cor. xiii. Moral beauty is more glorious and admirable than material beauty. The former is the life, the perfection of the latter. Of moral excellence, love is the crown. Love is the glory of the character of God, the sum of his perfections. Love in the believing soul is the image of the love of God, new-forming there by the Holy Spirit. Well might Jesus therefore say, that to him this love is beautiful. This is the beauty of all other beauties, the reflection of his own divine image. The gem is none the less beautiful, none the less valuable, though not set, though in the mine; and this love may be still in its incipient state in the heart, imbedded amid the corruption of our many infirmities, not yet set in the spiritual body, and nevertheless be beautiful in the eyes of Jesus. This love will not be more beautiful hereafter, even in heaven, than it is now. It may there shine with greater brilliancy, not with greater attractiveness. Overwhelmed with the sense of unworthiness, we feel that in us, that is, in our flesh, dwelleth no good thing, Rom. vii. 18; and can only say that amid these corruptions, we see nothing of a redeeming character but love to Christ, while even this is frail and inconstant, borne down too often by predominating infirmities. "Lord, thou knowest all things: thou knowest that I love thee." But on this love, even thus in its incipient state, Jesus looks with delight. This makes our society pleasant to him. Even where persons have no bodily beauty, loveliness of heart and manners will make us forget even their ugliness, and cause us to take more pleasure in their company, than we could do, if they had beauty without loveliness. Looking not on the outward appearance, but on the heart, our Lord welcomes to his presence and companionship all who possess this love. He says, "How much better is this love than wine!" that is, 'None can tell how much more delightful to me than the most exquisite enjoyments of sense, is this love shed abroad in thy heart by the Holy Spirit.' See chap. i. 2. Not only is our love thus agreeable to him: equally so are all those graces which are the fruit of the Spirit. Gal. v. 22; Eph. v. 9. How much better "the smell of thine ointments than all spices!" See chap. i. 3. It is indeed hard for us, oppressed as the pious heart ever is with the sense of deep, deep unworthiness, to realize that Jesus will receive us with open arms in prayer. But how can we hesitate when he encourages us by such representations as that contained in this verse? The impression produced on him by these graces of holiness, is more grateful than to us is the combined fragrance of all spices.

Ver. 11.—Thy lips, O my spouse, drop as the honey-comb: honey and milk are under thy tongue.

Here he would encourage us in communion with him by assuring us how pleasant to his heart is our language of prayer and praise. This comparison of agreeable speech to honey is very common in ancient profane authors, as well as in the Scriptures. "Pleasant words are as an honey-comb, sweet to the soul and health to the bones." Prov. xvi. 24; v. 3. "How sweet are thy words unto my taste! yea, sweeter than honey to my mouth." Ps. cxix. 103. "More to be desired are they than gold, yea, than much fine gold: sweeter also than honey and the honey-comb." Ps. xix. 10. Hence Xenophon was called the Attic bee; and in consequence of the beauty of the writings of Plato, a swarm of bees was fabled to have settled on his lips when an infant. Speaking of his ode, Pindar says, towards its conclusion,

> Amid the Æolian blasts of flutes,
> This honey mixed with milk I send.

Thus Homer says of Nestor,

> Words sweeter from his tongue than honey flowed.

An oriental poet mentions,

> "Those ruby lips whence honied sweets distil."

And again, "O grant me a draught of honey from the lotos of thy mouth."

Thus Milton's description of Belial:

> "His tongue
> Dropped manna, and could make the worse appear
> The better reason."

While the poison of asps is under the lips of the ungodly, Rom. iii. 13, honey and milk are under the tongue of the spouse. So Theocritus,

> "More sweet her lips than milk in luscious rills,
> Lips, whence pure honey, as she speaks, distils."

Nothing could express to the ancients more strongly than such comparisons, the idea of speech, sweet, pleasant, and captivating. The Holy Spirit would therefore assure us by this verse, that to Jesus no language, not even the highest praise of unfallen angels, is more delightful than the words of repentance, faith, prayer, and praise, offered at the mercy-seat by the contrite heart. Our Lord himself is included when it is said, "Joy shall be in heaven over one sinner that repenteth, more than over ninety and nine just persons, which need no repentance." Luke xv. 7. See Song ii. 14. He sees a fountain of this excellent discourse under the tongue. Out of the abundance of the heart the mouth speaketh; and this language of holiness from the lips of the redeemed can never fail, when the Holy Spirit is in the heart a well of water springing up into everlasting life. No music is richer, none more melodious, none more pleasing, than a chorus of infant voices in Jesus' praise; and we can readily see with what pleasure the hosts of heaven, and chief among them, our Lord, must hearken to the pious utterances of those who are now in this world, in the infancy of their spiritual being and eternal life.

<small>And the smell of thy garments is like the smell of Lebanon.</small>

That is, 'Come without hesitation to meet me in prayer, because thou mayest be assured, that nothing, not even the fragrance of Lebanon, can be more grateful to the human senses than is thy presence to me.' See ver. 6. Musæus speaks of "the heights of odorous Lebanon." Lebanon abounded in odoriferous trees of various kinds, from which fragrant gums were extracted, especially frankincense. Maundrell says, "It is clothed in fragrant greens from top to bottom." Its wine had a peculiar fragrance: "The scent thereof shall be as the wine of Lebanon." Hos. xiv. 7. On account of its fragrance, the wood of the cedars of Lebanon was used for making precious pieces of furniture, especially chests, for keeping rich garments. Odoriferous garments are thus mentioned in the Odyssey, lib. xxi. 52; and Calypso gave such to Ulysses, lib. v. 264. Speaking of an individual, Moschus says,

> Whose heavenly fragrance e'en afar exceeds
> The odours breathing from the flowery meads.

Hence the Psalmist, "All thy garments smell of myrrh, aloes, and cassia, out of the ivory palaces." And the patriarch "smelled the smell of his raiment, and blessed him, and said, See, the smell of my son is as the smell of a field which the Lord hath blessed."* As in chap. i. 3,

---

* The orientals endeavour to perfume their clothes in various ways. They sprinkle them with sweet-scented oils, extracted from spices, they fumigate them with the most valuable incense or scented wood, and also sew the wood of the aloe in their clothes. They are universally fond of having their garments strongly perfumed; so much so, that the perfume expressed the loveliness of Jesus and the pleasantness of his society to us; in this verse the fragrance of Lebanon, than which they knew nothing of the kind having greater richness, freshness, and excellence, sets forth the very great agreeableness of the

Europeans can scarcely bear the smell. The persons of the Assyrian ladies are elegantly clothed, and scented with the richest oils and perfumes; and the Jewish females did not yield to them in the elegance of their dress, the beauty of their ornament, and the fragrance of their essences. Such is Virgil's account of Venus:

> Thus, as she turned away, with roseate hue
> Her neck shone beauteous; and her locks bedewed
> With perfume of ambrosia, richly breathed
> Odours divine; graceful her flowing robe;
> And in her gait the goddess true appeared.
>
> *Æneid,* i. 403.

With this portraiture of the bride in the Song, we may compare Homer's description of Juno:

> "Self-closed, behind her shut the doors of gold.
> Here first she bathes; and round her body pours
> Soft oils of fragrance, and ambrosial showers:
> The winds perfumed, the balmy gale convey
> Thro' heaven, thro' earth, and all the aerial way:
> Thus, while she breathed of heaven, with decent pride
> Her ardent hands the radiant tresses tied:
> Part on her head in shining ringlets roll'd,
> Part o'er her shoulders waved like melted gold.
> Around her, next, a heavenly mantle flow'd,
> That rich with Pallas' labour'd colours glow'd:
> Large clasps of gold the foldings gather'd round,
> A golden zone her swelling bosom bound.
> Far-beaming pendants tremble in her ear,
> Each gem illumined with a triple star.
> Then o'er her head she casts a veil more white
> Than new-fall'n snow, and dazzling as the light.
> Last, her fair feet celestial sandals grace.
> Thus issuing radiant, with majestic pace,
> Forth from the dome th' imperial goddess moves.
>
> *Iliad,* xiv. 168.

humble-hearted saint to our blessed Lord. How can we hesitate in prayer, when Jesus takes as much delight in our society as ever Jew could take in the dewy fragrance of Lebanon.

How animating are the motives thus set forth for encouraging us to dwell at the throne of grace and to persevere in prayer! They are touching and tender in the extreme. Urging us to arise and come away from earth, by the greatness of his affection, as illustrated in chap. iv. 1—5, he instructs us that in the meanwhile, before the dawning of glory, we may find him by prayer on the hill of frankincense, and encourages us to meet him there as often as possible; because, though unworthy in our own eyes, he sees in us, as attired in his righteousness, no spot, nothing but beauty; because this is the only place of safety amid the dangers and enemies of the world; because his heart is enraptured with affection for us; because our love, with its attending graces, is more beautiful to his contemplation than we can now conceive; because our language, in contrition, prayer, and praise, is his greatest delight; because our presence altogether is more agreeable to him, than to our senses such fragrance as was wafted from Lebanon. O what a welcome does then ever await us at the mercy-seat!

VER. 12.—A garden inclosed is my sister, my spouse; a spring shut up, a fountain sealed.

As a seventh reason for encouraging us to meet him at the throne of grace, he states that his delights in the soul of the believer is as great as what is felt by us in enjoying the most beautiful garden. Ver. 12—15. See notes, chap. viii. 13. Thus Isaiah says, "Ye shall be as a garden that hath no water," Isa. i. 30; and again, "Thou shalt be like a watered garden; and like a spring of water, whose waters fail not." Isa. lviii. 11. So

Jeremiah—"Their soul shall be as a watered garden." Jer. xxxi. 12.* In Keats' Ode to Psyche, the spirit of the same illustration is adopted:

> "Yes, I will be thy priest, and build a fane
>   In some untrodden region of my mind,
> Where branched thoughts, new-grown with pleasant pain,
>   Instead of pines shall murmur in the wind:
> Far, far around shall those dark-cluster'd trees
>   Fledge the wild-ridged mountains steep by steep;
> And there by zephyrs, streams, and birds, and bees,
>   The moss-lain Dryads shall be lull'd to sleep;
> And in the midst of this wide quietness
> A rosy sanctuary will I dress
> With the wreathed trellis of a working brain,
>   With buds, and bells, and stars without a name,
> With all the gardener Fancy e'er could feign,
>   Who breeding flowers, will never breed the same:
> And there shall be for thee all soft delight
>   That shadowy thought can win,
> A bright torch, and a casement ope at night
>   To let the true love in."

President Edwards says, "Holiness, as I then wrote down some of my contemplations on it, appeared to me to be of a sweet, pleasant, charming, serene, calm nature; which brought an inexpressible purity, brightness, peacefulness, and ravishment to the soul. In other words, that it made the soul like a field or garden of God, with all manner of pleasant flowers; all pleasant, delightful, and undisturbed, enjoying a sweet calm, and the gentle, vivifying beams of the sun." Speaking of the church as

---

* "When a man dwells in love, the eyes of his wife are as fair as the light of heaven, she is a fountain sealed, and he can quench his thirst, and ease his cares, and lay his sorrow down upon her lap, and can retire home as to his sanctuary and refectory, and his gardens of sweetness and chaste refreshments."—*Jeremy Taylor's Sermons on Eph. v. 32, 33.*

a vine, the Psalmist says, "Why hast thou broken down her hedges, so that all they which pass by the way do pluck her?" In this passage, chaps. iv. 12—v. 1, there are four points brought out to view. 1. The holiness of the pious heart as set apart for God, ver. 12. 2. The heart thus hedged around by grace is occupied with the precious, odoriferous virtues of holiness, ver. 13—14, and by the Holy Spirit, who is within the soul as a fountain of water, John iv. 14—vii. 38, and whose influences are the very life and nourishment of these pious graces. Ver. 15. 3. The desire of the believer that his soul may be in readiness for the coming into our hearts of the beloved, by the Holy Spirit breathing on our graces and bringing out their fragrance. Ver. 16. 4. The consequence of this prayer—Jesus comes to dwell with us. Chap. v. 1. When keeping the soul thus guarded from the world, and against every one but Jesus, we enjoy the presence of the Spirit, and desire his operations in greater fulness—how great is our encouragement to prayer, in the assurance that even while we are yet asking, our Lord will come down into our souls, and take as much delight in our enlivened graces, as the beloved took in gathering the spices of the garden, and eating its precious fruits.

The Jewish gardens were generally hedged or walled, as indeed Josephus expressly states respecting the gardens near Jerusalem.* The idea set forth in these words, is the same with that in Ps. iv. 3—"Know that the Lord

---

* Speaking of a garden represented in the tombs of Thebes and other parts of Egypt, Wilkinson says, "The one here introduced is shown to have been surrounded by an embattled wall, with a canal of water passing in front of it, connected with the river. The small kiosks, or summer-houses, shaded with trees, stood near the water, and overlooked beds of flowers."—Vol. ii. 144.

hath set apart him that is godly for himself." Hence the acknowledgment made by Satan concerning Job: "Hast thou not made an hedge about him, and about his house, and about all that he hath on every side." The seclusion of the soul from the intrusion of the evil passions and evil spirits overrunning it in a state of nature, and the hedging of it around with the habits formed by Christian discipline, so that the virtues of piety may be undisturbed in their growth, is what the Scriptures really mean by sanctification. To sanctify, is to set apart from a common to a sacred use. In the East, wives are secluded with the greatest care from public gaze, for the company of their lords; and so far from looking on this restraint with disfavour, they seem to estimate the degree of their husband's affection by the watchfulness with which they are guarded. The most flattering epithet that can be applied to an eastern lady, is that of "the concealed treasure," "the guarded jewel," "the well-watched angel." The words, "a spring shut up, a fountain sealed," are a repetition of the idea in the foregoing part of the verse, expressing the sentiments of holy seclusion for Jesus, even more beautifully than does the garden enclosed. Sir John Chardin says, he has known springs locked up in divers parts of Asia on account of the scarcity of water. Among the Persians were fountains of which only the king and his eldest son might drink. Thus, says the Apostle, "Ye are Christ's." 1 Cor. iii. 23. No one has a right to our affections but Jesus. How entirely is the life of the Christian a hidden life; "hid with Christ in God;" hid from the world, as a spring shut up, so that they can neither see fully its excellence, nor reach it in such a way as to disturb or break it up at its source. The holy soul is a fountain of pious affections, shut up from the world, for the delight of him who has redeemed us with his blood, and sealed us with his Holy Spirit. The Spirit is the seal of the King of kings, set upon those spiritual fountains, holy hearts, in this wilderness, which are thereby shown to belong, not to the world, but to himself. The idea of holiness, as separation from earth and all things sinful, and as consecration to God, cannot be more neatly expressed, than by a garden hedged, a spring enclosed and sealed. Jesus will take delight in our society and welcome us to the throne of grace, according to the care with which our soul excludes all other affections, for the enjoyment of his love. This verse shows what the true saint is, or should be; and in its connection teaches that if we would enjoy the presence of Jesus in the heart, we must watch against the intrusion of sin. "Blessed are the pure in heart, for they shall see God." "If I regard iniquity in my heart, the Lord will not hear me." "Keep thy heart with all diligence, for out of it are the issues of life." Jesus takes delight in dwelling only in the soul that is a garden barred or hedged, a spring bolted, a fountain sealed. The same truth is expressed with even more strictness in the words, "Know ye not that ye are the temple of God, and that the Spirit of God dwelleth in you?" 1 Cor. iii. 16. Holiness requires that the soul be as exclusively devoted to God as the enclosed garden, or bolted spring, to its lord; or the temple, to him who dwelt between the cherubim. Over the door of the heart bolted against every one but Jesus, is written, "Holiness to the Lord." The dream of the heathen that each fountain had its divinity residing in it, is here realized. The Holy Spirit dwells in this fountain of the pious soul, and he is its guardian divinity.

VER. 13, 14.—Thy plants are an orchard of pomegranates, with pleasant fruits; camphire, with spikenard; spikenard and saffron; calamus and cinnamon, with all trees of frankincense; myrrh and aloes, with all the chief spices.

The three following verses give that with which this garden is occupied. The word rendered "thy plants" means not merely shoots and flowers, but anything issuing, or springing, or sent out from another; and therefore includes everything which is a product of the garden, or belonging thereto—the well of living waters with its streams, no less than the spikenard and all the chief spices. We understand the word "plants" to include all the things that follow to the end of ver. 15. The word "orchard" corresponds exactly to our word "paradise," and is of oriental origin, signifying the pleasure-gardens and parks, some with, others without, wild animals, around the residence of the Persian monarchs, planted with stately forest-trees and fruit-trees of every kind, well watered, and surrounded with a wall.* As mentioned by Xenophon, there was one of these belonging to Cyrus the younger, at Celænæ in Phrygia, through the middle of which ran the river Mæander. This in the text is mentioned as such a park or pleasure-ground, without the wild animals; and filled with trees and shrubbery, with the most beautiful flowers, the most delightful fruits, and the richest fragrance.

The pomegranate, still common in Syria and Persia, is considered delicious by travellers, and is highly prized. The bright and dark-green foliage of the pomegranate,

---

* "Behind these were the royal gardens, laid out in the most exquisite taste, and decorated with all that could gratify the eye, regale the ear, or satiate the most luxurious palate; the loveliest shade, the deepest verdure, grottoes of the most refreshing coolness, fruits of the most delicious flavour; cascades that never ceased to murmur, and music that never failed to delight."—*Maurice's Indian Antiquities*, i. 209.

and its flowers of a crimson colour, made it an object of desire in these gardens; while its large reddish-coloured fruit, filled with numerous seeds, each surrounded with juicy, pleasant-tasted pulp, would make it valuable as a fruit, in warm countries. See chap. iv. 3. With the pomegranate, thus mentioned for its beauty and sweetness, this garden has the most precious fruits in general. Besides, there are all the choice aromatic trees and shrubs —camphire and spikenard, spikenard and saffron; calamus and cinnamon, with trees of frankincense; myrrh and aloes, with all the chief spices. See chap. i. 12, 14. Earth can show nothing to man, more beautiful to the eye, no fruits more precious, no fragrance more delightful, than those combined in this paradise—a fitting representation of the graces of holiness centring in the believing heart, and making it a retreat where Jesus our Saviour loves to make it his abode.

VER. 15.—A fountain of gardens, a well of living waters, and streams from Lebanon.

In ver. 12 the "spring shut up" seems mentioned, like the "garden enclosed," for illustrating the idea of the holiness of the believer, or his separation and consecration to God; and to be independent of the idea intended in this verse. Here is mentioned the source whence is derived the life and fragrance of the fruits and shrubbery of this garden. A fountain of gardens means a very copious fountain, sufficient for watering many gardens. This fountain was the best possible. Instead of a reservoir filled with rain-water, as was often used, this pleasure-ground was enriched with a well or spring of running water, combining therewith streams cool, refreshing, and fertilizing, as those coming from Lebanon. These make the gardens of Damascus so enchanting. Their refreshing coolness is mentioned by the prophet: "Will a man leave the snow of Lebanon, which cometh from the rock of the field?" Jer. xviii. 14. Maundrell says, "There is a very deep rupture in the side of Libanus, running at least seven hours' travel directly up into the mountain. It is on both sides exceedingly steep and high, clothed with fragrant greens from top to bottom, and everywhere refreshed with fountains falling down from the rocks in pleasant cascades. The streams all uniting at the bottom, make a full and rapid torrent, whose agreeable murmur is heard over the place, and adds no small pleasure to it." Says another traveller, "We came into pleasant groves, by delightful rivulets that arose from springs, that made so sweet a noise as to be admired by king Solomon." We cannot see that any light is thrown on the real significance of this passage by a detailed description of "The pools of Solomon," about six miles from Jerusalem, on the route to Hebron.* This valley

---

* The following is from Maundrell: "This morning we went to see some remarkable places in the neighbourhood of Bethlehem. The first place that we directed our course to, was those famous fountains, pools, and gardens, about an hour and a quarter distant from Bethlehem, southward, said to have been the contrivance and delight of king Solomon. To these works and places of pleasure, that great prince is supposed to allude, Eccl. ii. 5, 6, where, among the other instances of his magnificence, he reckons up his gardens, and vineyards, and pools. As for the pools, they are three in number, lying in a row above each other, being so disposed that the waters of the uppermost may descend into the second, and those of the second into the third. Their figure is quadrangular; the breadth is the same in all, amounting to about ninety paces; in their length there is some difference between them, the first being about one hundred and sixty paces long, the second two hundred, and the third two hundred and twenty. They are all lined with wall, and plastered, and contain a great depth of water. Close by the pools is a pleasant castle of modern structure; and at about the distance of one hundred and forty paces from them is a fountain, from which, principally, they derive their waters. This the friars will have to be that sealed fountain, to which the holy spouse is compared, Cant. iv.

containing these pools, supposed the one referred to by Josephus, and mentioned by Maundrell, Hasselquist, and others, may be the site of the grounds described in the text, and has indeed got from Latin travellers the name of *Hortus Conclusus.* A modern, speaking of a monastery in the Levant, says, "There below my feet lay the convent garden, in all the fresh luxuriance of tropical vegetation. Tufts upon tufts of waving palms overshadowed the immense succulent leaves of the banana, which in their turn rose out of thickets of the pomegranate, with

12, and, in confirmation of this opinion, they pretend a tradition, that king Solomon shut up these springs, and kept the door of them sealed with his signet, to the end that he might preserve the waters for his own drinking, in their natural freshness and purity. Nor was it difficult thus to secure them, they rising under ground, and having no avenue to them but by a little hole, like to the mouth of a narrow well. Through this hole you descend directly down, but not without some difficulty, for about four yards, and then arrive in a vaulted room, fifteen paces long, and eight broad. Joining to this is another room, of the same fashion, but somewhat less. Both these rooms are covered with handsome stone arches, very ancient, and perhaps the work of Solomon himself. Below the pool here runs down a narrow rocky valley, enclosed on both sides with high mountains. This the friars will have to be the enclosed garden alluded to in the same place of the Canticles before cited. What truth there may be in this conjecture, I cannot absolutely pronounce. As to the pools, it is probable enough that they may be the same with Solomon's; there not being the like store of excellent spring-water to be met with anywhere else throughout all Palestine."

Hasselquist thinks this might possibly be the garden noticed in the text. Mariti says, "Nature has still preserved its original fertility in this valley. Although but little cultivated, the soil still produces a tolerable supply of cotton and various kinds of grain; there are also fine plantations of fruit-trees, affording the most juicy fruits in the country. Various flowers, and many fragrant plants, grow there naturally at all seasons, among which are thyme, rosemary, marjoram, salvius, persil, rue, ranunculuses, and anemones." Here may be found various rare plants not to be found elsewhere in Palestine, and which, as an old traveller suggests, may have been propagated from exotic plants which Solomon introduced into his gardens.

its bright green leaves and its blossoms of that beautiful and vivid red which is excelled by few even of the most brilliant flowers of the East. These were contrasted with the deep green of the caroub or locust-tree; and the yellow apples of the lotus vied with the clusters of green limes with their sweet white flowers. Fair branches and flowers, exhaling rich perfume and bearing freshness in their very aspect, become more beautiful from their contrast to the dreary plains outside the convent walls; and this great difference was owing solely to there being a well of water in this spot, from which were constantly drawn the fertilizing streams which nourished the teeming vegetation of this garden."

More beautiful was this spring than that classic fountain whose green, wild margin, with dew-sprinkled mosses, grows undisturbed:

> "Nor must the delicate waters sleep
> Prison'd in marble, bubbling from the base
> Of the cleft statue, with a gentle leap
> The rill runs o'er, and round fern, flowers, and ivy creep
> Fantastically tangled: the green hills
> Are clothed with early blossoms, through the grass
> The silvery zephyr rustles, and the bills
> Of summer birds sing welcome as ye pass;
> Flow'rs fresh in hue, and many in their class,
> Implore the pausing step, and with their dyes
> Dance in the soft breeze in a fairy mass;
> The sweetness of the violets' deep blue eyes
> Kiss'd by the breath of heaven, seems colour'd by its skies."*

This comparison is applied to the soul by Jesus himself: "The water that I shall give him, shall be in him a well of water springing up into everlasting life." John iv. 14. "This spake he of the Spirit, which they that believe on him should receive." John vii. 39. The fountain was the

* Childe Harold, iv. 116.

life of the garden; without this there could be no verdure, no growth, no flowers, no fragrance, no fruits, no refreshing shade. Trees not planted by these streams of water, had their leaf to wither, and brought forth no fruit. Ps. i. 3. Nothing could atone for the want of such a stream. Even so it is with the heart. The Holy Spirit is everything to our desolate and sinful souls. He is "as rivers of water in a dry place." Without his influences there can be no spiritual life, no fragrance of piety, no fruits of holiness. When his influences overflow from this hallowed fountain in the heart, every pious virtue thrives, this wilderness and solitary place is glad, and rejoices, and blossoms as the rose; and each grace of holiness becomes "as a tree planted by the waters, and spreadeth out her roots by the rivulet, and shall not see when heat cometh; but her leaf shall be green, and shall not be careful in the year of drought, neither shall cease from yielding fruit." Jer. xvii. 8. The Holy Spirit being thus the hidden spring of the life of holiness, Christian activity is as necessary for developing this life as exercise is for the growth of a child. Life and activity are inseparable. He who has enjoyed the Spirit, welling as a crystal fountain in his heart—

> "His life hath flowed
> From its mysterious urn a sacred stream,
> In whose calm depth the beautiful and pure
> Alone are mirror'd; which, though shapes of ill
> May hover round its surface, glides in light,
> And takes no shadow from them."*

These influences of the Holy Spirit are copious and overflowing; a fountain sufficient for many gardens; more healing to our blinded souls than the streams of Jordan to the leprous Naaman; giving that understanding which

* Talfourd's Ion, act i., sc. 1.

is a well-spring of wisdom to him that hath it; making the words of a man's mouth as deep waters, and the well-spring of wisdom as a flowing brook. Prov. xviii. 4. When a heathen could sing,

> Go to the silvery eddies
> Of pure Castalia's spring,
> And bathed in its pellucid waves
> Thy temple offering bring;*

we feel that much more shall we be fitted for the services of the heavenly sanctuary, by having our souls continually steeped in purer than Castalian dews by this perennial fountain of the Spirit, gushing forth in the heart, and bathing in its silvery streams the roots of all our virtues of holiness. And as Arethusa was fabled to have passed under the sea, and broken forth afresh in a distant island—so this fountain of the soul, passing unseen the sea of death, shall burst forth afresh beyond those gloomy waves, to flow with perennial and pellucid streams in the heavenly paradise.

VER. 16.—Awake, O north wind; and come, thou south; blow upon my garden, that the spices thereof may flow out.

These words give another feature of the heart which may meet Jesus with confidence at the throne of grace. Such soul has been just represented as a garden, lovely in his eyes, filled with the precious plants of the graces of holiness, and watered with the perennial and refreshing streams of the Holy Spirit; here the heart is set forth as having the desire, and using the corresponding means, for being in a state as agreeable and acceptable as possible to the beloved. All those precious plants are not sufficient to picture the loveliness of this garden: fountains and rills must crown the whole. Now, also,

---

* Euripides, Ion, 95.

cooling winds are introduced for making the abode in this pleasure-garden delightful, and scattering the balmy fragrance through its delightful retreats. The east wind is in Palestine generally withering and tempestuous; the west wind brings from the sea clouds of rain, or dark, damp air; the north wind is cooling and refreshing, its power being broken by the mountain-chain of Lebanon; the south wind, though hot, has its heat mitigated in the upland regions, and is never stormy. The north wind is called on to "arise," because it is more powerful and strong; the south wind to "come," as though it were the soft breathing zephyr. The north wind brought clear weather. "The north wind driveth away rain." Prov. xxv. 23. "Fair weather cometh out of the north." Job xxxvii. 22. Pliny says, that though cold and nipping, the north wind is the most wholesome wind that blows. The south wind was warm and moist. "Dost thou know, how thy garments are warm when he quieteth the earth by the south wind?" Job xxxvii. 17. And the oriental poet, "O gale, scented with sandal, who breathest love from the regions of the south, be propitious."* The bride here calls for the north wind, that thereby all clouds may be swept away, and the sky cleared; and for the south wind, that its genial influence might ripen the fruits of the garden, and draw forth the fragance of the flowers. Thus, Hafiz, as quoted by Dopke, "Send me with zephyrs, roses from thy cheek, that I may breathe the luscious fragrance of thy garden bloom."

The wind is on many accounts the best emblem of the Holy Spirit. Hence our Saviour says, "The wind bloweth where it listeth, and thou hearest the sound: so is every one that is born of the Spirit." John iii. 8. The identity of the Hebrew, Greek, and Latin words for wind,

* Songs of Jayadeva.

breath, and spirit, shows that the air has the nearest resemblance, of all created things, to the influence of the Holy Spirit, and is therefore a most appropriate illustration. The words of this verse are, then, a prayer that the heart may be prepared for the coming of Jesus, by the action of the Holy Spirit, like the north wind, sweeping away all gloom, error, unbelief, and mists of sin; and like the south wind, warming into vigorous life all the graces of holiness. To do this, is the prerogative of this sacred agent alone. Gloom overspreads the garden, and the flow of its spices is checked, not because the heavens above are changed, or the sun has ceased to shine, for these are as pure, and glorious, and life-giving as ever; but because clouds have arisen heavily, and intercept the genial influence from on high. Thus from the depths of that heart which in its natural state is like the troubled sea when it cannot rest, arise clouds that separate between us and our God; these influences the Holy Spirit removes by his power; and then, shines into our heart the light of the knowledge of the glory of God in the person of Jesus Christ;—then flows forth the fragrance of our holy virtues. After times of desertion, darkness, and decay, when the Spirit does thus clear the soul, and breathe thereon with more than the reviving power of the south wind, how delightfully is the holiness of the heart felt by all around, "as the smell of a field the Lord has blessed."

Let my beloved come into his garden, and eat his pleasant fruits.*

Having thus sought the preparation of the heart, the

---

* With this may be compared the following from Theocritus:

"And now in due return, O heavenly born!
Whose honour'd name a thousand fanes adorn,
Arsinoe gladly pays the rites divine,
Rival of Helen, at Adonis' shrine;

believer now prays that Jesus may enter there and enjoy the fruits of holiness. Thus, in the Gitagovinda, the lovely Kadha is in like manner invited to enter the garden or the embraces of her beloved: "Enter, sweet Kadha, the bower graced with a bed of asoca-leaves, the bower illumined with gay blossoms, the bower made cool and fragrant by gales from the woods of Malaya." "Pleasant fruits," or fruits of pleasantness, as in ver. 13, means all that are most delicious of fruits. The fruits of the garden are the products of the garden: and the fruits enjoyed by Jesus in the believing soul are those virtues which are there developed by the Holy Spirit: and the text means that our Lord should enjoy them as really as we enjoy the most delicious fruits by eating. Well would it be for us, could we feel that the garden spot of Jesus in the whole universe, is the heart of the saint; and the graces of the soul are to him a source of more exquisite pleasure than to us are the most precious fruits of the choicest garden. How valuable would we then feel those graces to be, and with what care would we cherish and

> All fruits she offers that ripe autumn yields,
> The produce of the gardens, and the fields;
> All herbs and plants which silver baskets hold;
> And Syrian unguents flow from shells of gold,
> With finest meal sweet paste the women make,
> Oil, flowers, and honey mingling in the cake:
> Earth and the air afford a large supply
> Of animals that creep, and birds that fly.
> Green bow'rs are built with dill sweet-smelling crown'd.
> And little Cupids hover all around;
> And as young nightingales their wings essay,
> Skip here and there, and hop from spray to spray,
> What heaps of golden vessels glittering bright!
> What stores of ebon black, and ivory white!
> In ivory carved large eagles seem to move,
> And through the clouds bear Ganymede to Jove."
> *Idyl* xv. 109.

cultivate them for this blessed friend, not for self-gratulation, or self-interest, not for the applause of the world, but for the approbation and love of our Lord.

CHAPTER V.

Ver. 1.—I am come into my garden, my sister, my spouse: I have gathered my myrrh with my spice; I have eaten my honey-comb with my honey; I have drunk my wine with my milk: eat, O friends; drink, yea, drink abundantly, O beloved.

This verse shows how promptly the prayer in the foregoing verse was answered. It is the eighth reason for meeting Jesus in prayer with preparation of the heart; because he will then come into the soul by his Holy Spirit, and bring around us a host of angels rejoicing to be our guard. When the heart is thus prepared, and anxiously desires the presence of Christ, "It shall come to pass, that before they call I will answer; and while they are yet speaking I will hear." Isa. lxv. 24. The fact of the existence of such desires for him, is evidence of his being with us; as in this passage, in immediate connection with the request, he adds, "I have already come, &c." He was present in the heart, though his presence was not felt; as "when Jacob awaked out of his sleep, and said, Surely the Lord is in this place, and I knew it not;" and when Jesus was present in the garden with Mary, and she knew it not. John xx. 14.

In the East, banquets are sometimes held in gardens; as Egmont and Heyman, when at the convent of Sinai, dined under the trees of the garden, with a number of the inmates, on one of their festival days. The ancients were in the habit of wearing chaplets of flowers on their heads at feasts. Thus in the book of Wisdom: "Let us fill ourselves with costly wine and ointments; and let no flower of the spring pass by us. Let us crown ourselves with rose-buds before they be withered," Chap. ii. 7. And in the Arabian Nights, a person is represented at Bagdad as buying myrtles, lilies, jessamine, and other fragrant flowers and plants, along with meat, wine, and fruit, as preparations for a repast. Milk and honey still form a luscious and common banquet among many Asiatic nations. Milk is mingled with wine for cooling the latter. Jael gave Sisera, when thirsty, milk to drink instead of water, as preferable; and Clemens Alexandrinus says, wine and milk is a very healthful and profitable mixture. Tibullus mentions "bowls of snow-white milk, mixed with wine." The words "my honey-comb with my honey," are possibly intended to express both the wild honey that was found dropping from trees, and that which was eaten in the comb and was consequently the most delicious. Gen. xliii. 11. In India, says Mr. Roberts, "the forests literally flow with honey; large combs may be seen hanging on the trees, as you pass along, full of honey." The same seems to have been the case formerly in Palestine. Here the beloved found the best honey in perfection, and both kinds, liquid and in the comb.*

The meaning of this verse, therefore, is, that the Lord Jesus comes into the heart prepared for him and desiring him, and draws from the enjoyment of the

---

* "Honey was of far more importance formerly than it is now. There was no sugar, and honey had to supply its place, besides being eaten in its primary state. Vast quantities of it must, therefore, have been consumed; and the importance assigned to it in Scripture becomes intelligible."—*Kitto.*

virtues blooming there, a pleasure that can be best illustrated to man by saying, it is like, in richness and exquisiteness, to the delight had in dwelling amid the fragrance, and feasting on the delicious fruits, of an oriental garden. The willingness of Jesus to answer prayer is set forth in many places of the Scriptures, but nowhere in language more encouraging than this. The idea is the same, and in expressions equally figurative, though not so amplified as here, in John xiv. 23, "We will come unto him, and make our abode with him;" and in Rev. iii. 20, "I will come in to him, and will sup with him, and he with me." Unbelief, blunting the spiritual apprehension of the soul, keeps us from feeling the power of these passages, and gathering from them due consolation. And in the same tone are the words, "Thus saith the high and lofty One that inhabiteth eternity, whose name is Holy, I dwell in the high and holy place, with him also that is of a contrite and humble spirit." Isa. lvii. 15. God is indeed everywhere present, but he is said to dwell in the places where his presence is manifested in brighter displays of his glory. Size of place, greatness of extent or space, is not requisite for a habitation for him. In comparison with him the grandest world and the most obscure retreat, the most widely extended garden and the contracted limits of the human soul, are equally mere spots; in his sight, the dimensions of the temple on mount Moriah, and of the heart which is a temple for the habitation of God through the Spirit, are marked by no difference worthy of notice. Of all other places, the redeemed soul was especially created for a shrine in which may shine forth the divine glory; and hence, when that glory is thus manifested in the heart, there God is said to dwell. The idea of a banquet and of feasting on the most delicious fruits, as in this verse, is added for illustrating to our comprehension the exceedingly great delight Jesus has in dwelling in such soul and enjoying its graces of holiness, thankfulness, and praise: as we say of the society of a cherished friend, his company was a feast, so the same mode of expression is used here. Even this delight does he take in answering the prayer of his people and manifesting his presence in their soul, when they have sought the preparation of the heart, and are awaiting him in humble faith. And when by his Holy Spirit thus bringing us into union with him by pervading and enlivening our affections, we feel his presence, how truly may he be said to be feeding on the fruits of this spiritual garden; and how deep our tranquil, heavenly enjoyment.

"Eat, O friends; drink, yea, drink abundantly, O beloved." These words, spoken by the bridegroom to his attendants, express the wish indulged by Jesus to have his own pleasure shared by others, here called "beloved ones." The angels and the heavenly host take a deep interest in redemption; there is joy in heaven among the angels of God over one sinner that repenteth; into these things the angels desire to look. They sang together and shouted for joy when the corner-stone of the earth was laid; they announced his coming at Bethlehem; they attended him at his resurrection and at his ascension; and when the Son of man shall come in his glory, all the holy angels shall be with him. Through all our pilgrimage, these are ministering spirits sent forth to minister for them who shall be heirs of salvation; and at death the soul is carried by the angels to Abraham's bosom. Such being the case, it is not strange that they should be represented as attending Jesus in his visits to the believing soul, and as being allowed to share with him the delight had in hovering around, contemplating and blessing those whose hearts are a sacred spot, a garden enclosed of the King of kings, filled with the fruits of those holy virtues which are the choicest plants in the universe of God. The fellows or associates in the work of redemption, above whom Jesus is anointed with the oil of gladness, include the angels of heaven. The words "drink, yea, drink abundantly," are precisely the same in the Hebrew, with those rendered "they drank and were merry with him," in Gen. xliii. 34. The latter means, to drink to the full, to hilarity. This kind of expression is common in the East—as in the following passage, quoted by Sir W. Jones: "They who walk in the true path are drowned in the sea of mysterious adoration, they are inebriated with the melody of amorous complaints." They simply mean that these holy angels have the privilege of sharing with him his delight in the sanctified soul. They attend on the saints and derive exquisite pleasure from hovering around us by the permission and command of our Lord. By meeting Jesus in prayer, among other motives here mentioned for encouraging us so to do, we have this as the crowning blessing, that there, on the mountain of myrrh and hill of frankincense, we have coming down into our heart the heavenly Shechinah, Jesus, through his Holy Spirit, encompassed with a crown-like host of angels. How great a glory and protection! Well may prayer be said to secure for us a wall of fire round about us, and a glory in our midst. "The angelic host of the Lord encampeth round about them that fear him, and delivereth them." The case of Elisha was but what is enjoyed by the humblest believer now, when, in the midst of perils, "behold, the mountain was full of horses and chariots of fire round about Elisha." 2 Kings vi. 17. Thus, for his encouragement, Jacob was permitted to have a view of the angelic bands which, though unseen, had been around him when "the angels of God met him; and when Jacob saw them he said, This is God's host." Gen. xxxii. 1. It was while Daniel was praying, that Gabriel, being caused to fly swiftly, came to him with a gracious promise, and the assurance that he was greatly beloved. Dan. ix. 20. The bereaved disciples were all with one accord in prayer, when the Holy Spirit came with a sound from heaven as of a rushing mighty wind. While prayer was made without ceasing of the church unto God for Peter, the angel of the Lord appeared to him, and brought him forth from prison. And "when Solomon had made an end of praying, the fire came down from heaven, and consumed the burnt-offering and the sacrifices; and the glory of the Lord filled the house." 2 Chron. vii. 1. And it was, when Jesus our forerunner had gone up into a mountain to pray, and as he prayed, that he was transfigured, and his face did shine as the sun, and his raiment was white as the light; and a bright cloud, the same that had dwelt between the cherubim, overshadowed them; and behold the voice of God out of the cloud. Matt. xvii. 1; Luke ix. 28.

How glorious was the sight in Eden, when amid the luxuriance of Paradise, man, just created, was overshadowed by the Shechinah, the dwelling-place of God; and around was gathered the innumerable company of angels—the Lord and all his attendants rejoicing in the work of his hands. The same Sovereign and his divine attendants take no less interest now in man formed anew by redemption; and hover over him with equal glory. The idea here may be best got by contemplating a beautiful, well-watered garden, Num. xxiv. 5, 6, as described in chap. iv. 12—15; or even like Eden, with the cloud that rested over the mercy-seat, dwelling in it as its light and glory; while an innumerable company of angels are gathered around in admiration and praise. And when, after seasons of withdrawal, in prayer, Jesus comes again into the garden of our hearts, it is as the coming down of the cloud of glory into the midst of Paradise to overshadow and enlighten it, surrounded by the host of his holy angels.

How encouraging are the motives here brought together for inclining us to prayer! How delightfully are they developed one after another, till ending in a blaze of glory, in the assurance that by faithful prayer we receive Jesus to dwell in our hearts by the Shechinah of his Spirit, and are encompassed by a guardian host of angels!

Ver. 2.—I sleep, but my heart waketh.

This passage, to the end of ver. 8, illustrates the exercises of the soul in a time of spiritual sloth and decay. After thus unfolding to us his love, he lets us, as in this passage, see our depravity and indifference. Our religious life consists of a series of revivals and of withdrawals by Jesus, for calling into exercise and putting to the test our graces. When under the influence of first love, we determine never to forget the Saviour, and think the thing almost impossible. After some experience of the deceitfulness of the heart, when at some subsequent period we have had our souls restored and made to lie down in green pastures, beside the still waters, we resolve again to be faithful in close adherence to our Lord, under the impression, that with our present knowledge of the workings of sin, and the glorious displays made to us of the loveliness of Christ, and of his love towards us personally, we shall now at length persevere;

but we soon find to our sorrow, that, left to ourselves, we are as unsteady and unfaithful as ever. It is surprising how quickly coldness will succeed great religious fervour. To the experienced believer it will not appear strange, that this divine allegory should bring this representation of indifference to the beloved into such immediate connection with the remarkable expressions of Jesus' love contained in the foregoing chapter. Where is the Christian who has not found the truth of this in his own experience? The three chosen disciples were overcome with lethargy even on the mount of transfiguration; and immediately after the first affecting sacrament, they not only fell asleep in Gethsemane, but all forsook Jesus and fled; while Peter added thereto a denial of his Lord, with profane swearing. While the bridegroom tarried, even the wise virgins with oil in their lamps, slumbered and slept. After endearing manifestations of Jesus' love, how soon do we find ourselves falling into spiritual slumber—often, like the disciples on the mount, under the full light of the presence of the Holy Spirit. And after periods of revival, in the same way will churches speedily show signs of sinking down into former coldness.

A Persian poet has almost exactly the same image: "Last night, my eyes being closed in sleep, but my good genius awake, the whole night, the live-long night, the image of my beloved was the companion of my soul."*

---

* Mr. Lane gives the following from odes of the Moslems, sung at their religious festivals. Its likeness to this part of the Song is obvious:

"O gazelle, from among the gazelles of El-Yemen!
 I am thy slave without cost;
 The phantom of thy form visited me in my slumber:
 I said, 'O phantom of slumber, who sent thee?'
 He said, ' He sent me whom thou knowest;

We see no necessity for supposing, with some, that Anacreon must have got from the Song the hint of his ode, in which Love is represented as standing at his door at midnight, and begging for admittance, lost in the dark, chilled and drenched with the dews. Cicero speaks of persons "semi-somni," half asleep, beholding the trite farces; and Seneca reflects on some who lay half asleep until mid-day. This phrase is sometimes used to express a sluggish, slothful man, also by Plautus. Here it implies that while the body was overcome with drowsiness, and thus insensible to surrounding things, the heart was unaffected, and still vigorous in its affections, though borne down and controlled by the action of the body. The medium of activity for the mind is through the body; hence, when the body is asleep, though the heart be awake, the individual is in a state of inactivity which cannot be broken till the body is aroused. The spiritual import of these words is therefore well expressed by John Owen: "Woful sloth and negligence are apt to prevail in us, in our meditations on heavenly things. 'Though our hearts wake' in a valuation of Christ, his love, and his grace, yet we sleep as unto the due exercise of faith and love towards him. Let them take heed of their aptness to forget endearing manifestations of special love. When God at any time draws nigh unto a soul by his Spirit in his word, with gracious words of peace and love, giving a sense of his kindness upon the heart by the Holy Ghost, so that it is filled with joy unspeakable and glorious there-

> He whom love occupies thee.'
> The beloved of my heart visited me in the darkness of the night:
> I stood to show him honour until he sat down.
> I said, 'O thou, my petition and all my desire!
> Hast thou come at midnight and not feared the watchman?'
> He said to me, 'I feared; but, however, love
> Had taken from me my soul and my breath.'"

on; for this soul, upon a temptation, a diversion, or by mere carelessness and neglect, which oftentimes falls out, to suffer this sense of love to be, as it were, obliterated, and so to lose that influencing efficacy unto obedience which it is accompanied withal; this also is full of unkindness. An account hereof we have in Cant. v. 1—6."*

> It is the voice of my beloved that knocketh, saying, Open to me, my sister, my love, my dove, my undefiled: for my head is filled with dew, and my locks with the drops of the night.

Our view of the nature of the Song makes it unnecessary for us to say anything in reply to those who view this whole passage as a narrative of what happened in a dream. These incidents, like the supposable incidents of allegories in general, are grouped together for the mere purpose of illustrating certain points of religious experience. This is done with remarkable beauty and delicacy, by this picture showing how a female treated a friend standing in the relation to her of a husband and a brother, as noted, chap. iv. 9, when he sued for admittance at night after a temporary absence. The connection seems to be, When I was sleeping, but my heart waking and intent on my friend, behold the voice of my beloved was heard knocking at the door, and saying, "Open to me, &c." The former clause expressed

---

* Madame Guyon speaks of the early part of her residence at Gex as being characterized by sweet and happy peace of mind, and the most intimate communion with God. She mentions, that a number of times she awoke at midnight, with such a presence and possession of God in her soul that she could no longer sleep, but arose and spent hours in prayer and praise, and divine communion. "I felt, even in my sleep, a singular possession of God. He loved me so much that he seemed to pervade my being, at a time when I could be only imperfectly conscious of his presence. My sleep is sometimes broken—a sort of half sleep—but my soul seems to be awake enough to know God, when it is hardly capable of knowing anything else."—*Life by Upham*, vol. i. 261.

the condition of the soul sunk down in spiritual drowsiness, sloth, and inaction. This sets forth the tenderness of Jesus in trying to rouse us from our slumbers, and have us to enjoy his society. How multiplied and tender are his terms of endearment—My sister, my beloved female friend, my dove, my perfect one. Chap. iv. 7. The word "perfect one," says Dopke, "does not mean physical beauty, as Kleuker thinks, but what we express by my angel, a pure innocent virgin." A glance will show that while these epithets are of unsurpassed tenderness, they are used as though with scrupulous care for guarding against the indelicate ideas some have tried to force from this passage. It might be thought that such affecting appeals would have moved in an instant the bride to welcome him with open arms. But to these he adds the fact of his being damp and chilly from the dew, which was very copious, especially in the latter part of the spring and the beginning of autumn. Maundrell says, "We were instructed by experience what the Psalmist means by the dew of Hermon, our tents being as wet with it as if it had rained all night." "My head is filled with dew, and my locks with the drops of the night." Could it be thought possible that such an appeal would be unsuccessful? There is a twofold reference—to his tender love for her, and to his condition as houseless, chilled, wet, and without a place of rest for the night.

Thus tenderly does Jesus appeal to us, for rousing us from our spiritual apathy and slumbers. He is all tenderness. Concerning all his dealings, we must say, "Thy gentleness hath made me great." Ps. xviii. 35. It is a sad evidence of the strength of our corruptions, that after such displays of his love, we should ever sink down into indifference. Even with grace in the soul, with the heart awake, we find ourselves falling asleep, borne down by the business of life, the charms of the world, or the infirmities of the flesh. This condition is one of outward comfort; everything around us is pleasant, as when reposing at night on our bed; and we are feeling the dangers incurred by the Christian through prosperity. Had the spouse been at this time suffering from pain or fear, so as to be incapable of sleep, and to feel the need of the presence and protection of the beloved, he would have found her watching for his return, and would not have been obliged thus to sue for admission. At such times, in our heartless indifference, how tenderly does he try to regain and rouse our love. What tenderness was there in the look he turned on backsliding Peter; and also in the words, "Simon, son of Jonas, lovest thou me?" It might be supposed that the simple words, "Behold, I stand at the door and knock," would be enough to make us leap from our spiritual slumbers, without such subduing language as is here used.

Ver. 3.—I have put off my coat; how shall I put it on? I have washed my feet; how shall I defile them?

These words mean, that as the bride had retired to rest, she could not put herself to the trouble of arising, even to let in the beloved. The bath is mentioned in the Odyssey, in connection with retiring:

> Give him the bath, arrange his couch with rugs
> Of warmth and costliness, and linen soft,
> There to await the golden-throned morn.

As Lady Montague assures us, the houses of the great ladies are kept clean with as much nicety as those of Holland, this pretence must appear still more frivolous. Taken as an illustration of the nature of the excuses formed by the soul for neglecting to receive Jesus at times of spiritual lethargy, these words are true and instructive. To us, it would seem impossible that the spouse could indulge or give such a reason. Yet the thing signified hereby has happened, how often, in our own experience. When, in our indifference to him, Jesus has stood near and allured by the tenderest influences, how often have we allowed personal ease, worldly pleasure, business, and indeed sheer indolence, to make us indifferent to his tenderness, and cause us to allow him to remain suing for admission to our hearts. The most trivial thing is enough to keep us from running to meet him in the duty of secret prayer, of the social meeting, of scripture-study and self-examination, of attending in the sanctuary, of giving to the cause of benevolence, of co-operating in Christian activity, of ministering to the necessity of saints. The same truth is illustrated in the conduct of those bidden to the supper, when "they all with one consent began to make excuse." Luke xiv. 18.

VER. 4.—My beloved put in his hand by the hole of the door, and my bowels were moved for him.

On the whole, the best explanation of the first clause of this verse, seems to us that which may be got from a statement of Wilkinson, taken with one in the "Mission of Inquiry to the Jews." "The folding doors had bolts in the centre; a bar was placed across from one wall to the other; and in many instances wooden locks secured them by passing over the centre, at the junction of the two folds. These locks were probably on the principle of those now used in Egypt, which are of wood, and are opened by a key furnished with several fixed pins, answering to a similar number, that fall down into the hollow movable tongue, into which the key is introduced when they fasten or open the lock." "He showed us the key of his cottage, commonly used for the door, which is nothing more than a piece of wood with pegs fastened in it, corresponding to small holes in a wooden bolt within. It is put through a hole in the door, and draws the bolt in a very simple manner. The large opening through which the key is introduced, illustrates these words in the Song." The words, "put in his hand by the hole of the door,"·we prefer reading, "withdrew his hand from the hole of the door." This, perhaps, is more strictly the meaning of the Hebrew, and gives a sufficient reason for her rising at that particular moment for opening the door to him. He might have removed the bolt and entered without her assistance; but after having put his hand through the aperture and made a movement towards opening, finding her still untouched by his very tender appeal, and treating him with indifference, he stopped, withdrew his hand, and departed. This roused her from her lethargy, and brought her to her senses. She had an ardent affection for the beloved, notwithstanding this exhibition of indifference. With the thought of his tenderness and her own unkindness flashing on her mind, the idea of losing his society, and having him to remain longer under the chilling dews, touched her heart, and roused into full vigour all her dormant love.

In this state of apathy, Jesus makes attempts for gaining admission to our hearts. The beloved did more than merely address the bride in endearing terms; he tried to open the door. Our Saviour not only "speaks to the heart of Jerusalem," but tries to unbar the entrance to the soul, that he may come in and sup with us, and take up there his abode. At times when, though the heart feels the value of Christ, faith and love, with their corresponding activity in his service, are slumbering, we find Jesus making efforts to arouse us by moving sweetly on the heart with his Holy Spirit, and by various gracious acts of his providence. Repeatedly may we have felt an influence on the heart, we could not tell how, or whence, surprising us in our coldness, coming even without our prayers, warming our affections, making us feel greater interest in spiritual things, and causing us to be sensible that it was indeed Jesus. He had truly come unsought. We were still in our slumbers, even yet hardly enough awake to feel the force of his whispers of love, so beautifully though inadequately shadowed forth by this touching language of the beloved. Circumstances of ease around us, gloom on the mind, drowsiness on the heart, made us reluctant to shake off our lethargy, and arise to give him a cordial welcome. We were precisely in the condition of a person partially aroused from sleep. His appeals failed to make a successful impression; and we were satisfied to quiet conscience with the most frivolous excuses. At length the influence felt moving on the heart began to subside; and the soul, instead of passing on to such full measures of the Holy Spirit as had been enjoyed in the presence of Jesus, found the light of his countenance withdrawing, spiritual impressions growing fainter, and the affections settling down into deeper torpor and gloom. Symptoms of his withdrawal began first to bring us to our senses. The fear of losing one who had so loved us, and had just been speaking to us so tenderly, moved our hearts towards him, and made us rise to give him a welcome. The three following truths are therefore embodied in this verse:—when we are in a state of spiritual coldness and indifference, Jesus often takes steps for arousing us from our lethargy, and gaining admittance to our hearts; continued neglect on our part will lead him to stop these exertions and withdraw; then when he is withdrawing do we, frequently, first awake to a sense of the desirableness of his presence, and the value of his love.

Ver. 5.—I rose up to open to my beloved; and my hands dropped with myrrh, and my fingers with sweet-smelling myrrh, upon the handles of the lock.

There is an interpretation of this verse which seems to us incorrect, and to have been suggested by a Roman custom:

> With tears, the ling'ring lover at the door
> Hangs flowery wreaths, and with perfume bedews
> The threshold, and impresses many a kiss.*

With this the idea would be, that the beloved had poured liquid myrrh profusely on the handle of the bolt or lock, and this it was that perfumed the hand of the spouse. But the more reasonable view is, that in her room were standing, according to the custom of the times, vases of perfumes as well as other presents, such as eastern ladies prepare for welcoming their lovers: as in Hafiz,

> "For me the angel of my heart prepares
> Chaplets and unguents, breathing fragrant airs."

With this compare Prov. vii. 17. In climates so warm as to keep persons almost constantly in a state of sensible perspiration, it is found a great comfort to have the palms of the hands and the soles of the feet in a comparatively dry state, particularly as to the hands, which would otherwise moisten whatever they handled. Perfumes, as mentioned by Pliny, were placed on the back of the hand as the coolest part of the body, and as causing their fragrance to exhale with greatest richness.† The free

---

* Lucretius, iv. 1171.

† "He was making his toilet for the day; and his hands were bedewed with the perfumes which his valets-de-chambre had poured upon them."—*Lamartine's Restoration of Monarchy in France*, vol. ii. 195.

use of odours by oriental ladies in meeting their loved ones, is mentioned in Esther, chap. ii. 12. Now in rising to meet her beloved, the spouse made use of these perfumes; and according to the usual custom, poured of them on the back of the hands, perhaps the more freely from her anxiety and haste; this perfume, thus so liberally used, bedewed the handles of the lock with its precious drops. The word "sweet-smelling," means liquid, or that which has wept drop by drop, tear-like, from the tree, and is consequently most precious. To use such perfume, and thus liberally, was the most palpable proof a bride could give her lover, of welcoming his presence. Hence, after the indifference of the spouse, as she wished, on awaking to a sense of her unkindness, to make the beloved feel how cheerfully she received him, she naturally used her very best perfume, and that very freely, so much so that it dropped on the handle of the bolt. For showing her love, there came to Jesus a woman having an alabaster box of very precious ointment. The text does then represent the anxiety of the soul, when awaked to a sense of the unkindness and guilt of its spiritual sloth, to meet Jesus with every possible demonstration of welcome and affection. We wish to make amends for past ingratitude and indolence. In the case illustrated by the spouse, the believer has the influences of the Holy Spirit, the liquid myrrh, resting sometimes even richly on his heart. Without these, there can be no earnest seeking after Jesus.

VER. 6.—I opened to my beloved; but my beloved had withdrawn himself, and was gone: my soul failed when he spake: I sought him, but I could not find him; I called him, but he gave me no answer.

At length, coming with a desire to give him a cordial welcome, the spouse opened the door for the beloved, but found that he had turned away, was gone. In the words, "my soul failed when he spake," we read the three latter, literally, 'because of his speaking,' or 'after his speaking.' Such may be the force of the preposition here used with the infinitive. The meaning would then be, not that her soul fainted, or she was overcome while he was speaking, but after, and in consequence of what he had said. Finding him gone, she called to mind his tender, affecting language, and was so overcome thereby as to be almost unmanned. Recovering herself, she began to seek him, but could not find him; she called, but got no answer.

It is dangerous for us to hesitate and delay when Jesus shows willingness to enter the soul again by his Holy Spirit. When he has been kind enough to seek us out in our decay, we should run with eagerness to meet him at the first intimation of his approach. Neglect to do so, leads to his withdrawal, and lays up for us periods of toil, sorrow, desertion, and humiliation. Grace in the heart may keep our affections vigorous; he will not gratify us with sensible proofs of his presence. The recollection of his kindness and his melting words of love during our period of sloth, affects us very deeply; causes our soul to fail; and arouses us to great exertions in seeking him for repairing the consequences of our neglect. By this carnal security and sloth, the believer has lost very many periods of delightful communion with Jesus, and been obliged to encounter painful difficulties, with seasons of darkness, reproach, and persecution.

VER. 7.—The watchmen that went about the city found me, they smote me, they wounded me; the keepers of the walls took away my veil from me.

The spouse had before sought the beloved by night in the streets, but under different circumstances. See chap. iii. 2, 3. In the former case, there was no treating of the beloved with neglect; and as she sought him from the impulse of deep affection, she found him almost immediately, without difficulty; here as the result of her neglect she encounters much unpleasantness and trouble. The watchmen treated her in an unworthy manner. Watchmen were customarily employed in Jerusalem; and their post was at the gates; at night watchmen were accustomed to perambulate the city. These represent the ministers of the Church, with whom the believer is naturally brought in contact, when suffering under spiritual desertion, and seeking Jesus in times of darkness and trial.

The watchmen viewed the spouse as a bad woman; for females were not allowed to go about the streets in the night. They smote her, wounded her, and took away her veil: the last is the greatest indignity that can be offered to an oriental lady. The meaning is, they did not recognize her claims to respectability; and treated her as one positively vicious. Her conduct, though not morally wrong, was unusual. As it was not customary for them to see a respectable female under such circumstances, they supposed no one could be reputable while acting thus. Hers was a manifestation of female devotion they had never yet seen. Christians animated by a holy zeal, under intense influences of the Holy Spirit, have often met with ill-treatment from their brethren, and even from the ministry, the watchmen of Zion who should help them in their search for the object of their affection, rather than treat them as destitute of suitable claims to be considered real lovers of Jesus. This disposition has not been confined to any one sect; it belongs to human nature, and has shown itself in men of every creed. Every pious exercise differing in vigour and degree from the current feeling of nominal Christians and the imaginary standard of particular churches, is viewed with suspicion, as distempered and spurious, as the offspring of fanaticism, however unmistakenly it may bear the marks of the Holy Spirit. In their fear of what is called fanaticism, some persons shun what are genuine religious affections. Many a poor soul, with a heart aching and burning to know more of Christ, has had its honest inquiries met with reproach or indifference. Hence, in every age, when spiritual decay has been prevalent, persons taking the lead in reviving evangelical religion have had to encounter ill-treatment and persecution. "Your brethren that hated you, that cast you out for my name's sake, said, Let the Lord be glorified: but he shall appear to your joy, and they shall be ashamed." Jesus himself was cast out from the synagogue; and, at last, put to death. Shall we mention Chrysostom, Luther? nay, the whole history of the Church is an illustration. Thus was Lady Guyon treated in France; Edwards at Northampton; and the Evangelical brethren of the present day, in Scotland. Every Christian communion has a general type of piety peculiar to itself; and many look with incredulty on any manifestation of holy affections of a kind at all different.

Ver. 8.—I charge you, O daughters of Jerusalem, if ye find my beloved, that ye tell him, that I am sick of love.

See remarks on chap. ii. 5—7. Leaving the watchmen who had ill-treated her, the spouse turns to the daughters of Jerusalem as more congenial friends. To them she opens her feelings; their interest she seeks to enlist. Thus the humble believer, received with coldness and repulse by those high in authority, turns away to find kindred spirits and sympathizing hearts among unknown brethren of a deeper religious experience.

We see here that holy love and holy joy do not always exist together in equal degree. There may be very much of the former during an absence of the latter. The soul may be sick of love to Jesus, while mourning the withdrawal of his presence, and struggling amid the darkness of temptation, obloquy and sorrow. Want of joy is no proof of the absence of grace. A beloved friend may be as devotedly loved when we are separated from him by distance and struggling with difficulties, as when we are peacefully enjoying his society. It were certainly unreasonable to doubt our love to him, or his love to us, because necessary duties of life often separated us. And in these hours when Jesus has left us, even though through our own neglect, we may still be comforted with the assurance of loving him, if we persevere in anxiously seeking him, even amid darkness, suspicion, and trial. We must assuredly love him, when able to adopt the words of Augustin, "What shall I say? what shall I do? whither shall I go? where shall I seek him? or when shall I find him? whom shall I ask? who will tell my beloved that I am sick of love?"

VER. 9.—What is thy beloved more than another beloved, O thou fairest among women? what is thy beloved more than another beloved, that thou dost so charge us?

The daughters of Jerusalem seeing the beauty of the spouse, knowing her character, and noticing her very fervent love, are naturally led to ask her what there is so peculiarly attractive in her beloved, what are his excellences more than those of any other. This inquiry prepares the way very fitly for the beautiful illustration that follows of the loveliness of Jesus. On the words "O thou fairest, &c.," see chap. i. 8. This question was put, not by foreigners, but by the daughters of Jerusalem. And when real Christians sometimes meet with those who have had brighter views than themselves of the loveliness of our Lord, they are ready to make the same inquiry, to ask what we see in Christ to make us speak of him with such fervour. Every person has some leading object of affection, on which the heart is devotedly set. For instance, the soldiers of Napoleon found this object in their emperor; and should they put this question, what must be the answer? What is Christ Jesus, the beloved of the saint, more than the beloved of those soldiers? Others have the heart set on a cherished husband, wife, or child: what is Christ more than these? Again, some, like the fair youth Narcissus, who became enamoured with the beauty of his own form seen in a pellucid fountain, make self the idol of their hearts; others fix their hearts on a heap of dust, called gold; while others in love with the beautiful, entwine around a work of imagination, a picture, or a statue, the warm affections of the heart. What is the beloved of the saint, Jesus, more than the beloved of these?

VER. 10.—My beloved is white and ruddy, the chiefest among ten thousand.

The principles guiding the interpretation of this whole passage to the close of the chapter, have been already explained. The nature of this description, and of the others like it in the Song, is precisely such as is seen in the exhibition of a piece of fine statuary or a beautiful painting. Should a person wish to represent to another the impression made on his own mind by gazing on the Apollo Belvidere, he must proceed on the same general principles here adopted, though his comparisons and language must be necessarily different. Persons of cultivated taste feel it is not improper to study finished works of art; and even in the present advanced stage of civilization, statues with little or no drapery are placed among the choicest productions of genius, and gazed on by thousands of both sexes, in company, without a blush or thought of anything indelicate. Does any one deem it an offence against good taste, to exhibit or to study the Apollo, the Venus de Medici, or the Greek Slave? Those who are willing to admire such undying productions, cannot with any consistency find fault with these portraits of the Song. The difference between the two cases is simply this—what statues do through marble, the Song does through words. These delineations in the Song give a picture of a noble human form, around which is thrown every drapery necessary to add to the beauty and gratify the most delicate taste. In defence of these exquisite delineations of the beautiful in the human form, we are not willing to plead, as might be justly done, that at the time the Song was written, its language was, in point of modesty, far ahead of the most refined nations; and that when our translation of the Bible was made, these passages were far above the general tone of English literature. We take rather the higher and stronger ground, that these representations are in perfect accordance with the constitution of the human mind, and with principles universally admitted in the fine arts. The sculptor wishing to represent the perfect beauty of the human form, portrays it by a resemblance of man wrought in marble. The custom of mankind is to set off the body with dress and ornaments drawn from different parts of the world, such as gold, gems, silks, plumes, &c. Why, therefore, should it be thought strange that the Holy Spirit should draw together beautiful objects from different quarters, for representing the beauty of the body? Beautiful attire invests the body according to a natural custom; why should not the same right be granted concerning an ideal body around which is thrown the drapery of the beautiful thoughts here grouped together. When it is said that such and such parts of the body are thus and thus beautiful, the meaning is, there is thrown over a human form a drapery and ornaments formed of the ideas suggested by these comparisons. These illustrations form a splendid drapery, the design of which is to set off with perfect grace, and heighten to the greatest possible degree, every beauty of the human form;—having done this, the Holy Spirit points to such portraiture, to such embodiment of beauty, and says, That may be an illustration of the beauty there is in Jesus. Wishing to set forth to mortal eyes the beauty seen in Christ, the wisdom of God, the Holy Spirit represents these not in marble that may be mutilated, and may perish, but in language that can never die; and gathers in this language the most beautiful comparisons and richest expressions possible. Could no other reason be given for inserting these passages in the Scriptures, this would be sufficient—that Christians of undoubted piety, deep experience, and great purity of heart, have found these illustrations of the loveliness of Christ, a source of instruction and unspeakable delight—not only not suggesting unhallowed thoughts, but feeding the soul with meditations kindred with those of heaven.

> "Ne from thenceforth doth any fleshy sense
> Or idle thought of earthly things remaine:
> So full their eyes are of that glorious sight,
> And senses fraught with such satietie,
> That in nought else on earth can they delight,
> But in th' aspec of that felicitie,
> Which they have written in their inward eye."*

Like pellucid rills from different springs, the trains of beautiful thoughts flowing from the various illustrations here mentioned, combine into one full stream, and inundate the soul with a flood of delight.

* Spenser's Hymn of Heavenly Beauty.

When it is said, the beloved is white and ruddy, the meaning is, that his complexion is the perfection of beauty and health. David was "ruddy, and withal of beautiful countenance, and goodly to look to." 1 Sam. xvi. 12. So beautiful is our beloved, that he is the chief among ten thousand; or, literally, he is lifted up as a banner among an innumerable host; that is, in a countless host the eye would naturally rest on him conspicuous and pre-eminent above all others, as it distinguishes a banner amid tens of thousands of people. When Milton would represent Satan as distinguished above his compeers, his words are:

> "He, above the rest,
> In shape and gesture proudly eminent,
> Stood like a tower."

In the muster of the fallen angels in hell, the imperial ensign

> "Full high advanced,
> Shone like a meteor, streaming to the wind,
> With gems and golden lustre rich emblazed:"

thus, towers Jesus above all others, the centre of attraction to whom all eyes must ever be turned, even amid the innumerable company of angels. The believer feels most truly, that wherever he goes, under all circumstances, Jesus is, like the banner in an armed host, the centre of attraction to which his eyes are always anxiously turned, the rallying point of his soul, full high advanced above all others; the splendour of his divinity burning with a brilliancy of glory richer than a meteor streaming to the wind, brighter than the cloud that rested on the mount of transfiguration. That mount, with the crown-like glory of the bright cloud then resting there, was distinguished above all other mountains; and thus, amid the hosts of heaven, Jesus is pre-eminent by the crown of glory and honour, the radiance of the divinity encompassing him as a sun. He is even now the sun by whose light all the youth of "the sacramental host of God's elect" move to do the brave acts of their spiritual warfare. To him are we exhorted to look, him to imitate, him to follow. In this grandeur and glory of his divinity, does he loom up before the soul in the hour of repentance, in trouble, in the valley of the shadow of death. In heaven he will be the conspicuous object to angels, no less than to the redeemed; for who besides him is there like him, even in heaven? In him are combined the divine and human natures; and this union gives rise to a development of glory, splendid and remarkable, as it is singular and grand.

In this verse, therefore, as introducing the following description, there are two general statements: first, that he has the beauty springing from the clearness of complexion and ruddy glow, bespeaking perfect health; and that there is something in his general appearance which would draw attention to him above all others, even amid an innumerable host.*

---

* Kitto gives from the Persian, the following description of the patriarch Joseph, with which this description of the beloved may be compared: "A beauteous youth, who eclipses the charms and graces of the houris of Paradise. His form, polished as the box-tree, erect as the cypress. His locks, falling in ringlets, sealing the mouth of wisdom, and arresting the feet of discretion. His forehead shining with immortal beams, surpassing both the sun and the moon. His eyebrows arched, and his eyelashes shading his sleepy eyes. His eyes beaming mildness, his eyelashes darting arrows. His lips smiling and shedding sweets, his lips dropping honey. His pearly teeth between his ruby lips, like the lightning playing upon a western sky. Laughing, he eclipses the Pleiades; smiles and jests dance upon his lips. Pearly drops hang upon his double chin; upon his rosy countenance a mole, as the dark ash in the midst of a garden. His arms like silver, and well proportioned; but the waist, for want of silver, slender."

VER. 11.—His head is as the most fine gold; his locks are bushy, and black as a raven.

The words rendered "the most fine gold," seem, from the original, to mean the choicest gold, such as kings laid up among their peculiar treasures—gold most carefully refined. Perhaps Rosenmüller's idea may be correct, when he understands them to express choice, pure, solid gold. Our apprehension of the meaning is, that the head of the beloved was so exquisitely beautiful, and an object of such pleasure to the contemplation of the bride, she could illustrate her feelings in gazing on it, in no better way than by saying, they were as delightful as they would be in contemplating a statue or bust, a head, sculptured by a finished artist from the finest solid gold. Beyond the ordinary pleasure had in gazing on a finished piece of sculpture from marble there is here added the pleasure had from contemplating the same wrought from the finest gold.

The word "locks" expresses the forelocks about the temples; the word "bushy" has received different interpretations, varying in their shades of meaning, but conveying the same general idea. The Septuagint translate, "his hair is like the young leaves of the palm." Dopke renders "palm branches." There is considerable uniformity in the shape of the leaves of the palms. They are generally feathery, or divided like the plume of a feather; sometimes the leaves are flag like, of a thin, flexible texture, and curl towards the extremities. The leaves of the Jaqua palm are sixteen or seventeen feet long, their extremities are curled like plumes; the ultimate divisions or leaflets flutter lightly and airily round the slowly balancing central leaf stalks."* The hair may be very aptly compared to the fine wavy young

* Humboldt's Aspects, 318.

leaves of the palm on their first bursting forth from the sheaths in which they are contained. The idea is, that his locks were full, in flowing clusters, like waving pendulous branches, with curls rising above one another in profusion. They were black as a raven; that is, of the purest and jettiest black. So Ossian, "Her hair was the wing of the raven." And the Persian poet—

> "Thy face is brighter than the cheek of day,
> Blacker thy locks than midnight's deepest sway."

And again—

> "Of black, e'en blackest hue, and unconfined,
> Her shadowy tresses wantoned in the wind."

VER. 12.—His eyes are as the eyes of doves by the rivers of waters, washed with milk, and fitly set.

See note, chap. i. 15. Here the eyes of the beloved are compared to doves, rather than to the eyes of doves, on account of what follows. In Ps. lxviii. 13, "The wings of a dove covered with silver, and her feathers with yellow gold," there is reference to those brilliant and sometimes golden reflections which the lustrous plumage of some doves exhibits. All in their true wild plumage, have iridescent colours about the neck; and often reflect flashes of the same colours on the shoulders: this is expressed in the clearest light, by saying, that these doves were more beautiful than when washed in streams of the purest water, pure and brilliant as though washed in a limpid brook, combining with the transparency of water the whiteness of milk. The same picture occurs in the Gitagovinda: "His passion was inflamed by the glances of her eyes, which played like a pair of water-birds with azure plumage, that sport near a full-blown lotus, on a pool in the season of dew." And again, "She whose wanton eye resembles blue water-lilies agitated by the breeze." Doves by such streams, represent beautifully the pupil of the eye, surrounded by its clear, healthful white; and the brooks of water seem mentioned for illustrating the eye as the fountain of tears, and the eyes of the beloved as suffused with the tenderness flowing from a spring deep in the heart of sympathy and love. The whole comparison represents the eyes as sparkling with vivacity, purity, and love of the greatest tenderness. The last words, "fitly set," are referred by some interpreters to the beautiful setting of a gem in a ring, perhaps to the precious stones in the breast-plate of the high-priest. The idea would then be, that while his eyes amid his clustering, waving, raven locks, were beautiful as doves sporting by the transparent streams around which gathered trees of rich foliage, those eyes were brilliant and perfectly set in his head, as gems fitly set by the most skilful artist in the finest gold. We prefer, however, to render the whole verse—'His eyes as doves by valley-rills of water, washed in milk, reposing by the full fountain streams.' The idea would then be that of milk-white doves in a rural vale, reposing quietly by rich, full streams, flowing from pellucid fountains.

VER. 13.—His cheeks are as a bed of spices, as sweet flowers: his lips like lilies, dropping sweet-smelling myrrh.

Besides fragrant plants and flowers, the Jewish gardens were occupied, in a considerable degree, with the growth of medicinal shrubs and herbs. The word *bed* here means a bed raised throughout, or at least in the middle; such a plat, thickly covered with sweet-smelling flowers in full bloom, was a most delightful object; and the spouse laying under contribution everything most beautiful in nature, says the pleasure felt by her in gazing on the cheeks of the beloved, could be best illustrated by the delight caused in viewing a bed filled with fragrant flowers.

She goes farther, however, and adds force to the idea. The next words, "as sweet flowers," rendered in the margin of our Bible, "towers of perfumes," do not seem to convey the idea intended by the original Hebrew. This word generally translated "tower," is used for an elevated stage or platform, in Neh. viii. 4, and ix. 4. It seems to mean trellises, and those of a towering height, covered with aromatic flowers. The whole verse would then read—'His cheeks are as banks or mounds of fragrant flowers, as towering trellises covered with aromatic blooms.' May this refer to the artificial terraces frequently covering the hills of Judea? In many places it is terraced continuously for miles. Steep hills are converted into numerous horizontal beds, rising successively till the top of the mountain forms the last. On ascending a mountain pass, a traveller counted sixty-seven terraces, which occupied the whole side of the hill; while considerably higher mountains were manifestly terraced all over by a proportionally greater number. These terraced sides formed hanging gardens, rising beautifully from the rich valleys, in the days of Israel's glory, when the scene must have been as fertile as now it is desolate, and as beauteous as now it is blasted. In this passage may the spouse therefore say, that the ruddy cheeks of the beloved excited a pleasure like that felt in gazing on beds of fragrant flowers, or contemplating those terraced hills covered with blooming aromatic herbs?

"His lips like lilies, dropping sweet-smelling myrrh." These words illustrate the beauty of his lips. There may be a reference here to a lily of deep red colour, mentioned by Pliny as much esteemed in Syria. That the colour as well as sweetness and general beauty of these lilies is referred to, appears probable from the following allusions in oriental poets: "Him whose lips are like a red lotos in full bloom;" "How can tulip-coloured wine be compared to the rubies of thy lips:" "I meditate on the fragrant lotos of her mouth, on her nectar-dropping speech, on her lips ruddy as the berries of the bimba." See chap. v. 5, on "sweet-smelling myrrh." Sir Thomas Brown supposes this refers to "the roscid and honey-drops observable in the flowers of martagons and inverted flowered lilies; and is probably the standing sweet dew on the white eyes of the crown-imperial, now common among us." This whole comparison, then, means that his lips are beautiful as those roseate lilies, distilling drops precious as the most precious myrrh, limpid as the morning dew.

VER. 14.—His hands are as gold rings set with the beryl: his belly is as bright ivory overlaid with sapphires.

The idea here is, not that his fingers were covered with golden rings, but that the fingers were as gold rings, rollers, or cylinders, and the nails were as the beryl set in those rings. The original word *tarshish*, here rendered *beryl*, means a precious stone, so called because brought from Tarshish. According to the Septuagint and Josephus, it is the chrysolite—that is, the topaz of the moderns, which is still found in Spain. This is a precious stone having a strong glass lustre. Its prevailing colour is wine-yellow, of every degree of shade. The dark shade of this colour passes over into carnation red, and sometimes, though rarely, into lilac; the pale shade of the wine-yellow passes into greyish, and from yellowish white into greenish white and pale green. This stone was highly prized by the Hebrews. To them no illustration could be more beautifully appropriate for giving an idea of the most finely formed hands, with fingers and nails of extreme delicacy, than to say they were gold rollers set with the beryl.

"His body is as bright ivory overlaid with sapphires."* The word body, rather than belly, is the proper one to be here used: it means the whole of the body from the shoulders downwards. The sapphire is a gem so called from its beauty and splendour. It is next in hardness and value to the diamond, and is mostly of a blue colour of various shades. In the choicest specimens it is of the deepest azure; and in others varies in shades of all degrees between that and the pure crystal brightness of water, without the least tinge of colour, but with a lustre much superior to crystal. The Hebrew word answering to "bright" in our version means something wrought, artificial work; and the idea intended therefore is, that his body excited feelings of beauty like those caused by gazing on a curious artificial work of ivory richly inlaid, even covered, with brilliant sapphires. For expressing the beauty of his body, the highly wrought finely polished ivory was not sufficient. It has a beauty combining with

---

* Homer has a like illustration:

> As when a Carian or Mæonian nymph
> With purple ivory tinges, for some steed
> An ornamental head-piece, stored it lies
> Of kings a treasure, charioteers a pride:
> Thus, Menelaus, was thy snowy form,
> Thy graceful thighs, stained with the trickling gore.
> *Iliad*, book iv. 142.

And Virgil:

> As when with purple, Indian ivory's tinged;
> 'Mid numerous roses snowy lilies blush;
> Her beauteous face a crimson flush suffused.
> *Æn.* xii. 67.

the whiteness and polish of ivory the splendour and glory of sapphires.

VER. 15.—His legs are as pillars of marble set upon sockets of fine gold; his countenance is as Lebanon, excellent as the cedars.

The phrase "silver legged" is common in Persia, to denote elegance of this limb. Thus Hafiz:

> "O thou whose polished legs like silver shine,
> My heart is ravished as thou bring'st me wine."

Ovid speaks of delicate marble feet. Aquila and Theodotion translate this, "his legs are pillars, or columns, of Parian marble." This was the whitest, purest, and best—that from which the Grecian statues generally were formed. "On sockets, or pedestals, of fine gold." These doubtless refer to the beauty of his sandals. From the many references to the beauty of sandals in the Latin and Greek poets, we take but one from Callimachus, in his hymn to Apollo:

> "A golden robe invests the glorious god:
> His shining feet with golden sandals shod;
> Gold are his harp, his quiver, and his bow."

Columns of fine marble, on bases of pure solid gold, were beautiful to the view; far more beautiful were his legs, with their costly, splendid sandals.

"His countenance is as Lebanon, excellent as the cedars." There are higher mountains than Lebanon, but none more truly deserving the epithet of Moses, "that goodly mountain, even Lebanon." Towering to a height of ten thousand feet above the sea, and deriving its name, not from the snow lying continually on its summits, but from the whiteness of its limestone rocks, "Lebanon presents us everywhere, with majestic mountains. At every step we meet with scenes in which nature displays either beauty or grandeur. When we land on the coast, the loftiness and steep ascent of this mountainous ridge, which seems to enclose the country, those gigantic masses which shoot into the clouds, inspire astonishment and awe."* "We were chiefly occupied with the view of majestic Lebanon. It is a noble range of mountains, well worthy of the fame it has so long maintained. It is cultivated in a wonderful manner, by the help of terraces, and is still very fertile. We saw on some of its eminences, more than two thousand feet high, villages and luxuriant vegetation; and on some of its peaks, six thousand feet high, we could discern tall pines against the clear sky beyond. At first the clouds were resting on the lofty summit of the range, but they cleared away, and we saw Sannin, which is generally regarded as the highest peak of Lebanon. The rays of the setting sun gave a splendid tint to the lofty brow of the mountain; and we did not wonder how the Church of old saw in its features of calm and immovable majesty, an emblem of the great Redeemer—'His countenance is as Lebanon.' The cedars of Lebanon excel those of all other lands. They are remarkable for the multiplicity and length of the branches, few trees dividing so many fair branches from the main stem, or spreading over so large a compass of the ground. No tree in the forest is more remarkable than the cedar for its closely woven, leafy canopy. Its mantling foliage—or overshadowing shroud, as Ezekiel calls it—is its greatest beauty, which arises from the horizontal growth of its branches, forming a kind of sweeping irregular pent-house. And when to the idea of beauty, that of strength is added, by the pyramidal form of the stem and the robustness of the limbs, the tree is complete in all its majesty and beauty."† Besides their uncom-

---

* Volney.   † The Scotch Mission of Inquiry.

mon size and beauty of shape and foliage, they send forth a balsamic odour, which seems to be meant by "the smell of Lebanon." With perfect elegance and taste, the beloved is compared to Lebanon and the cedars for dignity and grandeur; and afterwards the spouse is compared to Carmel and the palm-tree, for beauty and grace. Chap. vii. 5.

VER. 16.—His mouth is most sweet; yea, he is altogether lovely. This is my beloved, and this is my friend, O daughters of Jerusalem.

The mouth, or palate, together with the corresponding lower part of the mouth, is put for the voice. This may read, 'His voice is sweetness;'—that is, not merely pure sweetness, but so rich that its excellence cannot be better expressed than by saying, it is a combination of sweetnesses. Every possible beauty of sound and music is concentrated in the tones of his voice.

It will have been already noticed, that in this description there is a grouping together of objects and ideas of beauty and brilliancy, dazzling beyond expression, and beyond any power of conception by the unaided human mind. These different clusters of beautiful ideas are, like the various flowers brought from different places for forming a boquet, drawn together for giving us an idea of the cluster of glories centring in Jesus. Yet they are, after all, further from giving a perfect idea of his loveliness, than the various flowers gathered as specimens into a cluster, are from representing with anything like faithfulness, the richness of the tropical landscape from which they may have been gathered. All the things here used for comparison are rich and radiant with splendour. The head is more beautiful than a finished sculpture from the finest marble, it is a sculpture from the purest solid gold; the eyes have, besides the liveliness and tenderness of doves washing in a rural limpid stream, the brilliancy of gems elegantly set in gold; the cheeks have the fresh hues of beds of blooming, odoriferous flowers; the lips have the elegance of lilies distilling dew-like myrrh; the hands and fingers are cylinders of gold, the nails are precious stones; the body combines the beauty of ivory united with sapphires; the legs are pillars of the purest marble, set on bases of the finest gold; the countenance has the grandeur and majesty of Lebanon, the nobleness and excellence of the cedars. Were it possible for all these splendours and beauties to be united in any individual, how far would he transcend the fairest of the sons of men. Combine into a focus at the heart all the ideas and feelings of beauty gathered from all these objects of splendour, and then you have something resembling the delight had by the believer in contemplating the Lord Jesus. All these, however, infinitely more than these, are found in the person of him who is "fairer than the children of men." With this may be compared the language of Clytemnestra, on the return of Agamemnon:

> "Faithful—as dog, the lonely shepherd's pride;
> True—as the helm, the bark's protecting guide;
> Firm—as the shaft that props the towering dome;
> Sweet—as to shipwreck'd seamen land and home;
> Lovely—as child, a parent's sole delight.
> Radiant—as morn that breaks a stormy night:
> Grateful—as streams, that in some deep recess,
> With rills unhoped, the panting traveller bless;
> Is he that links with mine his chain of life,
> Names himself lord, and deigns to call me wife."*

How greatly was the beauty of the statues of Minerva and Jupiter, by Phidias, heightened by the fine carving, ornaments, and drapery of gold overlaying the figure formed with such majesty in ivory! The view of the

---

* Agamemnon of Æschylus, 828.

Apollo Belvidere gives pleasure even in the simple marble; how much more thrilling must be the impression, could all the splendid ideas here grouped together, be superadded to the majesty of the simple, unadorned marble. Even then we must go farther, and add the idea of life. The whole would then be no more than an emblematical representation of the Lord Jesus, of him in whom dwelt all the fulness of the Godhead bodily. As the Shechinah was surpassed by the glory shown forth in him who spake as never man spake; who healed the sick; who raised the dead; who was transfigured on Tabor; so, infinitely more is the glory of Jesus when on earth, transcended by the glory now investing him in heaven.

Hence after all that had been said, the spouse adds, "Yea," or beside all these excellences, he has so many others, that we must say, "he is altogether lovely;" more literally, 'his wholeness is delights'—his very constitution and nature consist of pure delights. As God, considered as exercising kind feeling towards us, is said to be 'love;' so Jesus, viewed as the source of happiness in us, or as the author of pleasing sensations in us, is said to be 'delights.' These constitute his very being as thus contemplated; there is nothing in him which does not cause delights. There is nothing in him which is not lovely; and there is nothing delightful which is not centred in him. The whole creation is a manifestation of the glory of God. The Jewish tabernacle was a model on a small scale, fitted by the same Creator, for illustrating the excellence of Jesus Christ, the maker of all things, as the Redeemer of men; and showing forth characteristics of the divine nature not seen in creation, and rendered necessary by a state of things among men, which did not exist when the world was made. The ancient Shechinah assumed different appearances, according to the character of God at the time; sometimes exhibiting the terrors of his justice, as in the flaming sword at the east of Eden, and in the consuming fire on the top of Sinai; at others, manifesting the loveliness of his mercy, as in the cloud which dwelt between the cherubim, in the temple. Under the old dispensation, this mysterious cloud was the type of him who is the atoning Redeemer, and "the brightness of the Father's glory."

We come very far short of attaining full views of the blessedness of Jesus, by taking only one aspect or representation of him at a time, instead of combining in one view all that the Scriptures shadow forth of his glory. At one time, we view him as a King; then, as Almighty; again, as a Lamb leading his flock to living waters; then, as the light of that world of glory. This mode of unfolding his character is necessary and wise. But in studying his excellences, let us not detach any one of them from the rest; let us view them as a glorious combination forming together one whole. The King crowned with many crowns is Jesus, but not the full development of the glory of Jesus. The Shechinah of the Holy City is Jesus; but this, however magnificent, does not constitute our Lord as he appears in his glory. And these detached characteristics, however beautiful when viewed alone, are far more grand when seen amid the cluster to which they belong. In forming a conception of Jesus, let us bring together into one person or individual all the detached representations given of him in the Scriptures—the Son of God, the King of kings, the King crowned with many crowns, the Judge on the great white throne, the Godhead coming with clouds, the Lamb leading his flock to living fountains of waters, the Shechinah of the holy Jerusalem, the tender friend weeping with his people in sorrow at the grave of Lazarus, the first born, the elder brother of the saints;—gather all these into one, so far as the mind is able to do this, and then we have something of what the Scriptures represent Jesus Christ as he is in glory. Yes, add to these the splendour of the burning bush, the grandeur of Sinai, the vision of Isaiah with its overpowering majesty, (Isa. chap. vi.,) the wondrous sight unfolded to Ezekiel, (chap. i.,) the vision of Daniel, (chap. vii. 9,) the cloud of glory that dwelt between the cherubim, the effulgence of the transfiguration, the appearance to Paul on the road to Damascus, the revelation to the beloved disciple at Patmos, the ideas of beauty grouped together in the Song, (v. 10—16,) the picture presented when he stood on the mount of Olives and wept over Jerusalem; when the mind can gather to its bosom all these ideas at once, it can feel all that God has now opened of the grandeur, glory, and loveliness of Christ. These rays, small, very small part though they are of his excellence, when gathered to a focus are overpowering. When thus attempting to comprehend even what is revealed of our Lord, the mind feels its incapacity, and sees the wisdom of having him revealed to us as God has done it in the Scriptures, by unfolding a part of his perfections at a time. We thus get a better comprehension of those detached scenes, and ultimately of the glory of Christ, by studying them independently, than could be done by having them all crowded into one. Yet, when the heart has studied them separately, it is anxious to rise to the highest conceptions possible of Jesus, by bringing these clusters of glories together; but it finds its powers to fail under the effort. These gems of truth are as fitly set in the Scriptures, as were the stones in Aaron's breast-plate; and with what effulgence do they beam, when the Urim and Thummim of the Holy Spirit kindles there his light; what a mellow radiance do they throw over all the intermediate truths and spaces of the word of God; the radiance poured abroad by the Spirit through these representations of the glory of Christ, lighting up all the other Scriptures with a more heavenly glow. And they light up all nature with a beauty and splendour before unseen. The Holy Spirit causes us as it were to see lamps of heavenly fire burning in everything around us, until all creation becomes to our view like the golden candlestick in the view of the worshipper in the sanctuary—every created thing, not only every star, but every tree, every flower, becoming a lamp more beauteous than gold, on which burns the richness of the splendour of the divine glory. To the eye of faith all this is reality. And to the soul whose vision has been purified by grace, the works of God convey sensations more delightful than could be experienced, were every bud, every blossom, every blade of grass, and every flower, a lamp burning with living fire.

> "The clouds that gather round the setting sun
> Do take a purer colouring from an eye
> Illumined with this inward purity:
> To such the humblest flower that blows can give
> Thoughts that do often lie too deep for tears."*

Substituting holy sensibility for mere literary taste, and the inward illumination of the Spirit of grace for the love of the beautiful, we may use the words of Wordsworth for expressing nobler emotions than they seem to have been intended to embody:

> "I have seen
> A curious child who dwelt upon a tract
> Of inland ground, applying to his ear
> The convolutions of a smooth-lipped shell;

* Wordsworth's Intimations of Immortality.

> To which, in silence hushed, his very soul
> Listened intensely; and his countenance soon
> Brightened with joy; for murmurings from within
> Were heard,—sonorous cadences! whereby
> To his belief, the monitor expressed
> Mysterious union with its native sea.
> Even such a shell the universe itself
> Is to the ear of faith; and doth impart
> Authentic tidings of invisible things;
> Of Him who formed and has redeemed them all.
> Thus by the Spirit led, whate'er we see,
> Whate'er we feel, by agency direct
> Or indirect, shall tend to feed and nurse
> Holy affections, fix in calmer seats
> Of moral strength, and raise to loftier heights
> Of love divine, our intellectual soul,
> And help the great Redeemer to adore."

In heaven we shall see that blessed one combining all these visions of beauty and glory in his one person, together with innumerable others of which the heart of man cannot now conceive.

> "Cease then, my tongue! and lend unto my mynd
> Leave to bethinke how great that beauty is,
> Whose utmost parts so beautifull I fynd;
> How much more those essentiall parts of his,
> His truth, his love, his wisedome, and his blis,
> His grace, his doome, his mercy, and his might,
> By which he lends us of himselfe a sight:
> His goodnesse, which his beautie doth declare,
> For all thats good is beautifull and faire."*

Thus contemplating our adorable Redeemer by a living faith, through the Holy Spirit, we say with humble exultation, in the language of the spouse, "This is my beloved, and this is my friend, my companion, O daughters of Jerusalem." So far from being ashamed of him, as in our unrenewed state, in him alone we now glory. He is the absorbing centre of our affections; his company is the desire and delight of our heart.

---

* Spenser's Hymn of Heavenly Beauty.

CHAPTER VI.

VER. 1.—Whither is thy beloved gone, O thou fairest among women? whither is thy beloved turned aside? that we may seek him with thee.

Such a description of the beloved might well make the daughters of Jerusalem anxious to see him, and inquire where he might be found. A judicious holding forth of the character and loveliness of Christ, has ever been the leading means of drawing sinners to the cross. The salvation of souls is effected by preaching to them Christ crucified. Great multitudes of people followed Jesus, because his fame went throughout all Syria. Had those who saw his mighty works and were the subjects of his healing power, said nothing, his name could not have been known abroad, and many whose lives were spared must have perished. "Ye are the light of the world. Neither do men light a candle, and put it under a bushel, but on a candlestick; and it giveth light to all that are in the house. Let your light so shine before men, that they may see your good works, and glorify your Father which is in heaven." Strange that there should be such backwardness among Christians in speaking to each other of their Lord, and of commending his grace to sinners. Love breaks through this icy restraint, even at the risk of being looked on with disfavour. While a relief to our own soul, this speaking of Jesus is often made a blessing to others. When the woman of Samaria "went her way into the city, and said unto the men, Come, see a man which told me all things that ever I did; is not this the Christ? Then they went out of the city and came unto him." John iv. 29. And what was the result of her so doing? "Many of the Samaritans of that city believed on him for the saying of the woman, which testified, He told me all that ever I did." Nor did the results of this conduct stop here. "They besought him that he would tarry with them; and he abode there two days. And many more believed because of his own word."

Ver. 2.—My beloved is gone down into his garden, to the beds of spices, to feed in the gardens, and to gather lilies.

All the gardens mentioned in Scripture, like those in the East of the present day, were not in any way connected with the residence; but were outside the several towns, and were from half a mile to a mile distant from the houses of the persons to whom they belonged. Josephus relates that Solomon used to go very early in the morning in great pomp to Etham, about two miles from Jerusalem, a pleasant place abounding with gardens and rills of water. In going to Jerusalem, they spoke of going up; in going from the city, they spoke of going down. The beloved had gone out to his garden to enjoy the beauty and fragrance of the beds of spices, "to feed,"— or as the same idea is expressed in chap. v. 1—to eat its pleasant fruits; to have his various senses regaled with the blooming flowers, the luscious fruits, the exhilarating fragrance, the beautiful scenes, the melody of the nightingales, "and to gather lilies." Thus Moschus, describing the beautiful Europa,

> "And from the meads thy fragrant banks that bound,
> Plucked the sweet lilies gaily blooming round."

And Virgil,

> "Come, beauteous youth, the nymphs in baskets bring
> For thee the loveliest lilies of the spring."

the

the like the seven golden candlesticks, Rev. i. 20, the
s here mean the churches of Christ; and the lilies

his saints, the pure in heart who shall see God. The spouse knew well the beloved's place of resort; and felt that though withdrawn from her, he was still among his churches and in the midst of his saints. Thither must she go to find him. Jesus may withdraw from the soul of the believer; he never forsakes his Church; and when our hearts are forsaken, we may be comforted by knowing, that if diligently sought, he will be found again in the spiritual garden of his Church, enjoying its delights and gathering to his bosom the lilies, his sanctified ones, that having their connection with earth broken off by death, they may lie nearer to his heart in glory, and adorn his heavenly home.

VER. 3.—I am my beloved's, and my beloved is mine; he feedeth among the lilies.

See chap. ii. 16. Throughout this whole scene we notice that after awaking from her sluggishness the spouse entertains ardent affection for the beloved, though his presence is withdrawn. Thus in times when we are without the sweet manifestations once had of the nearness of our Lord, love to him may remain ardent and unabated. The act of speaking concerning his loveliness and commending him to others, as in the close of the foregoing chapter, is attended with the happiest results to ourselves, and ends in our attaining again the full assurance of hope as here expressed.

VER. 4.—Thou art beautiful, O my love, as Tirzah, comely as Jerusalem, terrible as an army with banners.*

The very name of Tirzah, delight, bespeaks the beauty of its scenery. It is a city mentioned by Josh. xii. 24,

* The following description of a lady by her lover, is given by Kitto from an old Arabian romance: "The lovely virgin has struck my heart with the arrow of a glance, for which there is no cure. Sometimes she

remarkable for its elegance; and after the revolt of Rehoboam, chosen as the royal city, and preserving its preeminence till Omri founded Samaria. Jerusalem was beautiful for situation, the joy of the whole earth, called by Pliny the most beautiful city not of Judea only, but of the whole East. To these capital cites of Judea, rising majestically on its verdant hills, with towers, and walls, and palaces of marble white and pure, does the beloved compare the spouse, as Jesus himself compares his people to a "city that is set on a hill." A handsome Hindoo female is compared to the sacred city of Seedambaram. The words "terrible as an army with banners," mean terrible, or imposing and commanding, as a military host drawn up in battle-array under their several banners.

wishes for a feast in the sand-hills, like a gazelle, whose eyes are full of magic. She moves—I should say it was the branch of the tamarisk, that waves its branches to the southern breeze. She approaches—I should say it was a frightened gazelle, when a calamity alarms it in the waste. She walks away—I should say her face was truly the sun, when its lustre dazzles the beholders. She gazes—I should say it was the full moon of night, when Orion girds it with stars. She smiles—and the pearls of her teeth sparkle. The sun, as it sets, turns towards her, and says: Darkness obscures the land; do thou rise in my absence. And the brilliant moon calls unto her: Come forth, for thy face is like me, when I am at the full, and in all my glory. The tamarisk-trees complain of her in the morning and in the evening, and cry: Away, thou waving beauty, thou form of the laurel. She turns away abashed, and throws aside her veil, and roses are scattered from her soft fresh cheek. She draws her sword from the glances of her eyelashes, sharp as the sword of her forefathers; and with it, though sheathed, her eyes do slay. Graceful is every limb, slender her waist. Love-bearing are her glances, waving is her form. The damsel passes the night with musk under her veil, which draws inward fragrance from the fresher essence of her breath. The lustre of day sparkles from her brow, and by the dark shade of her curling ringlets night itself is driven away. When she smiles, between her teeth is a moisture composed of wine, of rain, and of honey. Her throat complains of the darkness of her necklaces."

According to Good, "In Persia, one of the most common epithets applied by a lover to his loved one, is synoymous with 'awe-striking,' or 'striking with fear.'" This expresses that characteristic of beauty and loveliness found pre-eminently in the bride, which so impresses the beholder with the sense of inherent dignity and majesty, as to strike with terror and repel bad men, while causing, even in the bosom of the beloved, feelings of respect and veneration. She possessed something more than beauty —beauty allied with majesty, dignity, and grace. Hence the strong language used in ver. 5, "Turn away thine eyes from me, for they have overcome me." See notes on chap. iv. 9.

On the last clause of ver. 5, see chap. iv. 1; on ver. 6, see chap. iv. 2; on ver. 7, see chap. iv. 3.

The same language, with little variation, is here repeated, that was used on a former occasion; as if for the purpose of assuring the believer that, notwithstanding our unfaithfulness and neglect, and the consequent withdrawal of Jesus from us for a season, the love of our Lord remains still unchanged.

VER. 8.—There are threescore queens, and fourscore concubines, and virgins without number.

There is no necessity for showing at large, that among females of an oriental court there is one superior in rank to the rest, and like Vashti, distinguished by wearing a royal crown, and by being called queen, in a distinguished manner; nor does it throw the least light on the significance of this passage, to point out particularly the difference between the queen, the lawful wife, and the concubines, and the daughters of Jerusalem, here called virgins. The import of the passage is clear. The beloved wishes to make the spouse feel the greatness and fervour of his love. In doing this he not only uses the illustrations of the foregoing verses, but goes on to show, that while he was surrounded by a numerous retinue of beautiful, noble, and splendid women of all ranks, she stood pre-eminent among them in his affections. The word "threescore" is used in chap. iii. 7, for an indefinite number; and he intends to say that he had around him countless ones to love, noble and dazzling as queens in their queenly attire, and other females of great attractions and different ranks, calculated to captivate the affections; amid such a company, could there be any room left in the heart for love to her who was dark as the tents of Kedar, who was lowly as the rose of Sharon, who had so lately treated with neglect him who had so many others to love? The next verse answers this inquiry.

VER. 9.—My dove, my undefiled, is but one; she is the only one of her mother, she is the choice one of her that bare her. The daughters saw her, and blessed her; yea, the queens and the concubines, and they praised her.

The meaning is—notwithstanding the number and personal attractions of the princesses and other splendid women of all ranks by whom I am surrounded, my dove, my undefiled, my perfect one, she in whom I can see no blemish, my angel, is the only one to me; the one that stands out by pre-eminence above all others; the favourite, the sole possessor of my heart. She is as dear to me as an only child to her mother; as her darling to her that bare her.*' While thus dear to the king, she was no object of jealousy to others. They all, with one consent, admired her beauty, and were not backward in her praise.

Thus in Ps. xlv. "kings' daughters were among thy honourable women;" or, as Horsley has it, "kings' daugh-

---

* In accordance with the expression, "She is the only one of her mother," we find that Priam interceding with Achilles for the body of Hector, says, he had fifty sons, but Hector was his favourite, literally "my only son:" Ὅς δὶ μοι οἶος ἔην.—*Iliad*, xxiv. 499.

ters are among the bright beauties of thy court: at thy right hand the queen has her station in gold of Ophir." Perhaps this might find an illustration in a modern court, with the peers in their coronets and the peeresses around the king; and she, the queen, the most beautiful, and the favourite, among them all. The object of the whole is to illustrate to the believer, the place held by him in the love of Christ. Our Lord is exalted far above all principality, and power, and every name that is named even in heaven; around him are an innumerable company that no man can number, of angels and spirits of just men made perfect, cherubim and seraphim, holy and glorious beings of every rank and grade; yet, among these, the soul of the redeemed is to him what the spouse was to the beloved, his perfect one, his darling, his angel—as we say of an object of special endearment—the one that stands out by pre-eminence above all others in that glorious host, loved with an affection such that human language can best express it by saying, such soul is *the* one, the sole possessor of the affections of his heart. See note on chap. iv. 5.

The glory of beings of a higher order is unfolded to us in the appearance of the angel at the sepulchre, whose countenance was like lightning, and his raiment white as snow; of the mighty angel who came down from heaven, clothed with a cloud, and a rainbow upon his head, and his face as it were the sun, and his feet as pillars of fire; of the angel who came down from heaven, having great power, and the earth was lighted with his glory; these are the noblest, highest, and most glorious order of creatures mentioned in the Scriptures; and hence the Apostle, in Heb. i., assuming the acknowledged principle that these are the most exalted rank of mere created beings, establishes the divinity of Christ by proving his superiority to angels. Yet to these shall the redeemed be superior in splendour, in rank, and in glory. We shall be glorious as she who appeared a great wonder in heaven, clothed with the sun, and the moon under her feet, and upon her head a crown of twelve stars. We shall be made like Christ as he is in glory, glorified with the glory he had with the Father before the world was. Who can know what was that eternal glory of God? Who, then, can know what is the glory now enjoyed by Jesus? Who, therefore, can tell what is the glory awaiting his saints in light? For "it doth not yet appear what we shall be; but we know that when he shall appear, we shall be like him, for we shall see him as he is." And when the Scriptures speak of him as the image of the invisible God, the first-born of every creature, the Creator of all things, even of the different orders of angels, Col. i. 16, as having in all things the pre-eminence; they show that while Jesus, our Redeemer, is truly God, the human nature he has taken into union with this divine nature, shall be exalted to a degree of glory beyond that of angels; and to this rank and glory his redeemed ones shall with him be raised. Thus the humble virgin was raised from a retired rural condition to a rank in the court of Solomon, and to a place in his affections, beyond that even of the queens surrounding him; thus was the Jewish orphan, though a captive in a strange land, raised to a position beyond the queen and all the fair young virgins in the oriental palace of Shushan; thus was Joseph drawn from his dungeon to receive a ring from the royal hand, and be arrayed in vestures of fine linen, and have a gold chain put about his neck, and be invested with the pre-eminence over all the land of Egypt; thus was Daniel raised from the condition of a Hebrew captive to be clothed with scarlet, and have a chain of gold about his neck, and be preferred before the presidents and princes; thus, He who was made a little lower than the angels, for the suffering of death, and took upon him the form of a servant, has been crowned with glory and honour, raised far above all principalities, and power, and might, and dominion, and every name that is named, not only in this world, but also in that which is to come, crowned with many crowns.

Nor in that heavenly court of the King of kings, will there be the least jealousy felt towards the redeemed thus honoured. The disposition which led John the Baptist to say with real pleasure, "he must increase, but I must decrease," the love which seeketh not her own, will there be the ruling principle of every bosom; and such will be the admiration and devotion towards Jesus by those holy intelligences, that they will rejoice with him as he then sees of the travail of his soul; and will be satisfied in the advancement in glory and honour, of his ransomed ones, his spiritual body, even beyond themselves. This exaltation of the redeemed cannot diminish their happiness; it will add thereto by the new field opened for their love and adoration, in the display thus made of the character of God.

VER. 10.—Who is she that looketh forth as the morning, fair as the moon, clear as the sun, and terrible as an army with banners?

Theocritus has a passage in the same spirit:

> As beams the beauteous face of dawning morn,
> When night retires; bright spring, when winter fades;
> Thus Helen golden moves among her peers.

In like manner Ferdusi:

> "Born of Afrasiab, there Manizah shines
> Bright as the sun, o'er gardens, groves, and streams."

And the Gitagovinda: "My soul remembers him who

disperses the gloom with beams from the jewels which decorate his bosom, his wrists, and his ankles: on whose forehead shines a circlet of sandal-wood, which makes even the moon contemptible, when she sails through irradiated clouds." Also Milton:

> "Eastward among those trees, what glorious shape
> Comes this way moving, seems another morn
> Risen on mid-noon."

Thus Spenser:

> "As far as doth the daughter of the day
> All other lesser lights in light excell;
> So far doth she in beautifull array,
> Above all other virgins beare the bell."*

The beloved still continuing his commendations of the spouse, and showing her superiority even to the queenly beauties of his court, adopts the interrogative form in this comparison, for giving it a stronger affirmative force. Having said she surpassed those around her, he proceeds to say that among the spiritual host of heaven, she stands pre-eminent, as the morning, the moon, the sun, among the starry host of night. The angels are called morning stars, Job xxxviii. 7; the saint is compared to the sun, the brightness of the firmament, Dan. xii. 3; and Jesus himself is represented as more glorious than the sun, for in Rev. xxi. 23, it is said the Lamb is the light of the

---

* Thus in Homer, Paris went forth from the palace to battle,

> In arms all glistering, as the beaming sun.—*Iliad*, vi. 513.

It is also said of Achilles, that he went forth, $\H{\omega}\varsigma\ \H{\eta}\lambda\epsilon\kappa\tau\omega\rho$ as the sun, gleaming with radiance. *Iliad*, xix. 398. In the Homeric Hymns we have,

> "Her lovely form with sudden radiance glowed,
> Her golden locks in wreaths of splendour flowed;
> Through the dark palace streamed a flood of light,
> As cloud-engendered fires illume the night
> With sudden blaze."—*Hymn to Ceres*, 278.

heavenly city, and so much more glorious than the sun is this light, that the city had no need of the sun, neither of the moon, to shine in it.

Believers are now in a process of change into this glory of Christ. 2 Cor. iii. 18. Hence in Job xi. 17, "Thine age shall be clearer than the noon-day; thou shalt shine forth, thou shalt be as the morning." She who was once as the lowly rose of Sharon and lily of the valleys, who was black as the tents of Kedar, is now glorious as the morning, the moon, the mid-day sun. She is here compared to the morning soon after day-break; then, to the moon as a yet brighter light; then, to the full splendour of the sun. When Diomedes went forth to battle, the goddess of wisdom distinguished him amongst the hosts of combatants by making a flame

> Blaze on his helmet and his shield, all pure
> And brilliant as the autumnal star fresh risen
> From mid the ocean waves.*

In the spiritual conflict of the present world, the believer bearing the helmet of salvation and the shield of faith, is distinguished by the light of the Holy Spirit kindled there by Christ the wisdom of God; but in heaven he will be invested with a splendour by which his present glory will be surpassed as far as the flame on the crest of Diomedes is surpassed by the light above the brightness of mid-day, in which Jesus appeared to Paul on the road to Damascus, or by the cloud which overshadowed him in the transfiguration. This outward glory of the saints in light is a reality, and is a consequence of that inward glory first wrought in the soul by the Holy Spirit. Splendour is more inseparably connected with holiness than radiance is with light. Holiness is light-like purity; and we may as soon conceive of

* Iliad, v. 5.

a blazing torch, or a sun without splendour, as a renovated soul of living holiness without that glory which shall be revealed in us, Rom. viii. 18, and with which Jesus our forerunner is already crowned. In rearing a triumphal statue commemorating a victory, the artist forms his conceptions of what is beautiful, and then embodies it in marble, which can be at best a mere cold resemblance: God forms not an ideal but a real holiness, after his own image, in the sanctified souls of his saints; and then embodies this in their spiritual bodies, for being pillars in the temple of their God, living triumphal statues, purer than transparent marble; for what must such statues be, when the very streets of the city where they will be placed, shall be paved with something better than marble, with something beautiful as golden glass.

VER. 11.—I went down into the garden of nuts to see the fruits of the valley, and to see whether the vine flourished, and the pomegranates budded.

The nut here referred to is probably the walnut, which Josephus says, grows wild on the borders of the lake of Gennesaret. This, the vines, and the pomegranates are put for the fruits of the garden in general. Thus Captain Norden, in describing the gardens of Cairo, mentions only palm-trees and vine-arbours, possibly because these were the most flourishing and remarkable of their productions. Their gardens were usually in low places, in valleys on the banks of brooks. Say the Scotch Mission, "When we reached the bottom of the valley, it was one complete garden of fruit-trees. The vines, the figs, pomegranates, peaches, citrons, quinces, and lemons were all budding or ripening in a most luxuriant manner. A clear brook flowing down the valley, gave freshness and beauty to every green thing."

The beloved gives, in the 11—13 verses, four statements showing the spouse what were his feelings during his withdrawal. He says, that when he left her, chap. v. 6, it was not in anger: but with kindly feeling and love unabated; only to withdraw to his favourite place of resort in the garden, and there amuse and occupy himself until such time as she might feel her unkindness, and seek again his presence; he was ready to welcome her return to his bosom at any moment. This language viewed as giving his feelings on leaving her, is of the same tender spirit with his words in chap. v. 2, and breathes the tenderest affection. Surely a love must be almost more than human, which could be thus calm and unabated under such a repulse. The love of Jesus, which this is designed to illustrate, is indeed more than human.

> "His love no end nor measure knows,
> No change can turn its course;
> Immutably the same it flows,
> From one eternal source."

This love is our life, the very spring of our being. Happy for us that its exercise towards us by our Lord, does not depend on our merit and watchfulness. Like the power which keeps the heart beating unconsciously without any act of our will, this divine love which began towards us while dead in sins, even before our being, continues to follow and bless us, even when unmindful of its source or its existence, and when unkindly forsaking the Redeemer. Even under neglect and repulse, Jesus turns away from us without anger; and leaves us until such time as we feel our unkindness, and seek again his presence and grace.

VER. 12.—Or ever I was aware, my soul made me like the chariots of Ammi-nadib.

While a particular explanation of this passage is very difficult, perhaps impossible, the general meaning in its connection seems clear. We cannot undertake to give the various interpretations. Dopke has stated and reviewed them at length. Amminadib is most probably the name of an individual, whose chariots were proverbial for swiftness; and the beloved means to say, that after thus withdrawing from the spouse without anger, with chastened affection—almost unconsciously, ere he was aware, his soul was filled with the desire of meeting her again, a desire so strong that it would have carried him to her arms with a swiftness that could be illustrated by nothing more appropriately than by the rapid, smooth-rolling chariots of Amminadib.

Such is the feeling of Jesus towards us, even when his presence is withdrawn, and the light of his countenance no longer felt. He changes not. When obliged by our neglect to turn away from us, he carries with him the same ardour of love that he manifested to us in our happiest hours of duty and affection; and when our love has grown cold, and our feet are wandering on the dark mountains, or our souls slumbering in the indifference of carnal security, he still has an affection which makes him ready to come and meet us at any moment, with the swiftness of the chariots of Amminadib? Yea, rather with the quickness of the wings of the morning, or of that all-present Spirit who flies to the bosom of every repenting believer, with a swiftness outstripping infinitely the wings of the morning or even the rapidity of thought. Though seeing it necessary for our good to hide his face, and even afflict us, he has all the while this strong yearning toward us; and every act however painful, has lying behind it, in his bosom, this deep affection and tenderness.

VER. 13.—Return, return, O Shulamite; return, return, that we may look upon thee. What will ye see in the Shulamite? As it were the company of two armies.

The word Shulamite, or Shulamith, is the feminine of he name of Shelomoh, or Solomon, and means the bride of Shelomoh, the prince of peace. The beloved calls on her to return, or rather this was the language expressing the feelings of his heart when separated from her. We would translate, "Return, return, that we may see in thee,—What shall you see in the Shulamith? A festive choir of rejoicing hosts." The interrogative form is thrown in for giving greater emphasis and beauty to the language. The beloved would say, that she whose loveliness in his eyes he had been illustrating by so many comparisons, was an object of more delightful contemplation to him, than bands beautifully attired, mingling in a sacred dance on a day of public rejoicing; or was a source of pleasure like that derived from such a sight; far greater than could be had from beholding any individual, however excellent: such as is felt from gazing on the combination of lovely forms, crowning with their elegance of form, shape, beauty of dress, and grace of movement, some public festal scene;* more beautiful than when on the

---

* In the scenes described by Homer as portrayed on the shield of Achilles, none would have been introduced but those deemed most attractive in his age, which could not have been long after the time of Solomon. Now, he has given such a scene as is noticed in the text, a place on that famous shield; and thereby we may know such was an object of beauty to the ancients, and proper to be used for illustrating anything which excited deep emotions of pleasure.

> "To these the artist added next a dance
> Drawn with surpassing skill, such as of old
> In Crete's broad island Dædalus composed
> For bright-haired Ariadne. There the youths
> And youth-alluring maidens, hand in hand
> Danced jocund, every maiden, neat attired
> In finest linen, and the youths in vests
> Well woven, glossy as the glaze of oil.
> These all wore garlands, and bright falchions, those,
> Of burnished gold in silver trappings hung:
> They with well tutor'd step, now nimbly ran

shore of the Red Sea, Miriam took a timbrel in her hand, and all the women went out after her with timbrels and with dances, Exod. xv. 20; than when David and all the house of Israel brought up the ark of the Lord, with shouting and with the sound of the trumpet, and with cymbals, making a noise with psalteries and harps, leaping and dancing before the Lord, 2 Sam. vi. 15; 1 Chron. xv. 26. As in chap. i. 9, the horse is the emblem of nobleness, energy, and activity in the believer; here, the reference is to elegance and grace of motion, as an element of beauty, while in the perfected saint perfect beauty is found. Thus, in something of a like train of thought, Byron says—

> "She walks in beauty like the night
> Of cloudless climes and starry skies;
> And all that's best of dark and bright,
> Meets in that aspect and those eyes."

As there is dignity, majesty, and grandeur in the calm movement of the evening sky, with its starry hosts, and therein is blended the beauty of darkness and of light; so this poet would say there was in her of whom he wrote, dignity, and majesty, and a blending of all that is beautiful. And in this passage the spouse is compared, if not to the starry hosts, to two hosts or companies rejoicing at a wedding, or on some festive occasion.

Poetry furnishes nothing of its kind more beautiful than the scene in the Fairie Queene, where, in a spot

> The circle, swift, as when, before his wheel
> Seated, the potter twirls it with both hands
> For trial of its speed, now, crossing quick
> They passed at once into each other's place.
> On either side spectators numerous stood
> Delighted."—*Iliad*, xviii. 590.

of singular loveliness, are espied, from the covert of a wood bordering "th' open greene,"

> "An hundred beauteous maidens lily white,
> All ranged in a ring and dancing with delight;"

and in their midst was placed

> "Another damzell, as a precious gemme,
> Amidst a ring most richly well enchased.
> Look! how the crowne which Ariadne wore
> Upon her ivory forehead that same day
> That Theseus her unto his bridale bore,
> Being now placed in the firmament,
> Through the bright heaven doth her beams display,
> And is unto the starres an ornament,
> Which round about her move in order excellent:
> Such was the beauty of this goodly band."

Now the spirit of the text implies, that the spouse was in the eyes of the beloved an object causing more pleasure than such scenes as these. With a delight of which this is the best, though faint resemblance, does Jesus view the sanctified soul, and the innumerable multitude constituting his redeemed Church. All things are present to him; and even now he sees that rejoicing host which no man can number, redeemed from all kindreds, and tribes, and people, and tongues, standing before the throne, clothed in white robes and palms in their hands; of all his varied works of creation, this is to him the most glorious. Is it strange that on a day of public rejoicing, a kingly father should view a brave, gallant, and victorious son with more pleasure than that felt from the presence of all the host besides. While king Edward, beholding from his tower the battle of Crecy, had proper feelings towards all his valiant followers who surrounded his son, with what especial 'delight did he watch the progress of that son; and after the victory, amid the bonfires, and lighted torches, and rejoicing of the soldiers, take the Black Prince in his arms, and say, "You are my true son, for loyally have you acquitted yourself this day, and worthy are you of a crown." Thus, from his watch-tower in the skies, the Captain of our salvation, our friend, our beloved, has his eye on every one of his saints; and when our conflict winds up with the victory over death, he will give us more than a father's greeting, while bestowing the crown of righteousness and glory which fadeth not away. Like the virgin among the hundred lily-like maidens of Spenser, "as a precious gemme amidst a ring most richly well enchased," the glorified soul, the redeemed Church, shall be in heaven an object of pre-eminent beauty to Jesus, a brilliant gem amid the golden ring of innumerable angels encircling as a crown the throne of the Lamb slain.

We may therefore be comforted by keeping in mind the four things here stated concerning Jesus on leaving us, when grieved away by our neglect: He withdraws, not in anger, but in love: he feels without ceasing, the strongest desire to return to us; he earnestly invites us to return; he continues still to view us with unabated love, even with greater pleasure than the angels, the hosts seen by Jacob at Mahanaim.

CHAPTER VII.

VER. 1, 2.—How beautiful are thy feet with shoes, O prince's daughter! the joints of thy thighs are like jewels, the work of the hands of a cunning workman; thy navel is like a round goblet, which wanteth not liquor; thy belly is like an heap of wheat set about with lilies.

THE language of chap. vi. 4—10, is for encouraging the spouse to come on, and not hesitate on account of her recent neglect of him; in chap. vi. 11—13, he states his feelings of unabated tenderness during the time of his withdrawal; the object of chap. vii. 1—9, is to show his love towards her is still the same.

"Prince's daughter" seems to mean daughter of a noble, a word signifying generous, noble-minded; and in the thought of an oriental, is closely connected with liberality in giving; it is spoken of character and conduct, and according to a common Hebrew idiom, expresses one who is herself noble, the same with noblewoman. The whole of this description is a fitting portrait of a woman of noble character and majestic mien—the original words, "prince's daughter," referring to the nobleness of her disposition, and the following part of the passage setting forth the majesty and beauty of her appearance.* Having referred to grace of motion in

---

* With these descriptions of the spouse in the Song, we may compare the celebrated ivory and gold statue of Minerva in the Parthenon, which was an effort by Phidias to embody his imaginary conception of that goddess. "The statue stood in the foremost and larger chamber of the temple. It represented the goddess standing, clothed with a tunic reaching to the ankles, with her spear in her left hand, and an image of Victory four cubits high, in her right: she was girded with the ægis, and had a helmet on her head, and her shield rested on the ground by her side. The height of the statue was twenty-six cubits, or nearly forty feet, including the base. From the manner in which

the last verse of the foregoing chapter, he naturally proceeds here to mention her feet and the elegance of her sandals. See chap. v. 15. Pindar speaks of "the silver-footed Venus;" and Milton of "Thetis' tinsel-slippered feet." Magnificent sandals constituted, in the East, a part of the dress of both males and females, who could afford to have them peculiarly costly; the oriental ladies were especially attentive to this fashionable ornament. The sandals of Judith were so brilliant that, notwithstanding the general splendour of her bracelets, rings, and necklace, these principally succeeded in captivating the ferocious Holofernes; for we are expressly told that "her sandals ravished his eyes." Judith xvi. 9. Lady Montague, describing her eastern dress, says her shoes were of white kid leather embroidered with gold. According to Pausanias, in the statue of Olympian Jupiter, the sandals of the god, as also his robe, were of gold—the latter wrought over with all sorts of animals and flowers, particularly lilies.

Plato speaks of the statue, it seems clear that the gold predominated over the ivory, the latter being used for the face, hands, and feet, and the former for the drapery and ornaments. The eyes, according to Plato, were of a kind of marble nearly resembling ivory, perhaps painted to imitate the iris and pupil; there is no sufficient authority for the statement which is frequently made that they were of precious stones. It is doubtful whether the core of the statue was of wood or of stone. The various portions of the statue were most elaborately ornamented. A sphinx formed the crest of her helmet, and on either side of it were gryphons, all, no doubt, of gold. The ægis was fringed with golden serpents, and in its centre was a golden head of Medusa. Even the edges of the sandals, which were four *dactyli* high, were seen, on close inspection, to be engraved with the battle of the Lapithæ and Centaurs. The shield was ornamented on both sides with embossed work, representing, on the inner side, the battle of the giants against the gods, and on the outer, the battle of the Amazons against the Athenians."—*Smith's Dictionary*, art. *Phidias*.

Our translation of these verses is, "How beautiful are thy feet in sandals, O noble woman. The contour of thy person is like the rounding of a necklace, wrought by the hands of a finished artist: thy waist is a round goblet that is full of rich spiced wine: thy body is a heap of wheat enclosed with lilies." The principles regulating the interpretation of this passage have been already explained. Introduction, and notes on chap. iv. 1—7, and chap. v. 9—16. The great misapprehension that prevails concerning these verses, has arisen from a misunderstanding of the spirit of the original. That seems to be expressed in this translation. We have shown, that as ancient statues of the gods were attempts to represent to human comprehension, certain ideas entertained concerning particular deities, so these descriptions of the Song are attempts to represent to the human mind the loveliness of Christ, and of the redeemed, by illustrations embodied in language, rather than in marble and gold. The statues of Olympian Jupiter and of Minerva by Phidias, were highly adorned, and among other things, with drapery of gold; and Cornelius Nepos states that it was customary in the statues raised to conquerors in the Olympic games, to represent them in the habits in which they had gained the crown.

The "joints of the thighs," did the original words mean what these express, would convey a finished idea of beauty and perfection; as the joints would then be compared to such work as the jewelled wheels of a watch. The word "joint" means, however, rounding, curvature; and the two words express the beautiful symmetry of that part of the person. There is now in existence a famous statue of Venus at Naples, to which the Grecian epithet "beautiful hipped" was applied.* The word

* Καλλιπυγκ.

"jewels" means necklaces, things on which great art was bestowed by the ancients. As Wilkinson remarks, "handsome and richly ornamented necklaces were a principal part of the dress of both men and women;"* and some idea may be got of the beauty of this allusion, by examining the illustrations of them he has given.† Thus we are able to see why the necklace should be mentioned in this connection, and with what delicacy of taste it is used for illustrating the graceful outline of the lower part of the body.

The original word rendered "navel," in the English version, expresses what we mean by the waist; and the roundness of the waist is compared to a goblet or bowl

---

* Ancient Egyptians, vol. iii. 375.

† The necklace was made sometimes to resemble a serpent coiled about the neck of the wearer, as was the case with that given as a nuptial present by Venus to Harmonia, which was ornamented in so elaborate a manner, that Nonnus devotes fifty lines of his Dyonysiaca to its description. This same necklace afterwards appears in the mythology, as the bribe by which Eriphyle was tempted to betray her husband. The beauty and splendour, as well as the value of necklaces, were enhanced by the insertion of pearls and precious stones, which were strung together by means of linen thread, silk, or wires and links of gold. Smith gives patterns of three splendid gold necklaces in the British Museum, that were found in Etruscan tombs; also a wood-cut exhibiting the central portion of a very ancient and exquisitely wrought necklace, which was found near Naples, in the sepulchre of a Greek lady. It has seventy-one pendants. Above them, is a band consisting of several rows of close chain-work, which we now call Venetian. The specimens of ancient chains which we have in ornaments for the person, especially necklaces, show a great variety of elegant and ingenious patterns, whose name expresses their fineness and delicacy as well as their minuteness. These valuable chains were commonly worn by women, either on the neck, or round the waist, according to a statement of Pliny. In a head of Minerva engraved from an antique gem, we see a necklace with a row of drops on the under side, which, when worn, arrange themselves upon the neck, like rays proceeding from the centre.—*Smith's Dictionary.* Articles—Monile and Catena.

filled with spiced wine made of myrrh and fragrant cane. The Hebrew word seems here to express what was known among the Latins and Greeks, as the crater. This was a vessel in which the wine, according to the custom of the ancients, who very seldom drank it pure, was mixed, and from which the cups were filled.* In oriental poetry, there are allusions entirely similar: "Graceful is every limb, slender her waist. Place a circlet of music on this breast, which resembles a vase of sacred water, crowned with fresh leaves, and fixed near a vernal bower."†

The beauty of the waist expanding upwards into the

---

* In the Homeric age, the crater was generally of silver, sometimes with a gold edge, and sometimes all gold or gilt. It stood upon a tripod, and its ordinary place in the dining-hall, was in the most honourable part of the room, at the farthest end from the entrance, and near the seat of the most distinguished among the guests. Craters were among the first things on the embellishment of which the ancient artists exercised their skill. Homer mentions among the prizes proposed by Achilles at the funeral games for Patroclus, a beautifully wrought silver crater, the work of the ingenious Sidonians, which, by the elegance of its workmanship excelled all others on the earth. According to Wilkinson, "Many of the ornamental vases of the Egyptians, as well as those in common use, were of alabaster, glass, ivory, porcelain, bronze, silver, or gold, and present the most elegant forms; and so strong a resemblance do they bear, both in shape and in the fancy devices which adorn them, to the productions of the best epochs of ancient Greece, that some might even imagine them borrowed from Greek patterns. We admire not only their forms, but the richness of the materials of which they were made—the colours and the hieroglyphics themselves, showing them to have been of gold and silver, or of this last inlaid with the more precious metal. Gold and silver cups were often beautifully engraved and studded with precious stones." We know the direct intercourse there was between the region of Sidon and Judea, and of Egypt and Judea; and hence we may know the goblets used by Solomon would be no less splendid.

† See the epithet, καλλίζωνει γυναῖκες· beautifully girdled women. *Iliad*, vii. 139.—*Od.* xxiii. 147. *Homeric Hymn to Mercury*, 446.

fulness of the bosom, is therefore most aptly illustrated by such a goblet, to the natural beauty of which is added the beauty of the richest spiced wine. The beauty of the form below the waist, what we often express by the word body, is set forth by "a heap of wheat enclosed with lilies"—a heap of wheat in a bed of full-blown lilies rising around and drooping over it. Putting together these illustrations, the costly goblet filled with choice wine and covered with rich devices, and the heap of wheat in the midst of a bed of lilies, we have in the mind a cluster of ideas of great beauty: thus beautiful was the impression made by gazing on the person of the spouse. Our view of this passage might receive confirmation by noticing the manner in which one part of the body is mentioned after another; first, the feet more beautiful in the elegant sandals; then the contour, the folds of the bridal dress falling around the hips, graceful as the curvature of a rich necklace wrought by a finished hand; next, the body like a heap of wheat encompassed with lilies; then, the waist expanding into the bosom, elegant as a goblet rounded gracefully upwards, and filled with the richest spiced wine.

VER. 3.—Thy two breasts are like two young roes that are twins.

See note on chap. iv. 5.

VER. 4.—Thy neck is as a tower of ivory.

See note on chap. iv. 4. In his Illustrated Commentary, on 2 Kings ix. 17, Kitto gives a drawing of a group of modern oriental towers, which adds to the elegance of the illustration here used. He remarks: "So far as we have examined the Hebrew word, it is always used wherever it is possible to understand that a tower of ornamental character is intended. The great beauty of many of the forms here given will not be disputed."

Josephus mentions the numerous towers of Jerusalem, that "were for largeness, beauty, and strength, beyond all that were in the habitable earth; they were of white marble, each stone was twenty-five feet in length, ten in breadth, and five in depth; these stones were so exactly united to one another, that each tower looked like one entire rock of white marble, so growing naturally and afterwards cut by the hands of the artificers into their present shape."* To such a structure, is the neck of the spouse compared, with the additional elegance that would be imparted by substituting in the materials ivory for marble.

Thine eyes like the fish-pools in Heshbon, by the gate of Bath-rabbim.

So Philostratus says, "Thou seemest to carry water as it were from the fountain of thine eyes, and therefore to be one of the nymphs." Heshbon was a town about twenty miles east of the point where the Jordan enters the Dead Sea. The ruins of a considerable town still exist at Heshbon, covering the side of an insulated hill, but not a single edifice is left entire. The view from the summit is very extensive, embracing the ruins of a vast number of cities. There are reservoirs here, which may be those mentioned in this verse. It was in the tribe of Gad, who desired this country because it abounded with pasturage, and with rivulets and brooks from which the pools of Heshbon were supplied. The pools of a place situated in such a country as that around Heshbon, would be likely to be supplied with water purer and fresher than

---

* Jewish War, book v. 4. 4.—"Here and there, the clustering blossoms of the orange or the nectarine, lay like foam upon that verdant sea. Minarets, as white as ivory, shot up their fairy towers among the groves; and purple mosque-domes, tipped with the golden crescent, gave the only sign that a city lay bowered beneath those rich plantations."— *Crescent and the Cross*, vol. ii. 154.

those of Jerusalem. Bath-rabbim was probably some neighbouring city to which the gate here mentioned led. These pools were remarkable for their purity and quietness—therefore a most fitting emblem of the clear, limpid eyes of those who are pure in heart. "Some varieties of gold and silver fishes," says a traveller in China, "were seen playing in ponds of pellucid water, upon a bottom studded with pebbles of agate, jasper, and other precious stones."

Thy nose is as the tower of Lebanon, which looketh toward Damascus.

Warburton says, "In the magnificent array of the mountains of Lebanon, with their various hills, glens, and crag-perched villages, each of those acclivities has a little tract of richly coloured vegetation hanging from its shoulders like a tartan cloak, and wears a fortress for its crown." This tower of Lebanon was probably a tower built on some part of that range of mountains in the frontiers of Israel, on an eminence overlooking the beautiful valley of Damascus, where "the vast and fruitful plain, with the seven branches of the blue stream which irrigates it, the city embosomed in gardens of surpassing richness, and overshadowed with the deepest verdure and richest luxuriance of oriental foliage, amid which rise towers and a forest of minarets of every form, the glittering lakes which reflect the heaven upon the earth, the majestic frame-work of the mountains—all combine to render this a terrestrial paradise." In such a landscape, a tower of white marble on one of the cliffs of Lebanon, would be an imposing feature—more so, from being on a commanding eminence overlooking such a landscape as that of Damascus. While the neck of the spouse is compared to the tower of David adorned with a circlet of the costly shields of heroes, and to a tower of ivory, her nose is compared to a tower rising in majesty on a noble eminence of Lebanon, and having associated with the grandeur of its position, the luxuriant beauty of the plain of Damascus. A fine, well-proportioned nose is most essential to beauty; and to this tower is compared the nose of the spouse.

VER. 5.—Thine head upon thee is like Carmel, and the hair of thine head like purple: the king is held in the galleries.

Philostratus has a similar comparison, though far less rich: "Thy head is a large meadow full of flowers, which are never wanting in the summer, and disappear not in the winter." Carmel is of beautiful shape, about twelve hundred feet high, and was in former days fruitful to a proverb. Hence its name Carmel, signifying a "fruitful field." "And when covered over with vineyards, olive-groves, and orchards of figs and almond-trees, not on the sides alone, but also along the table-land of its summit, would not Carmel, worthy of the name, appear an immense hanging garden in the midst of the land? And would not the beholder in other days at once understand the meaning of the beautiful description given in the Song —'Thine head upon thee is like Carmel.'"*

"And the hair of thine head like purple." The ancients used the word *purple* for expressing what was most beautiful in colour; and when it is said her hair, or tresses, is like purple, the meaning is, it was of the most beautiful colour. As Porphyry says, "the poets are accustomed to use purple for beautiful."† Thus Horace speaks of "purple swans;" Pindar of "purple wings,"

---

* Mission of Inquiry, 235.

† "Even the Tyrian purple was not one particular colour, but a class of animal dyes as distinguished from vegetable—varying in shade of purple, from the most faint to the most intense."—*Kitto's Ill. Com. Ex.* xxxv. 35.

and Virgil of "purple hair." And Spenser has, "the morrow next appeared with purple hair." Speaking of oriental females, Lady Montague says, "I never saw in my life so many fine heads of hair. In one lady's I have counted one hundred and ten tresses, all natural; but it must be owned that every kind of beauty is more common here than with us."

The word here translated "galleries," means full, flowing ringlets, or tresses, so called from their falling down or flowing; and in the words "the king is held in the galleries," the import is, the king is captivated with the beauty of her full-flowing tresses. Thus an oriental poet—

> "A thousand secret snares, like links entwined,
> Lurk in those ringlets waving to the wind."

The meaning of the whole verse is, her head of hair in its fulness had the beauty of Carmel, was of the richest colour, and with its full-flowing tresses, captivated the heart of the king.

VER. 6.—How fair and how pleasant art thou, O love, for delights!

Thus captivated, he exclaims—"How beautiful art thou, O love, and how fascinating in attractions." The beloved had enumerated numerous beauties of the spouse: the feet more beautiful in rich sandals, the outline of the hips graceful as the curvature of a most finished necklace, the waist elegant as a costly goblet filled with the finest wine, the body like a heap of wheat encompassed with lilies, her bosom like two young gazelles feeding among the lilies, her neck as a tower of ivory, her eyes pellucid and calm as the pools of Heshbon, her nose as a tower on a cliff of Lebanon rising over the landscape of Damascus, her head like Carmel in its richness and flowers, her hair full, flowing, and of the richest colour, and entrancing the king with the beauty of her tresses; having thus illustrated these several features of loveliness, he gives further utterance to his admiration by saying, as in this verse, that to all these was added the attractiveness arising from manners inexpressibly fascinating: how beautiful and how fascinating in attractions. Her general beauty of form and elegance of movement was lighted up by a living spirit within, which enabled her to know instinctively how to please and hold the beloved entranced with her attractive grace. She is represented as something more than an amiable nonentity, more than a mere Grecian statue, however perfectly finished. With more than mortal elegance of bodily form, she combined more than the fascinations which in an Aspasia could enthral the towering intellect of Pericles. The word "delights" expresses the characteristic which enabled the daughter of Herodias so to bewilder Herod by her accomplished graces, as to make him promise, under the spell, to give her even the half of his kingdom. It is recorded of Wilkes, that though the most homely man in the United Kingdom, no one could listen for a few moments to his conversation, without forgetting his ugliness in the attractiveness of his address. In the female character, this is far more powerful than mere inanimate beauty. Without it, beauty soon grows insipid and loses its charm; with this, homeliness is forgotten, and the individual becomes more attractive, the character more beautiful, even amid the decay of declining age. Hence, how greatly is our impression of the splendid character of the spouse heightened, when in addition to such grace of movement and beauty of form, she is said to possess manners so fascinating and attractive.

VER. 7.—This thy stature is like to a palm-tree, and thy breasts to clusters of grapes.

In this and almost all other Asiatic poems, the true eastern beauty is represented as being light as a fawn, tall as a cypress or cedar, slender as an arrow, erect as a palm-tree. The elegant slenderness of the beautiful Kadha is particularly mentioned, and repeated in frequent chorusses: "Surely thou descendest from heaven, O slender damsel, attended by a company of youthful goddesses; and all their beauties are collected in thee." The cedar, the cypress, the pine, and the palm-tree, from their general beauty, and more especially their erect and stately growth, offer a common source of imagery for elegance and dignity of person among oriental poets. Thus Hafiz—"Like the reed, my heart trembles to possess that soft waving pine-tree:" and another, "The graceful cypress yields to thee in grace." Homer compares the beautiful Nausicaa to a palm:

> "Thus seems the palm with stately honours crown'd
> By Phœbus' altars; thus o'erlooks the ground,
> The pride of Delos."*

The original word means simply clusters, and refers to the palm instead of the vine. When therefore the

---

* Odyssey, vi. 162. Humboldt says, "Palms are the loftiest and noblest of all vegetable forms, that to which the prize of beauty has been assigned by the concurrent voice of all ages. Smooth and polished stems of palms, carefully measured by me, had attained one hundred and ninety-two English feet in height. The port and physiognomy of palms have a grandeur of character very difficult to convey by words. Their lofty, slender, ringed stems, terminate in aspiring and shining either fan-like or pinnated foliage. The leaves are sometimes of a dark and shining green, at others of a silvery white on the under side; sometimes the middle of the fan or palmate leaf is ornamented with concentric yellowish or bluish stripes, like a peacock's beloved compares the stature of the spouse to a palm-tree, and her breast to its clusters, he gives the strongest possible illustration of her beauty. Now, the Holy Spirit has grouped these things together for enabling us to get some idea of the beauty which shall be revealed in the saints, and is already seen in them by Jesus. He does not merely say, we are beautiful in his eyes, as is the highest development of female beauty to us; but taking the most beautiful human form, cluster around it all the ideas of splendour drawn from feet with magnificent sandals, the splendid curvature of the most finished necklaces, the golden goblet filled with fragrant wine, the heap of newly harvested wheat set about with lilies, the two young twin roes feeding among the lilies, the tower of ivory, the pools in Heshbon, the marble tower on a cliff of Lebanon, looking towards Damascus, Carmel covered with flowers, the palm-tree with its golden clusters; to these, add the delights springing from the attractions of most accomplished manners and a loving

tail, and the leaves are flag-like, of a thinner and more flexible texture, and curl towards the extremities, while there is a fine play of light from the sun-beams falling on the upper surface of the leaves. The peculiarly majestic character of palms is given, not only by their lofty stems, but also in a very high degree, by the direction of the leaves. The more upright the direction of the leaves, or, in other words, the more acute the angles which they form with the upper part of the stem, the grander and more imposing is the general appearance of the tree. The fruits are large, egg-shaped, and beautifully coloured, resembling peaches, and tinged with a golden yellow, mingled with a roseate crimson. Seventy or eighty of them form enormous pendulous branches, of which each tree annually ripens three. This fine tree, the Piriguao palm, might be called the peach-palm. The fleshy fruits are, from the luxuriance of vegetation, most often devoid of seeds, and offer to the natives a farinaceous food, as yellow as the yolk of an egg, slightly saccharine, and extremely nutritious."—*Humboldt's Aspects*, 209.

heart; when we can form an idea of the ecstasy thrilling the soul, as all these different objects pour their star-like radiance of beauty bright upon the heart—then and then only, can we have some conception of the beauty, attractiveness, and loveliness, seen in his redeemed and sanctified people by our adored Lord. As the eye turned towards the sun is dazzled, and cannot take in the radiance; so the mind is dazzled with this beauty, and unable fully to comprehend it. For the love of Christ passeth knowledge. Of that love these brilliant comparisons are the illustration and nothing more.

Yet, if the saint is the bride of the Lamb, it must be expected he would thus view us, and thus love us. And as we naturally desire and try to remove everything unpleasant and like a failing in one thus loved—Jesus is doing even this for us in sanctification. The diamond, though exceeding in value more than a hundred thousand times its mass in gold, the most cherished treasure of kings and the most brilliant ornament of their crown, is of all precious stones "the meanest in its elements, the weakest in its structure, and the most perishable in its nature, a lump of coal, which it reduces to a cinder and dissipates into that insalubrious gas, which ascends from the most putrid marsh;" its native bed is among rough valleys, barren rocks, and desolate regions. He who can take such elements, so valueless, and perishable in themselves, and form them into a brilliant so dazzling, so precious, and so enduring, can take such elements as those found in the nature of fallen man, an offcast in this world of pollution, and form them into a gem which shall be the brightest ornament of heaven, and a peculiar treasure of the King of kings, set in the very front of his crown, worn on his heart.

VER. 8, 9.—I said I will go up to the palm-tree, I will take hold of the boughs thereof: now also thy breasts shall be as clusters of the vine, and the smell of thy nose like apples;* and the roof of thy mouth like the best wine for my beloved, that goeth down sweetly, causing the lips of those that are asleep to speak.

Having thus spoken of the loveliness of the spouse, the beloved here expresses the wish to gather her to his bosom, and assures her how agreeable her presence must be to him. These verses are but a statement of these ideas, in the highly figurative language of the orientals. The smell of the fruit of the citron-tree, for that is here meant by apples, was delightfully fragrant. The "roof of the mouth" is the same Hebrew word with that translated "mouth" in chap. v. 16, and means the palate, put by a common figure for the voice itself. The remainder of the ninth verse is not obscure in the general meaning, though it is difficult to explain satisfactorily some peculiarities here found in the original. We translate 'like that best wine for my best loved friend, which flows pure, and causes even the lips of those who are asleep to move gently.' The meaning seems to be, that the voice of the spouse was pleasant as the best wine, such as Solomon kept for some special friend, and which was so mild and rich as to go down sweetly, producing effects that continued long, and were so pleasant as to make the lips move and gently murmur in

---

* "Formerly it was usual to anoint the nostrils, which was reckoned very healthful and refreshing to the head; as well as was done, that they might give the more agreeable smell: and some sort of ointments, it seems, gave a smell like that of apples, which in some is very grateful and delightful; and Cicero observes, that the plenty and variety of apples, their pleasant taste and smell, show that they were only made for man: and indeed there was an ointment made of them, called *melinum;* so that the nostrils, being anointed with it, might well be said to smell apples; and which was accounted one of the best."—*Gill.*

sleep.* "A dream cometh through the multitude of business." Eccl. v. 3. As the thoughts and things which have engaged our attention during the day, give a colouring to the mind during sleep, and a direction to our dreams; so this wine was so mildly fitted to the tone of the system, was so delicious as to produce effects that continued during sleep, and caused pleasant dreams, and murmurs to steal over the lips of the slumbering, expressive of a pleasantness yet diffused by that good wine through our whole constitution. In accordance with this, is the representation of Mercy's dream by Bunyan, in the Pilgrim's Progress. The comparison is that of a delightful voice and its effects on the heart, to such wine. As the beloved says in chap. ii. 14, "Sweet is thy voice," and as his love is said to be better than wine, the most delightful of the pleasures of sense—these words show that nothing can be more pleasant to Jesus than the voice of his redeemed. See chap. ii. 14.

* Interpreters are divided concerning this passage; and though the general meaning is perfectly clear, there can hardly be an exposition given against which there may not be brought some objection. This word, "beloved," is indeed never applied to the spouse, but always to the bridegroom; and hence, even in this connection, designates a cherished friend. The ordinary import of the Hebrew word is one beloved, an acquaintance, a friend, a friend of the family, an intimate friend. The speaker wishing to illustrate the pleasantness of the voice of the spouse, does therefore say, that it is like the delicious wine which he kept for a most cherished friend—referring not to the spouse, but to some well-loved associate in the circle of his acquaintances. This seems to remove the difficulty, and set aside the necessity for dividing the passage so abruptly as is done by Rosenmüller, Delitzsch, and Dopke, who suppose the beloved to speak until the words, "like the best wine," and then the spouse to interrupt him by taking the sentence unfinished from his mouth, and saying, "that goeth sweetly to my beloved, &c." With this passage compare γέρουσιν ἄθετα οἶνον· wine drunk only by the chiefs, *Iliad*, iv. 259; as γέρουσιν ὅρκον· means an oath taken by the chiefs.—*Iliad*, xxii. 119.

And will our Lord thus take us to his bosom? "He shall gather the lambs with his arm, and carry them in his bosom," Isa. xl. 11; and every saint shall be treated with affection great as that shown to the beloved disciple who leaned on Jesus' bosom at the first sacramental supper. At the marriage supper of the Lamb, when the beloved drinks with us the new wine in his Father's kingdom, to that bosom shall we all be gathered; and if oppressed with a sense of unworthiness, we would know how agreeable our presence will be to him, we find the answer here given with a fulness leaving nothing more to be desired. In the state of heart here represented, is fulfilled the prayer of the Apostle, "That Christ may dwell in your hearts by faith; that ye being rooted and grounded in love, may know the love of Christ which passeth knowledge, that ye might be filled with all the fulness of God." Eph. iii. 17.

With this verse ends the general division of the Song, embracing the motives addressed to the soul for winning it away from earth, and particularly those drawn from the greatness of the love of Christ. In how full and glorious a manner does it conclude. The spouse had in the first verse earnestly longed for the kisses of his mouth; here that desire is gratified to the fullest possible extent, by the strongest assurances of love given from time to time, in various ways, and at last by the beloved's taking her to his bosom with the tenderest and deepest exhibition of affection. So true are the words, "Whatsoever ye shall ask in my name, that will I do, that the Father may be glorified in the Son. If ye shall ask any thing in my name, I will do it." John xiv. 13.

Ver. 10.—I am my beloved's, and his desire is toward me.

Here begins the third part of the Song, which shows the effects produced on the heart by these manifestations of Jesus' love. How naturally does the first follow from what has been mentioned. Thus cheered by our Lord, and lying in his bosom, well may the believer feel the full assurance of hope, and thus adopt the language of this verse. See notes on chap. ii. 16.

VER. 11.—Come, my beloved, let us go forth into the field; let us lodge in the villages.

A second effect of this love, is the desire to be much alone with Jesus in retirement. When we feel the loveliness of Christ, as here set forth, and realize the greatness of his affection towards us, we naturally desire to be with him apart from all things interfering with these communications of his love.

One most essential difference between the gardens of the Hebrews and our own, is that they are not in any way connected with the residence, but are situated in the suburbs, sometimes a mile distant from the house of the person to whom they belonged. See notes, chap. i. 16. To such a retreat did the spouse wish her beloved to withdraw, where there might be nothing to interrupt their love.

The heart naturally desires retirement with those sincerely loved. And shall not this be especially true of affection towards Jesus? The pleasures of solitude have ever been eagerly sought by multitudes; they are found only by the believer. He is never less alone, than when to the world he seems most alone, for there is he most uninterruptedly in the society of Jesus, his friend. All this he has in addition, while enjoying equally with the impious man of refined taste, the sweets of solitude and delights of meditation. How does the presence of an agreeable friend draw away our attention from the discomforts of an unpleasant scene, and throw richer beauties over one in itself attractive. So, with our beloved

Lord, solitude is delightful; doubly so, for there we can commune with him of all that is in our heart.

> "O solitude, come thou and with me climb
> Nature's observatory, whence the dell,
> Its flowery slopes, its river's crystal swell,
>   May seem a span; let me thy vigils keep
>   'Mongst boughs pavilion'd, where the deer's swift leap
> Startles the wild bee from the foxglove bell.
>   But though I'll gladly trace these scenes with thee
> Yet the sweet converse of an innocent mind,
> Whose words are images of thoughts refined,
>   Is my soul's pleasure; and it sure must be
> Almost the highest bliss of human kind,
>   When to thy haunts two kindred sprits flee."

It is not only almost, but altogether the highest bliss, when to those haunts two kindred spirits flee, and one of those is Jesus, gathering the humble soul of the believer more closely to his loving heart. There we are away from the distractions of the world; there we may have time for meditation, for study of the Scriptures, for contrition, for prayer, for praise. And while thus withdrawn from the world, even in sadness, like the disciples journeying to Emmaus, Luke xxi. 37, how often does he join himself unto us, and cause our hearts to burn within us, while unfolding to us the Scriptures by his Holy Spirit.

VER. 12.—*Let us get up early to the vineyards; let us see if the vine flourish, whether the tender grape appear, and the pomegranates bud forth: there will I give thee my loves.*

In this verse is mentioned the third effect of the love of Jesus on the heart;—we engage spontaneously in duties of holiness and love, such as are enjoined by our Lord, and in which we may consequently hope for his presence. "Early rising is, indeed, constantly indicated in Scripture, in conformity with the universal custom of the

East. The orientals generally rise very early in the morning. To be 'up with the sun,' is not in the East regarded as early rising. Every one who is not prevented by infirmity or sickness, from the ruler to the meanest of his subjects, is usually up and dressed by the morning dawn; and even in royal courts, the most important public business is transacted at a very early hour, before, in this country, even the workman rises to his labour. The women almost invariably rise even sooner than the men, often a good while before day."* Thus early did man in Eden awake to his duties, and converse with God. Thus Adam to our first mother—

> "Awake: the morning shines, and the fresh field
> Calls us; we lose the prime, to mark how spring
> Our tended plants, how blows the citron grove,
> What drops the myrrh, and what the balmy reed,
> How nature paints her colours, how the bee
> Sits on the bloom extracting liquid sweet."
>
> *Paradise Lost*, book v. 20.

And Virgil:

> But when, while Zephyrs whisper, summer sends
> The flocks to lowland meadows, wooded lawns;
> Then, with the morning-star, the cooling glades
> Fresh let us traverse, with the blushing morn,
> While yet the grass is hoary, and the dew,
> On tender herbage, grateful to the herd.
>
> *Georg.* iii. 322.

Jesus himself, in the morning, rising up a great while before day, went out and departed into a solitary place, and there prayed. Mark i. 35. Such was his activity; and this would he have us imitate. Indolence is no part of the Christian character; it had no place in man before the fall; it can have no place in heaven, where they rest not day nor night. Indolence is imperfection, and must

---

* Kitto's Bible Readings, 345.

therefore be crowded out from the soul as we advance towards perfection by sanctification. Love knows no weariness in serving its cherished object; and that love to Christ only can be genuine, which leads to activity in his service.

> "Thyself and thy belongings
> Are not thine own so proper, as to waste
> Thyself upon thy virtues, them on thee.
> Heaven doth with us, as we with torches do;
> Not light them for themselves: for if our virtues
> Did not go forth of us, 'twere all alike
> As if we had them not. Spirits are not finely touched,
> But for high purposes: nor nature lends
> The smallest scruple of her excellence,
> But, like a thrifty goddess, she determines
> Herself the glory of a creditor,
> Both thanks and use."*

Pre-eminently is this true of the grace granted to the saint. Not he who hoarded his talent in the earth, but those who improved their several gifts, received commendation and reward. The degree of our activity will be proportioned to the vigour of our love. Love to Christ was the constraining principle of the holy Apostle, who was in labours more abundant; and he says, "the grace of God which was bestowed upon me, was not in vain; but I laboured more abundantly than they all; yet not I, but the grace of God which was with me." 1 Cor. xv. 10. Activity without love is a spurious thing; equally so is love without activity. Hence, says Leighton, "Assurance is no enemy to holy diligence, nor friend of carnal security; on the contrary, it is the only thing that doth eminently ennoble and embolden the soul for all adventures and services. This confidence of love is the great secret of comfort, and of ability to do good

---

* Shakspeare, Measure for Measure, act i. sc. 1.

service. Nothing makes so strong and healthful constitution of soul as pure love. A heart thus composed goes readily and cheerfully unto all services, to do, to suffer, to live, to die, at his pleasure." While, therefore, love to Jesus makes us crave retirement with him, it animates us to untiring diligence in works of activity and self-denial, no less than of meditation and prayer. Thus did man give the Creator his love in Eden. In such ways must we give him our loves.

VER. 13.—The mandrakes give a smell, and at our gates are all manner of pleasant fruits, new and old, which I have laid up for thee, O my beloved.

This love prompts us to lay up for Jesus and consecrate to him our best gifts, as well as our diligent services. Kitto says, the Hebrew word here rendered mandrakes, has occasioned so much discussion as to evince clearly enough that we know nothing about it. Sir Thomas Browne has a curious dissertation on it in his quaint style.* The Abbe Mariti thus describes the mandrake: "At the village of St. John, in the mountains, about six miles southwest from Jerusalem, this plant is found at present as well as in Tuscany. It grows low like lettuce, to which its leaves have a great resemblance, except that they have a dark green colour. The flowers are purple, and the root is for the most part forked. The fruit, when ripe, in the beginning of May, is of the size and colour of a small apple, exceeding ruddy, and of a most agreeable odour. It is generally valued by the inhabitants as exhilarating their spirits when eaten." Perhaps Junius and Tremellius are not far wrong, when, looking to the etymology of the word, they render it "lovely flowers." By "gates" is probably meant the entrance to the kiosk or summer-house; and "pleasant

---

* Bohn's Edition, vol. i. 192.

fruits" means, as in chap. iv. 16, every delicacy the garden could afford. The meaning of the passage then is, that the spouse had already laid up in the summer-house every variety of fragrant flowers and luscious fruits, so that they could be had without the trouble of going to gather them, and would be to him an evidence of her forethought prompted by love.

Love ever hoards up for the object of affection the very best of everything that exertion can enable it to procure, without waiting to be asked. It seeks to anticipate every want, and takes delight in bestowing unexpected gratification. This feeling enters into the very essence of love, and is to it what vital warmth is to the body. Without it the affection cannot exist. Hence, love to Christ ever prompts us to hoard up spontaneously our choicest gifts for him. Whatever we possess, we wish him to have the first and the best of it. We feel hurt at the idea of his taking any secondary share. This was the principle sought to be inculcated on the Jews, when required to offer the first fruits. This made Gregory Nazianzen say, "If I have any possessions, health, credit, learning, this is all the contentment I have of them, that I have somewhat I may despise for Christ, who is altogether lovely and alone to be desired." This made a nobler than he exclaim, "I count all things but loss for the excellency of the knowledge of Christ Jesus my Lord."

CHAPTER VIII.

VER. 1, 2.—O that thou wert as my brother, that sucked the breasts of my mother! when I should find thee without, I would kiss thee; yea, I should not be despised. I would lead thee, and bring thee into my mother's house, who would instruct me: I would cause thee to drink of spiced wine of the juice of my pomegranate.

WE would translate these verses, 'O that thou wert as a brother to me, nourished in the bosom of my mother; should I find thee abroad, then would I kiss thee, nor would it be imputed to me as an impropriety. I would lead thee, I would bring thee to the house of my mother; thou shalt teach me how to gratify thy wishes; I will make thee drink of the spiced wine, of my fresh juice of the pomegranate.' These verses carry out the desire expressed in the last verse of chap. vii. Having spoken of manifestations of love she was able to make, in giving him her most delicious fruits and her choicest flowers, she is here carried away by the ardour of affection, and wishes it were possible to do towards him as she would desire. Were her relation to him different from what it was, she might give him demonstrations of love that would not be viewed by the world as improprieties. Hence she is led to wish he sustained to her the relation of a brother, for then, however ardent and multiplied her attentions, they could never be regarded as improper. On the words "my mother's house," see notes, chap. iv. 4. In that retirement she would learn from him what might be most agreeable, and with the alacrity of love manifest her affection by every possible attention.

The wines produced in the vineyards of Lebanon had a fragrant odour: "The scent thereof shall be as the wine of Lebanon." Hos. xiv. 7. The orientals frequently put spices into their wine to increase their flavour. Savary, in his Letters on Greece, states that various kinds of naturally-perfumed wines are produced in Crete and some of the neighbouring islands. Spiced wines were not peculiar to the Jews. The celebrated Persian poet, Hafiz, speaks of wine, "richly bitter, richly sweet." The Romans lined their vessels with odorous gums, to give the wine a warm, bitter flavour; and it is said that the Poles and Spaniards adopt a similar method, in order to impart to their wines a favourite relish. The juice of the pomegranate is often employed in the East, to give a pleasant sub-acid flavour to a variety of beverages; and where the laws of the Koran are not allowed to interpose, or their prohibitions are disregarded, a delicious wine is frequently manufactured from this juice alone. The spouse, therefore, means to say she would offer him the richest and most refreshing drink, her greatest delicacies.

The import of this verse is a desire that everything hindering the full and perfect interchange of affection between Jesus and our soul might be removed, and it were possible to enjoy his love to us and express our love to him, as we shall be able to do in heaven. Much as we may now long for stronger displays of his love, and to give stronger evidence of our love to him, we acquiesce in the present state of things, because we feel there would be an impropriety, no less than impossibility, in those overpowering exhibitions of love that belong to heaven. But this does not preclude us from feeling that, were it seen best by him, we would rejoice even now in those raptures which belong to heaven, where we shall be able to speak of his love in the strongest language, and give expression to it in the most exalted praise, without danger of exposing ourselves to the contempt of the world.

There shall our fellowship and communion with him be far more intimate and endearing than was possible on earth. The language of these verses expresses the real feeling of the pious heart. How often do even nominal Christians charge on brethren as an impropriety, or as a species of excess, exercises which are perfectly free from fanaticism, and spring from overflowing influences of the Holy Spirit on the heart. In the present world, we are not able to feel as we would wish to feel towards our Lord; we cannot speak of him as we would wish to speak of him; we cannot do as we would wish to do towards him. We are prevented by our position among those who are unable to understand these things; by the remaining corruptions of the heart; by the peculiar duties now resting on us; and by the relation Jesus must necessarily bear to us in the present world. Well may the wearied heart, with so many obstructions between us and the object of our love, desire that they may be removed, and that our relations to him may be made such as to give us the power to gratify perfectly our affection.

Ver. 3, 4.—His left hand should be under my head, and his right hand should embrace me. I charge you, O daughters of Jerusalem, that ye stir not up, nor awake my love, until he please.

See notes on chap. ii. 6, 7. These verses seem here mentioned, as though the happy state expressed by them was viewed by the soul as a blessed and satisfying foretaste of what may be expected hereafter, and as much as is best or possible for us in this world.

Ver. 5.—(Who is this that cometh up from the wilderness, leaning upon her beloved?) I raised thee up under the apple-tree: there thy mother brought thee forth: there she brought thee forth that bare thee.

According to our reading of this passage, the daughters of Jerusalem say, 'Who is this coming up from the wilderness, leaning on the beloved?' Answering this question, the beloved says to the spouse, as though for the purpose of reassuring her, by calling to mind that she was truly his rightful wife, 'Under the citron-tree I gained thine affection; there thy mother pledged thee; there she that bare thee betrothed thee.' This is one of the verses which cannot be explained but on the supposition that this poem is an allegory. We do not know that it throws any light on this passage to remark, that among many nations the Cydonian apple was sacred to love; or to notice the golden apple which Paris adjudged to Venus, who is sometimes represented in her statues with an apple in her hand. Theocritus has the following:

> "First I beheld thy beauties, blooming maid,
> When o'er the hills, in every charm arrayed,
> Thy mother led thee, and thy fingers fair
> Plucked the wild hyacinths that blossomed there.
> And I was guide to thee along thy way."

This verse gives the seventh result flowing from the divine love. Though we cannot now enjoy what we could desire, and what shall be enjoyed in heaven; though the delightful scenes now had must be interrupted, yet we are permitted to go up from this wilderness leaning on the beloved; we feel that underneath us are the everlasting arms; in all circumstances he sustains us; and throughout our pilgrimage we are thus upheld by him who first found us, raised us up, and took us into covenant relation, "under the apple-tree," as in chap. ii. 3, under the shadow of Christ. Here is, 1. The blessed privilege enjoyed by the believer, of going up from this world towards heaven, leaning on the beloved; 2. The soul who enjoys this privilege, is the soul that has been found by the beloved under the shadow of Christ; 3. There he first awaked and won our love; 4. There we were given to him by the one who had the right to dispose of us. What force do the last three considerations give to the first. Had she who was leaning on the beloved the right to lean there as his espoused wife? Yes, as is clearly shown. Have the believers that go up to heaven, the right to lean on Jesus, as his bride, the wife of the Lamb? Hence we see why the language changes so abruptly from the daughters of Jerusalem to the beloved; as though he would say, She has this right, because under such and such circumstances, and in such a place, she was betrothed to me by her mother's hand.

He on whom we are leaning, found us under the citron-tree, Jesus Christ. See notes, chap. ii. 3. There did he awaken us first to his love. This love is shed abroad in our hearts by the Holy Spirit, who is given unto us. The awaking of this love within us is the giving unto us of a new life. It introduces us into a new world, leads us to lean on new objects for comfort and support, and fits us for enjoying even the presence of God. Could the intellect of a man be imparted to an inferior creature, it would not more exalt his nature, than does the love of God elevate degraded and imbruted man. Before Jesus found us, our condition was truly forlorn. Like a poor, wayworn pilgrim in an oriental desert, under the withering heat, we had with Hagar sat down to die, Gen. xxi. 16; but we saw one who was as the shadow of a great rock in a weary land; to him we turned, and under his shadow we sat down with great delight; there one touched us, greater than the angel who was sent to the disheartened prophet, 1 Kings xix. 5; there God called on us to arise from our despondency; there he opened our eyes, and caused us to see a well of living water, and made us go in the strength of that food onward to the mount of God, where he had appeared, not in the terrible darkness of Sinai, but in the mercy of

Calvary and gentleness of Zion. There, beneath the dropping of his blood, were we given away to him in covenant relation, by one who had the right to dispose of us, even God the Father—given to him as the purchase of his blood; and with a tenderness infinitely surpassing that with which the beloved disciple fostered the mother of Jesus, committed to his care by the dying Saviour on the cross, did our precious Redeemer from that hour take us into his own fortune, his own bosom, his own home.

Thus found by Jesus, quickened by him to his love, and given to him by the Father, we are led away from our disconsolate condition, up from this wilderness, to the city of the living God. The wife looks to the husband for wisdom, for protection, for support; she leans on him in confidence and love. Thus lean we on our blessed Lord. He gives us support, wisdom, protection. With Israel, we feel there is none like unto the God of Jeshurun, who rideth upon the heaven in our help; and underneath us are the everlasting arms. Deut. xxxiii. 26. On him we lean in repentance, in temptation, in trial, in sorrow, in times of desertion by the light of God's countenance, or of persecution by the world, in sickness, in death, in the judgment, in our entrance into the heavenly city, and in our presentation, amid the splendours of his court, to the king of glory.

VER. 6.—Set me as a seal upon thine heart, as a seal upon thine arm.

This alludes to jewels having the name or portrait of the beloved person engraved on them, and worn next the heart, or on the arm. In the pictures of the eastern princesses and heroines, there is sometimes a large square jewel on the fore-part of the arm, a little below the shoulder. "When all the persons had assembled in the divan, every one remained sitting or standing in his place without moving, till in about half an hour came two kapudschis, one of whom carried the imperial signet-ring, and presented it to the grand vizier, who arose from his sofa, and received the signet-ring with a kind of bow, kissed it, put it on his hand, took it off again, and put it in the bag in which it had been before, and placed both in a pocket at the left side of his kaftan, as it were upon his heart."* According to Roberts, "When a husband is going to a distant country, the wife says to him, 'Ah! place me as a seal upon thy heart;' that is, let me be impressed on thy affections, as the seal leaves its impression upon the wax. Let not your arms embrace another; let me only be sealed there." There may possibly be a reference here to the stones in the breast-plate of the highpriest, and those worn on his shoulders.

These words do therefore give as the eighth result of the divine love, the desire to lie continually near the heart of Jesus, and be perpetually in his remembrance. Feeling thus the love of Christ, and the privilege of leaning on him, we pray to have ever a part in his intercession. How comforting to know that we have one in heaven to intercede for us. This is often overlooked; but as we grow in love we feel more and more the preciousness of this truth. How glorious a position is that of the gem on the finger of the king, how inseparable from his presence. "Thou shalt be a crown of glory in the hand of the Lord, and a royal diadem in the hand of thy God," Isa. lxii. 3; "They shall be as the gems of a crown." Zech. ix. 16. Here the saint desires to be a seal so precious as to be borne on the heart. A believer writes thus, concerning his experience at a certain time: "I never felt so strongly and sensibly that I had a place

---

* Rosenmüller.

in his loving heart. It seemed to my spiritual perception, as though my soul had passed not only into his bosom, but far away into his very heart, and my sensations were such as they would be, were the thing possible, were I lodged in the centre of his heart with love, such love as belongs to Jesus only, above, below, around, within me, the air, the light, all, the very richness of love, my heart buried thus in the fountain of life and love, and feeling tenderly, exquisitely, the beating of the heart of Jesus in the outgushings of that love in the Holy Spirit springing up within me as a fountain of water unto eternal life. Never may I forget these sensations. They seemed the delicious perfection of union with Jesus, my soul like a spark of light, a star of flame, broken off from the sun of righteousness and wandered afar, but returning towards its centre, till passing into the depths of this fountain of light, it reposes at the very centre, lost to all things else, and calm amid the quiet splendour of eternal peace. This coalescing of our soul with the spirit of Jesus, this oneness with him, is the perfection of sanctification, the end to which the death and intercession of our Saviour lead: 'That they all may be one, as thou, Father, art in me, and I in thee,' John xvii. 21; 'I in them, and thou in me.' Ver. 23. Faith gives such a substance to these truths as to make me feel just as I must feel, if my heart were lodged in the very centre of the heart of Jesus. It is something more than being gathered in his arms and carried in his bosom, than being set as a seal on his heart. It is the consciousness of being one with Jesus, of resting in Jesus, heart in heart. Here is the full meaning of the words, 'His soul shall dwell in goodness,' Ps. xxv. 13. 'Shall lodge in goodness,' in that fountain of life, the streams issuing from which are, according to the condition of those they reach, goodness, mercy, compassion, or love."*

The seal has generally engraved on it some device commemorating something which is most valued by the possessor: the soul of the saint is such a seal; on it is traced that which is a commemoration of the glorious mercy of the King of kings; and so peculiar is the engraving, that whoever sees it will know to whom the soul belongs. Rev. ii. 17. The seal is set in gold; and our spiritual body is the golden setting for the precious seal of the renewed heart, on which the Holy Spirit is now engraving by sanctification the lineament of our Lord. It is not only allowable, but the duty of the saint to pray, that we may be with Jesus where he is, to behold his glory. John xvii. 24. And in what way can we more clearly and comprehensively offer this prayer, than in the language of this verse.

> For love is strong as death; jealousy is cruel as the grave: the coals thereof are coals of fire, which hath a most vehement flame.

Rather translate—'Devoted affection is unrelaxing as

---

* "The love of God, and of God alone, was my soul's great business. I seemed so entirely lost in God, as to have no sight of myself at all. It seemed as if my heart never came out of that divine ocean. Oh! loss, which is the consummation of happiness, though operated through crosses and deaths! I could say with the Apostle Paul, that Christ lived in me; and that I lived no more. Every inward motion, originating from self, seemed to be taken away and lost; so much so, that all the soul's movements and actions were now in God, under the dominion of his will, and entirely in union with him; the soul living in and of God, as the body lives in and of the air it breathes. Human language cannot well describe this state. God only knows perfectly what it is. Souls, who are in this state, are very precious in the sight of God, though outwardly there is nothing which especially attracts notice. They are the little ones of the earth;—meek, humble, quiet. Their humility, however, does not wholly protect them from the world's opposition, they are not unfrequently the objects of the worlds scorn and rage."—*Madame Guyon.*

the realms of the dead; its flames have the energy of lightning-flames, which have the fiercest blaze.' These words illustrate the devotion of this love to the object of affection, the Lord Jesus. The privilege, the glory, the happiness of being thus set as a seal, appears such, that the believer is ready to sacrifice everything for its attainment. While the various endowments of the soul are representations of the excellences of God, every affection of a pure and exalted cast is the image of what our devotion should be to him; and then this devotion is the image in return of what God's love is towards us. All other loves were intended as subsidiary to this love to God, and streams for feeding its strength. Of this love pre-eminently may be said what Coleridge has sung of a subordinate passion:

> "All thoughts, all passions, all delights,
> Whatever stirs this mortal frame,
> Are all but ministers of love,
> And feed his sacred flame."

There is a law in nature that the attractive power of bodies is proportioned to their size or quantity of matter; and the attractive power of lovely objects depends on the amount of loveliness centred in them. Now, what is the loveliness centred in Christ? In him is not only every thing actually, but everything possibly lovely. He is the citron-tree, as it were continually putting forth fresh successions of buds, blossoms, and fruits of beauty; the fountain of life and loveliness. What must, therefore, be the attractive power with which he draws holy souls towards him and binds them to him? This nothing can withstand. The devotion will be in proportion to the degree of the love. Love is devotion. So lovely does Jesus seem, so great his attractiveness, so numerous our obligations to him, that we rejoice to "count all things

37*

but loss" for him. The inquiry on every point of duty, is not whether the performance of it is difficult, dangerous, or even seemingly possible; but simply, "Lord, what wilt thou have me to do?" The practicability of a duty is felt, to be properly judged of, not by the appearance it presents to our judgment, but by the command of our Lord. If he has commanded, we go forward, fearing nothing that may seem to lie in the way. The true principle was stated by the Duke of Wellington, when, in reply to a person who asked whether his knowledge of things in India would not lead him to recommend the friends of missions to drop their work as hopeless, he said, "Your business is to look only to your marching orders—Go ye into all the world, and preach the gospel to every creature."

True, the amount of our contributions may seem small and swallowed up like a rain-drop in the ocean; our efforts may seem unimportant, hardly felt if put forth, or missed if withheld; yet we hesitate not, but go forward, feeling that whatever result may attend our labours, we are grateful for opportunities of showing our love to Jesus, even though the exertions be unattended with any further results. Truly, as Leighton says, "This love makes the soul delight in the hardest tasks and greatest difficulties, where it may perform God service either in doing or suffering for him. The greater the task, the more real is the testimony and expression of love, and therefore the more acceptable to God. If times be for suffering, love will make the soul not only bear, but welcome the bitterest afflictions of life, and the hardest kinds of death, for his sake. In a word, there is in love a sweet constraint, or tying of the heart to all obedience and duty."

CHAPTER VIII. 7.

VER. 7.—Many waters cannot quench love, neither can the floods drown it: if a man would give all the substance of his house for love, it would utterly be contemned.

These words set forth the tenth effect flowing from the love of Christ—the power thereby imparted to the soul of withstanding everything that would draw us away from the Saviour. The ninth effect, mentioned under the second division of verse sixth, shows the devotion of this affection; this verse illustrates its power. The power of anything must be determined by looking at the resistance which it may be able to overcome. And what does this love in the heart overcome? Against it are combined mighty influences, the world, the flesh, and the devil. Cherishing for the blessed Saviour a devotion strong as death, the saint finds himself surrounded by enemies who would crush or uproot this love, and bar the way effectually against our ever becoming able to attain the enjoyment of the divine glory in heaven. This host of foes avail themselves of our every instinct, impulse, passion, and feeling, taking advantage of every weakness and every opportunity for injury to us that can be conceived. But, "in all these things we are more than conquerors through him that loved us;" for the love of Christ constraineth us; and we can do all things through Christ who strengthens us. Our position is now very different from what it was in Eden, where there was but a single propensity on which the tempter could work, and every facility was offered for resistance. But had we never fallen, the energy and power of this love could not have been so fully seen. Its power does not appear so great in keeping holy beings in their sphere, as in taking hold of the fallen, and carrying them up through all these opposing influences, to their proper place beside the throne of God, and reinstating these lost stars in their orbits, never again to wander, never to fall or grow dim. The excellence of a vessel, the power of its machinery, is shown by the angry tempests amid which it can live, and the stormy waves through which it urges its way. Devotion in the pilot to his duty cannot avail, unless the vessel be sea-worthy, its engine perfect and strong. This divine love is the motive-power of the soul in its passage over the angry waters of life's tempestuous sea. The force of the elements combining for its destruction may be seen in the fiery persecutions which marked the course of Jesus through this life, and have marked the track of his people in every age. Yet has this love ever proved sufficient to carry even the frailest bark of humanity in which it has been lodged, safe through all surges into the haven, where the wicked cease from troubling and the weary are at rest. Never, in a single instance, has one foundered in the depths of that sea which shall never give up its dead. Sometimes amid sorrow and temptation, like the disciples in the storm on the sea of Galilee, we may be sore afraid, and cry, "Lord, save us; we are perishing;" yet shall we ever find Jesus is with us: and when in jeopardy, like the Apostle, we beseech the Lord even thrice that the peril may depart from us, if he does not say unto the wind and the waves, "Peace, be still;" he will at least say, "My grace is sufficient for thee." Herein lies the power of this love. While this grace with its attending love continues in vigorous operation in the soul, we are safe, however heavy the surges and violent the storm; if its power be diminished, our peril proportionally increases; were it withdrawn, we must inevitably perish. This has been happily illustrated by Bunyan, when "the interpreter took Christian by the hand, and led him into a place where was a fire burning against a wall, and one standing by it, always casting much water upon it to quench it; yet did the fire burn higher and hotter; at the back of the wall was a man with a vessel of oil in his hand, of the which he did also continually cast, but secretly, into the fire." Hence we say with the Apostle, "I am persuaded, that neither death, nor life, nor angels, nor principalities, nor powers, nor things present, nor things to come; nor height, nor depth, nor any other creature, shall be able to separate us from the love of God, which is in Christ Jesus our Lord."

VER. 8.—We have a little sister, and she hath no breasts: what shall we do for our sister in the day when she shall be spoken for?

Rather read, 'We have a young sister, and she hath not yet reached womanhood: what shall we do for our sister with reference to the day when she shall be spoken for in marriage.' These are understood by us as words of the spouse to the beloved. In her exalted position as the spouse of Solomon, she does not forget those allied to her, who are yet in their natural, humble position. This represents the interest felt and manifested by the believer, in prayer to the Lord Jesus, for those who are yet in their native impenitent state. From Matt. xii. 50, we see that all are here meant who may be brought to do the will of God; and hence all impenitent persons in general, no less than those of our own household. An interest for the salvation of the souls of others is a characteristic of genuine grace. The evidence of right feeling is right action. Right action will show itself in prayer and efforts for the good of souls. He who is crucified to the world, and he only, estimates the world aright; and truly enjoys it. He feels for the miseries of others, not from the promptings of natural benevolence, but from the impulse of love to Christ. It is delightful to pray and labour in the cause of benevolence; especially to pray and labour for those we love. The believer will seek the salvation of his impenitent friends, by going to Jesus, and making interest for them in prayer; if they are young, not yet arrived at years of discretion, he will be training them up and attending them with his prayers, that when they do reach proper years, they may be ready to receive the divine blessing. In such labours, we should not be discouraged because our efforts may be small, and apparently promise little reward. Duty is ours; results are with God. Trifling acts are often the cause of much happiness, and issue in most important consequences.

> "The blessings which the weak and poor can scatter
> Have their own season. 'Tis a little thing
> To give a cup of water; yet its draught
> Of cool refreshment, drained by fevered lips,
> May give a shock of pleasure to the frame
> More exquisite than when Nectarian juice
> Renews the life of joy in happiest hours.
> It is a little thing to speak a phrase
> Of common comfort, which by daily use
> Has almost lost its sense; yet on the ear
> Of him who thought to die unmourned, 'twill fall
> Like choicest music."*

In Chrysostom's introduction to his homilies on the rich man and Lazarus, are the following admirable sentences. "As the springs run when no one uses their waters; as the fountains pour forth when none draws from them; as the rivers flow on although no one drinks from their waves; so must the believer discharge his whole duty, though no one gives attention. Though by our efforts none may be converted, yet thereby are the impenitent kept from going on as freely in sin. I have not raised the sick, but I have rendered stronger the healthful; my discourse may not have recalled any from vice, but it has

* Talfourd's Ion, act i. sc. 2.

made the virtuous more careful. Moreover, he who hears to-day and resists, may to-morrow hear and obey; he also who despises this message to-day and to-morrow, may, after a longer time, attend carefully to these instructions; for the fisherman may often draw an empty net through the whole day, but in the evening, when about to depart, take the fish that had till then escaped. Were we to suspend business and sit down in idleness, when unsuccessful in our undertakings, our whole life would be lost, its spiritual as well as temporal advantages. Were the husbandman to suspend all labour on account of one, or two, or many disasters from unfavourable weather, we should all perish from famine; and did the mariner abandon the sea even on account of many tempests, the business of navigation would cease, and all the conveniences thence derived to society be excluded; and were men to act in reference to the various employments of life as too many Christians act in reference to the interests of religion, all things would go to ruin. When the husbandman has repeatedly sown the same field without a successful harvest, he returns again to the tillage of the same ground, and in a single year reaps a full reward for all his labours; and the merchant, though he has suffered many wrecks, again fits out his vessels, and embarks in the same enterprise, with no better prospects of success than the former. It is so with men in every calling. Since they exercise so much diligence and perseverance in temporal things, the issue of which is uncertain, shall we, when our exhortations are unheeded, be at once discouraged? When his vessel is wrecked, the mariner finds none to relieve his poverty; and when the tempest, deluging his grounds, destroys the harvest, the husbandman must bear his wants. It is not so with us. Although the hearer may not receive the seed of the word, nor bring forth the fruit of obedience, you shall receive from God a recompense as great when he disobeys, as you would have received had he been obedient. You did what you could. We are not responsible for our hearers being persuaded, but only for their being properly exhorted: to admonish is our duty, to be persuaded is theirs. Let the limit of your exhortation be the obedience of him who is exhorted. The devil is constantly opposing our salvation, though gaining nothing thereby, and injuring himself by his zeal. So great is his phrenzy, that he often undertakes impossibilities, and assaults not only those whom he may hope to supplant and overthrow, but those who are probably superior to his devices. When he heard that Job was commended by the omniscient God, he hoped to be able to overthrow him; nor did the deceiver cease his various efforts and devices for destroying this just man, even though God had commended so highly the integrity of his saint. Tell me then, shall we not be ashamed, shall we not blush, if, when the devil never despairs of our destruction, but constantly expects it, we despair of the salvation of our brethren? The devil does not retire from his assault against us, even when God forbids. Will you then abandon your brethren, when God is encouraging and urging to their aid?"

Ver. 9.—If she be a wall, we will build upon her a palace of silver: and if she be a door, we will inclose her with boards of cedar.

The spouse having thus interceded with the beloved for her sister, receives from him the encouraging answer contained in this verse. It is the usual parabolic mode of speaking in the East. The imagery here used was probably drawn from the walls of Jerusalem and from the temple. The spouse had been compared to a city such as Tirzah; illustrations drawn from turrets and doors is here applied to her sister. Josephus states, that on the walls of Jerusalem, thirty feet high and built of stones fifteen feet broad and thirty feet long, there were one hundred and ninety towers, "solid as the wall itself, wherein the niceness of the joints and the beauty of the stones were no way inferior to the holy house itself."* Such towers added very much to the strength and beauty of the city; and formed as they were of white marble, must, together with the temple, make the holy city "the beauty of the whole earth." The Hebrew word means a battlement or turret. There were on the walls battlements three feet high. The reference may be to these, though more probably to something in the time of Solomon, like the turrets here mentioned. Nothing could be more elegant than such turrets made of silver. The other allusion here seems to refer to the peculiar beauty of some doors, possibly to those of the temple. 1 Kings vi. 31—35: "For the entering of the oracle he made doors of olive-tree; the lintel and side-posts were a fifth part of the wall. The two doors also were of olive-tree;

---

* Jewish War, book v. 4. 8. According to Diodorus Siculus, the walls of Nineveh were one hundred feet high, and so broad that three chariots might be driven abreast on them. They were furnished with fifteen hundred towers, each two hundred feet in height. The gates of ancient cities were often of great size, sometimes of brass, and flanked by towers adorned with sculptures, as at Koyunjik. May this have something to do with associating a door with a turret in the text?

Speaking of the emperor Akber's efforts to adorn the city of Agra, Maurice remarks, "The castle itself, the largest ever erected in India, was built in the form of a crescent along the banks of the Jumna; its lofty walls were composed of stones of enormous size, hard as marble, and of a reddish colour, resembling jasper, which at a distance, in the rays of the sun, gave it a shining and beautiful appearance. It was adorned with many stately porticoes, galleries, and turrets, all richly painted and gilded, and some even overlaid with plates of gold."— *Indian Antiquities*, vol. i. 208.

and he carved upon them carvings of cherubims, and palm-trees, and open flowers, and overlaid them with gold, and spread gold upon the cherubims, and upon the palm-trees. So also made he for the door of the temple posts of olive-tree, a fourth part of the wall. And the two doors were of fir-tree: the two leaves of the one door were folding, and the two leaves of the other door were folding. And he carved thereon cherubims, and palm-trees, and open flowers; and covered them with gold fitted upon the carved work. And he built the inner court with three rows of hewed stone, and a row of cedar beams."* Such doors would certainly supply materials for a very suitable comparison. The meaning of the whole verse would then be, that to fit this sister for her new position, a glorious change should be wrought in her character, great as that in a wall like the walls around Jerusalem, on which should be raised turrets of silver; or

---

* In the Crystal Palace, at London, in 1851, "the Russian court abounded in beautiful works of Malachite stone, out of which many gorgeous articles of furniture were wrought, whereof two folding-doors composed of many thousand pieces, and of the estimated worth of £9,000, deserve especial mention."

The gates of the Baptistery of St. John at Florence, may show, that this comparison of the spouse to a door was intended to give a very strong illustration of the beauty of holiness in the soul, and of the exquisite workmanship of the Holy Spirit. The first of these gates was finished about the middle of the fourteenth century, after a labour of twenty-two years; it contained twenty-four panels, and the bas-reliefs represent the life of John the Baptist from his birth to his death. The second gate, which together with the third, was made in the succeeding century, was divided into twenty-eight panels representing scenes and persons of the New Testament. The third gate exhibits two parts divided into ten panels containing bas-reliefs taken from the Old Testament. Varchi calls this gate a marvellous work, and perhaps unique in all the world; D'Agincourt considers it one of the most precious monuments of modern art: and Michael Angelo judged it worthy to be "the gate of Paradise."

as that in an ordinary door, which should be so overlaid with cedar, and finished, as to be beautiful as the doors made by Solomon for the temple. Her nature should be adorned with ornaments, giving more beauty and strength than turrets of silver, or a richly carved door of the most elegant cedar.

Believers shall be made pillars in the temple of God, Rev. iii. 12; here, such are compared to towers of silver built on a wall of white marble, and to the richly wrought door of the temple, of carved cedar and olive adorned with gold. The Holy Spirit, at work on the soul in sanctification, is developing graces of holiness, which are rising over the heart, like towers of silver on the holy city's walls. The spouse is said to be beautiful as Tirzah, elegant as Jerusalem: these were lovely, indeed, when the morning sun fell on their towers, even though of white marble; how much more so would they have been, had those towers been of silver. Who, then, can tell what will be the glory of the soul, when beautiful as these imperial cities with walls and towers of marble, it shall have the virtues developed by sanctification, rising there purer than turrets of silver, lighted up by the splendour of heaven, and over it shall be spread the holiness which is the carved work of the Holy Spirit, richer, more elegant, than the carving of cherubim and palm-trees, and open flowers on the olive, and cedar, and gold of the doors of the temple.

VER. 10.—I am a wall, and my breasts like towers: then was I in his eyes as one that found favour.

The meaning of this verse is, that the change promised by the beloved to the younger sister, had already been wrought in the condition of the spouse; and the consciousness of this furnished her with grounds for indulging the assurance of continuing to enjoy his favour. In the eighth, ninth, and tenth verses, these four considerations are distinctly stated: 1. Those truly actuated by the love of Christ, show an interest, by effort and prayer to Jesus, for the souls of the impenitent, ver. 8; 2. Two grounds of encouragement are then noticed—the promise of God to work the necessary change in the unrenewed; and 3. Our experience of his gracious power in having wrought such change in ourselves, ver. 9, 10; 4. Then, by reference to our own state, finding that God has shown favour to us, we are encouraged to pray and labour for the salvation of others. There can be no stronger ground of encouragement than the declaration of God, yet our faith may receive confirmation by seeing that word fulfilled. This confirmation becomes the strongest possible, when that confirmation takes place, not only under our eye, but in the very experience of our heart. We should consider effort for the salvation of souls a hopeless thing, were it not for the two considerations here presented—the promise of God, and the experience of his regenerating and sanctifying power in our own sinful hearts.

VER. 11, 12.—Solomon had a vineyard at Baal-hamon: he let out the vineyard unto keepers; every one for the fruit thereof was to bring a thousand pieces of silver. My vineyard, which is mine, is before me: thou, O Solomon, must have a thousand, and those that keep the fruit thereof two hundred.

There have been many conjectures concerning the locality of Baal-hamon. Some have supposed it situated near Baalbec; others, probably with more reason, in Palestine, at no great distance from Jerusalem. A knowledge of its exact situation is perfectly immaterial, and can throw no light on the truth here embodied in the allegory. These pieces of silver were doubtless shekels, each in value about fifty-six cents of our money. It seems probable that the vineyard consisted of a thousand vines, each required to afford a shekel to the owner; for we see that Solomon received a thousand shekels from this vineyard, and we learn from Isa. vii. 23, that a thousand silverlings, or shekels, was the profit of a thousand vines. The vines of Johannisberg are valued at a ducat—about an American dollar—each, according to Michaelis, who thinks that, with allowance for the change in the value of money, this price was high even for a valuable vineyard. The whole income of this vineyard would then have been worth between five and six hundred dollars to Solomon. While those who were tenants were obliged to pay this rent, the spouse speaks of a vineyard which was her own, but which she would nevertheless so keep under her own control and manage, as to be able, while paying the keepers equitable wages, to offer yearly to the king a thousand pieces of silver as a testimonial of her love.

Viewed in connection with the parable of the labourers in the vineyard, Matt. xx. 1, and xxi. 33, these verses illustrate the truth, that we are all the stewards of God, and that all our property, intellectual endowments, and influence, are things intrusted to us by God, who will require of us an account of our stewardship; they furthermore show that were we, like the spouse in reference to her vineyard, under no requirement or command to give to Jesus, yet would we, under the impulse of this love, give him of our possessions everything that could be spared from the necessary demands made on us by justice to others. The spirit of Jesus, our example, is a spirit of liberality.* In 2 Cor. viii. 9, the word grace means

---

* "An improper use must be called an abuse. Were we pilgrims in a distant land, unable to live happily save in our native country, being miserable in our wanderings, and desiring to end our wretchedness, did we wish to return to our country, we should be obliged to use conveyances by land or by sea, for reaching and enjoying our home; but did

liberality; "Ye know the liberality of our Lord Jesus Christ, that, though he was rich, yet for your sakes he became poor, that ye through his poverty might be rich." There is an error among men concerning the nature of the title by which they hold their property. When any man has such claim on a property as to remove at will, under the just sanction of the law, one tenant after another, and place others in their stead, we consider him the legal owner, whatever the ejected tenants may think of their claims; and we feel that the law would not justify him in doing so, unless the possessions were righteously his. Now, God is daily giving us proof of this very kind, that all we have and hold belongs not to ourselves, but to him. At will, he makes one rich and another poor; causes riches to take wings and flee away; removes men from their possessions by death, and causes their wealth to pass into the hands of others; nor does any person think of questioning the justice of these proceedings, or his right to dispose of us at his will. Everything we have, belonging thus to him, and being held in trust, we cannot repress a liberal spirit and refuse contributions to his cause, without committing a breach of trust and incurring a responsibility fearful to be met in the judgment.*

---

the pleasures of the journey and the conveyance of the vehicles delight us so that we might fall into the enjoyment of what we ought only to use, we would grow unwilling to hasten the journey, and becoming involved with those dangerous comforts, would grow alienated from the land whose pleasures could make us blest: thus, in this mortal life, aliens from the Lord, would we return to heaven, our home where we may be truly blest, we must use this world, not enjoy it; that the invisible things of God may be seen, being understood by those things which have been made, that is, that we may understand eternal and spiritual things by things sensible and temporal."—*Augustin. Dé Doct. Christ.*, book i. 4.

* " Be charitable before wealth make thee covetous, and lose not the glory of the mite. If riches increase, let thy mind hold pace with them;

But were there no divine command, and no obligation thus resting upon us, love would seek to pour its riches, its all, at the feet of Jesus, and feel such consecration the highest privilege. With such a spirit, the richest blessings are connected. "Honour the Lord with thy substance, and with the first fruit of all thine increase; so shall thy barns be filled with plenty, and thy presses shall burst out with new wine." Prov. iii. 9. "For this thing the Lord thy God shall bless thee in all thy works, and in all that thou puttest thine hand unto." Deut. xv. 10. "He that soweth bountifully shall reap also bountifully." 2 Cor. ix. 6. On whom is the blessing pro-

and think it not enough to be liberal, but munificent. Diffuse thy beneficence early, and while thy treasures call thee master. Give not only unto seven, but also unto eight—that is, unto more than many. Though to give unto every one that asketh may seem severe advice, yet give thou also before asking; that is, where want is silently clamorous, and men's necessities, not their tongues, do loudly call for thy mercies. For though sometimes necessitousness be dumb, or misery speak not out, yet true charity is sagacious; and will find out hints for beneficence. Acquaint thyself with the physiognomy of want, and let the dead colours and first lines of necessity suffice to tell thee there is an object for thy bounty. Spare not where thou canst not easily be prodigal, and fear not to be undone by mercy; for since he who hath pity on the poor lendeth unto the Almighty Rewarder, who observes no ides but every day for his payments, charity becomes pious usury, Christian liberality the most thriving industry; and what we adventure in a cock-boat may return in a carrack unto us. He who thus casts his bread upon the water shall surely find it again; for though it falleth to the bottom, it sinks but like the axe of the prophet, to rise again unto him. If avarice be thy vice, yet make it not thy punishment. A slave unto mammon makes no servant unto God. Covetousness cracks the sinews of faith, numbs the apprehension of anything above sense, and, only affected with the certainty of things present, makes a peradventure of things to come; lives but unto one world, nor hopes but fears another; makes their own death sweet unto others, bitter unto themselves; brings formal sadness, scenical mourning, and no wet eyes at the grave."—*Sir Thomas Brown's Works*, vol. iii. 90.

nounced by the Judge in the last day, "Come, ye blessed of my Father, inherit the kingdom prepared for you from the foundation of the world"? On those who fed the hungry, who gave drink to the thirsty, who sheltered the stranger, who clothed the naked, who visited the sick, who sought out the prisoner. While the Magdalen may then rejoice in having followed him from Galilee to Calvary, to minister unto him; and Mary in having broken the box of alabaster at the feet of Jesus; and Joseph of Arimathea in having given to the outcast corpse of him who through life had not where to lay his head, a peaceful resting place in his own new tomb; we may equally rejoice, as he says, "Inasmuch as ye have done it unto one of the least of these my brethren, ye have done it unto me."

VER. 13.—Thou that dwellest in the gardens, the companions hearken to thy voice: cause me to hear it.

The Hebrew puts it beyond doubt that these words are addressed to the spouse, as we suppose by the beloved. "Our first parents had for their residence a beautiful garden, which may have had some influence upon their immediate descendants, in giving them a predilection for such situations. People in England will scarcely be able to appreciate the value which the orientals place on a garden. The food of many of them consists of vegetables, roots, and fruits; their medicines, also, being indigenous, are most of them produced in their gardens. Here they have their fine fruit-trees, and the constant shade; and here they have their wells and places for bathing. See the proprietor, in his undress, walking around his little domain; his fence or wall is so high no one can overlook him: he strolls about to smoke his shroot, to pick up the fruit, and cull the flowers; he cares not for the world;

his soul is satisfied with the scenes around him."* See notes on chap. i. 16. Before the fall, "the Lord God took the man and put him in the garden of Eden, to dress it and keep it." Gen. ii. 15. The Church is now his spiritual Eden; and the saint is placed in this spiritual garden, to enjoy it and feed on its healing fruits, but not, therefore, to lead an idle life. It is his privilege to enjoy it; his duty, to be engaged in dressing and keeping it. Then do we find the presence of our Lord pleasant to us, and him ready to receive us into communion with himself. Those actuated by the love of Christ feel an interest for the impenitent, and show liberality in the cause of our Lord; and those thus acting are encouraged by Jesus to prayer. The words "vineyard" and "garden" were often used interchangeably by the Jews; the expression, "thou that dwellest in the gardens," is probably applied to the spouse in consequence of her care of the vineyard mentioned in the foregoing verse; and hence this faithfulness on her part is connected with delight and readiness on the part of the beloved to hear her voice in praise and prayer. Those animated by this love, while showing its genuineness by effort and liberality in the cause of Christ, have a lowly opinion of themselves, and need encouragement to come to their Lord. And how sweetly does the beloved address this language to the heart. See notes on chap. ii. 14. Not only has he given us exceedingly great and precious promises; he sends his Holy Spirit into our hearts for constraining us sweetly to the mercy-seat. And in times of trouble, when we feel the insufficiency of the world, and are driven to the necessity of going to the throne of grace, he is but using such dispensations for saying unto us, "Let me hear thy voice." To him no less pleasing is the voice of praise. And that we may

---

* Roberts.

never fear he will grow weary with us, he addresses to us these cheering words.

VER. 14.—Make haste, my beloved, and be thou like to a roe, or to a young hart upon the mountains of spices.

See notes, chap. ii. 17. The Song concludes with the same sentiment expressed in different words, and repeated with emphasis, in Rev. xxii. 7, 12, 20. "Behold, I come quickly:" and "Surely I come quickly." These words are properly the answer to the desire of the spouse in the text, sent by the beloved from his dwelling-place on the mountain of myrrh and hill of frankincense, where he abides till the day breaks and the shadows flee away. Thus encouraged to dwell at the mercy-seat, in confidential and constant communion with our Lord on earth, we are becoming fitted for being with him in heaven; and this fitness, combined with the displays of his love before mentioned, carries with it a stronger and stronger desire for the enjoyment of his glory, as it shall be revealed when the Lord perfects that which concerneth us, at his second coming. To this, as the ultimate, absorbing desire of the soul, do all these assurances of the love of Jesus lead. As the book begins with a burst of desire for the love of Christ, as that love can be enjoyed only by his intimate friends, chap. i. 2, it ends with a prayer for the hastening of the time when we shall no longer see him through a glass darkly, but face to face; when there shall be nothing to interfere with the manifestation of his love to us, and the expression of our love to him: this desire is expressed, and its intenseness shown, by the prayer that he would hasten that happy day, and come with the celerity of a roe, or a young hart bounding over the mountains of spices, and at every step shaking fragrance from the dewy boughs. When Jesus came forth from the ivory palaces, all his garments smell of myrrh, aloes and cassia: how fragrant will they be when the sacred perfume of his divine nature shall, at his second coming, flow forth around him more boundless, more life-giving, than the atmosphere which encompassed him when in human form on earth. Truly his presence will be more delightful than that of a gazelle through mountains of spices. To the sentiments of chap. ii. 17, is added, "mountains of spices," for associating with the second coming of the beloved every possible idea of delight; and well may he be said to come as a gazelle or fleeting fawn, for his words are, "I come quickly." Rev. xxii. 20. And, "As the lightning cometh out of the east, and shineth even unto the west, so shall also the coming of the Son of man be." Matt. xxiv. 27. To this promise the Holy Spirit has taught us to pray, "Even so, come, Lord Jesus."

To this period, it would be strange if the believer did not look forward with the greatest interest. In regeneration, we were betrothed to the beloved; that day is to be the day of our espousals with "Him who loved us and gave himself for us." Jesus himself has taught us to view it as the time of our redemption, of the full, glorious, and eternal completion of our salvation. Taught by this blessed Redeemer, the Apostle was comforted in the midst of his chains, by being able to say, "Our citizenship is in heaven: from whence also we look for the Saviour, the Lord Jesus Christ; who shall change our vile body, that it may be fashioned like unto his glorious body." Phil. iii. 20. Were Sir John Franklin, with his companions, yet living, and aware of the efforts made for his deliverance, with what earnestness would he long for the appearance of those sent to rescue him from the desolation of the polar regions, and for the day when he could see again the long lost friends awaiting him in his native country: Amid the wintry desolations of the curse in this world of sin, we know that Jesus our beloved has gone away into heaven, to receive a kingdom unto himself, and return the second time without sin, for the salvation of his saints; and insensible indeed must we be to his love, could we cease to anticipate that period with emotions of unspeakable delight. Æschylus draws an affecting picture of the sad consequences of war, when speaking of the siege of Troy, he says, Mars sends back to friends at home from the so-called field of glory, sad relics burned in the funeral fire, wept with bitter tears, urns filled with ashes, all that remains of what was once men in the vigour of youth.* But when

> "The day shall come, the great avenging day
> When sin's proud glories in the dust shall lay
> And Satan's power and Satan's self shall fall,
> And one eternal ruin swallow all;"†

and the Captain of our salvation, the King "crowned with many crowns," shall come for our final deliverance, he will bring to us—what?—the sad relics of mortality, gathered from the tomb where they had been so long mouldering, formed by his creative power into a body flushed with perennial youth, like the glorious body of him who is glorified with the glory he had with the Father before the foundation of the world. To that period of deliverance from the bondage of corruption into the liberty of the glory of the sons of God, of release from our warfare with sin, the period that puts an end to the separation from him whom our soul loveth—we may well look

---

* Agamemnon of Æschylus, 402.   † See Iliad, iv. 164.

forward with earnest longings; and as much as the glory of that unending day, and the splendour of that resurrection morning, surpass the brightness of any day on earth, so much more earnestly "our soul waiteth for the Lord than they that watch for the morning; I say, more than they that watch for the morning." Ps. cxxx. 6.

Animated by these cheering assurances given us by Jesus, the Creator of all things, the soul contemplates the world and the heavens, under the light of the great deductions of modern philosophy, and sees amid these ruins, traces of magnificence and grandeur big with the promise of future glory. "If the man of clay has been honoured with such magnificent apartments, and fed at such a luxurious table, may not his undying and reasoning soul count upon a spiritual palace, and sigh for that intellectual repast at which the Master of the feast is to disclose his secrets. In its rapid and continued expansion, the mind, conscious of its capacity for a higher sphere, feels, even now, that it is advancing to a goal more distant and more cheering than the tomb. Its energies increase and multiply under the encumbrances of age; and even when man's heart is turning into bone, and his joints into marble, his mind can soar to its highest flight, and seize with its firmest grasp. Nor do the affections plead less eloquently for a future home. Age is their season of warm and genial emotion. The objects long and fondly clasped to our bosom have been removed by Him who gives, and who takes what he gives; and lingering in the valley of bleeding and of broken hearts, we yearn for that break of day which is to usher in the eternal morn—for that home in the house of many mansions which is already prepared for us—for the promised welcome to the threshold of the blest, where we shall meet again the loved and the lost, and devote the eternity of our being to the service of its Almighty Author."*

"He which testifieth these things, saith, Surely I come quickly. Amen. Even so, come, Lord Jesus." "Make haste, my Beloved, and be thou like to a roe or to a young hart, upon the mountains of spices."

* North British Review, No. 11, art. 8. "The Revelations of Astronomy."

THE END.

WILLIAM S. & ALFRED MARTIEN,

606 Chestnut Street Philadelphia,

Publish the following valuable works:

I. NOTES ON SCRIPTURE. By Joel Jones, LL.D. 1 vol. 8vo.

II. FAIRBAIRN'S TYPOLOGY OF SCRIPTURE. 2 vols. 8vo. $3 00

III. THE CRUCIFIXION OF CHRIST. By Major D. H. Hill. 1 00

IV. MAN, MORAL AND PHYSICAL; or, the Influence of Health and Disease on Religious Experience. By Rev. Joseph H. Jones, D. D. 12mo. - - . 1 00

V. HODGE'S COMMENTARY ON ROMANS. 12mo. - 75

VI. COMPLETE WORKS OF REV. EDWARD PAYSON, D. D. With a Portrait. 3 vols. 8vo. - - - - 3 75

VII. WINES' COMMENTARIES ON THE LAWS OF THE ANCIENT HEBREWS. Fifth edition, 8vo. - - 2 50

VIII. LIFE OF THE REV. DANIEL BAKER, D. D. With a fine Portrait. 8vo. - - - - - 1 25

IX. LIFE AND SERMONS OF DR. BAKER, 3 vols. 12mo. 3 25

X. BROWN'S COMMENTARY ON THE FOUR GOSPELS. 12mo. - - - - - - - 50

XI. CONSIDERATION OF THE SERMON ON THE MOUNT. By Major D. H. Hill. Third edition. 12mo. - - 75

XII. ANGUS' BIBLE HAND-BOOK. An Introduction to the Study of Sacred Scripture. Fifth edition. 12mo. 1 25

XIII. THE PENTATEUCH; or the Five Books of Moses: and the Book of Joshua. With an original and copious Critical and Explanatory Commentary. By Rev. Robert Jamieson, D. D., of Glasgow. - - - 75

XIV. THE HISTORICAL BOOKS, FROM JUDGES TO ESTHER. With a Commentary. By the same author. - - 75

XV. THOLUCK'S COMMENTARY ON THE PSALMS. 8vo. 1 25

*** Any of the above works will be sent by mail free of postage, on receipt of the price.

NEW AND ELEGANT EDITION

OF

SCOTT'S COMMENTARY.

JUST PUBLISHED, A NEW EDITION OF

SCOTT'S COMMENTARY ON THE BIBLE,

In Five large quarto Volumes, large type, and neatly bound.

In sheep, ...	$12 50
In half calf, ...	15 00

The capital excellency of this valuable and immense undertaking, perhaps, consists in following more closely than any other the fair and adequate meaning of every part of Scripture, without regard to the niceties of human systems; it is in every part of the expression, a Scriptural Comment. It has, likewise, a further and a strong recommendation in its originality. Every part of it is thought out by the author himself, not borrowed from others. Further, it is the comment of our age, presenting many of the last lights which history casts on the interpretation of prophecy, giving several of the remarks which sound criticism has accumulated from the different branches of sacred literature, obviating the chief objections which modern annotators have advanced against some of the distinguished doctrines of the gospel, and adapting the instructions of Scripture to the peculiar circumstances of the times in which we live. Accordingly, the success of the work has been rapidly and steadily increasing wherever the English language is known.—*Bishop Wilson.*

The Rev. Thomas Hartwell Horne, author of "The Introduction to the Critical Study of the Scriptures," remarks in reference to the above notice, that "To the preceding just character of this elaborate Commentary, the writer of this deems it an act of bare justice to state, that he has *never consulted it in vain on difficult passages of the Scriptures.*"

Already one hundred thousand copies of this work have been sold, and the constant and increasing sale proves the high estimation in which it is deservedly held. The present edition is superior to any that has yet been issued, not only having all the author's final corrections, but also a number of useful Tables, a Concordance, Family Record, &c., together with the advantages of large type, and substantial binding.

☞ Ministers and congregations, when purchasing in quantities, will be supplied upon very liberal terms, which will be made known upon application to the publishers,

WILLIAM S. & ALFRED MARTIEN,
No. 606 Chestnut street,
PHILADELPHIA.

www.ingramcontent.com/pod-product-compliance
Lightning Source LLC
Chambersburg PA
CBHW031959300426
44117CB00008B/828